NEW PERSPECTIVES
ON NARRATIVE PERSPECTIVE

SUNY series, The Margins of Literature
Mihai I. Spariosu, Editor

NEW PERSPECTIVES
ON NARRATIVE PERSPECTIVE

EDITED BY

Willie van Peer
and Seymour Chatman

State University of New York Press

Published by
State University of New York Press, Albany

Printed in the United States of America

For information, address the State University of New York Press, 90 State Street, Suite 700, Albany, N.Y. 12207

Production by Diane Ganeles
Marketing by Patrick Durocher

Library of Congress Cataloging-in-Publication Data

New perspectives on narrative perspective / edited by Willie van Peer and Seymour Chatman.
p. cm. — (SUNY series, the margins of literature)
Chiefly papers presented at a conference held June, 1995 in Zeist, The Netherlands.
Includes bibliographical references and index.
ISBN 0-7914-4787-1 (acid-free paper). — ISBN 0-7914-4788-X (pbk. : acid-free paper)
1. Narration (Rhetoric)—Congresses. I. Peer, Willie van. II. Chatman, Seymour Benjamin, 1928– III. Series.

PN3383.N35 N45 2001
808.3—dc21

00-027694

10 9 8 7 6 5 4 3 2 1

Contents

Part III: Applications and Case Studies

Part IV: Comprehension

Part V: Effects and Consequences

Illustrations

Figures

Tables

Acknowledgments

This volume contains new studies on narrative perspective. Most of the chapters were first presented at an international conference, "Narrative Perspective: Cognition and Emotion," in Zeist, the Netherlands (1995). The conference was organized and sponsored by the Netherlands Graduate School for Literary Studies, whose financial and logistic support is gratefully acknowledged here. We also wish to thank Sage Publications for permission to reprint Uri Margolin's chapter, which appeared in *Language and Literature* 5, no. 2 (1996).

Introduction

Willie van Peer and Seymour Chatman

Consider the following quotation:

> As in *Rashomon*, perspective took hold. More formally: Sometimes what we are left to deal with are not the facts . . . but the different stories people tell as a way of articulating and making sense of the uncertainties and complexities that matter to them.[1]

This is not a piece of film criticism, nor some literary or philosophical reflection on cultural matters. It appears in a book on policy analysis, and it demonstrates the often unrecognized centrality of *narrative* in present-day thought. Roe (1995), its author, argues that objects and techniques studied by literary theory can provide important insights into the complexities of public policy issues—budget problems, animal rights, and global warming—not the kind of things usually associated with literature.

Whether or not one agrees with Roe's (1995) concrete narrative analyses of the issues concerned,[2] we can hardly deny that his proposal deserves close attention. Even if (as Lyotard's (1984) postmodernist philosophy asserts) the Great Narratives—of history, philosophy, and culture are dead, clearly narratives continue to play a central role in our societies. They play a crucial role in a number of social institutions, such as the press, the courts, the doctor's office, corporate headquarters, and capital buildings. Hence a better understanding of how such narratives are constructed, processed, and function in the lives of individuals and groups will augment our sensitivity to how issues are explained, but will also allow us to better grasp alternative ways of thinking.

The present volume focuses on one crucial issue in narrative theory: perspective; Roe's (1995) insight neatly illustrates the value of such an understanding. Narratives are *texts* about events structured in time. They are about agents who act in real or fictional worlds, responding to their inner drives as well as to external circumstances. Narratives typically start with imbalances that protagonists attempt to redress. Usually these attempts lead to complications, setbacks, crises, and ultimately to success or failure. Whether it is a couple attempting reconciliation, a knight in quest of the Holy Grail, or a poor boy overcoming his humble conditions, all such narratives, be they simple or complex, rely on a similar underlying structure.

The study of such structures has a long history, dating back to Aristotle's reflections on plot (*mythos*) in his *Poetics*, but it received its first major theoretical impetus in the work of Propp (1928). Propp analyzed the underlying structures of about a hundred Russian fairy tales, and came to the conclusion that they turned on a set of abstract rules that could account for their systematic resemblances. Propp's method remained somewhat speculative, however, and his work was developed by a whole movement of structuralist analysts that constituted the birth of narratology, a new branch of literary studies. Though considerable progress in narrative theory has been made, there are still some questions that have not been probed; for instance, although we possess good intuitions and insights into narrative structure, we are still unable to generate stories by computer. We also know little about what goes on in readers' minds or what effects such reading creates. Nor do we have enough reliable knowledge of the role that narratives play in societies at large. In short, despite half a century of research, we must confess the limitations in our understanding of narratives. Our goal in this volume is to move the field forward by bringing together some of the important recent developments that have taken place in the study of narrative perspective. We believe that the various contributors have mapped out new territory that will shape research questions over the coming decade.

One reason for bringing out this volume is that the study of narrative has been undertaken in different disciplines that until recently have had little contact with each other. The range of those disciplines is impressive. In anthropology, for instance, Geertz's (1983) book contains a chapter "From the Native's Point of View," pleading for an "interpretive" anthropology in which the perspective of the other culture is thoroughly represented. In a similar vein, but with respect to a Western culture, Lavie (1990) describes the oppositions and tensions under Israeli military occupation of the West Bank through an analysis of the narratives produced by different sides in the conflict. In philosophy, there is Ricoeur's great project (1984). In ethics, Greenspan (1995) argues in favor of the "perspectival appropriateness" of moral sentiments, while Nussbaum (1990) has pleaded for an ethics informed by the various and multifaceted perspectives of narrative literature; this notion has also led her into the domain of jurisprudence (1995). In psychology, Herman (1995) has attempted to link narrative structure to Chomsky's universal grammar. William Chafe is convinced that "narratives provide evidence for the nature of the mind."[3] In sociology, Liebow (1993) constructs a description of homelessness on the basis of narratives told from the perspective of homeless women. In history, a whole new area of investigation, called "oral history," has sprung up: Josselson and Lieblich (1995) is one of the many titles that fit this category. In a similar vein, Zeldin (1994) offers a history of intimacy, based largely on a corpus of women's narratives, collected over the years. More generally, White (1973) has opened a new way of looking philosophically at history, the so-called narrativist view of historiography, which has been propagated by (among others) Canary and Kozicki (1978) and Mitchell (1981).

These examples are far from exhaustive. What all of these approaches reveal is the power of narratives as structuring devices to convey human experience. But they have not been taken far enough; there is still no recognition of the need to address the general question, How and under what conditions do narrative provides such powers to convey widely varied human experience?

The ubiquity of studies in narrative also presents other problems, one being the fragmentation of insights and methods. Communicating the results of such studies across disciplinary borders has been hampered by institutional barriers and historical traditions. Thus, by producing ever more information, we reached a state in which much unnecessary overlapping of effort occurs, because specialists do not learn about methods used in other disciplines. The present study argues the case for *more* interdisciplinary research. We believe that the present monodisciplinary dissipation of views and approaches is not beneficial to progress. It is, in our view, precisely the comparison and even contestation of theories and methods that may help us to overcome our present limitations. The comparison of various approaches to narrative as illustrated in this volume highlights problematic issues that need to be clarified. Here are two examples:

Assumption 1: Narrative Is a Monolithic Category

First, the approaches of different disciplines operate under the (tacit, but wrong) assumption that a narrative is a narrative. Especially in the "narativist" models in history, law, and philosophy, this has been a serious problem. The representation of the past is simply and basically a "narrative," so the argument goes. Similarly, justice in the courtroom emerges from the various narratives that are told. This implies that knowledge about the world is nothing more than a construction of the mind and that those narratives that are cast in the most attractive form capture our imagination and form great metanarratives that become the standard form of our self-image. While there is a kernel of truth in these implications, it has been radicalized and exaggerated. Obviously not just *any* narrative can be told about history or about a legal case. By overextending the idea, narrativism has detracted our attention from a more fundamental question, like, What *kind* of narrative is this? Some narratives are more trustworthy than others: medieval lives of saints, for example, should not always be believed at face value. Nor should the propagandistic stories of totalitarian regimes be given much credit. Surely it is not very helpful if "narrative" is used as an all-encompassing accrediting term. There are marked differences between various types and subtypes of narratives.

The obvious place to look for finer narrative distinctions is literary theory, which has generated a considerable body of text categorizations. Especially in genre theory one may find relevant information, for instance, in Fowler (1982), Hempfer (1973), and Schaeffer (1989). Obviously a satire is different from a myth, which in turn is different from a romance or an epic. When historians, for example, declare that histories are to be understood as different narrations of historical events, one would expect them to utilize recognized subcategorizations of narrative types, showing how the structure of one such historical narrative resembles that of a saga, while another resembles a legend. These differences are so obvious, and their relevance for historical study seems so evident, that one wonders why they have been applied so infrequently.

The present volume concentrates on one particular aspect of narrative, namely *perspective*. By this we mean the location from which events in a story are presented to the reader. “Location” here can have both a literal and a figural meaning. Literally, “perspective” refers to the spatiotemporal coordinates of an agent or observer; figuratively, it signifies the norms, attitudes, and values held by such an agent or observer. We believe that the application of narratological models in the various disciplines benefits from a clear awareness of the kind of perspective that does or does not hold it together. Without such awareness, it is often difficult to relate the narrative as a text to the social or historical constructs under scrutiny.

Assumption 2: Understanding Narrative

Another problem concerns the application of narrative models in disciplines that simplistically assume that the understanding of narrative is self-evident and unproblematic. Hegel’s philosophy of history presents the development of Oriental civilizations from a Western perspective, but these civilizations have their own narratives about themselves and about the West. How is one to reconcile these different perspectives? Recent globalization—through the economy and through the spread of the mass media and information technology—makes such self-restricting narrativization no longer tenable. The crucial difficulty in dealing with the diverse narratives of the twentieth and twenty-first centuries is their mutual incompatibility and even incomprehensibility. In this sense the term *postmodern condition* indeed captures something of the puzzlement and emotional alienation that results from the breaking up of closed societies or unified narrative traditions.

Again, however, the mere observation of this condition is not enough. We cannot allow ourselves to float helplessly in this sea of narrative debris; the consequences are simply too dire, and the demand too urgent for a more accurate investigation of how people deal with narratives in the real world. Consider, for example, the world of difference between people’s reactions to everyday narratives told as part of family life, and to televised news stories or radio talk shows informed by various ideological signatures. How do people treat these narratives? How are they influenced by specific textual devices? How do they construct chains of causal attribution? What is the role of emotions in shaping or accepting these narratives? When and why are narratives experienced as "convincing" or "persuasive"? These are questions that need to be addressed if we wish to progress beyond the mere declaration that narratives provide people with "food for thought."

Some examples from the present volume may illustrate the complexities involved. Van Oostendorp presents empirical evidence that readers do not always process narratives without making mistakes. Dixon and Bortolussi, laying the groundwork for a psychonarratology, argue that there are good reasons to start from a model in which readers treat narrators as resembling everyday partners in communication as much as possible. But even under such a definition, miscommunication may occur, as is well attested by Coupland, Giles, and Wiemann (1991). If we want to progress in our understanding of the way in which narratives shape and constitute our cultural world, we will have to develop more accurate descriptions of textual devices that create a perspective, but also of how readers process and comprehend them. As to reader psychology, the present volume shows the kind of advances being made through the close cooperation of scholars from various disciplines.

Consider, furthermore, the question of identification. It is often assumed that part of the power of narratives lies in the potential for identification with the protagonists. But what if there are multiple agents in a narrative? Do people keep track of their separate movements? What is the nature of such identification, and why do readers get involved in it in the first place? According to Graesser and his colleagues, it is not enough to ask these questions; cognitive psychology can provide the tools necessary for answering them. Another question is whether identification always and necessarily takes place, or what sort of conditions trigger it. That invokes a whole new set of intricate questions; Do some conditions overrule others or are they taxonomically equal? At present cognitive and emotional aspects of identification are only partly understood, and much more work awaits us if we are to understand how narrative perspective influences reader or spectators' attitudes, norms, and values.

All in all, these results lead to the conclusion that it is false to assume that understanding narratives is unproblematic, and thus the fallacies of both assumptions just cited plunges us into an entirely new situation. The study of narrative perspective has entered a stage in which interdisciplinary cooperation has become inevitable. Though more is needed, some real progress has already been made in the elaboration and sophistication of traditional narratology.

One dimension of progress is the change from the tendency to categorize whole texts manifesting a specific perspective to more detailed analyses of perspectival complexity. It is a move from "global" to more "local" phenomena, from "macro" to "micro." It is evident in several contributions to this volume, notably in the ones by Fludernik, Gerrig, De Jong, and Morrow that the older typological approach needs to be complemented by more detailed textual analyses. Although such an analysis is in itself not new—witness the works by Bal (1977, 1985); Banfield (1982, 1987); Chatman (1986, 1990, 1995); and Leech and Short (1981)—it remains an important task of contemporary narratology.

Beyond this, however, there is also a need to move from a concentration on (the textual) product to an appreciation of the production *process*. Earlier approaches were usually concerned with questions regarding the type of perspective manifest in a particular text, which was considered a characteristic of the finished product. More recent attempts describe the ongoing interaction between narrator and narratee in order to articulate a particular perspective. Figuratively speaking, one could call such analyses "on-line," in contrast with earlier "off-line" models. Research modeled on the on-line approach is often better able to detect slight inconsistencies in perspectives, as Shen demonstrates. It goes beyond older models by allowing more fine-grained analyses that bring to light the subtle interplay between various linguistic and compositional devices. The change from product-analysis to process-analysis changes the basic research model from the question, *What* is the perspective in this story? to *How* is perspective in this story brought about? Obviously both questions are valid, but new research shows that the former question often presupposes the latter.

While such inquiry has occurred within the field of literary studies itself, there is at least one point in which the present volume differs fundamentally from earlier publications.[4] This is the cooperation of humanities scholars with social scientists in studying narrative perspective: collectively they have laid bare several crucial issues. One is whether the general assumptions and hypotheses developed in literary theory are tenable when one looks at the behavior of real readers. Narratologists have often taken a lot for granted, and have not shied away from normatively stipulating the kind of effects that *should* follow from linguistic devices establishing a particular narrative perspective. Concrete psychological research into how real readers react to such devices, however, shows that these theoretical claims are sometimes untenable. As Prince argues, it is better not to assume too much, but instead to examine the actual behavior of readers, viewers, and listeners. Such research requires cooperation between humanists and social scientists, so that narratological theories can be probed by the sophisticated testing methods of experimental psychology. As long as theories remain purely speculative, they are not worth much: speculation is cheap and easy, but does little to advance our understanding of the world. It is precisely the separation of true from partly or wholly false speculations that is at the heart of a scientific enterprise. On the other hand, science is dependent on ideas, and ideas start out as intuitive speculation. Cooperation between the humanities and the social sciences thus results in more than the mere sum of two independent skills. Instead, it produces a symbiosis of interlocking feedback and hence of mutual enlightenment.

Compare, for instance, the move toward semantic precision that some of the chapters in this present volume. Carroll's contribution suggests a bold new move to define the nature of the concept of "narrative." Starting from the old assumption that narratives consist of an ordered description of events related in such a way that earlier events are *at least causally necessary conditions* for later events and state of affairs, he argues that readers of narratives have the ability to sense: readers do sense a range of possibilities of what may happen next, "forming expectation on the basis of what events are possible, given earlier events in the story." His use of the tools of analytic philosophy enriches traditional definitions of narrative, and thus offers a more accurate description of our intuitions, which thereby becomes testable. A cognitive psychologist like Graesser shows how readers are indeed able to keep track of narrator and characters' speech and knowledge. The point here is that such issues get much more adequate treatment if the problems are pursued by a consortium of scholars from different disciplines. Without literary theory, cognitive psychology has little to say about narrative, and Graesser readily admits as much. But without the rigors of empirical testing, much of literary theory remains underspecified. Philosophical and linguistic approaches introduce more semantic precision, after which it becomes easier to scrutinize the validity of concepts. The furthest end of the spectrum of rigorous analysis is presented by experimental psychology, where theoretical notions are subjected to the severest of tests. But, obviously, such tests are meaningless without a constant dialogue with literary studies that provided the concepts to psychologists in the first place.

Interdisciplinarity is often only a catchword, invoked to dodge problems in one's own field by "exporting" them to another field. One is often justified in looking with some suspicion upon claims in this direction. Real interdisciplinary research, by contrast, demands effort and patience in understanding the other's assumptions and working methods. The energy required to learn how to apply theoretical insights and research methods from other disciplines is often so taxing that people prefer to stay at home rather than travel the hard road into largely unknown territory. Not so in this volume. It is the result of concrete cooperation between linguists, literary and film scholars, philosophers, and psychologists. Humanities scholars came to the awareness that assumptions about the effects of narrative perspective needed more than just intuition, however ingeniously supported by textual citation. If texts display various ruptures in the presentation of perspective, how can we account for readers' constructions of a coherent perspective? Scholars are beginning to realize that our theoretical claims about narrative perspective are not entirely free from contradiction. If traditional narratology provided us with no clear answers to such questions, then it seems legitimate to look to other methods that may be able to describe and explain the phenomena concerned. This development also emerges as a spin-off of reader response theory and of the empirical study of literature.

The search for methods that could clarify readers' processing strategies leads almost directly into psychology, which possesses methodological tools designed to probe the problems at hand. Psychology teaches one not to trust one's intuitions, but instead to put them to independent tests designed to determine whether an intuition is valid or not. At the conference in Zeist, the Netherlands, literary scholars found among psychologists a friendly atmosphere in which genuine interest in the questions of literary theory were alive.

On the part of the social scientists, interdisciplinary cooperation was felt necessary for similar reasons. Experimentation with texts had been going on for a while in psychology, often with great skill and creativity. However, most of the texts employed in investigating readers' processes were artificially constructed, geared exactly to the needs of the experiment at hand. Such texts remain primitive in a certain sense, and in any case lack the complexity, ambiguity, and stylistic sophistication that literary texts generally possess. To that extent, the materials employed lessen the validity of the experimental results. Cognitive psychologists became aware of the necessity to complement their research with "real" texts. Naturally, they turned to literary studies, the more so since in that discipline efforts toward empirical research had been going on for a while.

There was also a second reason why literary studies presented an interesting partner to the psychologists. The field had a long tradition of studying and analyzing the nuts and bolts of texts. Since psychologists are not only interested in readers' general reactions to texts, but in how they process specific textual elements, literary studies offers a powerful toolkit for the description of text structures, such as narrative perspective. Cognitive psychologists knew about readers, but not much about texts, while literary scholars knew a lot about texts, but rather little about readers. Thus, collaboration between literary studies and psychology became feasible and mutually profitable.

Of course, not all relevant issues can be covered in a single volume like this one; for example, there are broader cultural and political issues that could only be hinted at. The complications involved in the use of a "we" perspective, for instance, are quite staggering, as Margolin's detailed analysis shows. Obviously the use of such a "we" perspective is widespread, for instance, in political propaganda. It may be remembered, as a particularly grim example, that Hitler's *Mein Kampf* makes abundant use of a "we" perspective. The incisive analyses by Elias and Scotson (1965) of the use of such perspectives in social conflicts help clarify the social implications of the opposition between "us" and "them," but their analysis of the semantics of the pronouns remains crude, and the pragmatic implications of such perspectives are underanalyzed. Setting up a perspective of us versus them is one of the most frequently employed strategies in the political arena. Margolin's analysis also reveals a number of striking differences between the literary and everyday uses of a we-perspective. How literary narratives might contribute to a group perspective remains unclear and certainly requires detailed further study.

How different subcultures within a society erect and maintain images of each other is very complex, and we therefore argue strongly for more research in this area, especially given the increase in ethnic and cultural diversity in most Western societies. As the chapter by Van Peer shows, it is by no means impossible nor unlikely that different cultural groups view each other with a high degree of impartiality, and his historical example of Euripides' *Medea* reveals well enough how such an attitude is already found at the roots of Western civilization. Similarly, Sack's contribution provides analytical instruments for the automatic identification of an ideological point of view in intergroup perception.

The importance of perspective for wider social issues has recently also been shown by O'Neill (1994: 94-95): ambiguous focalization in some New Testament narratives has prompted quite different translations, which in turn suggest wider latitude for interpretation. Perspectival ambiguity has thus led to divergent interpretations of the words and deeds of Jesus, fostering disagreement over the interpretation of religious texts. As we know well from history, such divergences have sometimes stirred intergroup conflict and violent confrontations. A more detailed study of narrative perspective in the original Greek text would reveal the fundamentally ambiguous nature of many passages in this religious text and hence explain the various differences in opinion over its content. Such textual structures should be complemented by psychological research. Focalization theory attempts to explain *attribution*, but how can one properly study this effect without the appropriate knowledge of attribution theory? Gerrig signals the tendency of readers to commit the fundamental attribution error (FAE) described by Ross (1977). If the study of perspective is to make further progress, one will have to include the way in which real readers attribute motivations to protagonists' actions. All of these cases exemplify the need for cooperation across disciplinary borders. We believe that the rewards of such interdisciplinary exchange and cooperation are great enough to warrant the extra effort.

There is yet another reason why an interdisciplinary approach to the study of narrative is necessary, namely, that narratives often take on a life of their own and continue to be believed, even when the facts they narrate are wrong or misguided. Many stories, we know, were (and are) told about people from ethnic groups other than our own. Many of the debates over multicultural or gender issues involve narratives that go largely uncontrolled. Sommers has, for instance, fleshed out the origins and biases in various stories about wrongdoings to women in our society. She calls such myths "noble lies," such as the increase in wife battery at Super Bowl time, or the "statistics" that four to five million women are abused every year in the United States. Reading her analyses one cannot help but wonder how people come to believe such extravagant stories, so grossly inaccurate and statistically absurd that they should immediately raise eyebrows. Similarly, Sowell (1995) reveals the impact that narratives coined by so-called liberal intellectuals have had on social policy in the Western world, with (according to him) detrimental results.

In such a situation, studying narratives for their own sake runs the risk of forgetting one crucial characteristic of narratives, namely their capacity for transferring experience. The power of narratives lies in their potential to increase reader and viewers' experiential bandwidth, and to deepen their emotional sensitivity and their social commitment. Experience with different narrative perspectives, fictional as well as nonfictional, allows us to view the world from different locations, angles, and value systems. This experience helps us determine whether a new instance of perspective is believable or deceitful, for example, it can refute the arguments of Holocaust revisionists. If history is nothing but narratives, does that mean that "all narratives are equal," that they all have equal access to reality, that they are all equally true? Himmelfarb (1995) has analyzed the situation poignantly by asking what the ultimate consequences of the radical postmodern vision will be, a vision in which everything should be decentered, dehumanized, and deconstructed. Can one really deconstruct the Holocaust, she wonders, without coming close to a denial of the horrors involved? If, as White has argued,[5] "there are no limits to the kinds of stories the historian might choose to tell and no grounds on which to reject one or another mode" (quoted in Himmelfarb; 144), how can one still attempt to get at the truth?[6] If, however, it turns out that stories cannot be proliferated endlessly and at random, as in the case of the Holocaust, then perhaps we have to call a halt to the tendency to cut off narratives from real life, as the postmodernists have been wont to do.

This has further ramifications for the way in which narratives inform us about our experiences. If there is no meaning to these experiences, no coherence to these narratives, then indeed people may feel helpless and alienated. But do narratives indeed have this effect? As Himmelfarb puts it: "To pluralize and particularize history to the point where people have no history in common is to deny the common humanity of all people" (154). In our view, that is a greatly impoverished view of narratives. It does not do justice to the immense richness we obtain through the various perspectivations possible in story telling. The relativist, postmodernist, and deconstructivist views may be interesting as an academic exercise, but they bear little relationship to the world at large. In that world, people do derive meanings from narratives, and they do find coherence among different narratives. In Dickens (1859), the novel that so eloquently makes the case for workers' rights, there is an unpretentious public library; the readers visiting it "wondered about human nature, human passions, human hopes and fears, the struggles, triumphs and defeats, the cares and joys and sorrows, the lives and deaths, of common men and women! They sometimes, after fifteen hours' work, sat down to read mere fables about men and women, more or less like themselves, and about children, more or less like their own" (90). Reading narratives, partaking in different perspectives, argued Dickens, ultimately informs us about ourselves, about our human nature and universal predicament. To understand narrative perspective is to understand human beings.

An Overview of the Volume

These conclusions are taken up and developed further in the various contributions in this volume. Though they come from across several disciplines they all share a common concern for the study of narrative perspective, despite different theoretical orientations and specific research methods. Because the variation in approaches faces matters of definition as one of the primary obstacles in cross-disciplinary dialogue, the volume opens with a section on conceptual matters. In order to communicate one needs clarity about the concepts one employs. That is what the three chapters in this first part attempt: to strive toward a higher semantic precision of the concepts employed. A presupposition for being able to communicate about "narrative perspective" is what we mean by "narrative." Although this may seem plain at first sight, and for most everyday situations, we will not encounter problems, there are also situations that are not so simple. While we may not hesitate to call *War and Peace* or *Buddenbrooks* narratives, things become complicated immediately once one considers questions like: Should one consider jokes as narratives? Can a narrative consist of one sentence only? How do we distinguish narratives from a description of events? We may inspect such borderline cases in order to more closely analyze our intuitions, so that we develop a better grasp of the concepts with which we are supposed to work. Part I opens with a clarification of the notion of the narrative as articulated by Carroll (chap. 1), after which the notion of perspective is analyzed by Prince (chap. 2). Traditional definitions of these notions as well as common conceptions have left some crucial terms underdefined, or indeed suggested that we should prefer more open-ended definitions. Both Carroll and Prince argue that there is value in attempting more rigorous definitions. As later parts of the volume demonstrate, semantic precision of the concepts used in narratology is a prerequisite for testing them empirically. However, in the attempt toward rigorous conceptualization, one may easily overlook unintended (perhaps also unwanted) consequences of a particular definition. Phelan (chap. 3) points out such problems of terminological precision in the tradition of Prince and Chatman.

Part II extends the conceptual issue by tracing the historical roots and developments of narrative perspective. Learning how narrative perspective operates in different cultures, at different times, may enlighten the very functions that specific perspectival forms fulfill. Traditional approaches to narrative perspective held the view that before the nineteenth-century point of view was largely confined to authorial narration. Experimentation in novels such as Flaubert's *Madame Bovary* (1856–57) led, according to this theory, to a proliferation of new types of narrative perspective. In a sense, this is correct and the chapters by Fludernik and Margolin (part IV) testify to the general adequacy of this notion. However, the traditional view is no longer unchallenged if one applies the principles of microanalysis retrospectively. As the chapters in this part demonstrate, we have every reason not to underestimate the extent to which complexities in narrative perspectives were already present in earlier historical periods. De Jong (chap. 4) describes the origin of some complex devices for creating perspective at the very beginnings of Western civilization, that is, in classical Greek literature. Adamson (chap. 5), explores how such devices manifested themselves in the Renaissance, and particularly in Puritan texts. Fludernik (chap. 6), finally, traces the elaborations of narrative perspective at the end of the twentieth century. Together these chapters draw attention to the rich possibilities of narrative perspective in Western literature, distinguishing between variations and constants. A balanced account of both will yield a deeper understanding of the way in which narrative perspective functions in literary and other texts.

Part III demonstrates, by the exemplification of a number of case studies, how narrative perspective operates. Chatman's (chap. 7) analysis exemplifies some of the shifts from global to local orientations that have been outlined before. Contrary to earlier approaches, which tended to minimize the differences between various media (i.e., literature and film), studying the way in which irony plays a role in Conrad's *Secret Agent* (1923) and its BBC television adaptation, Chatman reveals the fundamental differences between both media. What is a powerful tool for establishing a character for one medium may be unavailable to another, so that "adaptations" may distort central ingredients of the other medium, or make the reconstruction of characters' motives and inner world a more hazardous event. How such processing activities take place in spectators' minds is demonstrated by Andringa and her colleagues (chap. 8). As their results indicate, however, narratologists would be well advised not to overestimate the effects of narrative perspective on empathy. Shen (chap. 9) shows how at the textual level there is also a need for caution and modesty. She outlines concrete textual devices that show ruptures in the overall structure of narrative perspective, impeding readers' construction of a unified and coherent perspective. Given Van Oostendorp's (chap. 10) findings that readers have but limited resources in updating incoming information when reading news stories, the kind of literary complexities highlighted by the other case studies clearly puts high demands on readers' involvement with the text. The ultimate test of our theoretical understanding of such complexities may come in the application of software for automatic text analysis. Sack (chap. 11) shows how one may proceed in the automatic detection of an ideological perspective in news reports. By systematically testing the algorithms he has developed, one gets a much better idea of how agents and their positioning, and their actions and norm systems create that conglomerate we usually call "ideological point of view." Operationalization through computational mechanisms provides an important complement to the more intuitive textual analyses usually informing the study of narrative texts.

Part IV explores issues of comprehension; How is narrative perspective processed? Nünning (chap. 12) underlines the constructive character of perspective. What we designate as perspective is actually the result of the cognitive activities of readers. What this involves is the construction of a mental representation of the underlying semantics offered by the text. Morrow (chap. 13) extends this notion into the domain of actual representations that real readers construct, demonstrating the "situation model" that readers generate while reading. Morrow shows how this model does not apply to spatiotemporal issues alone, but extends to the inner world of story protagonists. Margolin (chap. 14) subsequently discusses how we comprehend the complex we-perspective. Since there are various routes toward comprehension of such complex cases, Margolin shows that we need more elaborate analyses than had hitherto been assumed. Especially the oscillation of the we between "I + you" and "I + other" presents great obstacles to a straightforward designation of referentiality in reading we-narratives. Whether these obstacles are insurmountable or not depends on the cognitive resources of readers. Hence the question arises about the necessary mental equipment for performing complex comprehension tasks in reading narratives, a question addressed by Graesser and his coauthors (chap. 15). Since we know the differences among the resources that readers bring to this task, one might wonder whether the demands involved in comprehending a narrative perspective are not too great for most readers. All the evidence points in the direction of a limited, but well-developed capacity to flesh out the various threads that constitute a narrative perspective, at least in "typical" short story narratives. Whether that holds as well for the more complex case that Margolin discusses or for the more radical experiments treated in the chapter by Fludernik remains to be seen.

The final section investigates consequences and effects of narrative perspective. In order to better chart these, one obviously needs a model that adequately represents narrative communication. Dixon and Bortolussi (chap. 16) present such a model, introducing a distinction between "text" and "effect," the latter being the product of the interaction between texts and readers. The authors propose a psychonarratology operating on the simplest of assumptions, that is, that readers construct the narrator on the model of a partner in everyday conversation, unless, of course, particular elements in the text tell them to deviate from this assumption. Their research reveals that readers indeed search for a unitary location and focalization, that they act on Grice's maxims striving toward cooperation with the narrator, and that they attribute to the narrator properties that will facilitate communication, such as familiar cultural schemata. Miall and Kuiken's (chap. 17) examination complements this model by drawing attention to the aesthetic effects that may be created when the perspective moves beyond existing cognitive models of the world. They argue that a situation model that excludes the cognitive and emotional workings of foregrounding devices is insufficient to explain readers' reactions to literary texts. They offer compelling evidence that in the course of reading, efforts at constructing a perspective are repeatedly disrupted, prompting not only an updating of information, but also an emotional reshaping of the meaning and impact of the narrative.

While the previous chapters already indicate the give-and-take between text and reader, the research by Gerrig (chap. 18) clarifies this issue even further by making a distinction between an "external" perspective that readers "bring" to the text, and an "internal" perspective that they must "discover" within the world of the text. While traditional narratology may have overemphasized the textual nature of perspective, reader response approaches may have swung to the other extreme, assuming that the reader attributes everything to the text. Gerrig shows that we are under no obligation to choose between these alternatives, as there is good evidence in favor of *both* processes. Although this complicates matters considerably, and although a strictly causal method may be inadequate to account for the effects that are produced by narrative perspective, it is not the case that such effects are random. Given certain parameters, they can be predicted. Participation in the world of the narrative, an activity most readers readily become involved in, has consequences for the reader. Studying these consequences is an integral part of narrative theory. Such consequences are situated in a wider framework of social justice in the final chapter of this section. Van Peer (chap. 19) considers how textual perspective may conflict with the perspective that readers bring to reading.

The volume concludes with an epilogue, in which Short (chap. 20) reviews the general thread of the various contributions, linking them to theoretical goals in the study of narrative perspective, and critically scrutinizing the various methodological roads that may help us achieve these goals.

Notes

1. Roe (1995: ix).

2. The authors of this volume recognize that Roe's proposal is ingeneous and innovative, and that it should receive every bit of attention it deserves. However, they also consider the proposal to be flawed by similar shortcomings, which are discussed later in this introduction. If further work in narrative policy analysis is to overcome these shortcomings, it will have to take into account the issues that are at the core of the present volume. At a more local level of the narrative text, issues of deictic center, of focalization, or of the use of foregrounding devices should be inspected. And these should be related to the psychological processes involved, for instance, the construction of causal attributions, the updating of situation models, or the role of emotions in reshaping narrative perspectives.

3. "Some Things that Narratives Tell Us about the Mind," in Britton and Pellegrini (1990: 79).

4. This is true perhaps with the exception of Gerrig (1993).

5. White, "Historical Emplotment and the Problem of Truth," in Friedlander (1992: 37ff.).

6. On the notion of truth, see Van Peer (1998).

Part I

Concepts

1

On the Narrative Connection

Noël Carroll

Narrative is a topic of increasing interest across the humanities and the social sciences today. Even philosophers like Rorty and MacIntyre invoke it, often against something they call "theory." However, although the notion of narrative frequently figures in many discussions in the university, it is not often defined. The purpose of this chapter is to advance a characterization of our ordinary concept of narrative in terms of one of its crucial ingredients, and to explore some of the ramifications of that definition in light of how we might begin, in part, to understand narrative comprehension.

Of course, narratives come in many different sizes and shapes. What is called a "narrative history," for example, may mix different expositional forms, including not only narration, but argument and explanation. Likewise, a novel may contain elements of commentary, description, and decoration in addition to strictly narrative elements. It is not the purpose of this chapter to define such large-scale units of discourse. My aim is much more modest. I would like to attempt to define something more discrete—what I call "the narrative *connection*."

I suspect that when we call more large-scale discourses, such as histories or novels, narratives, we do so because they possess a large number of narrative connections or because the narrative connections they contain have special salience or a combination of both. I will not speculate on what proportion of narrative connections a discourse must possess or on what degree of salience said connections must exhibit in order for a large-scale discourse to be called a narrative. At present, I am only concerned with characterizing the nature of the narrative connection.

If this is all I intend to do, does this justify my previous claim about characterizing narrative? I think that it does. For fundamental to our identification of a given novel or history as a narrative is its possession of narrative connections. Histories and novels may contain more than narrative connections. But it is their possession of these connections that leads us to call them narratives. Thus, even if we are not prepared to say what proportion and what degree of salience of narrative connections provide grounds for calling a history or a novel a narrative, the possession of these connections is an essential feature of anything that we would want to call a narrative. Therefore, we need a characterization of the narrative connection before we attempt to explore the grounds upon which we call large-scale mixed discourses narratives.

Defining the Narrative Connection

The first step in defining the narrative connection is to consider its proper domain. I hope that it is uncontroversial to say that the domain of narrative discourse is at least comprised of events and states of affairs. I will assume this much. However, the statement—"There was an old lady who lived in a shoe"—is not a narrative, although it describes a state of affairs. Why not? Because narratives contain more than one event and/or states of affairs. Narratives represent a series of events and/or states of affairs. Thus the first necessary condition for what constitutes a narrative representation is that it refer to at least two, though possibly many more, events, and/or states of affairs. "There was an old lady who lived in a shoe" is not a narrative, but "There was an old lady who lived in a shoe that was very small, so she went looking for a boot" looks more like a narrative, since this involves two things, a state of affairs—living in a shoe—and an event—"searching for a boot."

A narrative connection represents a series of events and/or states of affairs. Mention of a *series* here implies that narratives contain the citation of two, but possibly more, events and/or states of affairs. But is any series of events and/or states of affairs a narrative? Here, following the lead of linguistics, let us test our intuitions against an example. Is the following a narrative?

"The Tartar hordes swept over Russia; Socrates swallowed hemlock; Noël Carroll got his first computer; Jackie Chan made his most successful movie; and dinosaurs became extinct." Is this a narrative?

I suspect that almost everyone will agree that this is not a narrative. Why not? One reason is that this particular discourse, though is contains more than enough events and states of affairs to qualify as a narrative, fails to be about a unified subject. It seems as though it is about disconnected subjects. Thus, I hypothesize that to count as a narrative connection, a discourse representing a series of events must be about a unified subject (though, I admit, more will have to be said about what makes a subject unified).

Of course, saying even this much allows that a narrative may be about more than one unified subject. Large-scale narratives, such as a history of France, will often be about more than one subject; and narratives of all sizes may develop parallel stories concerning different subjects; moreover, in addition, narratives may contain nonnarrative material. But to qualify as a narrative connection, the discourse must manifest at least one unified subject. Perhaps so much is implied by calling the phenomenon under discussion the "narrative *connection*." That is, the events and/or states of affairs must be *connected*; they cannot simply be a list of *disconnected* events and/or states of affairs.

Now test another example against your intuitions: "The president talked to his adviser; the president ate a piece of cheese; the president jogged; the president waved to reporters." This discourse string takes note of apparently more than one event and it appears to have a unified subject—namely, the president's activities. But let me suggest that it is not a narrative. Why? Because it lacks a discernible temporal order. One cannot divine the order in which the preceding events occurred. Perhaps, the president jogged in the morning, then ate the cheese, and on the next day he talked to his adviser and, at the same time, waved to the reporters. From a logical point of view, assuming the president did do all these things, the discourse string as a whole would be true whether the president jogged first and then waved to the reporters or vice versa. But narrative structure makes demands over and above logical structure. Narratives mandate that the events and/or states of affairs represented be perspicuously time-ordered. A narrative is not simply a series of events arranged helter-skelter; a narrative is at least a *sequence* of events, where sequence implies temporal ordering.

Perhaps my example is a little confusing. Some may feel that the previous recounting of the president's activities is, in fact, time-ordered. But I submit that if you think that, then it is because you are assuming that the order of the sentences represents the order of the events in question. But why assume that? If you look closely at the discourse string in terms of the information it carries, I suspect that you will quickly realize that all of the activities notated could occur at the same time. The discourse string is underdetermined with respect to the time-ordering of the events, even if initially it seems natural to suppose that they are occurring sequentially.

"John jumps; Mary sings; Harold bleeds" is not self-evidently a narrative not only because a unified subject eludes us, but also because it yields no reliable insight into the order of these events. Likewise, "The Tartar hordes swept over Russia; Socrates ate hemlock; Noël Carroll got his first computer; Jackie Chan made his most successful movie; and dinosaurs became extinct" is not a narrative not only because it lacks a central subject, but also because it does not even conversationally implicate a perspicuous, reliable time-ordering of the events it recounts. The narrative connection requires both a unified subject and a perspicuous temporal order where by a perspicuous temporal order I mean retrievable one. This, of course, does not mean that the temporal order must be stated outright in the discourse string. Context and the knowledge that the intended, informed audience brings to the discourse may be enough for the intended reader, viewer, or listener to derive a perspicuous temporal ordering from an example.

So far I have alleged that a narrative connection is comprised of a series of events that is both possessed of a unified subject and is perspicuously time-ordered. Moreover, it is important to realize that the requirements of a perspicuous time-ordering and that of a unified subject do not amount to the same thing. This can be seen by comparing the following two strings of discourse: "The Eastern Roman Empire falls in 1453; the American Constitution is accepted in 1789; Russia is defeated in 1905"; and "Hume publishes 'Of the Standard of Taste'; Hume fails to secure a professorship." Neither is a narrative because the first lacks a unified subject, though it is temporally ordered, whereas the second, though apparently possessing a unified subject (viz., Hume), lacks a perspicuous time order—which came first: the failure to secure a professorship, or the publication?

For classificatory purposes, following White (1965), we might call our first example—"The Eastern Roman Empire falls . . . etc."—an "annal." An annal is not a full-blooded narrative. On the other hand, it is not altogether without temporal order. So perhaps we should call annals members of the class of "story forms," where story forms are any sort of temporally ordered discourse. But with respect to the annal, its principle of organization is simply temporal ordering.

However, the annal is not the only kind of story form. The *chronicle* is another. A number of theorists, including Croce, Danto, and Dray (1985, 1993) have used this term. I am using it in the way in which White (1965: 222) does. Where temporal ordering is combined with a unified subject, we arrive at a somewhat more complex structure than the annal which has been called the "chronicle." For example, "The French Revolution occurred in 1789; Napoleon became emperor in 1805; Napoleon was defeated at Waterloo in 1815, after which the Bourbons were restored." This possesses a perspicuous temporal structure, as well as a unified subject, namely, French history.

In this example of a chronicle, each event is explicitly dated. However, in order to qualify as a chronicle, it is not necessary that the temporal order be made absolutely explicit in the text, so long as the reader, viewer, or listener is able to derive a reliable temporal order from it. Had our earlier example stated "First the President talked to his adviser; then he ate a piece of cheese; then he jogged; and, finally, he waved to the reporters," then this would be a chronicle, rather than an annal, for even though the temporal structure is somewhat imprecise, it nevertheless affords a rough order of occurrence.

Or, in some cases, it may be appropriate to presume that the temporal order is implicit for a target audience. Thus, "Kennedy is assassinated; Johnson becomes president" qualifies as a chronicle for informed audiences who are able to fill in the temporal order. A discursive representation that (temporally, but noncausally) connects at least two events in the career of a unified subject such that a reliable temporal ordering is retrievable from it (and/or from the context of enunciation) is a chronicle. Chronicles are certainly more complex structurally than annals. But are chronicles full-fledged narratives?

I conjecture that they are not, although I realize that this is open to terminological dispute. The reason why I think that a mere chronicle is not yet a narrative is that it does not display any connection other than that of temporal succession between the events it recounts. If I say "I woke up; later I dressed; still later I went to class," I suspect that most people would agree that this falls short of a full-fledged narrative. But why isn't it a narrative properly so-called? To put it vaguely—because the connection among the events alluded to by it is not tight enough.

Of course, as noted, this might be a controversial conclusion. Some theorists, like Prince (1982: 145), might be willing to call this a narrative. However, I think that it is more profitable theoretically to discriminate between different sorts of temporal discourses or, as I call them, "story forms"—between, for example, annals, chronicles, and narratives proper. Having more distinctions at least has the advantage of affording more fine-grained structural insights. And what we have been talking about are important structural differences no matter what labels we finally settle upon.

On my view, narratives proper require more than simply temporal ordering as a principle for connecting events and/or states of affairs. But in order to motivate my taxonomy, it is necessary for me to specify the nature of the connection I have in mind rather than simply saying that it is more than merely a matter of temporal ordering.

What is the connection that obtains between events and/or states of affairs in a narrative proper? One popular candidate is causation. This seems to be eminently plausible, since narratives typically represent *changes* in states of affairs, and change implies some subtending causal process.

"Creon had Antigone executed; consequently, his son committed suicide, which caused his wife to commit suicide, and, as a result, Creon felt anguish." This is a narrative. It has a unified subject, Creon, and it is perspicuously time-ordered. But in addition to begin time-ordered, the events are also causally linked. Earlier events in the discursive string are the causes of the later events in the string in the sense that the earlier events supply sufficient grounds, all things being equal, for the occurrence of the later event. This is certainly a "tighter" connection then mere temporal ordering. Is it the secret of the narrative connection?

It is not, if what we are after is the generic or comprehensive connection between earlier events and/or states of affairs and what follows. Admittedly, in some narratives, causation of this sort is what supplies the connection between earlier and later events. But causation in this sense—the sufficiency sense—is too strong a relation to hypothesize as the relevant connection operative in *all* narrative linkages. Were the relation causal on this understanding, that would suggest that earlier events in narratives causally entail later events. And although this may obtain in some cases, it does not obtain in all cases, nor does it seem to me to obtain in even most of the typical cases.

Most narratives are not strings of causal entailments; instead, the earlier events in a sequence of events underdetermine later events. We read that a thief enters a bank and robs it; in the next scene, as he exits the bank, he is apprehended by the police whom we subsequently learn have been watching him all along. The first event did not entail the second event. Indeed, we may even be surprised by the appearance of the police when the thief leaves the bank. Nevertheless, "the thief enters the bank to rob it, but subsequently, as he exits, he is apprehended by the police" is a narrative, though, strictly speaking, the first event is not the cause of the second event. Although robbing the bank is causally relevant to the arrest, it does not causally entail the second event. That is why we cannot think of all narratives on the model of a series of causal chains in which earlier events and/or states of affairs function as the efficient causes of succeeding events and/or states of affairs.

Looking at the preceding counterexample concerning the thief and the bank may suggest a way of modifying the causal account. The first event does not causally entail the second event, but the second event brings with it the causal information—the presence of the police observers—that explains the second event—the arrest—when it is combined with the first event—the robbery. We can call this addition, following Dray, a "causal input." Dray discusses the causal input in the second edition of his (1993: 93–94) book, extrapolating the notion of a causal input from chapter 11 in Danto's *Narration and Knowledge*. On this model, the narrative connection is a matter of the first event and/or state of affairs + a causal input + the second event. Does the casual input model yield a general picture of the narrative connection?

I think not, and again the problem is that it is too strong. Consider this narrative (which I borrow from Danto and Dray, albeit in a modified form):

> Because the town refused to surrender, the invading army laid siege to it; because the message reached them that their base of operations was under attack, the besiegers soon withdrew, but, in withdrawing, their campaign fell into confusion.

This seems to be an acceptable narrative. However, not every successive event in it can be subsumed under either the causal or causal input model. The first connection in the story—the refusal to surrender/the siege—is arguably causal; the second connection-the message/the withdrawal—possibly involves a causal input; but the last connection—the withdrawal/the confusion—is a causally underdetermined. Withdrawing from the siege might have integrally contributed to the campaign falling into confusion. But it does not necessitate it. Withdrawing troops does not causally entail falling into confusion. Nevertheless, this last connection seems like a legitimate narrative connection. Indeed, this sort of connection appears quite often in narratives. But it does not fit either the deterministic causal model or the causal input model. Thus, we need a characterization of the narrative connection that is not as strong as those provided by these models.

Since narratives represent change, it is natural to think that the narrative connection has something to do with causation. But it is too demanding to expect that, in all cases, the narrative connection involves an earlier event that causally necessitates the succeeding state. But though the earlier event need not be the cause, in this sense, of succeeding states, it is not causally irrelevant either. What might the narrative connection be if it need not be the sufficient cause of successive states, but is also somehow causally relevant to successive states? One obvious relation fitting these desiderata is that the earlier event and/or state of affairs in a narrative connection is a causally necessary condition for successive states (or a contribution to such a causally necessary condition);[1] that is, more precisely, the earlier event in a narrative connection is *at least* a necessary or indispensable contribution to a sufficient, though nonnecessary, condition for the occurrence of the relevant later event in the narrative complex. Or, it is, at least, what Mackie (1976, 1980) calls an "INUS condition," that is, an *i*nsufficient but *n*ecessary part of a condition that itself is *un*necessary but *is* sufficient for an effect event. (Throughout this chapter, when I refer to the causally necessary conditions in the narrative connection, I have INUS conditions in mind inasmuch as they are necessary ingredients in the relevant causal networks under discussion.)

Referring to our robbery example, had not the earlier events cited obtained, the later events would not have obtained, though the earlier events in question do not guarantee the occurrence of the later events. In other words, had the robber not been pilfering the bank, *ceteris paribus,* the police would not have arrested him, but his robbing the bank, at that point in the story, did not guarantee his being arrested. (Here we are obviously talking about token causation, not type causation.)

Likewise, in the preceding story about the withdrawal of the army, the retreat from the town can be understood as a causally necessary condition for the army in question falling into confusion when it did. Other factors may also have conspired to cause the disarray of the army. But the preceding story tells us that a causally necessary condition for this particular instance of disarray was that the army was in the process of withdrawing. That is, if that army at that time had not been withdrawing, it would not have fallen into disarray.

Similarly, that the thief robbed the bank is a causally necessary condition for his arrest. Had he not robbed the bank, all things being equal, he would not have been arrested by the police observers when he was. The robbery was a necessary condition for his arrest.

On the strict, deterministic causal model of the narrative connection, the earlier events in the narrative necessitate the succeeding events and/or states of affairs. On the causal input model, the earlier event plus some causal input necessitate the succeeding event. But, as I have noted, the narrative relation is often weaker than that of necessitation or causal entailment. Rather, in a great many cases, earlier events merely function to make later events causally possible. Insofar as the earlier event is generally of the nature of a causally necessary condition (or a contribution to such a condition), the later event is often not predictable.

Many events share the same causally necessary conditions. The hero is rushing to save a child from an oncoming truck. This opens up the possibilities that either the child will be saved from the truck, or not. That the oncoming truck is rushing at the child is a necessary condition for both the event of the child's destruction or its being saved by the hero. The earlier event does not necessitate the outcome, but it is, all things being equal, a necessary condition for either of the alternative outcomes.

The reason why we hesitated to identify causation as the relevant connective for all cases of narrative connection was that we noted that very often the earlier events and/or states of affairs in stories underdetermine the events that follow them. Hypothesizing that the earlier events and/or states of affairs are at least causally necessary conditions, however, cannot be defeated by this objection, since *x*'s being a causally necessary condition for what follows is consistent with the appearance of a wide range of events and/or states of affairs. Moreover, hypothesizing that the earlier event is at least a *causally* necessary condition (in the sense of an INUS condition) coincides with the intuition that many have that narrative has something to do with causation (if only because it is concerned with processes of change).

Of course, in saying that the earlier event in a narrative connection is *at least* a causally necessary condition in the sense stipulated, one leaves open the possibilities that sometimes the relation may be stronger causally. Sometimes the earlier event may be the cause of a subsequent event and/or states of affairs in the sense of necessitation, or sometimes a series of earlier events and/or states of affairs may be jointly sufficient for the production of a later event. I do not preclude these possibilities in some cases. Rather, I deny that they supply an account across the board of the narrative connection. A better candidate for that account is that the earlier event and/or state of affairs in a narrative connection is at least a causally necessary condition or ingredient for bringing about later events (or a contribution to such a condition). This way of approaching the matter holds only that earlier events must figure in the causal network that gives rise to later events, but allows that it can figure in that network not only as a sufficient condition but as weakly as simply a causally necessary condition (or as a contribution thereto) that is indispensable to the sufficient but nonnecessary cause of the relevant later events.

Once it is proposed that the earlier events in a narrative are at least causally necessary conditions (in the sense of INUS conditions) of later events (or contributions thereto), it is natural to wonder whether this hypothesis isn't itself too strong. Perhaps it is too stringent to require that the earlier events be *causally* necessary conditions. Might they not be just necessary conditions?

Consider this putative narrative: "Aristarchus hypothesized the heliocentric theory thereby anticipating Copernicus' discovery by many centuries." This appears to have a unified subject—the heliocentric theory—and it is time-ordered—first Aristarchus hypothesized the heliocentric theory and then Copernicus had the same insight centuries later. Moreover, if this is what we might call a "narrative of anticipation" ("or prefiguration"), then the first event, Aristarchus' discovery, is a necessary condition for the anticipation (or prefiguration) of the second event, Copernicus' discovery. Thus, if this is a narrative, then it appears that a necessary condition, rather than a causally necessary condition is all that we need to require of a narrative connection.

Yet if there is no line of influence stretching from Aristarchus' discovery to Copernicus', I, at least, find it strained to think that this a narrative. It is an interesting series of events. Indeed, mention of the second event in this series retrospectively reveals something of the significance of the earlier event, and, as we shall see, retrospective significance is a frequently recurring feature of narrative. However, where the events bear no sort of causal relation to each other, they seem more of the order of coincidence than of narrative, at least if you agree that narrative involves changes in the career of a unified subject, where change is a function of causal processes. Of course, you may not be persuaded by this, in which case you may prefer to conjecture that the earlier event in the narrative connection is only a necessary condition of the later events rather than that it is a causally necessary condition. However, I predictably feel that this formulation is too loose.

Assuming that the narrative connection involves the earlier event in the sequence playing the role of at least a causally necessary condition, the narrative connection is structurally more complex than the chronicle. However, the narrative connection bears an obvious relation to the chronicle, since this connection will imply a chronicle of events, that is, a time-ordered sequence of events. From any narrative connection proper, one can retrieve a time-ordering of the relevant events. A narrative connection, in other words, entails some chronicle, although a mere chronicle does not entail a narrative. Similarly, both a narrative proper and a related chronicle will imply some annal, though no annal strictly entails a chronicle or a narrative connection. In this way, our story forms are ordered hierarchically.

Of course, the order of presentation, as it is locally articulated, of a narrative connection—that is to say the story as told (or, what the Russian formalists called the *syuzhet*)—may deviate from the chronological-causal structure of the narrative connection itself (from what the Russian formalists called the *fabula*), since the exposition may involve all sorts of devices such as the flashback, the flash-forward, the hysteron proteron, and so on.[2] Nevertheless, in the narrative proper, the narrative connection (or *fabula*) should be retrievable from the exposition. If it is not, there is no narrative.

In the preceding paragraph, I introduced the idea of a *local articulation*, like a flashback. However, narratives as a matter of discursive practice, are globally articulated in what might be called a "forward-looking manner." Once we are in a flashback, for example, the events are told in a temporally progressive way. They are not told backward, so to speak. This differentiates narratives from mere explanations of the form: *x* at *t3* because of *y* at *t2* because of *z* at *t1*. "The battle was lost for want of a horse and the horse was wanting for lack of a horseshoe" is not a narrative, though "King Philip could find no shoe for his horse and could not ride into battle and as a result the battle was lost" is a narrative. The forward-looking aspect of narrative here is what might be called a "discursive," rather than a "logical" requirement, of this particular story form.[3]

Summarizing my arguments, then, a narrative connection obtains when 1) the discourse represents at least two events and/or states of affairs 2) in a globally forward-looking manner 3) concerning the career of at least one unified subject 4) where the temporal relations between the events and/or states of affairs are perspicuously ordered, and 5) where the earlier events in the sequence are at least causally necessary conditions for the causation of later events and/or states of affairs (or are contributions thereto). I say that the earlier events must be *at least* causally necessary conditions in order to allow that they may also be sufficient or jointly sufficient conditions for the later events. Basically, what I am saying is that the earlier events fall into the causal network that gives rise to the later events where the weakest, but perhaps the most frequent, way of figuring in that causal network is as a causally necessary condition (or a contribution thereto) for the causation of later events. That is, the earlier event in the narrative connection must be causally relevant to the effect event.

Moreover, I have added parenthetically that the earlier events and states of affairs may merely be contributions to a causally necessary condition. This last qualification is meant to accommodate the fact that many of the descriptions and depictions of states of affairs in narratives may not themselves present causally necessary conditions for what is to come, but only elements of a causally necessary condition. For example, we may be told that a character was born in a humble neighborhood in Arkansas. Later we are told that he became president of the United States. Here the humble birthplace of the president is not itself a causally necessary condition to his presidency, but only a contribution to setting forth such a condition, since it is a requirement for the presidency that the candidate be an American citizen, which condition is satisfied by being born in Arkansas, however humbly. A great many of the details we encounter in narratives are of this sort; they do not constitute causally necessary conditions for later events, but are contributions to the characterization of such conditions.

In passing, I mentioned that a typical effect of a narrative is retrospective significance. That is, later events in a narrative disclose the significance of earlier events. For example, in the historical narrative "The Allies and the Central Powers had fought themselves to a standstill, but then the Americans entered the war and, as a result, Germany was defeated," the significance of America's entry into the war is made clear in terms of its contribution to the defeat of Germany. In this narrative, the significance of America's entry into World War I is foregrounded as a turning point in that conflict. The end of the story, so to speak, makes prior mention of America's entry into the war pertinent. It discloses the significance of that event; it makes the relevance of the inclusion of that event in the story clear. Likewise, a later event in the *fabula* of *Oedipus Rex*, the plague, makes an earlier event in the story, the murder of the stranger at the crossroads, retrospectively significant. Moreover, as this example perhaps suggests, it is the fact that narratives track causal networks that most frequently enables us to identify their subjects as unified, since we usually colligate or collect elements of a narrative under the overarching umbrella of some causal network. In narratives, causal relations are standardly the cement that unifies the subject of the story.

The account that I have offered of the narrative connection should help explain the phenomenon of retrospective significance. The earlier events in the narrative connection are at least causally necessary conditions of later events in the story. Thus, when later episodes are added to the story they reveal the relevance and importance of earlier events in terms of the causally necessary roles they play—something that may not be evident when these events and/or states of affairs are first mentioned. Consequently, the characterization of the narrative connection I have offered can explain the phenomenon of retrospective significance that is typically observed to attend reading, viewing, or listening to narratives. On the other hand, retrospective significance, though a typically recurring and explicable feature of narrative, should not be mistaken as the mark of narratives, a view that Danto (1985) would appear to hold. For the temporally ordered discourse "Aristarchus hypothesized the heliocentric system and then centuries later Copernicus discovered it again" affords the apprehension of retrospective significance—it indicates the point of mentioning Aristarchus' discovery in light of Copernicus'—but it is not, as I have argued, a narrative proper inasmuch as it lacks a narrative connection.

Earlier I justified the taxonomy involving annals, chronicles, and narrative connections proper, rather than accepting any time-ordered series of events as constituting a narrative, on the grounds that it provides us with more theoretical precision. Now that I have developed my account of the narrative connection, I can perhaps offer a more powerful consideration on behalf of this taxonomy. It is this: when confronted by specimens of annals, chronicles, and narrative connections proper, and asked which most accords with what one expects of a full-blooded narrative, I predict that most respondents will choose the narrative connections proper. Narrative connections proper correspond best to our intuitions about what a narrative is. Moreover, this is because our intuitions are rooted in a vague sense that narratives have something to do with changes of state and, thus, with causation. Other theorists may suggest that we deal with the preference for narrative connections proper by saying that they possess greater degrees of narrativity. But reverting to my earlier argument, I think that it is more enabling theoretically to talk about different structural variations, notably the structural variations between annals, chronicles, and narrative connections proper.

Perhaps a related consideration in favor of my view of narrative is that narrative is a common form of explanation. In ordinary speech, we use narratives to explain how things happened and why certain standing conditions were important. Narrative is capable of performing this role because it tracks causal networks. The rationale for citing earlier events in the course of an explanatory narrative is that they play some role in the etiology of the events we wish to explain. To perform that role they must minimally belong to the causal network, a requirement that can be satisfied by their being a causally necessary ingredient (or a contribution thereto). Thus insofar as what we call narratives are explanatory, it seems advisable to regard narrative properly so-called as connected to causation and not merely as temporal succession.

Some Objections

This account of the narrative connection is likely to draw forth a number of criticisms. Though I cannot anticipate them all, let me mention a few. In literary studies, it is often customary to talk about narratives not only in terms of temporal and causal relations, but also spatial relations. However, I have not included spatial relations in my characterization of the narrative connection. Is this a problem?

Most narratives do involve spatial relations. However, since I am attempting to get at the essential features of our concept of narration, I do not invoke spatial relations, because it seems to me that there can be narratives bereft of spatial relations, though, on the other hand, narratives bereft of temporal and causal relations seem to be unfathomable to me. Consider this example: "This morning I was upset because I thought that I had forgotten how to add, but then I remembered that 2 + 2 = 4 and now I am so very happy." This seems to be a narrative to me, or, rather, to possess a narrative connection, but it doesn't involve spatial relations, since, of course, "I" might be a disembodied spirit. Nor is this simply an invented example. In various religious narratives we are frequently told of spirits and spiritual forces who undergo changes of state.

Another objection to my view involves a counterexample. Suppose we hear a story of the sort we are all likely to categorize as a full-blooded narrative—at least up to the last line of the story. But, then, the last line says that everything has transpired in a logically possible world where there are no causes, just coincidences. In the world of the story, there are no causally necessary conditions. So, according to my view, there are no narrative connections in the story, and, hence, it is not a narrative, properly so-called.[4]

This is an ingenious example. However, my temptation is to bite the bullet and to say that it is not a narrative. It looked like a narrative up until the very end, but then it turned out not to be. Is this simply arbitrary or question begging? I think not.

If one is attracted to this counterexample, it may be because one thinks that a tale being told is some kind of story, and that my claiming that it is not is simply dogmatic. However, I too can agree that it is a story—it is a chronicle on my accounting. It is not a narrative properly so-called, but it is still a representative of a story form. We thought at first that it was a narrative, but by its conclusion we realized it is a chronicle. Thus, denying it the status of a narrative is not as drastic or counterintuitive as it may sound at first, since I am not claiming that the example fails to be any kind of story; it just fails to be a full-fledged narrative. Indeed slotting it under the category of the chronicle may even be attractive, since it says precisely what story form it belongs to.

A related counterexample might be to imagine a race of alien peoples who have no concept of causation. They string together event ordered series untethered by causal connections. On my account, these people would not have narratives even though they might spend most of their time recounting past events to each other. But once again, this sort of counterexample does not seem to be problematic to me. On the one hand, it seems clear that these people would not have our concept of narrative, and that is the concept I am trying to unravel. And, on the other hand, if we knew more about the kind of stories they tell, we might be able to identify them in terms of story forms other than narrative.

Literary and cinema scholars are apt to be distrustful of my characterizations because they are often concerned with modernist or avant-garde narratives. These are often antinarratives, like Kathy Acker's *Pussy King of the Pirates*, which are designed to disrupt or to subvert ordinary narrative connections. These sorts of practices do not accord with my characterizations, since they are expressly intended to violate the standard conception of narrative. But, in that sense, these practices themselves must presuppose something like the ordinary concept of narrative in order to negate it. Such practices are parasitic on the ordinary concept of narrative. But so much concedes that there must be an ordinary concept that functions as their, so to speak, foil. I would argue that that is what my conception of the narrative connection models. Thus, practitioners and critics of the avant-garde antinarrative, oddly enough, need something like my concept of the narrative connection as a condition of possibility for their own practices and, in that way, they will confirm my theory, or something very much like, if only backhandedly.

The picaresque is another genre that literary critics advance as a counterexample to theories like mine. However, this is to enter the debate over the identification of what I earlier called "large-scale discourses." Picaresques, like *Tom Jones*, may recount the diverse adventures of a character over a long period of time and many of these events may not cohere in a connected causal network. That is certainly true. However, none of the best-known picaresques are totally bereft of narrative connections. Actions and events within given episodes standardly evince what I have called "narrative connections," not to mention the fact that there are often, even if not always, narrative connections between episodes. Thus, at least the best-known picaresques will not be discounted as narratives proper on my characterization of the narrative connection. They will have some narrative connections, even if they contain fewer connections than other genres like the classical detective mystery or the thriller.

Narrative Comprehension

Having outlined a theory of the narrative connection proper and having considered some objections to it, the question arises about whether this theory can contribute anything to our understanding of narrative comprehension. I think that it can. Comprehending a narrative involves following it. But following a narrative involves anticipation. It involves having a sense of where the narrative is headed. But what is the nature of this anticipation? In what sense does the reader, viewer, or listener intuit the direction in which the narrative is headed?

Where ideas about outcomes are at issue, it is natural to think in terms of prediction. And sometimes when reading, viewing, or listening to a narrative, we do predict what will come next. But this is not our typical posture toward future episodes in a narrative. For as I have already noted, generally the earlier events in a narrative underdetermine the later events. Prediction would be a feasible mental state for readers, listeners, and viewers typically to be in if deterministic causal models of narration were persuasive. That is, presented with causes, we would predict the effects. But I have suggested that very frequently the connection between earlier and later events in narratives is not that of a strict causal chain. Indeed, typically, earlier events in a narrative underdetermine later events. So *prediction,* in any strong sense of the term, seems to be an unlikely characterization of the sort of anticipation that characteristically accompanies narrative.

But if prediction is not the core of narrative anticipation, what is? On my account of the narrative connection, earlier events raise certain possibilities, rather than others. They, so to speak, open a range of possibilities about what might happen next. From the point of view of the reader, viewer, or listener, this is a matter of encouraging a range of expectations. Following the story involves having a broad sense of where it is headed—a broad sense of what might happen next—rather than having a definite sense of what will happen next (as would be the case with prediction). Thus, narrative anticipation is structured in terms of the reader, listener, or viewer's possession of a range of possibilities. When later events are then entered into the narrative, the audience finds them intelligible just because they accord with or fall into the range of possibilities suggested by the earlier events in the story.

This is not to say that the reader, listener, or viewer has an array of concrete possibilities before her mind as she processes the narrative. Rather, earlier events open a range of possibilities and when later events arrive, we recognize that they fall into that range. If ensuing events fail to fall into that range and are not recuperated by the addition of causal inputs, the narrative will appear to be incoherent and unintelligible. Following a narrative with understanding is a matter of seeing how the states of affair that obtain in the narrative are possible, given the earlier events in the narrative. This involves, in short, recognizing that the earlier events presented conditions for the realization of the later events. Specifically, it involves recognizing that the earlier events were causally relevant conditions (or contributions thereto) for the occurrence of the pertinent later events in the story at hand.

These conditions make later events possible. Our sense of the direction of the narrative—of its intelligible unfolding—is rooted in our sense of what kinds of events are possible, given other events. Of course, causally necessary conditions can branch in many different directions. Many subsequent itineraries are possible. One causally necessary condition will support an indeterminate range of consequences. But, of course, this is consistent with the fact that our sense of the direction of a narrative may also be very indeterminate. Remember that following a narrative is not typically a matter of prediction.

On the other hand, that the direction of the narrative is indeterminate does not mean that it is wide open—that just anything can follow anything else. For the causally necessary conditions that access some lines of development, exclude other lines of development. So while earlier events open a range of possibilities, they also preclude (save the addition of extenuating causal inputs) other possibilities. Our sense of the direction of the narrative is not typically precise—we do not typically predict future narrative events with exactitude. But our sense of the direction of the narrative is not altogether without shape, even in the initial stages of narration. Presented with a boy and a girl, we entertain the possibility that they may or may not subsequently become lovers, but we do not, without the addition of more information, anticipate that Mars will explode. The presentation of a boy and a girl is not a causally necessary condition for a planetary eruption.

That our sense of the direction of a narrative is typically indeterminate fits in with our hypothesis about causally necessary conditions. That is, an indefinite though not wide-open sense of direction is what one would expect if the basis of the narrative connection is generally only a matter of causally necessary conditions (in the sense of INUS conditions), or contributions thereto. Or, alternatively, that the narrative connection depends primarily on such causally necessary conditions explains why our sense of the direction of a narrative is generally indeterminate (though not unbounded). Of course, as narratives proceed, piling up more and more causally necessary conditions, the range of possible subsequent events shrinks. We expect subsequent events to fall in the intersection of those events made possible by the combination of the antecedent causally necessary conditions. Indeed, the compilation of causally necessary conditions may be so exhaustive that we treat them as jointly sufficient and predict subsequent events. But even when prediction becomes feasible, it is the special case and not the norm of narrative anticipation. That is, it is not what we are generally involved in doing when we follow a narrative, even if it is what we do at certain points in a narrative, especially with respect to penultimate episodes.

Rather, narrative anticipation is a matter of forming expectations on the basis of what events are possible, given earlier events in the story. Where do these expectations come from? Lots of places, including our knowledge of the world (our knowledge of what is causally possible in everyday life), our knowledge of what is possible within the conventions of a certain narrative genre, and our knowledge of what is thought possible given the beliefs of the culture in which the narrative is composed. These expectations are not always—indeed, possibly rarely—consciously articulated. Metaphorically speaking, they are like opening certain directories for access in our mental computer. I leave it to the psychologists to discover the actual mechanics of this process. Suffice it to say that the addition of such causally necessary conditions to the narrative prepares us mentally for certain kinds of possibilities rather than others, and when one of those possibilities is realized by subsequent events in a narrative, we find it intelligible if it accords with one of the kinds of lines of possibility we have been primed to expect.

Following a narrative involves understanding what is going on in the narrative. This is a matter of assimilating what is going on into a structure—of integrating earlier and later events into a structure. That structure is comprised of possibilities opened by earlier events in the discourse that function at least as causally necessary conditions. The sense of intelligibility that attends the narrative connection is a matter of the later events falling into the range of possibilities opened by or proponed by earlier events.

Stated negatively, following a narrative is a matter of not being confused when later events arrive in a narrative. Stated positively, following a narrative involves a sense of the direction of the narrative as it unfolds, and a sense of intelligibility or fitness when earlier events are conjoined with later events in the narrative. These events can all be explained by the hypothesis that earlier events in narratives are at least (and perhaps typically) causally necessary conditions (or contributions thereto) for the later events in the story. We are not confused by later events in a narrative because they fall into the range of possibilities opened by earlier episodes that function at least as causally necessary conditions (or contributions thereto). Or, if we are confused, that can generally be explained by pointing out that the subsequent events do not appear to fall into the range of possibilities for which the earlier events have prepared us. When we follow a narrative successfully that is because we find subsequent events in the narrative rationally acceptable. The criterion of rational acceptability here is whether the subsequent events fall into the range of possibilities opened by earlier events and/or states of affairs in the narrative.

Likewise, when we say we have a sense of the direction a narrative is taking, we mean that its destination is roughly defined by the possibilities that the representation of earlier events and states of affairs have opened up. Figuratively, we might say that the narrative is "headed toward" those possibilities (and "away from" the ones precluded by earlier events and/or states of affairs).

Moreover, when the arrival of subsequent events in a narrative strikes us as intelligible or fitting, that is because they accord with our sense of what is possible, given earlier events. This does not mean that we are not often surprised by subsequent events in a narrative. I was surprised when I learned who the culprit was in the movie *The Usual Suspects* and in its spiritual forebear, the novel, *The Murder of Roger Ackroyd*. However, once the culprit was revealed, I recognized that he fell into the range of possibilities opened by earlier scenes, even though I had not explored that particular possibility in my own thinking about these cases. Moreover, being surprised is consistent with there being causally necessary conditions in the narration that are, so to speak, stylistically recessive. In the cases of *The Usual Suspects* and *The Murder of Roger Ackroyd*, we might say that they were downright "hidden."

In this chapter, I have tried to develop a definition of the narrative connection, which connection I think is fundamental to our concept of narratives—to the way in which we go about categorizing large-scale discourses as narrative. The most controversial aspect of that theory, I predict, is my contention that the basis of the narrative connection is that earlier events and/or states of affairs are at least causally necessary conditions (in the sense of INUS conditions), or contributions thereto, for the occurrence of later events in the relevant stories. I have attempted to defend this hypothesis by contrasting the narrative connection with annals and chronicles, and by an appeal to our intuitions about narrative. I have also tried to use this notion to characterize and to explain aspects of narrative comprehension, especially narrative anticipation and its role in following a narrative. If these explanations are attractive, it is my hope that they will make my hypotheses about the nature of the narrative connection even more compelling to you.[5]

Notes

1. Gallie (1964, chap. 2) first proposed that the earlier events in narratives might be construed as necessary conditions for later events, though his comments are very laconic and undeveloped. I have refined his approach by talking about *causally* necessary conditions as well as by attempting to support the hypothesis argumentatively and by developing it in greater detail. I have also profited greatly from Gallie's discussion of following a narrative, though I hope that I have extended it and clarified it somewhat.

2. For discussions of the *syuzhet/fabula* distinction, see Chatman (1990) and Bordwell (1985).

3. I owe my recognition of the need to acknowledge the forward-looking aspect of narration to comments made by audience participants at the University of Leeds.

4. I owe this objection to Gregory Currie.

5. I would like to thank Gregory Currie, Elliot Sober, Berent Enc, Ellery Eels, James Phelan, David Bordwell, Susan Friedman, Sally Banes, Graham McFee, Matthew Kieran and my audiences at the University of Leeds, and the University of Sussex for their helpful comments and criticisms.

2

A Point of View on Point of View or Refocusing Focalization

Gerald Prince

There have been many—perhaps too many—definitions of narrative points of view (cf. van Rossum-Guyon [1970] and Prince [1987]). Some are restrictive, like Genette's (1980, 1988), who prefers to use the term *focalization* and limits its domain to questions of *mood* (or "vision") as opposed to questions of *voice*, "who sees (or perceives)" and not "who speaks." Others are expansive, like Lanser's (1981) or, more recently, Ronen (1994) and O'Neill's (1994). According to Lanser points of view spring from the relations between narrator, narratee, narrating, and narrated. Ronen, although she often relies on Genettean terminology, argues that a "perspective can be described in terms of *perceptual restrictions* on a character, in terms of the *ideological attitudes* of an external focalizer, or in terms of a *logic of action*" (183–84) and she further specifies that "an omniscient narrator in a zero act of focalization (with no apparent restriction on his field of focalization) necessarily manifests a restriction on selection" (182). As for O'Neill, he maintains, in a thought-provoking book, that everything, in every narrative, is *primarily* focalized by an agent external to the narrated (87) and he goes on to argue that this focalization is itself embedded in that of an *implied author* (96). He could, no doubt, have argued that the latter, in turn, is embedded in the reader's focalization (cf. 102), and so on and so forth.[1]

In what follows, I would like to put forth a restrictive account of point of view based mainly on Genette's work and on Chatman's more recent proposals (1986, 1990).[2] In fact, it will hardly be more than a restatement; but it will allow me to underline some of the advantages of a restrictive, as opposed to expansive, stance and to make a few general comments about the possible effects of particular uses of point of view on cognition or emotion.

I have, not surprisingly, hesitated about the terminology to adopt. Partly because of its relative vagueness (and sometimes because of its overly strong visual connotations), the locution "point of view" has encountered many rivals (including perspective, angle of vision, filter and slant, focus of narration, and focalization) and some of these have themselves generated a substantial vocabulary and even led to a multiplication of narrative entities; for instance, Bal refers not only to a focalizer and a focalized but also to a *focalisataire* or "focalizee" (1977: 38)! Since I was unable to think of a satisfying neologism, I decided to remain faithful, by and large, to Genette's terminology—which has been very influential—and to supply any number of paraphrastic formulations whenever I thought it convenient or pertinent.

There are two basic ways in which a narrative situates the information it provides about the narrated world. Either the narrative presents (the narrator reports) what some (one or more) of the entities in that world are perceiving of the situations and events narrated ("She heard people speaking a strange language") or it does not ("As the weather was very fine, the people on the farm had dined more quickly than usual, and had returned to the fields"). Focalization obtains in the first case—it is roughly equivalent to Chatman's "filter"—but does not obtain in the second.

Note, first, that the verb "perceive" is to be taken in a broad rather than narrow acceptation: to apprehend with the senses (to see, hear, touch, etc.) or with the mind, or with something like their equivalent. In other words, what is perceived may be abstract or concrete, tangible or intangible—sights, sounds, smells, or thoughts, feelings, dreams, and so on.

Note also that the entities can but need not be characters: everything may be presented in terms of a nonanthropomorphic instrument—say, a camera—located in the narrated world (the narrated diegesis). Of course, the same or different situations and events can be presented according to the "perceptions" of the same or different entities (giving rise to cases which, following Genette, we might differentiate as fixed, variable, and multiple focalization). Moreover, in what may be dubbed compound or, more generally, collective focalization, a given set of elements can be perceived simultaneously—and identically or differently—by any number of entities (as in "John,

Mary, and Sally saw Peter walking toward them," or in "Janet thought it was a turtle and Larry thought it was a stone," or in "[W]e knew we were fated, before the ebb began to run, to hear about one of Marlow's inconclusive experiences"). Sometimes—and this occurs quite frequently in movies—at least one aspect of a situation or event is focalized while, simultaneously, at least one other aspect is not: a character perceives a strange sound but cannot see what we are shown to be its source. We might then speak of partial focalization. Sometimes, as in "One of them saw Catherine hiding behind the bushes," the text does not specify the entity functioning as focalizer. We might then speak of unspecified focalization. And sometimes, it proves impossible to determine whether or not situations and events are filtered through an entity's perception. We might then speak of undecidable focalization. As for the cases presenting "what might be or have been seen or perceived—if only there were someone who could have adopted the requisite perspective on the situations and events at issue" (Herman 1994: 231), the cases sometimes studied under the rubric of a hypothetical point of view and involving, for instance, something like a Balzacian observer, traveler, or *promeneur* who *would* see x, hear y, think z, they do not really constitute instances of focalization since no entity belonging to the narrated is actually engaged in its perception.[3]

Note further that, as Genette made clear, "the commitment as to focalization is not necessarily steady over the whole length of a narrative" (1980: 191). Not only can one focalizer (reflector, center of consciousness, or holder of a point of view) yield to another one within the space of a few words (as in "John watched Mary, who stared back at him, wishing he would stop") but focalization itself may obtain and then vanish from one sentence to the next or even within a single sentence ("Jane saw Robert and thought that he looked tired: she did not know that he was faking"). Indeed, it is only in a general way that a given narrative may be said to be or not to be focalized, or to adopt one mode of focalization or another. Even in *The Ambassadors* we find such passages as "This was the very beginning with him of a condition as to which, later on, as will be seen, he found cause to pull himself up" ("violating" fixed internal focalization) and in "The Killers" such sentences as "He had never had a towel in his mouth before" ("violating" external focalization).

Finally, note that, contrary to the position of, say, O'Neill, who stipulates that "*the narrator is always a focalizer*, having no choice *whether* to focalize or not . . . only *how* to do so" (1994: 90), and contrary, as well, to the more "moderate" stance of narratologists who have argued that the narrator is *sometimes* a focalizer (cf. Chatman [1978], Lintvelt [1981], or Prince [1982]), in terms of the position I am adopting, the narrator—even an *intradiegetic* and *homodiegetic* one like Des Grieux in *Manon Lescaut*—is *never* a focalizer. This in no way means that the narrator does not have a "point of view," a certain (individualized or anthropomorphic) attitude, outlook, or vision of things, a slant (to speak like Chatman [1990]), a more or less specific "take" on what transpires *diegetically*. He or she (always) does, of course, and is often not shy about formulating it explicitly. The narrator of *The Brothers Karamazov*, for example, endeavors to make his feelings about Alyosha clear and takes no fewer than two long pages to do so: "I would only beg the reader not to be in too great a hurry to laugh at my young hero's pure heart. I am far from intending to apologize for him or to justify his innocent faith on the ground of his youth, or the little progress he had made in his studies, or any such reason. I must declare, on the contrary, that I have genuine respect for the qualities of his heart. . . ." and so forth. Furthermore, this is not so much because the situations and events narrated are always (significantly) *past* with regard to the narrator or even because the latter cannot perceive them physically (cf. Chatman, [1986: 194]). Cases of (fictional) anterior or simultaneous narration and cases of homo- or heterodiegetic narration in real time (as in live radio or television broadcasts of some catastrophe, parade, or sport event) might provide counterexamples and so might passages like the following from Beckett's *Malone Dies*: "For it is evening, even night, one of the darkest I can remember, I have a short memory. My little finger glides before my pencil across the page and gives warning, falling over the edge, that the end is near." In these lines, as Nelles remarks, "the narrator's seeing and conceiving appear to be identical with the character's, and there is surely no 'back then' involved" (1990: 370–71). Rather, if the narrator is never a focalizer, it is simply because, qua narrator and regardless of his or her (homo- or hetero-, intra- or extra-) diegetic status and narrational stance, s/he is never part of the *diegesis* she presents. Qua narrator, s/he is an element of *discourse* and not *story* (of the narrating and not the narrated) whereas focalization is an element of the latter. To paraphrase Chatman slightly, in the case of a movie, the camera (or whatever) does not focalize situations: it *presents* them (at such and such a distance, from such and such an angle); similarly, with a painting, the painterly narrator does not focalize a scene but presents it to us; and, with a verbal narrative too, the narrator is an instrument of presentation and not focalization (cf. 1990: 155–56).

The restrictive definition has, I think, several advantages (and, of course, I cannot see any of its possible disadvantages). In the first place, and apart from applying equally well to narrative fiction or nonfiction in any media, it is based on a simple criterion. Whereas even Genette's account, for example, sometimes seems to hesitate between a characterization founded on *who perceives* (e.g., internal or external focalization, character or noncharacter) and one founded on *what is perceived*—as Nelles puts it, either the narrator has no access to the character's thoughts "or has (and is limited to) access, or has (but is not limited to) access" (1990: 368)—and whereas other useful and influential typologies (like Doležel [1973] or Lintvelt's [1981]) seem to rely on the position (e.g., center, front, or periphery) and the nature of the focalizer but also on the situation and status of the narrator, my discussion links focalization only to the perception of the narrated by (or through, or "with") an entity in that narrated.

Second, by restricting itself to that sole determining criterion, the discussion makes it clear that focalization is just that: it does not result from or (partly) consist of various other features of the narrating or the narrated but combines with them variously to yield different narrative strategies. Furthermore, by maintaining a strict distinction between "who speaks" and "who perceives," narrator and focalizer, the discussion also makes it clear that focalization is autonomous with regard to medium of presentation, though, obviously, different configurations of the latter can manifest the presence or absence of different modes of focalization. "Harriet did not see Jessica leave the room" indicates that Harriet is not a focalizer; "Peter liked to be on the second floor of the library" is quite different from "Peter liked to lurk on the second floor of the library"; and when the adult autodiegetic narrator of *Marie-Claire* says: "My father often took us to a place where there were men drinking wine," the inference is that the child-protagonist functions as a focalizing instrument.

Third, from a slightly more formal point of view, the restrictive definition has the advantage of placing focalization squarely in the domain of the narrated or story. In narrative-grammatical terms (cf. Prince [1987]), the phenomenon would thus be accounted for in the *structural* or "story" component of a narrative grammar (the finite set of rules generating the macro- and microstructures of all and only sequences of narrated situations and events). Significantly, definitions involving as focalizers not only narrated entities but also narrators entail a more complicated grammar without yielding more powerful descriptions, since focalization would have to figure in both the structural component and the *narrating* or "discourse" one (the finite set of rules operating on the generated structures and accounting for "narrative discourse"). As for definitions like O'Neill's, which make of focalization "very evidently a phenomenon of discourse rather than story" (95), they imply that the grammatical description generated in the story component would be operated on by a focalization rule in the discourse component and, thus, they more than suggest that situations and events are always describable independent of the way in which they are focalized. Which is surely not the case. . . .

Fourth, and perhaps most important, by not limiting a priori the power of focalizers, the definition respects theoretic potentialities as opposed to common sense or to generic imperatives. It is linked to the possible rather than to the plausible, the acceptable, the ordinary. Granted, human beings are not (usually) able to read other people's thoughts, their physical perceptions are (spatiotemporally) limited, and they cannot see the future. Cameras too (and tape recorders) suffer from many limitations. But, theoretically, nothing prevents focalization from yielding the same kind and amount of information provided in cases of nonfocalized *omniscient* (or quasi-omniscient) narration. In fact, many fictional human beings *are* endowed with the capacity to perceive other entities' reflections and feelings. It happens—memorably—in *A la recherche du temps perdu* as well as in lesser works like Giraudoux's *Bella,* Barbusse's *Feu*, Marivaux's *Paysan parvenu,* Crébillon's *Egarements du cœur et de l'esprit*, and Shelley's *Frankenstein*: "Clerval at first attributed my unusual spirits to joy on his arrival, but when he observed me more attentively, he saw a wildness in my eyes for which he could not account." According to the restrictive definition, focalization would not merely cover cases of so-called (fixed, variable, or multiple) internal point of view, cases of external point of view (in which the focalizer—character, actor, or instrument—perceives only tangible elements or events), and cases in which the focalizer perceives *no* such elements or events; it would also cover cases in which no perceptual restrictions whatever apply. As for nonfocalized material, it too could be restricted to the tangible or the intangible or not be restricted at all. I have left for last a few comments on the *difference* focalization makes. In theory, as my discussion emphasizes, focalization need not entail any change in the kind or amount of information provided (except that this information would be marked as focalized). In practice, of course, focalization conventionally entails various restrictions and limitations (e.g., human focalizers can only guess the intentions of other characters; they do not know what will happen; their perceptions are biased, partial, and inaccurate) and, besides, it also often obeys more locally motivated rules (e.g., with the focalizer being unable to read or unable to understand this language or that one). On the other hand, both in theory and practice, the recourse to a character as a focalizer does affect the relative status of characters in a narrative, if only because it endows the focalizer with a specific attribute (which would distinguish him or her from any nonfocalizing character). Similarly, the adoption of certain modes of focalization can have certain consequences for processing and interpretation. Thus, should the narrator remain covert and should something like an external point of view be used, it would be up to us ("readers") to assess the feelings of the characters (if any), the meaning of their actions, the very significance of the situations presented; should something like fixed internal point of view be used, it would be up to us to determine whether (and in what sense) it distorts "what is"; and should something like multiple internal point of view be used, it would be up to us to find out which one of the resulting accounts (assuming they are different) is closest to the truth.

As my phrasing suggests, this should not be taken to mean that focalization per se necessarily affects interpretation and response, and cognition and emotion, in specifiable ways or, even, that it affects them at all. It has (often) been argued that a "character who is also a focalizer has a special claim not only on readers' attention but also on their sympathy: for, as Bal [1977: 138] observes, in such a case, "the reader watches with the character's eyes and will, in principle, be inclined to accept the vision presented by that character" (O'Neill 1994: 96). Perhaps! In principle. But what if the character's opinions are antithetical to mine, his motives repugnant, his values repulsive? Besides, it has also (often) been argued that the reader tends "to treat a character-focalizer's perspective cautiously as being subjective" (87) and that "the more easily graspable as a character [the focalizer is], the more the reader will in turn feel authorized to question the focalizer's vision" (89). Perhaps! Again, I am not so sure. For my suspicions to be aroused, shouldn't there be some textual (or contextual) indication that (reliably) contradicts the character's perception or differs from it or, at the very least, shouldn't there be some sign implying the possibility that, in certain situations, this perception may be skewed? After all, even when a focalizer proves repeatedly fallible (to use Chatman's expression [1990]), much that he, she, or it perceives may simply not be put into question. In Sartre's *Age de raison*, for instance, Daniel Sereno is notoriously in bad faith; but, to my knowledge, no one has ever doubted the accuracy of the geographic information filtered through him. More generally, I am not sure that we necessarily consider focalized information as less trustworthy than nonfocalized data, a focalizer's view as less valid than a narratorial one. What if the narrator is unreliable? Or what if, in a historical rather than fictional narrative, his or her "circumstantial credibility" is low (he is a careless historian; she is an "ideologue")?[4] What if the narrator seems more unreliable than the focalizer seems fallible? Or, even, what if the heterodiegetic (and covert) narrator seems thoroughly reliable but the focalizer also seems accurate and yet their views do not quite coincide?

I think that we—(literary) narratologists—have too often taken conventional and locally persuasive claims about how we understand and react to focalizers and focalizations for universally true statements. I also think that we need an empirically/experimentally grounded theory of narrative functioning—in other words, a narratology that is also a psychonarratology (see Dixon and Bortolus, chap. 16 of this vol.)—to account for what actually is the case. Indeed, the development of such a theory is perhaps the most important task of narratologists today.

Notes

1. The general opposition I have sketched antedates Genette, Lanser, and O'Neill. It is the opposition between those who, from James (1979) and Lubbock (1921) on, consider "point of view" to refer to a specific technique (as in "point of view narrative") and those who take it to refer to the general attitude or outlook governing any presentation of situations and events.

2. I have also profited from Nelles's (1990) analysis of the Genettean model and from Sanders's (1994) fine thesis on narrative perspectives.

3. Similar to passages rendered in terms of such a "traveler" are passages rendered according to the perceptions that *anyone*—in a certain position, at a certain distance, and from a certain angle—would have ("From the top of that gigantic building, one can see the entire valley"; "On that day, the ocean looked like an enormous gray stain"; and "Just before the entrance to the city, the river gently flows between two rows of rocks").

4. On this topic, see Cohn's (1990) interesting discussion.

3

Why Narrators Can Be Focalizers— and Why It Matters

James Phelan

Introduction

Like Prince in the previous chapter, I want to take another look at the various concepts swirling around the term *focalization* and to propose a new way of thinking about the relation between the term and the concept. Not surprisingly, perhaps, my proposal will be an alternative to Prince's. Although I admire his effort to join forces with Chatman and to offer a restrictive definition that will increase the clarity and economy of narratology, I shall argue that the Prince/Chatman position achieves that clarity and economy at the expense of an inadequate account of what narrators can do. In the Chatman/Prince view, narrators cannot perceive the story world but can only report on it. In my view, this limitation on narrators fails to explain their role in influencing the perceptions of *narratees,* implied audiences, and flesh and blood readers. Furthermore, studying the Prince/Chatman view of narrators reveals some problems in the underlying principle upon which it is based: the explanatory power of the story/discourse distinction. In what follows, I will develop my alternative view that narrators can be focalizers and suggest that adopting that view has at least two significant consequences: It reminds us that the story/discourse distinction is a heuristic construct rather than a natural law, something we've invented to aid our understanding of narrative, not an intractable phenomenon establishing impermeable boundaries between narrative commentary and characters' actions. Adopting the view that narrators can be focalizers opens up an avenue to talk about an important but neglected aspect of homodiegetic and *autodiegetic* narration: the self-consciousness of the narrator.

Shaw, in a recent discussion of Chatman, has made a related argument that has helped advance my thinking here. But where Shaw wants to consider the phenomenon of "loose narrators," that is, narrators who *seem* to enter story space, I want to argue that even when narrators remain clearly in discourse space, they perform acts of *perception* that ought to be called "focalization." And where Shaw takes his discussion in the direction of realism and history, I take mine in the direction of narrator-character interactions. In his reply to Shaw, Chatman acknowledges that the terms *story space* and *discourse space* are metaphors and that narrative artists have shown that narrators can enter story space and characters can enter discourse space. But my point—and, I believe, Shaw's—is that in Chatman's argument about narrators' inability to perceive the story/discourse distinction *functions* much more like a law of nature than a convenient metaphor.[1]

The Focalization Debate and the Prince/Chatman Position

In order to ground the discussion in narration itself, I would like to begin by considering the following passage from Nabokov's *Lolita*, in which Humbert Humbert summarizes the first long car trip he has taken with Lolita. The reasons for my choice of this passage and for this narrative will become evident. (Shortly, we shall also have a look at the opening of Dickens's *Dombey and Son*, a passage that Chatman uses to illustrate some of his points.)

> And so we rolled East, I more devastated than braced with the satisfaction of my passion, and she glowing with health, her bi-iliac garland still as brief as a lad's, although she had added two inches to her stature and eight pounds to her weight. We had been everywhere. We had really seen nothing. And I catch myself thinking today that our long journey had only defiled with a sinuous trail of slime the lovely, trustful, dreamy, enormous country that by then, in retrospect, was no more to us than a collection of dog-eared maps, ruined tour books, old tires, and her sobs in the night—every night, every night—the moment I feigned sleep. (1848: 177–78)

As Prince's able summary of the debate over focalization makes clear, contemporary narratologists would offer a wide range of descriptions of the perspective in this passage. Genette and his followers would say that it contains variable focalization, beginning as internal focalization (the vision belongs to Humbert the character) and moves in the last sentence of the passage toward zero or free focalization (the vision belongs to Humbert the narrator) with a final move back to Humbert. Bal (1977, 1985) and her followers would emphasize, among other things, that the passage has both *focalizers* (the narrating-I and the experiencing-I) and *objects of focalization* (the *focalized)*, and that the movement of the latter—from Humbert to Lolita, to the "lovely, trustful, dreamy, enormous country," and then back to Lolita is as significant as the movement of the former. Rimmon-Kenan (1983, 1989), Lanser (1981), and others would emphasize that the movement of focalization includes not just a shift of vision but also a shift in emotive, psychological, and ideological perspective: where Humbert the character focuses first on the effects of his physical passion on himself and then on the passage of time on Lolita's body, Humbert the narrator focuses on the negative effects of Humbert the character's passion on her psyche. O'Neill (1994) would point to the implied Nabokov as the ultimate focalizer of the passage. Chatman (1978, 1986, 1990, 1995) would eschew the term *focalization* and say instead that the passage moves from being filtered through Humbert the character to being slanted through Humbert the narrator with a final return to the filter in the second half of the last sentence. Prince (1982, 1987, 1990) would say that the first part of the passage is focalized through Humbert the character, while the last sentence, with its shift to Humbert the narrator's report of his present understanding, contains no focalization—until its last half that is again focalized through Humbert the character.[2]

In the midst of this diversity of explanations and emphases, we may lose sight of the fact that the debate about focalization begins with an insight praised by all participants: Genette's (1980) observation that the most commonly used term to refer to narrative perspective, *point of view,* conflates two distinct concepts: vision (who sees?) and voice (who speaks?) (186). (In *Narrative Discourse Revisited*, Genette remarks that the question, "Who sees?" is more adequately formulated as "Who perceives?" [1988: 64].) One of the reasons why the debate has gone on so long, I believe, is that Genette himself takes his insight in a relatively unhelpful direction. After proposing that the term *focalization* replace *point of view*, Genette proposes a typology not according to the distinction between who sees and who speaks but according to the criterion of *how much narrators see and know in relation to characters.* Thus, he describes three kinds of focalization:

1. zero focalization (appropriately renamed "free focalization" by Nelles): omniscient narration, for instance, in Fielding's *Tom Jones*, where the narrator perceives and knows more than any character
2. internal focalization: objective narration, for instance, in the fiction of Henry James, where the narrator perceives and knows only what the central consciousness perceives and knows
3. external focalization: center of consciousness narration, for instance, in the fiction of Hammett, where the narrator perceives and knows less than the protagonist.[3]

I say that this proposal is relatively unhelpful because it reproduces the problem that Genette wants to solve: though it separates "who sees" from "who speaks," it conflates two other concepts: "who sees" and "what (or how much) is seen."[4]

A significant advantage of the Chatman/Prince position is that it abandons Genette's *relational* typology with its conflation of the *who* and the *what* and moves back to the clearer distinction between who perceives and who speaks. The disadvantage of the position is that it inadequately describes the capacities of narrators. In Chatman's view, the key distinction is that narrators can report on the story world but they cannot literally see it. Thus, he would maintain that in the passage from *Lolita*, Humbert the narrator remembers but does not see Lolita; instead, the narrating-I only reports how the experiencing-I once saw her and how he now retrospectively thinks of the whole situation. Chatman's own example is the opening of Dickens's *Dombey and Son*:

> Dombey sat in the corner of the darkened room in the great armchair by the bedside, and son lay tucked up warm in a little basket bedstead, carefully disposed on a low settee immediately in front of the fire and close to it, as if his constitution were analogous to that of a muffin, and it was essential to toast him brown while he was very new. (1848: 1)

Chatman comments that

> the narrator is not to be imagined as literally *contemplating* the new baby and deciding, in that contemplation, that he resembles a muffin. . . . The narrator, in this case omniscient and unidentified, is a reporter, not an "observer" of the story world in the sense of literally witnessing it. It makes no sense to say that a story is told "through" the narrator's perception since he/she/it is precisely *narrating*, which is not an act of perception but of presentation or representation. . . ." (143)[5]

For Chatman, what is true of heterodiegetic narrators is ultimately true of homodiegetic narrators as well:

> The heterodiegetic narrator *never* saw the events because he/she/it never occupied the story world. The homodiegetic or first-person narrator *did* see the events and objects at an earlier moment in the story, but his recountal is after the fact and thus a matter of memory, not of perception. (145)

Shortly after this passage, Chatman indicates why he is so insistent on the difference between perception and reporting: "*if we are to preserve the vital distinction between discourse and story*, we cannot lump together the separate behaviors of narrator and character under a single term" (ibid., my italics). Needless to say, the rhetoric of Chatman's sentence presupposes that we want to preserve the distinction. Furthermore, the logic of the sentence indicates that, for him, the distinction between story and discourse is one between two ontologically different worlds or, to adopt his own metaphor, two impermeable membranes. Homodiegetic narrators such as Conrad's Marlow and Brontë's Lockwood, he writes, cannot "pierce the discourse membrane to experience the story world directly" (144).

Prince offers his own version of Chatman's position, while advancing several new justifications for it. As I just noted, Prince decides to retain the term *focalization*, but by restricting it to entities in the story world, he makes it "roughly equivalent" to Chatman's term *filter* (2). Prince introduces the concept of focalization by identifying the two ways in which a narrative reveals information about the narrated world: the narrator either reports what some entities in that world are perceiving—or does not. "Focalization obtains in the first case . . . but does not obtain in the second" (ibid.). Prince reveals his own reliance upon and faith in the story/discourse distinction at a key point in the essay. Having proposed his definition, Prince acknowledges that

> cases of (fictional) anterior or simultaneous narration and cases of homo- or hetero-diegetic narration in real time . . . might provide counterexamples and so might passages like the following from *Malone Dies*: "For it is evening, even night, one of the darkest I can remember, I have a short memory. My little finger glides before my pencil across the page and gives warning, falling over the edge, that the end is near." (5)

But Prince dismisses these possible counterexamples with one fell swoop of the story/discourse distinction:

> if the narrator is *never* a focalizer, it is because *qua* narrator and regardless of his or her (homo- or hetero-, intra- or extra-) diegetic status and narrational stance, s/he is never part of the diegesis s/he presents. *Qua* narrator, s/he is an element of discourse and not story (of the narrating and not the narrated) whereas focalization is an element of the latter. (ibid.)

Referring directly to Chatman, Prince adds that "with a verbal narrative, . . . the narrator is an instrument of presentation and not focalization" (6). In other words, Prince's point that narrators cannot be focalizers is based on the same logic as Chatman's point that narrators cannot perceive: the story/discourse distinction establishes boundaries that limit the powers of narrators. Thus, although Prince's terms would be different, he would agree in principle with Chatman's analysis of the passage from *Dombey and Son*.

Why Narrators Can Be Focalizers

Let me repeat that the Chatman/Prince position has genuine appeal and is a welcome improvement over Genette's typology: as Prince says, it is based on a simple criterion (perception inside the story, or reporting in the discourse), and that simple criterion allows for greater clarity and economy in narratological theory. Nevertheless, I think that their discussion of narrators inadequately captures the dynamics of narration as it is experienced by readers. If narrators are, in effect, blind to the story world, then audiences must be too. Or, more formally, if narrators cannot perceive the story world, then narratees, *implied readers,* and flesh and blood readers, who get much of their access to that world through a narrator, also cannot perceive that world—or can do so only through a focalizing character darkly. This conclusion suggests an impoverished conception of the act of reading narrative, something that is especially surprising from the thinker who introduced us to the concept of the narratee and from the one who synthesized the communication model.

Indeed, the distinction between perceiving and reporting—or, in the case of homodiegetic narrators, between perceiving and remembering—is ultimately impossible to maintain unless we reduce all narrators to reporting machines ("Hello, my name is HAL, and I will be your reporter for this narrative"). Happily, neither Chatman nor Prince is inclined to make that reduction (just as neither one of them nor I would insist that all narration must be understood as coming from a human agent). A human narrator, I submit, cannot report a coherent sequence of events without also revealing his or her perception of those events. The story/discourse distinction itself helps to explain why. From the perspective of story, the distinction implies that any coherent sequence of events can be reported in more than one way; from the perspective of discourse, it implies that any narration takes only one of many possible paths through the story world. Consequently, any path marked by the narrator's perspective (whether we call it "slant" or "focalization") will be not only a report on the story world but also a reflection of how the narrator perceives that world which, in turn, influences how audiences perceive that world. In other words, as the narrator reports, the narrator cannot help but simultaneously function as a set of lenses through which the audience perceives the story world. Of course, the narrator's perceptions may be unreliable or partial, but just as a character cannot act without revealing something of him or herself, a narrator cannot report without also revealing his or her perceptions. Indeed, because Chatman and Prince see the narrator as doing something parallel in discourse space to what focalizing characters do in story space, they implicitly admit that the distinction between reporting and perceiving is impossible to maintain. Chatman does suggest that the parallel between the powers of narrators and characters is not exact when he introduces his distinction between "slant" and "filter": "I propose *slant* to name the narrator's attitudes and other mental nuances appropriate to the report function of discourse, and *filter* to name the much wider range of mental activity experienced by characters in the story world—perceptions, cognitions, attitudes, emotions, memories, fantasies, and the like." But a little reflection on Tristram Shandy, Lucy Snowe, Pip, Humbert Humbert, and others, will yield the conclusion that this range of mental activity has been shown by narrators as well. But this is not to say that every passage of narration is ultimately focalized through the narrator: when the narration leaves the narrator's perspective for a character's, then the focalization shifts; the audience doffs the narrator's lenses and dons the character's.

To illustrate these points, let us return to the opening of *Dombey and Son*. I have no quarrel with Chatman's claim that the narrator is not literally in story space contemplating the baby and "deciding, in that contemplation, that he resembles a muffin" (141). But notice that Chatman assumes presence to be a necessary condition for perception. It is a plausible assumption, but the passage from *Dombey and Son* suggests that it is not warranted. The striking quality of the muffin metaphor tellingly reveals the simultaneity of report and perception. The narrator is taking the muffin path through this scene rather than, say, the steak-and-kidney-pie path or the clay pot path—and his taking this path reflects his perception of the story world. Most important, the narrator's act of reporting/perceiving provides a perception for the narratee, the implied audience, and the flesh and blood reader. The passage illustrates what Chatman's strictures about narrators lose sight of: the wonder of narrative (especially fictional narrative) is that, by convention, narrators can—and do—perceive, can and do act as our lenses on the story world, without being physically present in it.

In short, narrators can be focalizers. Determining focalization is just a matter of answering the question *who perceives*? It works just as well for homodiegetic as it does for heterodiegetic narration—and it works for second-person narration. The opening of *Dombey and Son* is a passage in which the narrator is the perceiver and, thus, the focalizer; in the following passage, also quoted by Chatman, the focalizer is Mr. Dombey:

> [He] would have reasoned: That a matrimonial alliance with himself *must,* in the nature of things, be gratifying and

> honorable to any woman of common sense. That the hope of giving birth to a new partner in such a house, could not fail to awaken a glorious and stirring ambition in the breast of the least ambitious of her sex. That Mrs. Dombey had entered on that social contract of matrimony: almost necessarily part of a genteel and wealthy station, even without reference to the perpetuation of family firms: with her eyes fully open to these advantages. (2–3)

In the passage from *Lolita,* the first sentence is focalized not through the narrator but through Humbert the character, while the first half of the last sentence is focalized through Humbert the narrator. Second-person narration is typically focalized through the "you," whether that you is a disguised form of "I" or a character external to the narrator. Its striking effects stem from the discourse's apparent insistence on merging the narratee, and the protagonist—and sometimes the flesh and blood reader—in that you.

Why It Matters

The first consequence of recognizing that narrators can be focalizers is that we can develop a revised view of the possible vision/voice relationships. In place of Genette's typology or revisions of it such as that offered by Nelles, I propose the following set of combinations:

1. narrator's focalization and voice, as in the first passage from *Dombey and Son*
2. character's focalization and narrator's voice, as in the first sentence of the passage from *Lolita*
3. character's focalization and voice, as in stream of consciousness narration
4. blends of narrator's focalization and voice with character's focalization and voice as in *free indirect discourse* or in the middle sentences of the passage from *Lolita*
5. narrator's focalization and character's voice, as when a naive narrator unwittingly takes on the voice of another character

The other consequences of my view can best be explained through a closer look at the last sentence of the passage from *Lolita*:

> And I catch myself thinking today that our long journey had only defiled with a sinuous trail of slime the lovely, trustful, dreamy, enormous country that by then, in retrospect, was no more to us than a collection of dog-eared maps, ruined tour books, old tires, and her sobs in the night—every night, every night—the moment I feigned sleep. (177–78)

As just noted, the first part of the sentence is focalized through Humbert the narrator ("I catch myself thinking today"). What is most striking about the sentence, though, is something that can not be seen from the Prince/Chatman perspective with its interdiction on narrators as focalizers: when Humbert the character's focalization enters in the second half of the sentence ("by then, in retrospect, [the country] was no more to us than a collection of dog-eared maps, ruined tour books, old tires, and her sobs in the night—every night, every night—the moment I feigned sleep)," the narrator's focalization does not drop away. Instead, the narrator's focalization contains the character's. The source of this effect can be found in the syntax, which clearly indicates that everything in the sentence is included in what Humbert catches himself "thinking today." The syntax is sufficient to produce the effect, but it is reinforced by the temporal ambiguity of the phrase, "in retrospect," which can refer either to a retrospect from the narrator's present moment or to a retrospect from the character's.

Thus, although it is only the narrating-I who draws the conclusion that their journey had defiled the country, it is both the narrating-I and the experiencing-I who envision Lolita sobbing "every night, every night." In other words, at the end of this sentence, we have the counterpart in focalization to what Bakhtin has, in matters of voice, labeled *double-voicing:* dual-vision or dual-focalization (I avoid the term *double-vision,* since its negative connotations are likely to make readers do a double-take). It is worth emphasizing that in cases of dual-focalization generally and in this case in particular, story and discourse overlap: Humbert the narrator is perceiving the sobbing Lolita and his own former self—through the eyes of that self.

This dual-focalization has several important effects. Because Humbert the narrator is not just remembering, as the Prince/Chatman position would have it, but also focalizing, we have a very rich understanding of *why* Humbert-the-narrator concludes that Humbert-the-character's pleasure trip defiled the country. The dual-focalization also provides the basis for us to conclude that Humbert is absolutely sincere in the severity of his self-judgment—or that his insincerity is very skillfully disguised. The technique, which occurs in other present-tense passages in *Lolita*, is also a marker of the way in which Humbert himself is aware of the distance between his present and his former self—and in that way is also a marker of his self-consciousness. In homodiegetic and autodiegetic narration, because we have only the narrator-character as the explicit agent for the construction of the narrative, one can almost always argue that the narrator is in self-conscious control of the narrative. And here we see one way of talking about the limits on Humbert's self-consciousness. Assuming that he is not so deceitful as to plan to switch motives for his telling, we can conclude that he is not in complete control of every self-representation he makes in his narrative.

It is also of course possible for an author to shift the focalization from a narrating-I to an experiencing-I for the purpose of showing that the narrating-I still perceives himself and the events as the character did; such narration, which is, in fact, the kind we have at the beginning of *Lolita*, may still contain a high degree of self-consciousness, if the narrator feels the need to justify him- or herself. And determining the degree of narratorial self-consciousness has many consequences for our understanding of narrator/implied author relationships. If we think that Humbert is self-consciously attempting to fake his remorse, we will also assume that Nabokov wants us to recognize that attempt. If we think that Humbert's self-consciousness does not extend that far, we will also infer that Nabokov, at least to some extent, endorses Humbert's movement toward remorse. Although I do not think that the question of a homodiegetic narrator's self-consciousness can be definitively determined by studying focalization, I would suggest that focalization provides some indication of self-consciousness. Extrapolating from this passage and from others like it in *Lolita*, I would propose, first, that shifts in focalization between the narrating-I and the experiencing-I are indicators of self-consciousness—not infallible or exclusive indicators but important ones nonetheless. Extrapolating further, I would propose that the kind of overlapping of story and discourse that we see in this sentence from *Lolita*, an overlapping rooted in the mingling of narrator and character's focalization, is another indicator of self-consciousness: a narrator who is aware of the distance between his current and former self is also likely to be aware of himself constructing the story of how he moved from one place to the other.

The importance of dual-focalization and its overlapping of story and discourse in *Lolita* emerges even more clearly as we consider the dynamics of the larger narrative. Humbert Humbert's narration begins and ends in the present tense. The focalization and voice of the opening invocation and of the closing address to Lolita belong to Humbert the narrator. That opening invocation conjures up Lolita as "light of my life, fire of my loins" before Humbert turns and offers "the ladies and gentlemen of the jury" "exhibit number one" for his defense (11). The closing address, on the other hand, is part of Humbert's self-condemnation and his wish that his confession might "make [Lolita] live in the minds of later generations" (311). In short, Humbert the narrator begins with one purpose, to exonerate himself, and ends with another, to confess his crimes and to make some gesture of expiation through the confession itself.

The source of Humbert's change, as we can see in the passage just discussed, is not only in the past events but also in his narration of them: in reperceiving the events, in mingling his perspective now with his perspective then, and in thinking about what he is saying and how it is affecting an audience, Humbert develops (or at least claims to develop) a new relation to those events. In so doing, Humbert becomes (claims to become) a transformed character. Thus, discourse is very much part of the story as Humbert the narrator's self-conscious act of telling apparently effects the further evolution of Humbert the character.

Furthermore, our own final decisions about Humbert are dependent upon the judgments we make about the interaction of the narrating-I and the character-I—and about the degree of his self-consciousness about their relation. We may take him at his word and feel that the telling of the story has led him to recognize the horror of his crimes against Lolita. In this view, we will find one important limit on his self-consciousness: he did not deliberately set out to show this progression in the motives for his narration. Alternatively, we may believe in Humbert's sincere desire to repent but find that he remains blind to the ways in which his confession continues to objectify Lolita. In this view, we will also have to determine the extent to which Nabokov either recognizes or shares Humbert's blindness so that our decisions about the extent of Humbert's self-consciousness will also entail decisions about the extent of Nabokov's. Yet another possibility is that we may decide that Humbert's expression of guilt and of the desire to expiate are themselves just two more manipulative moves on his part. In this view, his self-consciousness would be very great—as would Nabokov's distance from him. And of course there are other plausible interpretations to consider.[6] But regardless of which interpretive decisions we make, we will need to come to terms with the recognitions that Humbert's discourse is as much a part of the story as the history of his interactions with Lolita and that this overlap of story and discourse complicates our thinking about the narrator's self-consciousness.

In summary, then, I want, like Prince, to claim for my proposal about focalization the advantages of simplicity and clarity. In my view, focalization is not a complicated matter of the relation between narrators' vision and knowledge and characters' vision and knowledge but a straightforward question of who perceives. It matters that narrators can be focalizers because this view allows us to account more satisfactorily for the complex dynamics of narration, enabling us to recognize the role that narrators play in influencing audience's vision of the story world and to recognize such phenomena as dual-focalization. Regardless of whether these claims will be universally accepted, I hope that my effort here can help us recognize that an existing theoretical construct such as the story/discourse distinction can both enable and disable our efforts to think through the consequences of particular new insights such as Genette's division of vision and voice. In that spirit, I invite Prince, Chatman, and other narratologists to help me think further about the theoretical contribution I have attempted to offer here.

Notes

1. See Shaw (1995a, 1995b), Chatman (1995). See also the continuation of the debate in the exchange between Pohler (1996) and Shaw (1996).

2. As Prince's summary of the debate indicates, this paragraph does not include all of the proposals about how to understand focalization; see also Nelles (1990), Edmiston (1989), Ronen (1994), and Herman (1994, 1995). Herman and Ronen's suggestive work deserves a special mention here because they are concerned not just with the debate among narratologists but also with rethinking the concept of focalization from the perspective of possible-worlds theory.

3. For an excellent exposition of the logic of Genette's position along with intelligent proposals for some slight modifications, see Nelles. Unlike Nelles (1990), however, I think that conceiving of focalization as a relation of perception/knowledge among narrator and character muddies rather than clarifies the questions of who speaks and who perceives.

4. In order to be fair to Genette (1980), I should also stress the fact that his move fits the logic of his approach. Genette sees focalization as part of the larger category "mood" (as opposed to either "tense" or "voice"), and under mood, he considers the *degrees* by which things are seen, reported, done, and so forth. His relational typology with its concerns about degrees of vision and knowledge is very consistent with this conception of mood.

5. Shaw also cites this example in his debate with Chatman, claiming that Dickens's "loose narrator" here "*imitat[es] the role* of someone who has happened upon the scene" (1995b: 99). Like Shaw, I think that Chatman's account of the narrator as only a reporter is inadequate, but I don't think it's necessary to view him as imitating an observer. As I will explain in the next section, I think that his function of reporting necessarily entails a function of perceiving.

6. Of course all of these interpretive decisions have important consequences for our view of the ethics of reading *Lolita*. For an essay that combines a useful overview of the debate about the novel with an important intervention in that debate, one that reclaims the novel for feminist readers without becoming complicit with the worst side of Humbert-the-character, see Patnoe (1995).

Part II

History

4

The Origins of Figural Narration in Antiquity

Irene J. F. de Jong

> The smile of daybreak was just beginning to brighten the sky, the sunlight to catch the hilltops, when a group of men in brigand gear peered over the mountain that overlooks the place where the Nile flows into the sea at the mouth that men call Heracleotic. They stood there for a moment, scanning the expanse of sea beneath them: first they gazed out over the ocean, but as there was nothing sailing there that held out hope of spoil and plunder, their eyes were drawn to the beach nearby. This is what they saw: a merchant ship was riding there, moored by her stern, empty of crew but laden with freight. This much could be surmised even from a distance, for the weight of her cargo forced the water up to the third line of boards on the ship's side. But the beach!—a mass of newly slain bodies, some of them quite dead, others half-alive and still twitching, testimony that the fighting had only just ended. . . . They stood on the mountainside like the audience in a theater, unable to comprehend the scene: the vanquished were there, but the victors were nowhere to be seen.[1]

This passage reads like the gripping opening of a thriller. It is, however, the beginning of an ancient Greek novel, the *Aethiopica* by Heliodorus, which can probably be dated in the fourth century A.D. It was this passage that Bernd Effe, a classical scholar from Konstanz, Germany, used in 1975 to argue that "at least rudimentary" figural narration, that is, the presentation of events through the eyes of characters inside the story, is found as far back as antiquity. The prevailing opinion among literary historians and narratologists is that, whereas authorial and first-person narration are as old as storytelling itself, figural narration is a relatively recent invention:

> . . . the figural novel made its appearance late in the history of the novel: around the second half of the nineteenth century. Once invented, it became prominent in a very short time. Three factors contributed to its development: a philosophical principle (the desire for objectivity), a narratological innovation (the strict and consistent application of one and the same perspective), and a new theme (the conscious and subconscious). (Stanzel 1966: 39, my translation)

Returning to Heliodorus' opening, we see that he is indeed looking at the events, or rather the scene, through the eyes of the characters, in this case a group of Egyptian bandits. The narrator takes care to motivate their knowledge (that the ship was "laden with freight" could be "surmised from") or, when it cannot be motivated, restrict it (they are "unable to comprehend the scene"). In other words, the passage displays 'the strict and consistent application of one and the same perspective."

In the same paper Effe explicitly denies the existence of figural narration in earlier narrative texts, notably the epics of Homer and Virgil; even in the long first-person passages that these epics contain (when Odysseus and Aeneas recount their earlier adventures), the narrators make generous use of their hindsight knowledge and hence are virtually omniscient.

Effe was not the first to deny the Homeric epic the technique of figural narration. The same view had been voiced in even stronger terms by Auerbach in his highly influential *Mimesis*. He bases his case on the long digression on Odysseus' scar in the *Odyssey* (19.393–466). Odysseus has come back to his palace after twenty years, but in view of the presence of more than a hundred suitors, has to remain incognito until the right moment to take his revenge. Book 19 describes a nightly encounter between Odysseus, disguised as a beggar, and his wife Penelope, in the course of which the queen offers her guest the service of having his feet washed. This chore is performed by Odysseus' old nurse, Euryclea, who recognizes her master by a scar on his leg. At this dramatic moment the narrator inserts a long digression on how Odysseus got this scar, which is linked to the main story as follows:

> the old woman took up the shining basin
> she used for foot washing, and poured in a great deal of water, the cold
> first, and then she added the hot to it. Now Odysseus
> was sitting close to the fire, but suddenly turned to the dark side;
> for presently he thought in his heart that, as she handled him,
> she might be aware of *his scar*, and all his story might come out.
> She came up close and washed her lord, and at once she recognized
> *that scar*, which once a wild boar. . . . [beginning of the digression][2] (386–93)

According to Auerbach:

> the entire story of the scar [might have] been presented as a recollection which awakens in Odysseus' mind at this particular moment. It would have been perfectly easy to do; the story of the scar had only to be inserted two verses earlier, at the first mention of the word scar, where the motifs "Odysseus" and "recollection" were already at hand. But any such subjectivistic-perspectivistic procedure, creating a foreground and background, resulting in the present lying open to the depths of the past, is entirely foreign to the Homeric style; the Homeric style knows only a foreground, only a uniformly illuminated, uniformly objective present. (1953: 7)

Elsewhere, I have argued that Auerbach's analysis of the passage is not the only possible one (de Jong 1985). The digression can also be taken as the recollection of *Euryclea*, who is an even more logical candidate than Odysseus: as soon as she sees the scar, the incident comes back to her in a flash. Thus the "subjectivistic-perspectivistic" procedure might not be inconceivable for Homer after all.

In this chapter I would like to look at the existence of figural narration in classical literature on a somewhat larger scale. I will attempt to modify the picture sketched by Stanzel, Effe, and Auerbach by arguing that figural narration occurs before Heliodorus, in fact, as far back as Homer.[3] The discussion of my examples is preceded by a brief theoretical section, in which I undertake to explain why scholars have failed to detect figural narration, and introduce the instrument by which to find it. In my conclusion I will indicate why this particular narrative perspective is actually very much at home in Greek culture.

Theoretical Preliminaries: From Figural Narration to Embedded Focalization

Why are scholars convinced that figural narration is foreign to the Homeric style, indeed to all narrative styles up until the Greek novel of late antiquity? One explanation might be that in Greek painting, too, perspective is a relatively late invention and one that was barely developed. But, as Wellek and Warren (1977: 125–35) have argued, it is a tricky business to relate technical developments in one art form to those in another.

Another possible explanation—which applies only to Homer—is that complexity of perspective is a feature of *written* texts only: the "silent speech" of writing serving as a model for unspoken thought in narrative.[4]

A third explanation—which again only applies to Homer—concerns the author's worldview, more specifically his concept of human nature. As we have seen, the new theme of "the conscious and subconscious" was, according to Stanzel, one of the driving forces behind the development of figural narration in the nineteenth century. This process was then strengthened in the twentieth century through the work of Freud. It is logical that a narrative technique that makes us see events through the eyes, or consciousness of a character, is bound to flourish at a time when so much more is known about the human mind. When we keep this correlation in the back of our mind, it is also easy to see why figural narration is thought to be foreign to the Homeric epics: psychological analysis per se is largely absent from these texts, and Homeric characters manifest themselves primarily through their words and deeds, not through their thoughts (e.g., as do the characters of Joyce or Woolf). Indeed, the very concept of a central consciousness has long been denied to Homeric man as a result of the theory of Snell on the discovery of the mind (1953[1946]): Homeric characters are seen by the narrator (and themselves) as a combination of limbs (knees, hands, etc.) and mental organs (heart, diaphragm, etc.), while it was not until the time of the lyric poets that the idea of "the mind" (as a central, unifying principle) was "discovered." Even though

Snell's theory has now been largely abandoned, and Homeric psychology has been shown to be much more complex,[5] the *communis opinio* that Homeric heroes are doers rather than thinkers has not encouraged a search for figural narration, where, in the end, a character's mind is central.

The fourth, and in my view most important, factor that has prevented scholars from recognizing figural narration is the tendency to employ typologies when describing the narrative style of texts. Thus Effe, using the typologies of Stanzel (1966) and Friedman (1967), is content to characterize Homer as neutrally omniscient (with a number of passages of first-person narration). Similarly, Booth (1961) in his analysis of authorial narratives like Homer, the Bible, and Boccaccio, leaves room for inside views, where the narrator reveals to us the thoughts and emotions of characters, but he considers these an aspect of authorial narration, rather than a different form of narration.[6]

The disadvantages of this "typology thinking"[7] are—synchronically—that it lacks the flexibility to do justice to the text as a whole and—diachronically—that it presents us with a much more jerky history of narrative techniques than necessary. It is for this reason that I prefer the more flexible model proposed by Bal (1985), which provides the tools for a close—indeed, if necessary sentence-by-sentence—analysis of narrative texts.

I will not spell out this model in detail here, but rather concentrate on giving the equivalent of figural narration. To do this, I will first give a more in-depth description of figural narration. Stanzel (1984: 47–62) lists as its main characteristic that events are not presented by a narrator, but mirrored in the consciousness of a character (a reflector), who is not aware that she is the mediator of a story. This means that we are looking at the events from a temporal and spatial point inside the story, that these events are emotionally colored, and that the understanding of what is going on may be limited. In Bal's model this same narrative situation is called "secondary" or "embedded focalization": events are focalized by a character, who is not, however, the narrator of her own perceptions, thoughts, and emotions. These are presented to us by the primary narrator-focalizer.

Let us now take a look at instances of embedded focalization in classical literature, which derive from four Greek authors, and analyze the way in which the choice of this narrative perspective shapes the emotional and cognitive response of the readers of these texts.

Homer

The first author is Homer (9th–7th century B.C.). The examples of embedded focalization derive from book 23 of the *Odyssey*. Odysseus has finally come back to Ithaca and eventually killed the suitors. All this time he has operated in the disguise of a beggar, since returning to his palace openly would have meant death at the hands of the more than one hundred suitors. In his disguise he even spent a whole evening talking with his wife Penelope without revealing to her his true identity. At the beginning of book 23 Penelope has just been told that Odysseus is back and is waiting for her in the great hall:

> [Penelope] came down from her chamber, her heart pondering
> much, whether to question from a distance <the man supposed to be> her dear husband,
> or to go up to him and kiss his head, taking his hands.
> But then, when she came in and stepped over the stone threshold,
> she sat across from him in the firelight, facing Odysseus,
> by the opposite wall, while he was seated by the tall pillar,
> looking downward, and waiting to find out if his majestic
> wife would have anything to say to him, now that she saw him.
> She sat a long time in silence, and her heart was stupefied.
> At one time she would look at him full in the face,
> at another she would fail to recognize him since he wore poor clothes.[8]

The passage opens with Penelope's embedded focalization, her hesitation about whether to remain cautious to the end and first to question the man supposed to be her husband, or whether to believe the good news right away and embrace him (lines 86–87). In the end, she decides to do nothing at all and silently seats herself opposite Odysseus. We now enter the mind of Odysseus, who likewise remains silent, and we learn that he wants his wife to be the first to speak (lines 91–92). Turning to Penelope again, the narrator explains to the narratees—not to the characters in the story, who soon will take Penelope to task about her silence—why she does not speak: Odysseus is still wearing his beggar clothes, the very clothes he had been wearing during the evening of their interview, and these prevent her from properly recognizing him (lines 94–95). It will be another one hundred lines before the final recognition takes place.

It is clear from this passage that the Homeric narrator is quite capable of abandoning his omniscient perspective and looking at events through the eyes of characters. We find all of the characteristics of figural narration: a position inside the story (we look with Penelope at Odysseus, with Odysseus at Penelope, and then with Penelope again at Odysseus), subjectivity (Odysseus and Penelope are referred to in the passages of embedded focalization not by name but as "husband" and "wife"), and limited knowledge (we are made to share Penelope's hesitation about whether the man in front of her really is Odysseus).[9]

Herodotus

My second author is Herodotus (fifth century B.C.). The example is taken from the first Book of his *Histories* (chaps. 8–12), the story of how the Lydian king Candaules lost his throne to his servant Gyges (I am paraphrasing here while quoting—in italics—the instances of embedded focalization):

> Candaules was very much in love with his own wife and one day suggested that his favorite servant Gyges should look at his wife while she was naked, in order to confirm that she was the most beautiful woman in the world. Gyges answered that this seemed to him a bad and lawless idea: "Men have long ago made wise rules for our learning; one of these is that we, and nobody else, should see what is our own." In this way, he tried to make the king change his mind, *for he feared that some ill to himself might come of it.*

In his speech Gyges stresses the moral side of the issue, while the embedded focalization gives us, the narratees, the real, personal reason for his hesitation to comply with the king's request: he fears for his own skin.

> Candaules insisted and the servant obeyed, but in the act the woman *saw him as he passed out of [her bedroom] and perceived what her husband had done*. But shamed though she was, she never cried out nor let it be known that she had perceived anything, *for she had in mind to punish Candaules*; for among the Lydians and most of the foreign peoples it is held to be a cause for great shame that even a man should be seen naked. For the moment she did nothing, but the next morning called Gyges, who, *supposing that she knew nothing of what had been done*, came at her call.

The narrator now embeds the focalization of Candaules' wife, and we learn not only that she has seen Gyges, but also that she intends to take revenge on her husband; hence she does not reveal that she has seen his servant. The woman's strategy works, as the ensuing inside view in Gyges' head shows: he thinks her unaware of his having watched her. Had he known what the narratees know, he would never have come.

> The queen said to Gyges that either he had to kill Candaules or himself be killed. Gyges begged her not to force him to make such a choice; but when he could not make her change her mind, and *saw that dire necessity was in very truth upon him either to kill his master or himself be killed by others*, he chose his own life. He obeyed and followed the queen into the chamber (for he could not by any means escape, and either he or Candaules had to die). He killed the king, thus acquiring for himself the throne and the queen.

The interesting point in this final passage is the triple repetition of the idea that Gyges has to kill Candaules or be killed himself. The first time, it is the queen who presents him with this harsh truth; the second time, Gyges' embedded focalization (note the reference to Candaules as "his master") shows us that he has exactly understood the queen's message; the third time, it is the narrator himself who reiterates the dilemma in the form of an explanatory comment ("for he could not"). This third instance is superfluous from a cognitive point of view (by now the narratees know exactly what alternatives are open to Gyges), but is highly important emotionally: the narrator exculpates Gyges from his murder, accepting the latter's conclusion that in effect he had no choice.

We see that Herodotus does indeed make use of embedded focalization or figural narration—something denied by some Herodotean scholars[10]—which confronts us with the characters' (secret) thoughts and limited understanding, thereby greatly increasing the depth, tension, and irony of the story.

Jane Austen's Emma

At this point I would like to insert a brief digression to counter possible skepticism regarding the examples of figural narration discussed so far, which some might find too brief and insignificant to be convincing. I suggest that we now take a look at a passage from Jane Austen's *Emma*, a novel that is regarded by most scholars as an example of figural narration, in particular by Stanzel (1982: 150) who sees it as a borderline case between authorial and figural narration:

> (A) As she [Emma] sat one morning . . . a note was brought from Mrs. Goddard, requesting, in most respectful terms, to be allowed to bring Miss Smith with her. (Miss Smith is introduced as follows:)
>
> (B) She was a very pretty girl, and her beauty happened to be of a sort which Emma particularly admired. She was short, plump and fair, with a fine bloom, blue eyes, light hair, regular features, and *a look of great sweetness*; and before the end of the evening, Emma was as much pleased with her manners as her person, and quite determined to continue the acquaintance.
>
> (C) *She was not struck by any thing remarkably clever in Miss Smith's conversation, but she found her altogether very engaging—not incoveniently shy, not unwilling to talk—and yet so far from pushing, shewing so proper and becoming a deference, seeming so pleasantly grateful for being admitted to Hartfield, and so artlessly impressed by the appearance of every thing in so superior a style to what she had been used to, that she must have good sense and deserve encouragement.* (The visit of Mrs. Goddard and Miss Smith is concluded as follows:)
>
> (D) [Emma] had particular pleasure in sending them away happy. The happiness of Miss Smith was quite equal to her intentions. *Miss Woodhouse* [Emma] was so great a personage in Highbury, that the prospect of the introduction had given as much panic as pleasure—but the humble, grateful, little girl went off with highly gratified feelings, delighted with the affability with which *Miss Woodhouse* had treated her all the evening and *actually* shaken hands with her *at last!* (my italics)

We successively get: (A) a passage of neutral narration by the narrator; (B) the introduction of a character by the narrator, which already contains an element of figural narration ("a look of great sweetness"); (C) the further introduction of this character via Emma's focalization; and (D) Miss Smith's focalization of Emma (note the deferential reference to her as "Miss Woodhouse," expressive elements like "actually," "at last," and the exclamation mark, suggesting her excitement), which is clearly embedded in the narrator's own focalization (note the reference to Miss Smith as "the humble, grateful, little girl").

It is clear that the stretches of figural narration in *Emma* are much longer than those of the ancient texts discussed so far, but the principle of authorial narration *alternating with* figural narration or, in Bal's terminology, a primary narrator-focalizer embedding *from time to time* the focalization of his characters, is the same. Such an analysis seems to me to be preferable to Stanzel's borderline case *between* two narrative situations and his assigning *Emma* a fixed point on his "typological circle." In this way we can better trace the gradual development of figural narration, both in quantity, complexity, and refinement, from the *Iliad* and *Odyssey*, via *Emma*, to, say, *Mrs. Dalloway*.

Thucydides

My third classical author is Thucydides (ca. 460–400 B.C.). While in the case of Homer and Herodotus classical scholars have been slow to spot inside views, *The Peloponnesian War* presents a very different situation. A monograph by Schneider (1974) shows how Thucydides tends to place the readers in the position of the characters, allowing them to share their experiences, doubts, and deliberations. In other words, Thucydides makes lavish use of the mode of figural narration. To illustrate this, I have chosen a passage from book 1. A conflict between Corcyra (present-day Corfu) and Corinth has arisen, culminating in a sea battle. In the first round, the Corcyreans, who are assisted by ten Athenian ships, are defeated. After an interval, the fighting resumes (the instances of embedded focalization are italicized):

> (A) The Corcyreans, (B) *fearing that they [the Corinthians] might attempt to make a landing on their island*, came out to meet them with every available ship, including the ten Athenian ships as well as the remainder of their own fleet. (C) It was already late in the day, . . . , when suddenly the Corinthian ships began to back water. (D) They had *seen in*

> *the distance twenty more Athenian ships approaching.* 1.50.4–51.4

The episode begins in (A) with the narrator's presentation of an action by one party, the Corcyreans, which is motivated through embedded focalization (B). In (C) he turns to the other party, the Corinthians, because they do something unexpected ("suddenly"). Again, the action of these characters is motivated through embedded focalization (D). What is interesting here is that a crucial piece of information, that is, the arrival of twenty more Athenian ships, is presented through the eyes of characters. The effect is that we are as surprised as the Corinthians inside the story.

> (E) These [Athenian ships] had been sent out later from Athens to reinforce the original ten. (F) It was this new force that the Corinthians saw. (G) They *suspected that they came from Athens, and thought that there might be still more behind the ships that were visible.* (H) Therefore they began to withdraw. (ibid.)

The narrator now goes back in time and first, in (E), explains the sudden presence of the twenty Athenian ships. After a recapitulation of (D) in (F), he adds in (G) what goes on in the minds of the Corinthians when they see the ships: lacking the information that the narrator had just provided the narratees in (E), they can only "suspect" that the ships come from Athens. They also think—mistakenly, as we know—that there may be even more ships. Note that, strictly speaking, the narrator in (D) has intruded on the focalization of the Corinthians, saying that they had seen "*twenty* more *Athenian* ships approaching." The reason for the intrusion is clear: to avoid confusing his readers. Thus (G) is a clear instance of figural narration, in that we are confronted with the Corinthians' restricted understanding of the situation. In (H) the narrator recapitulates (C).

> (I) The Athenian ships were not seen by the Corcyreans, because at their position visibility was not so good, and (J) they were amazed when they *saw the Corinthians backing water.* . . . (ibid.)

The narrator now turns to the Corcyreans and having first set out, in his omniscience, what they did *not* see (I), he presents in (J) their "amazed" focalization of the action that had been described in (C), that is, the sudden withdrawal of the Corinthians. The narrator is so eager to make us experience the events from the perspective of the characters involved that he does not hesitate to go over the same ground twice.

> (K) . . . until some people *sighted them* [the 20 new Athenian ships] *and shouted that there are ships coming up over there*. (L) Then they [the Corcyreans] also withdrew, (M) *since it was already getting quite dark*, and the Corinthians turned and definitely broke off contact with them. (N) In this way they separated and the sea-battle came to an end at nightfall. (ibid.)

Only in (K) do the Corcyreans also focalize what the Corinthians had focalized before them in (D): the arrival of the twenty Athenian ships. Again the narrator takes pains to make us see the events through the eyes of the characters in the scene, turning to a vivid present ("there *are* ships coming up") and using a mimetic element suggestive of the actual words spoken, "over there"; in other words, the events are clearly presented from a temporal and spatial position within the story, which is one of the major characteristics of figural narration. The Corcyreans also retire (L), an action that is motivated through embedded focalization (M): whereas in (C) the narrator had noted that it was "late," the Corcyreans now perceive that it is getting "quite dark" (and hence that it is useless to continue fighting). The progression of time is here presented via the perception of characters inside the story, another sign of figural narration. In (N) the narrator concludes the episode, looking at both parties at the same time.

This example illustrates how figural narration plays an important role in Thucydides: we look at events through the eyes of the people involved; follow the pace of their perceptions (some parties seeing things before others); and share their misunderstandings, their fears, and their amazement. It is an interesting paradox that Thucydides, who is generally heralded as the first scientific and objective historian of European history, achieves this effect through his lavish use of a highly subjective narrative mode.

Apollonius Rhodius

My last text is the *Argonautica* of Rhodius (third century B.C.). The example is taken from the third book of this Hellenistic epic, which describes the love affair between Jason, the Greek hero sent out on the dangerous mission of acquiring the Golden Fleece, and Medea, the daughter of the king who possesses that Golden Fleece. They are about to have their first rendezvous and Medea, killing time by playing games with her maidservants, eagerly awaits Jason's arrival (the instances of embedded focalization are italicized):

> (A) Despite the games, Medea's spirit could not be distracted to other thoughts [viz. than those concerning Jason]. Whatever game she played, none gave her pleasure or kept her amused for long, but she kept breaking off, unable to concentrate. Nor could she keep her eyes fixed on the crowd of maidservants, but constantly she turned her face away and peered into the distance along *the paths*. (B) Often indeed did her heart within her breast seem to shatter, *whenever she was unsure whether what she seemed to hear speeding past her was the sound of a foot or of the wind*. (C) Soon, however, he appeared to her as she desired, (D) *like Sirius leaping high from Ocean; it rises brilliant and clear to behold, but to flocks it brings terrible misery*. Just so did the son of Aison [Jason] approach her, *brilliant to behold*, but his appearance roused the distress of luckless desire.[11] (948–61)

In (A) we move inside Medea's head. The passage is best analyzed in terms of Cohn's "psychonarration" (1978: 21–57): it is the narrator who puts Medea's confused state of mind into words; she herself probably would not have been able to do so. At the end of the passage, the plural "paths" indicates that we are now starting to look at things through Medea's eyes: she does not know the direction from which Jason will approach. In (B) we get a wonderful instance of embedded focalization, which manages to convey Medea's manifold emotions and perceptions to us in just a few words: she is not sure *whether* she has heard anything (or is merely imagining it); she is not sure *what* she has heard, footsteps or merely the wind; and, finally, she fears that Jason may pass her without her noticing it. In (C) he appears. I would like to draw attention to the fact that instead of "Jason appeared" we find "he appeared," this, again, suggests Medea's focalization: for her, there exists at this moment only one person in the world. As Stanzel notes: "The continuous substitution of the personal pronoun for the name is a decisive step from the authorial to the figural domain" (1984: 189). In typically epic fashion, Medea's perception of her beloved is then intensified and magnified through a simile (D): in her eyes he is like a brilliant star. At the same time, the narrator intrudes upon Medea's focalization, telling us that this star brings "terrible misery" (heat and fever) to flocks, just as Jason will bring Medea the "distress of luckless desire" (her falling in love, through an arrow shot by the god Eros, has been described from the very beginning in terms of pain, and Jason/the star will only bring an intensification of love's burning heat). The omniscient narrator even calls her desire "luckless," anticipating the tragic end of her affair with Jason (she will give up her family for him, kill her own brother, and yet be deserted by him). This foreshadowing, placed strategically at the moment when Medea's greatest desire is fulfilled, greatly adds to the pathos of this unhappy love story.

We see how Rhodius exploits the technique of figural narration for purposes of the typically Hellenistic theme of love, thereby anticipating many modern novels that will later deal with the same subject, using the same narrative perspective.

Conclusions

I hope these examples have made amply clear that figural narration is found in classical literature, indeed that it is effectively used by different authors for a great variety of purposes. Upon reflection, it is not surprising that this type of narrative perspective is represented in Greek literature. After all, what is figural narration other than the technique of placing oneself in the position of another, and looking at life through the eyes of another. This is exactly something at which Greek culture excelled, with its philosophers arguing first against and then for the same proposition, its female dramatic roles being written and performed by men, and its litigants accusing others and defending themselves in speeches written by ghostwriters.

Notes

I wish to thank Will van Peer for his suggestions, Mrs. B. Fasting for her correction of my English.

1. I quote from the translation by Morgan in Reardon (1989).

2. I quote from the translation of Lattimore (1991), with minor modifications.

3. Compare also Lohmann (1992).

4. Compare Martin (1986: 39).

5. For modifications of Snell's theory, see Latacz (1984); for a plea for psychological depth in Homeric characters, see Griffin (1980: 50–80).

6. Compare also Stanzel's (1965: 146–47) brief discussion of the report of thoughts (Gedankenbericht) in authorial narration.

7. Stanzel has recognized the problem and stressed the possibility of the "dynamisation of the narrative situation" (1984: 63–78); yet in the end he still insists on giving texts a place on his "typological circle."

8. I quote from the translation by Lattimore (1991), with minor modifications.

9. More examples of Homeric embedded focalization are discussed in De Jong (1987: 101–48, 1994).

10. Compare, for instance, Long: "Pohlmann had already pointed out that we learn the character and intentions of figures in the Herodotean stories by being told what they say and do, not by being told what they think. This mode robs the author of one of his most effective devices—the glance into the mind of the characters" (1987: 17). Long here (and cf. 186–87) shows himself unaware of the study by Montgomery (1965), who has collected (but hardly analyzed) all Herodotean instances of mental activity (*seelische Vorgänge*). Long's analysis of the Gyges and Candaules story (1987: 9–38) is otherwise highly rewarding.

11. I quote from the translation by Hunter (1993), with minor changes.

5

The Rise and Fall of Empathetic Narrative: A Historical Perspective on Perspective

Sylvia Adamson

Introduction

Since the 1960s, when Booth rejected as "irrelevant to literary judgment" the works of "innumerable scholars who have traced in endless detail the . . . *erlebte Rede* . . . from James to Robbe-Grillet" (1961b: 60), Anglo-American critics have come to recognize what German and French commentators had already known, that this style lies at the heart of the major questions that Booth was addressing (1961). In particular, its management is now seen as crucial to the affective and cognitive aspects of narration which he characterized as the tensions between "sympathy and judgment" (1961a: 243–66) and "reliable and unreliable" narration (311–74).

Yet despite the recent attention lavished on *erlebte Rede* (or *style indirect libre*, or *internal focalization*, or, to use my own addition to its catalogue of titles, *empathetic narrative*[1]), our understanding of it has been compromised by the general exclusion of a historical dimension from critical discussions. By and large, commentators have been content to repeat without further inquiry the early accounts of Bally (1912) and Lips (1926), in which the style is seen as a product of the nineteenth-century novel, where it arose as a device for representing the "point of view" of one or more of the protagonists.

It has been my contention that many of the ongoing debates about the form and function of empathetic narrative can be, if not resolved, at least illuminated, by looking beyond the boundaries of both the novel and the nineteenth century. In previous papers (Adamson 1994a, 1994b, 1995), I have argued the case for seeing it as a historically evolving form that has a different value (in the Saussurean sense) at different points in its history. In the present chapter I want to compare its values at the two end points of its historical evolution in English: the seventeenth century, when it first emerged as a distinct narrative style in autobiographical writing, and the late twentieth century, when it was borrowed back from the novel into the nonfictional genres of history and documentary journalism.

To establish a reference point for these comparisons, it may be as well to start with an example of the style in what is generally accepted as its canonical form and genre. As a tribute to Dorrit Cohn, who played a key role in reconciling Anglo-American criticism to the analysis of what she called "narrated monologue," I'll take my example from a text that played a key role in her 1966 account:

> (A) It was true. God was almighty. God could call him now, call him as he sat at his desk, before he had time to be conscious of the summons. God had called him. Yes? . . . He had died. Yes. He was judged. A wave of fire swept through his body. . . . His brain was simmering and bubbling within the crackling tenement of the skull. . . . His soul sank back deeper into depths of contrite peace. . . . Ah yes, he would still be spared; he would repent in his heart and be forgiven; and then those above, those in heaven, would see what he would do to make up for the past. (James Joyce, *A Portrait of the Artist as a Young Man,* 1916: 142–4)

Though Cohn rightly regards the early twentieth century as the moment when this style of writing became a standard or unmarked mode of narration for most third-person novels (1966: 107), its emergence as a distinct narrative type—by which I mean its use as the staple style for a whole narrative span—took place over a century earlier.[2] Empathetic narrative can be seen as a reflex in prose genres of the Romantic period's more general drive toward giving literary expression to what Bate christened "the sympathetic imagination" (1945). The act of sympathizing—defined by Johnson as "to feel with another; to feel in consequence of what another feels"[3]—had become a key concept in the ethics and aesthetics of the late eighteenth century precisely because it offered a way out of the moral and epistemological limitations of ego-centered consciousness. To cultivate fellow-feeling was both an exercise in altruism and a route to vicarious knowledge, allowing the self to extend the range of its own experience by viewing the world from another perspective. The role of the writer was to inculcate sympathetic activity in the reader by demonstrating it in himself.

In the case of empathetic narrative, a double perspective is reflected in the very grammar of the style. Typically, the pronoun marks the narratee as other ("he" or "she") and the tense marks the event as distant ("was") but the other linguistic forms that canonically encode the locutionary agent's perspective—by which I mean his temporal, epistemic, or emotional stance toward the reported event—are used empathetically rather than egocentrically, being focalized on the narratee instead of on the narrator. In (A), for instance, the "now" refers not to the moment of narrating but to the moment of the narratee's experience, the exclamations—"ah, yes"—express his emotional response, and the declarative modality of "it was true" represents his epistemic certainty.[4] The empathetic narrator is thus at least halfway to the position that Keats prescribed for "the camelion poet," who "is continually infor[ming] and filling some other body" (*Letters of John Keats*, ed. H. E. Rollins [1958, 1: 386–88, 403–4]). In Cohn's words: "the author creates the illusion that . . . he experiences the present *with* the character . . . [and] thus plunges the reader into the here and now of the experiencing consciousness" (1966: 106). But a degree of separation remains, as signaled by the selection of "he was" rather than "I am," and empathetic narrative is not necessarily uncritical toward the viewpoint it represents. As Cohn observed (111), the form can be used ironically as well as lyrically. In what is probably the first full-scale example of third-person empathetic narrative in the English novel, Austen's *Emma*, the ironic mode predominates, and even in Joyce's *Portrait of the Artist as a Young Man* (which Cohn like many other commentators assigns to the lyrical mode) emotional alignment is accompanied by a certain cognitive skepticism. Readers of (A), for instance, do *not* typically assume that the narratee "had died" or "was judged" or that "his brain was simmering and bubbling"; we interpret these statements as a record of the protagonist's subjective experience rather than (and sometimes in violation of) the objective facts of the world of the novel, a point more fully discussed in Adamson (1995). As we shall see, this pattern is already established in the style's seventeenth-century avatar.

The Birth of a Style—The Narrative of Experiential Memory[5]

Because (A) constitutes the canonical type of empathetic narrative in general critical consciousness, its first-person variant (configured "I-was-now" rather than "he-was-now") has consistently been treated as the exceptional case. But in fact it appears to have been the primary case, at least in the English literary tradition. The earliest instance I have found of empathetic narrative being used consistently as the staple style for a complete narrative span occurs in a text that differs from (A) in being both first-person and nonfictional, Bunyan's *Grace Abounding* (1666). The fostering conditions for this development lie in the seventeenth-century interest in consciousness and specifically the form it takes in English Puritanism.

To a Cartesian, the defining role for the self is as subject of an act of consciousness: I believe I exist when I have the experience of thinking (and for this reason, as Lyons has persuasively argued [1982: 104], Descartes' *Cogito* should be translated into English with the progressive aspect: "I am thinking" not "I think"). The grammar of Puritan consciousness has a different specification: the verb of consciousness is typically transitive and the self is simultaneously its subject and object, so that the Puritan experience of self takes the form described by the Baptist Jane Turner as "self-examination, self-watching, self-judging, self-humbling" (1653: 185). As Turner's terms imply, the result of self-examination is often self-alienation and the typical relation between subject and object selves is summed up in Goodwin's suggestively titled *Auto-Machia* or *The Self-Conflict of a Christian* (the English translation is from Josuah Sylvester's *Tobacco Battered* [ca. 1614]):

(B) I sing my SELF; my *Civil-Warrs* within;
The *Victories* I howrely lose and win. . . .
My Selfe I followe, and my Selfe I fly:
Besides my Selfe, and in my Selfe am I. (lines 7–8, 203–4)

Puritan consciousness presents a psychological analogue of the civil wars played out on seventeenth-century battlefields and it is quite normal for Puritan writers to decompose their conflicted self into distinct warring factions representing Grace and Sin. Most characteristically the automachia is expressed as a temporal split, laid out in narrative form, focusing on the experience of conversion as the pivot between unregenerate and regenerate phases of self-being. The result is the emergence of a new genre, which the Presbyterian Richard Baxter saw as a powerful rival to existing literary genres:

> (C) The report of one Souls Conversion to God. . . . [is] as far better than the Stories of these grand Murderers, and Tyrants, and their great Robberies, and Murders called Conquests, as the Diagnosticks of Health are than those of Sickness. (Cited in Haller 1938: 101)

Baxter explicitly dismisses the kind of protagonist and events celebrated in such Elizabethan "poppit-plays" as *Tamburlaine*, just as Goodwin rejects the martial hero of nationalist epic ("I sing not heer AENEAS . . . I sing not CAESAR"), revising the Virgilian formula, "arms and the man I sing," to "I sing my SELF." In the new epic of consciousness, the hero is the writer's own soul, and the conversion narrative, as the account of its self-conquests, provides the Puritan counterpart to the external narratives fostered by other ideologies.

Grace Abounding is probably the most celebrated of these conversion narratives, and in its preface Bunyan explicitly accepts and justifies the program I have just sketched out:

> (D) It is profitable for Christians to be often calling to mind the very beginnings of Grace with their Souls. . . . O the remembrance of my great sins, of my great temptations, and of my great fears of perishing for ever! They bring afresh into my mind the remembrance of my great help, my great support from Heaven, and the great grace that God extended to such a Wretch as I.
>
> My dear Children, call to mind the former days, the years of ancient times; remember also your songs in the night, and commune with your own heart. . . . Yea, look diligently, and leave no corner therein unsearched, for there is treasure hid, even the treasure of your first and second experience of the grace of God toward you. Remember, I say, the Word that first lay hold upon you; remember your terrours of conscience, and fear of death and hell: remember also your tears and prayers to God; yea, how you sighed under every hedge for mercy. Have you never a Hill Mizar to remember? have you forgot the Close, the Milk-house, the Stable, the Barn and the like, where God did visit your Soul? (John Bunyan, *Grace Abounding to the chief of Sinners*, ed. R. Sharrock, London: Oxford University Press, 1966: 4–5 [first published 1666])

The reiterated keyword here is *remember*. For the Puritan, introspection almost always entails retrospection: the act of consciousness takes the form of an act of memory, which provides distinct roles for the subject/object components of the double self. As this passage shows, the difference between the self that remembers and the self remembered is both psychological and theological: the remembering self has attained grace, which separates it in kind as well as in time from the remembered self; the remembered self is unregenerate, and of value solely for its exemplification of what it is like to be in a state of sin. Thus the gap between narrating and narrated selves takes on an ideological force: the narrated self is not only past but categorically other. At the same time, Bunyan expresses the need to lessen this gap. The redeemed man is urged to revisit his past sinfulness, both for his own sake and for that of others: for him such memories reinforce his gratitude for the contrasting grace he has been given; for others they may act as a warning of the tribulations of the unredeemed state. The task for memory, then, is to re-create the past in all its experiential vividness, the more so since the objective coordinates of time, place, and circumstance ("the Stable, the Barn and the like") provide simply the context for the significant events, which are subjective: the Puritan pilgrim makes progress not through successive actions but through successive stages of consciousness.

It is not surprising then that empathetic narrative made its historical debut within this narrative genre as the technical means of realizing its aims—to report on consciousness in the mode of experiential memory. The form it takes can be gauged from (E):

> (E) And *now* was I both a burthen and a terror to myself, nor did I ever so know, as *now*, what it was to be weary of my life and yet afraid to die. Oh, how gladly now would I have been anybody but myself! Any thing but a man! and in any condition but mine own! . . . But O how did my Soul at this time prize the preservation that God did set about his People! Ah how safely did I see them walk, whom God had hedged in! they were within his care, protection, and special providence: though they were full as bad as I by nature, yet, because he loved them, he would not suffer them to fall without the range of Mercy: but as for me, I was gone, I had done it; he would not preserve me, nor keep me, but suffered me, because I was a Reprobate, to fall as I had done. Now did those blessed places that spake of *Gods keeping his people*, shine like the Sun before me, though not to comfort me, but to shew me the blessed state

> and heritage of those whom the Lord had blessed. (47–49, Bunyan's italics)

The dominant tense of this passage—the past tense—encodes the perspective of the narrating Bunyan, writing to inform his "dear Children" of events that took place at least fifteen years before; but the other markers of perspective are all focalized on the narrated Bunyan, for whom the reported events are part of current experience. His point of view is represented temporally (in the proximal deixis of adverbials such as "at this time" and the reiterated "now"), emotionally (in the exclamatory constructions and the interjections of despair and envy "oh" and "ah"), and, most strikingly of all, at the epistemic level. From the vantage point of the narrating self (and his contemporary readers) statements such as "I was gone" and "[he] suffered me . . . to fall" are known to be false. They can only represent the temporary delusions of a past despair. But Bunyan does not here qualify such statements with "it seemed" or "I thought." Instead he replicates the epistemic certainty of his past self's belief.

The similarities of form and effect between (E) and (A) are, I hope, sufficiently striking to establish them as variants of the same style; but we still need to account for the historical emergence of the second variant, which involves accounting both for the linguistic leap by which a style based on the grammatical configuration *I-was-now* gave rise to one based on *she-was-now* and for the genre leap by which the style moved from autobiography to novel. The answer seems to be that the leap was made initially where the gap between genres was at its narrowest. For if (E) represents not the general genre of autobiography but the specific subgenre of conversion narrative, (A) represents an equally specific subgenre of the novel, the *Bildungsroman*, and in its literary lineage the *Bildungsroman* is a direct descendant of the conversion narrative. Essentially it is a secularized equivalent, in which education replaces conversion as the plot-mechanism and social accommodation replaces spiritual salvation as the postulated goal. In both genres, the narrative traces the tribulations and backslidings that promote the growth of consciousness in a protagonist whom the reader is invited simultaneously to identify with and judge. It is not surprising then that when third-person empathetic narrative first established itself as a distinct narrative type, the *Bildungsroman* was the type of novel in which it did so.[6]

If this sketch of the early history of empathetic narrative is substantially correct, it provides the basis for proposing a general model of literary history in which stylistic change (here from the grammar of *I-was-now* to *she-was-now*) is triggered by genre transfer (here from conversion narrative to *Bildungsroman*) which is in turn triggered by an ideological shift (here from the Puritan valorization of experiential memory to the Romantic valorization of imaginative sympathy). It's a model that is tested and, I will argue, supported by more recent events in the history of narrative perspective.

The Death of a Style?—The Narrative of Social Solidarity

Three hundred years after Bunyan, empathetic narrative again became the site of a genre innovation, when, in the 1960s, New Journalism was created by importing the style of (A) into the nonfictional genres of documentary reporting and history. Attacked as a "bastard form, having it both ways, exploiting the factual authority of journalism and the atmospheric license of fiction" (Wakefield 1966: 89), New Journalism was less a bastard than a self-declared orphan, ideologically at odds with both of its parent genres. It represents, on the one hand, a reaction against the style of reporting found in (F):

> (F) On 22 October the Pentagon was beseiged by some 10,000 demonstrators for two days; 2,500 troops with fixed bayonets supported the police in protecting the Pentagon, and a total of 681 arrests were made. On 14 November some 3,000 people demonstrated against the war during a visit to New York by Dean Rusk, the Secretary of State; 46 arrests were made and some 25 people hurt in scuffles with 1,500 police. More organized protests were staged in New York for three days in early December. Demonstrators tried to disrupt conscription centres in the city, but the police were well prepared and kept a tight control over the crowds. Three hundred people were arrested. (*The Annual Register* for 1967, ed. I Macadam, London: Longman, 1968: 176)

The "factual authority" of this narrative type can be seen as no more than a rhetorical ploy. By suppressing all linguistic markers of his own spatiotemporal and epistemic perspective, the historian-journalist creates the illusion that what he narrates is a matter of public knowledge rather than of private belief, objective fact rather than subjective interpretation. Benveniste describes this style as one in which "les événements sont posés comme ils se sont produits à mesure qu'ils apparaissent a l'horizon de l'histoire" ["events are set down just as they occurred, matching the way they appear on the horizon of history"] adding the cautionary footnote "bien entendu l'énonciation historique des événements est indépendante de leur vérité 'objective' " ["of course the historical style of recounting events is not dependent on their 'objective' reality"] (1966: 240–1). A New Journalist, by contrast, wants to acknowledge that what constitutes an "event" or "fact" of history is largely determined by the interpreter's point of view; and, more radically, that all events occur first as experience, which means that a history like (F) becomes necessarily falser as it becomes more objective (*no one* on 22 October 1967 experienced "681 arrests"). This is an epistemological position that brings New Journalism close to the novel of consciousness. Where it diverges from narratives such as (A) and (E) is in the desire to combine a perspectived event with a *democratized* perspective.

In both the conversion narrative and in the *Bildungsroman*, the focalizer is typically a single consciousness, either the elect soul on the path to spiritual salvation, or "the problematic individual" coming to terms with "concrete social realities."[7] And the implicit élitism in this model becomes overt in *Portrait* and in other late examples of the genre, where the focalizer is frequently the figure of the alienated artist. In the English novel at least, group focalizers are rare and where they do appear the representation is almost always satiric or reductive, as in Eliot's rendering of "the mind of St Ogg's" in *Mill on the Floss.*[8] New Journalism adopted a polemically different stance: it not only replaced the individual focalizer with a group but typically selected the group from a subculture or counterculture that rejects or is rejected by establishment norms. The Puritans, of course, constituted just such a subculture in the seventeenth century; but both audience and narrator of the conversion narrative were members of that culture. The problem in the modern period lies in the fact that subcultures have typically been documented by establishment narrators writing for establishment readers. Hence Wolfe's view that "the voice of the narrator . . . was one of the great problems in non-fiction writing" (1975: 31ff.). It is not accidental that the works recognized as genre-defining for New Journalism were Capote's "nonfiction novel" of a pair of drifters-turned-murderers (*In Cold Blood*, 1965) and Mailer's *Armies of the Night* (1968), which epitomizes the whole historical development of the focalized consciousness in its transformation of the autobiographical "I" into a narrated "he"—the protagonist "Mailer"—who merges his individual perspective with the group perspective of his companions on the 1967 anti-Vietnam War protest march. Here's how he translates one of the historical events of (F) into the experience of those involved in it. "The demonstrators" are as anonymous as they are in (F), but in Mailer's narrative they are centres of consciousness instead of mere numbers:

> (G) Night was on. The demonstrators were entering the last few hours of their march on the Pentagon. They were tired, exceptionally tired, they felt vulnerable—their aggression, their ability even to defend themselves now used up by endless calls over the hours for more adrenaline; yes the mood was pacifistic, almost saintly, but very weak. In the night they were all close to each other. Quietly. They were waiting. The walls of the Pentagon bulked large. (Norman Mailer, *Armies of the Night,* London: Weidenfeld and Nicolson, 1968: 281)

The affinity in effect with (A) and (E) is obvious and the shift from the *he-was-now* formula of (A) to the *they-were-now* of (G) seems to be a minimal change. But other stylistic consequences follow, as witness the following examples:

> (Ha) it just might be possible to write journalism that would . . . read like a novel. . . . This was the sincerest form of homage to The Novel and to those greats, the novelists, of course. Not even the journalists who pioneered in this direction doubted for a moment that the novelist was the reigning literary artist, now and forever. All they were asking for was the privilege of dressing up like him . . . until the day when they themselves would work up the nerve and go into the shack and try it for real. . . . They never dreamed of the approaching irony. (Wolfe 1975: 22–23)

> (Hb) working mash wouldn't wait for a man. It started coming to a head when it got ready to and a man had to be there to take it off, out there in the woods, in the brush, in the brambles, in the muck, in the snow. . . . Junior and his brothers, about two o'clock in the morning they'd head out to the stash, the place where the liquor was hidden after it was made. (32)

(Hc) And now it was 1969 and they were in the dock at the Old Bailey, and witnesses were giving evidence against them. And finally there was the judge, Mr. Melford Stevenson, telling them: "In my view, society has earned a rest from your activities." (*The Independent,* 1995)

(Hd) They had a dream. They had a vision. A vision of Britain where neither the harsh market supremacist policies of Margaret Thatcher, nor the idiocies of outdated socialism prevailed. There had to be a middle way. But it was not to be. (*The Daily Mail,* 1987)

(He) The operation now entered its most dangerous phase. Two or three holes appeared in the roof and prison officers were creating them. (*BBC News*, 1990)

In (Ha) Wolfe sets out the program of New Journalism as seen from the perspective of its early exponents. As in (A), the empathetic narrative here encodes the narratee's perspective, not only temporally ("*now* and forever" and "the *approaching* irony") but also epistemically ("might be possible" and "of course") and evaluatively ("those greats"). The only difference from (A) is that the focalized consciousness is plural, the narratee, as in (G), is "they" rather than "he." (Hb) is more radical both socially and technically. Reporting on the activities of illegal distillers in Inglehollow, Wolfe adopts their language variety along with their perspective and the perspective itself is generalized: where the focalized consciousness in (Ha) is that of a specific group of New York journalists, in (Hb) it belongs to a more nebulous entity that we might identify as "the Inglehollow community," analogous to "the mind of St. Ogg's," but here presented without apparent condescension. Wolfe comments: "I was feigning the tones of an Ingle Hollow moonshiner, in order to create the illusion of seeing the action through the eyes of someone who was actually on the scene and involved in it, rather than a beige narrator" (1975: 32).

The remaining examples testify to the diffusion of this style from self-conscious innovators, such as Mailer and Wolfe, into the practice of workaday journalism in daily newspapers (illustrating, in passing, its geographic diffusion from America to Britain). In (Hc), the journalist follows in the path of Capote's *In Cold Blood* (1965) by taking up the perspective of convicted criminals, in this case the notorious gangland killers, the Kray twins. The death of

Ronald Kray in 1995 prompted this reconstruction of the moment of the Krays' downfall twenty-five years earlier, in an empathetic narrative in which the experiential past progressive replaces the simple past tense of historical record ("were giving evidence" instead of "gave evidence"),[9] the year 1969 is interpreted as "now," and the sentencing judge is viewed as if across the courtroom from a position "in the dock" ("*there* was the judge"). In (Hd) the referent of "they" has broadened out from specified individuals to a group, in this case, the short-lived British Social Democratic Party (SDP), whose demise is here reported. The reporting newspaper, *The Daily Mail*, though politically far to the right of the SDP, adopts their evaluative perspective on the other parties ("harsh" and "idiocies") and their assessment of their own prospects ("there *had to be* a middle way") before passing the verdict of history in the final sentence. Finally, in (He), from a BBC News report on the 1990 riot in Strangeways Jail, the focalizer is both nonspecific and discontinuous (the nonspecificity being the factor that licenses and facilitates the discontinuity). The event is reported in perspective, but the perspectives of the two sentences are—in naturalistic terms—mutually exclusive. The second sentence seems to represent the viewpoint of reporters gathered on a neighboring rooftop, seeing first "two or three holes" and then the emerging prison officers;[10] but the first sentence aligns itself rather with the prison officers *inside* the jail—they are the agents of "the operation" and it is from their point of view that it is categorized as both "now" and "dangerous."

It can be argued of course that what (Ha-e) illustrate is stylistic borrowing rather than stylistic change, since their procedures, however innovative within nonfiction, can all be paralleled within the novel before the middle of the century. Joyce, for instance, abandoned the "beige narrator" for the idiom of his child-protagonist in the early part of *Portrait*, Woolf used a disembodied perspective—the viewpoint of the *genius loci* almost—in *Kew Gardens* and elsewhere, and both she and Lawrence experimented widely with the kind of kaleidoscopic technique we see in (He).[11] But the emergence and diffusion of New Journalism involves more than the simple trickle-down of highbrow techniques into popular genres. Or, more accurately, trickle-down is rarely simple. Different genres have different objectives, which are liable to leave their mark on borrowed forms, and, on the simplest level, the popularization of a form alters its frequency of occurrence, which may in turn alter its value within the system. Both outcomes are, I believe, detectable in this case and significantly they affect not just the peripheral features of empathetic narrative but the *was-now* configuration, the paradoxical tense of narration, which many commentators have regarded as the central feature of the style's linguistic identity.[12]

In the conversion narrative, the dual temporality implied by the *was-now* paradox is to be interpreted literally. The narrative fuses the perspective of the remembering self for whom the experience is past and the perspective of the remembered self, for whom it is present. When empathetic narrative migrates into the *Bildungsroman*, the nonpresent tense metaphorizes from temporal to epistemic meaning, *was* becoming the marker of fictionality rather than pastness and the *was-now* combination becoming the marker of sympathetic imagination rather than experiential memory. What the two genres have in common is that the narratee's "now" is embedded within the larger perspective of the narrator and the discrepancy between the two may be actualized, either in the silent ironies of (A) and (E) or in explicit commentary, as in (I):

> (Ia) Yet whether sincere Conversion *began now* or before or after I was never able *to this day* to know.

> (Ib) All sorts of things, in fact, *now seemed* to *come* over him, comparatively few of which his chronicler *can hope* for space to mention.[13]

But with the genre shift into New Journalism, this dual perspective becomes ideologically something of an embarrassment, implying, as it does, the presence of a privileged narrator distant from, and superior to, those whose experience he narrates. This, coupled with the journalistic imperative to convey a "sense of events that is immediate, personal, close to the pulse of present history" (Johnson 1971: 46) results in a fitful but frequent abandoning of the traditional distancing past tense:

> (J) And so all of a sudden, in the mid-Sixties, here comes a bunch of these lumpenproles, no less, a bunch of slick-magazine and Sunday-supplement writers with no literary credentials whatsoever in most cases—only they're using all the techniques of the novelists, even the most sophisticated ones—and on top of that they're helping themselves to the insights of the men of letters while they're at it—and at the same time they're doing their low-life legwork, their

"digging," their hustling, their damnable Locker Room Genre reporting. (Wolfe 1975: 39–40)

This is Wolfe reporting the outraged response of the literary establishment to the emergence of New Journalism. But only the explicit date ("the mid-Sixties") read in conjunction with the date of the report's publication (a decade later) marks it as an event of past time. The verbs throughout are in the present tense. *Is-now* has replaced *was-now* as the tense of narration and all that marks (J) as empathetic rather than egocentric perspective is the absence of an I, which permits the spatial deictics ("here" and "comes") and evaluative terms ("lumpenproles" and "damnable") to be interpreted as anchored in the narrated "they." This is the feature that Wakefield appeals to when defending Wolfe from the charge of sharing the "youth culture" perspective recorded in his account of stockcar racer Junior Johnson. Wakefield argues that the ending, quoted in (K), is "an evocation of the feelings of the people he has been describing rather than his own," but linguistically his defense rests solely on Wolfe's pronoun selection: "It is "their" America Wolfe is talking about not his" (1966: 88)[14]:

(K) . . . up with the automobile into their America, and the hell with arteriosclerotic old boys trying to hold onto the whole pot with arms of cotton seersucker. Junior!

Even where the *was-now* paradox is retained, it changes its value. Consider the following passage:

(L) In the nineteenth century and early part of the twentieth the success of England as an imperial nation combined with romantic ideas about language being the expression of a people's genius would engender a triumphalist and patriotic attitude to English. The language was now not so much to be improved but preserved as a great national monument and defended from threat. . . . As the demographic shift in the English-speaking population moved away from Britain, the twentieth would be declared the American century, and the Empire would strike back.

Excerpted from the introduction to an academic history of the English language,[15] (L) testifies to the contemporary spread of empathetic narrative from New Journalism itself into other forms of nonfictional narration. In this passage *was-now* is the narrative tense throughout, appearing either in its canonical form, as in the middle sentence, or in the form of "would"—which, in earlier empathetic narratives, represents a narratee's predictive "will" backshifted to signal that it is embedded in a narrator's distancing "was" (e.g., "would be spared," "would see" in (A) or "would not suffer," and "would not preserve" in (E)). But is this the function of the verb forms in (L)? Does this narrative, like earlier instances of the style, represent the narratee's perspective? For the middle sentence, the answer may be yes, since the evaluative language ("great" and "threat") alongside the temporal adverb "now" could be said to express the "triumphalist and patriotic attitude" of the late Victorians described in the previous sentence. But it is not so easy to extend this reading to the sequence of "would engender," "would be declared," and "would strike back" since the events encoded here are not predictions available to any nineteenth-century consciousness. The narrative of (L) is in this sense as omniscient and abstracted from local experience as the narrative of (F).

Two explanations seem possible. What we see in (L) may be a further stage in the delocalization of perspective seen in (G) and (H). The only focalizer we could posit would be "the spirit of the age," as if history has become its own witness.[16] A second explanation is that *was-now* has undergone a further change in value: a temporal marker in autobiography, an epistemic marker in the novel, it may, in New Journalism and its descendants, be in the process of turning into a pragmatic marker, signaling not so much a doubling of perspective as a choice of register. In examples such as (G) and (H) it is the sign of "committed reporting," in (L) it is a disclaimer of the stuffiness of academic prose.

The choice between these interpretations (which may not be mutually exclusive) must await further research, but what seems clear in either case is that by disturbing existing style-genre correlations New Journalism has blurred the oppositions within the repertoire of styles of narration and triggered a fundamental form-function realignment within empathetic narrative itself. In cases like (J) and (K), the style retains the function of expressing perspective but loses the narrative tense that distinguished it formally from other styles of narration (e.g., the historic present); in cases like (L), the distinctive tense form is retained, but seems to be shedding its traditional function of representing "the here and now of experiencing consciousness."

Notes

1. My justification for the term *empathetic narrative* is given in Adamson (1994a). A comprehensive list of alternative names is provided by Brinton (1980). Their sheer number and diversity raises the question of whether we are dealing with a unitary phenomenon or a cluster of related styles. This issue, though an important one (I partly address it in Adamson [1994a]), does not affect the argument of this chapter. *Empathetic narrative* as used here will cover the range of Banfield's "represented thought" and Brinton's "represented perception."

2. Throughout this chapter, it will be important to bear in mind the distinction between sentence type and narrative type and between sporadic and consistent use of a style. For instance, Austen is not the first author to use sentences of third-person empathetic narrative, but there has been no serious challenge to the claim that she is the first to make it the staple style of a whole novel, thereby establishing a new narrative type. For a discussion of the concept of stylization and of one method of quantifying the notion of stylistic consistency, see Adamson (1994b).

3. See the entry for *to sympathize* in Johnson's *Dictionary* (1755). The difference from PDE usage should be noted. A continuous semantic slippage has operated in this field, turning *sympathy* into a virtual synonym of *pity*. The sense of identifying with another, which predominates in Johnson's definition, was taken over for most of the twentieth century by *empathy*, but among younger speakers that too is now often used as a synonym of *pity*.

4. I hope that these and other readings offered in this chapter are relatively uncontroversial. I have no space to address the question of how and how securely the interpretation of represented perspective is arrived at. For a range of opinions on the degree to which it is grammatically encoded, discoursally cued or pragmatically inferred, see McHale (1978), Banfield (1982), Ehrlich (1990), Sternberg (1991), and Fludernik (1993).

5. For a detailed account of the research summarized in this section, see Adamson (1994b).

6. Constraints of space prevent an extended discussion of this phase of the style's history. A more detailed account might show even more graduality in the genre shift, with a third-person *Bildungsroman* being preceded by a first-person form, notably in the work of Godwin. For Godwin's account of sympathy as an ethical concept, see his *Enquiry Concerning Political Justice* 4.x; for his use of first-person empathetic narrative, see Kittel (1992: 334–49). Anglo-American criticism has been somewhat reluctant to engage with the concept of *Bildungsroman* (for reasons not unlike those that delayed its engagement with *erlebte Rede*). For an overview of the current state of research, see Hardin (1991), especially the essay by Bannet, which establishes the importance of the genre for female novelists in England. The sym-

biotic evolution of empathetic narrative and *Bildungsroman* in the German tradition—from Goethe to Mann—is too obvious to require comment.

7. This is from Lukacs's definition of *Bildungsroman*. See Hardin (1991: xvi).

8. The French tradition, by contrast, has some notable experiments in group perspective, most importantly by Zola; compare also the chapter by Margolin.

9. For the role of *imparfait* and past progressive as markers of empathetic narrative, see Ehrlich (1990) and Fleischman (1990).

10. There's a striking similarity to the much commented on opening to Hemingway's *The Killers:* "The door of Henry's lunchroom opened and two men came in" (discussed in Fillmore [1981: 164]).

11. For interpretations of the use of depersonalized focalization in Woolf, see Banfield (1987) and Fludernik (1993: 387–95); for an account of the ideological basis of Lawrence's shifting perspectives, see Baron (1998).

12. See, for instance, the discussions in Hamburger (1973), Bronzwaer (1970, 1975), Banfield (1982), and Fleischman (1990). For my own account, see Adamson (1995).

13. The bearing of these sentences on theoretical controversy (Ia is from Baxter's *Reliquiae Baxterianae* and Ib from James's *The Ambassadors*) is discussed in Adamson (1994a: 200).

14. A third-person present tense empathetic narrative is also found in American fiction of the 1960s, notably in the work of Pynchon. Further research is needed to determine the direction of influence between the two genres.

15. From *The Cambridge History of the English Language 4: 1776 to the Present Day*, ed. S. Romaine, Cambridge: Cambridge University Press (1998: 1).

16. Compare the semantically similar formulae of "The *twentieth century saw* the Empire strike back," and "*1998 witnessed* France winning the World Cup," now so common as to have lost all overtones of personification.

6

The Establishment of Internal Focalization in Odd Pronominal Contexts

Monika Fludernik

As Banfield (1982) demonstrated in her pioneer study, internal focalization, Stanzel's reflector mode,[1] is established by means of a deictic center in which SELF correlates with the Bühlerian *origo* (Bühler 1934) of the reflector character, the protagonist whose internal perspective dominates the text of the textual segment in question. Stanzel's reflector mode and traditional accounts of internal focalization operate on a macro-structural level, defining the constitutive focalization for larger textual units, Banfield's application of the deictic center to the representation of consciousness shifts the emphasis on a microstructural level, that of the sentence-by-sentence projection of SELF. The absence of a narrator in RST (Represented Speech and Thought) clauses is an interim small-scale effect, since the speaker qua narrator reemerges in every sentence of indirect discourse. Banfield's model therefore opens the way to a radical redefinition of point of view in terms of small-scale reorientations of focal perspective. Her proposals allow one to anchor internal perspective in the minutiae of spatial/temporal deixis, lexis, syntactic patterns, and other features that are linguistically relatable to a deictic center, rather than in the questions of perception and (access to) knowledge that constitute focalization in the classic accounts of Genette (1980, 1988), Rimmon-Kenan (1983, 1989), or Chatman (1986, 1990, 1995). This has recently been noted by Pier (1995), who even argues that the classic account of focalization is superseded by a narratology of speech and thought representation.

Issues of focalization or point of view have entered a new phase of intensive scholarly debate, specifically in the area of further refinements of Genette's model (the line from Bal [1977, 1985] to Ci [1988], Nelles [1990], and Edmiston [1989]), and attempts to reconceptualize narrative perspective have been made by Chatman (1990) and, most recently, by Jahn (1996). Whereas those seeking to refine the Genettean model have tried to make Genette's proposals more stringent and logically consistent,[2] Chatman and Jahn attempt to anchor perspective in critical evaluations of where the standard model has failed. Chatman, but also Prince (chap. 2 of this vol.), institutes a major fissure between the narrator (discourse) and the reflector character (story level), distinguishing between the narrator's slant (which is mainly ideological) and the character as filter. This reminds one of the distinction between *vision sur (vision du dehors)* and *vision avec* (Pouillon 1946), but specifically reserves the visual metaphor for the character: the narrator only speaks; only the character can see or perceive. Jahn, by contrast, like Phelan (chap. 3 of this vol.) allows both narrators and characters the faculty of perception. Jahn redefines perception, however, to include much more than vision, knowledge, and ideological stance. In particular, he tries to incorporate consciousness with the constellation, arguing that perception (which includes any kind of ideation) necessarily involves memory and that the narrator cannot, therefore, speak without seeing: "James's narrators see before they speak, and they speak in order to make us, the readers, see" (262).

In *Towards a "Natural" Narratology* I have myself entered into this debate, although focalization takes up a relatively marginal role within the cognitive model that I propose. In terms of natural narratology large-scale focalizations simply surface as cognitively constituted schemata. Dominant internal perspective corresponds to the EXPERIENCING schema, dominant neutral perspective to the VIEWING schema, and zero focalization is rooted in omnicommunicative TELLING. Each of these schemata is dominated by a holistic prototypical constellation, and TELLING in particular allows for various generically motivated realizations, including autodiegetic and prototypically bardic narrative romance narration. These schemata, however, do not exist in and by themselves and they do not correspond with texts. On the contrary, such schemata, in my model, are said to be accessed as projections or interpretative models on the basis of small-scale linguistic features that trigger readers' establishment of narrators, reflectors, and observers and then anchor these within a cognitive structure that embraces prototypical schemata as situations in which such existents can be embedded. Macrofocalizations such as internal perspective can be overturned at each and every point by contradictory linguistic features that require updating, compelling efforts of reinterpretation, and renewed projections of alternative or modified schemata.

Jahn's emphasis on consciousness is particularly insightful in terms of the crucial importance of internal perspective, filters, or reflectors; the whole debate about focalization became necessary as a consequence of reflectoral narrative. No longer could the narrator (whether homo- or heterodiegetic) be held responsible for the main perspectival orientation of such texts. The main issue in all of the models has therefore always been how to account for the presentation of characters' consciousness, or for the lack of such insight. Omniscience or zero focalization as the default term documents this theoretical enmeshment with consciousness, establishing an internal and external point of view as, basically, (a) unlimited access to a protagonist's ideation and (b) absolute refusal of access as the two major focalizations. In cognitive terms these dichotomies are not particularly fruitful, however. External perspective operates exclusively in the heterodiegetic realm: all first-person natural narrative ends up being reinterpreted in accordance with the narrator's suppressed emotions (Cohn & Genette 1992; Fludernik 1996). External perspective therefore simply describes what is the prototypical human scenario of limited access to others' ideations, and the variability of zero focalization allows itself to be reduced to the factor of personalization of the narrator-figure: if the narrator is conceived of in terms of a human person sharing the fictional world with the characters, albeit only in the margins of the story, then the same limitations apply and the prototypical homodiegetic narrator (who has proved to be particularly recalcitrant material in Genette's formulation of the focalization schema) or peripheral first-person narrator appear on the scene; if the narrator is heterodiegetic, access to characters' consciousness is in principle unlimited but its actual deployment remains strategically selective. In particular, focalization interrelates with the issue of omnicommunicativity (omniscience, i.e., how much the narrator is prepared to communicate to the reader) and the entirely different issue of perspective on the characters' consciousness. The latter factor relates to a choice between *vision du dehors* and *vision avec* (or any combination of these), that is to say, to the decision of how much slant or filter the narrator is going to allow. To the extent, however, that filter starts to dominate, the narrator-figure will tend to become backgrounded and make way for a (temporary) shift toward or into internal focalization. The major dichotomy in relation to perspective is therefore the organic one of access or nonaccess to another's consciousness, supplemented by the distinction of, on the one hand, the mediating representation of that consciousness and, on the other, the quasi-immediate rendering of that consciousness. The first dichotomy is an absolute one (either access or nonaccess, although these options can alternate within a text); the second is definitely a gradual one—indeed it spans the entire scale of thought representation from psychonarration through various intermediary forms to interior monologue at the other end of the scale. Narration and focalization on this cline correlate precisely in terms of linguistic economy of the deictic center; and it is here that small-scale linguistic strategies rewrite the point of view models of classic narratology. These are, however, rewritten and not supplanted—they resurface as projections and holistic interpretative schemata that have been triggered in the reading process by these linguistic minutiae. Focalization in the old terminology therefore remains a valid narratological concept, but it has been relocated on a different level and subsumed under pragmatic interpretative conditions of textual processing. Focalizations are interpretations and not essential features of texts.

In this chapter I want to demonstrate the importance of linguistic features related to the deictic center in what are unfamiliar contexts of narration. The texts that I analyze employ "odd" personal pronouns in the function of the anaphoric marker relating to SELF in Banfield's framework. In the standard cases of internal focalization, a reflector character usually shows up as *he* or *she*, and these anaphora are linked to a network of deictic expressions relating to this he or she as their deictic origo.[3] Stanzel's figural narrative situation typically defined a third-person narrative in which the protagonist, male or female, served as the focal center of perception and ideation, thus evoking an illusion of immediate, unmediated, representation of his or her experience.

Consider the following example, where the thoughts of the child, the younger of the two "babu's sons," and his excitement over the cricket match are rendered in the passage:

> The little one now looked sorry for himself. The match had begun. He stood by the heap of the boys' clothes which lay

> on the side of the hockey ground. He wished he were as big as Chota. Then *he* would be asked to play. Also then he could wear shorts like him. And he would look *like a real sahib* because he was not so dark as Chota. . . .
>
> The little one could have cried at that moment. *But the game, the play—Bakha was going to score a goal.* (Anand 1940: 114)

Anand's *Untouchable* is the story of Bakha, the sweeper's son, and deals with one day in the life of this youth, a day that in its incidents documents Bakha's anguish at the Hindu caste system, his anger at his Hindu superiors, as well as his naive admiration and adoration of kindly Hindus and especially the British sahibs. The novel alternates between zero focalization and brief passages of internal focalization, and its overall consonant (Cohn 1978) representation of Bakha's mind-set makes it a typical case of narration on the authorial-figural continuum (Stanzel 1984). In the passage just quoted we get a brief inside view of the child's aspirations, which are similar to Bakha's. The linguistic features establishing the child as the deictic center have been highlighted in the quotation: the anaphor he, the childlike expression "like a real sahib," and the truncated syntax of the final clause (indicating the child's excitement). The shifted "was going" makes this a sentence of narrated perception.

The passage is a typical instance of psychonarration ("he wished"; "he could have cried") developing into free indirect discourse, with the shift from Bakha's dominant perspective to the "little one's" marked by "looked sorry for himself" in the first sentence: this indicates that Bakha notices the obvious disappointment of the child, but the perception is a generalizable one. By means of a description of the external situation (the child standing by the heap of clothes that the players have dropped) the narrative provides a neutral transitional passage before introducing the child's thoughts.

The establishment of the deictic center is here an interim affair and it does not affect the dominant focalization on Bakha in the rest of the novel. No macrostructural narrative situation emerges from this interlude, except to signal the variability of internal focalizations within the framing narrative discourse in zero focalization. To treat the passage as, merely, a few clauses of free indirect discourse, however, does not do justice to their significance in the narrative. A window on the little boy's mind is here opened. Unlike passages of speech representation in free indirect discourse, this opening makes a qualitative difference within the text, triggering empathy with Hindu children in their enthusiasm for the Sahibs, an enthusiasm that they share with the novel's protagonist. Bakha's aspirations are dignified as a consequence of this generalization and no longer expose him to the accusation of insolent presumption by an untouchable toward his social superiors.

In the homodiegetic realm, the deictic center of the protagonist's SELF has been identified as the experientiality[4] of the so-called experiencing self (Stanzel 1984: 208–9) of the first-person narrator. Since the autodiegetic narrator has unlimited access to her memories of earlier experiences, the establishment of the deictic center in this case is complicated less by the relation of linguistic elements with an unfamiliar experiential center of consciousness, but by the separation of the distanced evaluative perspective and of the quasi-immediate immersion within the first-person protagonist's past experience. That separation can be difficult in practice, as Adamson's examples from Bunyan (chap. 5 of this vol.), demonstrate. In present-tense narratives such separation becomes even more complicated, since evaluative statements are no longer supported by the distancing deixis of the past tense.[5]

Another difference in the relation of homo- and heterodiegetic texts concerns the extent of internal focalization. Reflector mode narratives are comparatively rare in the homodiegetic realm; most first-person texts typically foreground the dynamic interaction between narrating and experiencing selves.[6] Again, it is generally present-tense narrative that constitutes the large majority of homodiegetic texts in internal focalization, and there seems to be a decided preference for the short story format.

Ingoldby's "To Be a Pilgrim" illustrates these conundra very well. The narrator is meeting Purseglove, a woman, at her hotel with the intent of murdering her. The story mostly consists of impassive narrative clauses ("We both drink. I eat and drink. My drinking makes me drunk" [1994: 452]) and of the protagonist's impressions, thoughts, and memories that are simultaneous with the description of events:

> Alone but not alone; the staff are so discreet. (453)

> I'm edgier than ever. If she hasn't seen the car then she'll be told I got the message. She may be leaning from a win-

> dow: Stubble features can't look up. Or showering: for her own delectation and not mine. Purseglove's body—confidence is everything—I've seen it, been there, no great shakes. (451)

Only very rarely does the narrating self assert itself:

> In other places I drink with flunkies. I downmarket myself, act the chameleon, imply that I am nearer them than us. Sometimes they go for it, they are bored as Purseglove's bored; a new face to match crack up. (453)

Since this refers to recurring habits of the protagonist, it might be part of the narration filling in on the background. Nevertheless, in the context of the story one can just conceivably imagine the protagonist thinking about what he usually does.

The last point is a crucial one. Not the linguistic markers (these are indistinguishable in the first-person realm) but their pragmatic interpretation is at stake: Is this a reportative passage or does it represent the protagonist's thoughts; is this a metafictional comment, or a rendering of the protagonist's musings?

Second-person narratives[7] also allow for the establishment of internal perspective through the deictic center, and they do so essentially on the same lines and in the same contexts as third-person narratives. In this way they share features of heterodiegesis in the Genettean mode. On the other hand, the case is complicated in second-person fiction by the possibility of having an identity relationship between the you-protagonist and the current discourse addressee. Narratives that employ a consistent strategy of address in the form of imperative clauses therefore lend themselves less readily to a reflector mode reading than do present-tense texts in the second-person form that lack the imperative morphology or discourse features such as "I want to tell you." Consistent uses of "I" entrench the narratorial voice and therefore counteract the establishment of a second-person deictic center.

Second-person internal focalization can be anchored in expressive features of the Banfieldian kind, but it is additionally enhanced by generic and pragmatic frames relating to common uses of the second-person pronoun. Generic (or gnomic) "you" which, like "one," frequently connotes "anyone" rather than a specific addressee (and indeed often pragmatically refers to the speaker[8]) helps to induce empathy in the reader. Sometimes the "you" is taken to be "anyone" for long stretches of text until specific attributes of the you are mentioned that force one to construct a protagonist for the story.[9] Moreover, uses of the second-person pronoun in the context of self-address and pervasive uses of "you" in passages of free indirect discourse additionally help to support a reading of internal focalization in a second-person text.[10] A typical example of a second-person reflector-mode narrative is the following:

> You always did look with your mouth.
>
> The sun-warmed pebble, salty-smooth against your tongue. Oh Jesus, she's swallowing something again—your Mammy prising open your mouth like you did to Tiny, the Jack Russell. Come on, now, spit it out, spit it out. Your gums aching from clenched teeth, sand in your eyes from your tussling. What's got into you, at all? Mammy embarrassed before her friend. Do what your Mammy says—her nails clawing at your jaw—spit it out, now. She won't be vexed. Its smoothness, its grainy smoothness against your flesh. Now I'm warning you—that note of dying patience in Mammy's voice. The struggle would soon be over, you would have to yield to her nails and sharpening tongue. Open up, come on, now. (O'Reilly 1994: 93)

The first sentence, in a paragraph by itself, is definitely distanced, but the entire second paragraph renders the "you's" experience of having a pebble in her mouth and the struggle with her mother from her exasperated internal perspective. The linguistic markers of the deictic center are obvious: "Mammy" in reference to the protagonist's mother; definite articles for new reference items ("*The* sun-warmed pebble"); familiarizing demonstrative that ("*that* note of dying patience"). The syntax also, in juxtaposing the mother's reprimands with the sensations and thoughts of the daughter, serves to emphasize the reflector mode. The passage operates in the same way as would a third-person she narrative, but the use of the second-person pronoun enhances the empathizing effect, making it even easier for the reader to view the world from the perspective of the reflector figure.

I now turn to two very special cases, that of "one" and "it." They are the least likely to allow for internal focalization: who could empathize with "anyone"? "It" refers to an object (and objects don't have minds). The comparative ease with which even "one" and "it" in some texts trigger a reading of an incipient internal focalization therefore illustrates how linguistic features and a pragmatic anthropomorphic context can join to produce a reading on the lines of a deictic center filled with "one" and "it," a deictic center that operates exactly like "he" or "she" in the standard case.

"One," once one starts to think about it, seems to be the more amenable of the two to being used in a reflector-mode environment. "One," particularly in some British uses, frequently disguises reference to "I" or "you"[11] and it occurs relatively often in passages of free indirect discourse:

> Bakha noticed the ardent, enthusiastic look that lighted up the little one's face. The anxiety of going to school! How beautiful it felt! How nice it must be to be able to read and write! *One* could read the papers after having been to school. *One* could talk to the sahibs. *One* wouldn't have to run to the scribe every time a letter came. And *one* wouldn't have to pay him to have one's letters written. (Anand 1940: 38)

Here Bakha's yearning for learning to read and write is rendered in a passage in which this ability is described as a generally desirable amenity. Bakha foregrounds the practical use of literacy; only once does his personal interest (being able to talk to the Sahibs) interfere, and even at that point the use of "one" camouflages Bakha's self-interest.

In English there exists, as far as I have ascertained, no consistent narrative in the "one" form, but French and German authors have been more forward in exploring this possibility for their experimental purposes. There is at least one novel that uses French *on* in a fairly regular fashion: Monique Wittig (1964), and Roche (1966) also employ *on* as a narrative pronoun in some segments of the novel.[12] In German literature the Swiss author E. Y. Meyer has produced a complete narrative with the German "man" ("one"), where man refers to the male protagonist. *In Trubschachen* (1973), however, does not have any decisive markers of internal focalization; on the contrary, the interpretation of interiority is triggered, if at all, by the fact of having "man" refer to the protagonist. This suggests that the protagonist regards his decisions about where to go for a walk and when, what to eat at the hotel, and so forth, in the light of touristic experience that is intrinsically a generalizable one. German passages of "man" as insets within standard heterodiegetic narrative in the reflector mode or in passages of free indirect discourse are much more common. Joseph Roth's *Radetzkymarsch* (1932) and a series of novels by Gerhard Meier,[13] another Swiss author, are much more typical of the narrative use of "man," a use that squarely corresponds with the English example from Anand that I just quoted.

As with "you," which—in its generalized reading—occurs in very similar environments and is indeed replaceable with "one," the crucial point for reading "one" or "you" as a deictic center is whether the pronoun refers to a specific character whose consciousness can then be accessed via the deixis:

> Meet in expensive raincoats, on a pea-soupy night. Like a detective novel. First, stand in front of Florsheim's Fifty-seventh Street window, press your face close to the glass, watch the fake velvet Hummels inside revolving around the wing tips; some white shoes, *like your father wears*, are propped up with garlands on a small mound of chemical snow. ("How to Be an Other Woman," Moore 1986: 3)

> Il pleut. *On* joue dans la classe. *On* tient les mains du petit garçon qui s'appelle Guy Romain et qui est assis à côté. *On* se met cheval sur le banc et *on* chante, maman les petits bateaux qui vont sur l'eau, en se penchant l'un vers l'autre pour faire le bateau. C'est comme ça qu'*on* ne voit pas déboucher ma soeur qui vient de donner le signal de la fin de la récréation et qu'*on* reçoit une gifle de chaque côté de la figure, ça résonne et la tête brimbale. (*L'Opoponax*, Wittig 1964: 11)

> It is raining. *You* are playing in the classroom. *You* are holding the hands of the little boy whose name is Guy Romain and who sits next to *you*. *You* straddle the bench and sing Maman les petits bateaux qui vont sur l'eau, bending together to make a boat. This is how *you* fail to notice Sister who has just given the signal for the end of playtime and *you* receive a slap on both cheeks, it rings in *your* ears and makes *your* head spin. (Wittig 1966: 8)

In the first example the highlighted "like your father wears" definitely establishes the "you" as a protagonist; in the second example *on* acquires specific reference to a single protagonist when this *on* is said to hold the hands of Guy Romain (not all the children can hold his hands at the same time), and it must be Catherine herself, and only she, who receives the slap on her face, not the children in general.

My second case is that of narrative "it," and I need to say right away that this pronoun occurs only in incipiently narrative contexts, in the odd margins of heterodiegetic novels, and in (as far as I know) one science-fiction text.[14] Walter M. Miller's "I Made You" (1954)[15] introduces the robot-protagonist as "it" ("It had disposed of the enemy" [1954: 485]). That robot acquires a name ("Grumbler"), which is first introduced in a dialogue on the intercom. Whereas the active Grumbler operates under the cover of "it," its human antagonist is referred to as "the feeble thing in the cave" (ibid.). Grumbler's feelings are described by means of psychonarration ("It hated sound and motion" [ibid.]; "And it knew the nature of the world" [487]) and quite extensive passages of free indirect discourse: "Tomorrow, when the enemy was gone, it would drag the trailer back to the main feeders for recharging, when the sun rose to drive the generators once again" (483).

Two more classic texts in the British canon are Isherwood's *A Single Man* (1964) and John Fowles's *Mantissa* (1982). Both novels start with a passage in which the protagonists, half-awake George and the patient recovering from a coma, are referred to as "it," and in both cases the characters' consciousness is rendered by means of brief bursts into free indirect discourse and, in Fowles's case, psychonarration. Thus, Isherwood's "it" steps on the scales and exclaims (whether as interior monologue or as free indirect discourse is a moot point): "still a bit over 150 pounds, in spite of all that toiling at the gym!" (8).

The preceding much condensed survey over the establishment of a deictic center in "odd" pronominal contexts was designed to demonstrate two things. On the one hand, it served to corroborate the importance of linguistic signals for the establishment of internal focalization. "That" in "all that toiling at the gym" immediately gives away George's perspective and anthropomorphizes the referent of "it," despite that referent's unpromising pronominal shape. The implicit anthropomorphic projection is, however, aligned with the function of the deictic center as a rendering of consciousness, and that function establishes an interpretative frame. The linguistic signals, and this is my second point, in and by themselves merely invoke a deictic center and its "attached" consciousness; the interpretation that links that consciousness with a human protagonist and establishes him or her as a reflector character cannot be monitored by a purely textual or linguistic level but requires the reader's active processing on the basis of cognitive schemata. Such schemata link consciousness with anthropomorphic prototypes, situate the protagonist's worldview within the plot situation of the text, and additionally allow interpretations that mimetically motivate and explain the specific thought acts of the protagonist. Thus, in the case of Bakha, his recourse to the impersonal "one" in Kazuo Ishiguro's *The Remains of the Day* (1990) correlate with the butler's self-aggrandizement and his aping of the bygone modes of aristocratic life and manners.[16] Depending on what kind of pronoun is used, such odd pronominals access various familiar schemata (inanimacy and generalization) and those are counteracted on the interpretative level by the attribution of consciousness (which is by definition anthropomorphic) and the establishment of specificity (consciousness, if mimetically verisimilar, is deemed to belong to an individual personal experience[17]).

The centrality of consciousness for the establishment of internal focalization and the macrostructural interpretative or constructivist pragmatics that subtends the narratological classification of such SELFs in their specific textual environments therefore suggest that classical models of focalization or point of view may require extensive redefinition and restructuring. Such rewriting of the canonical formulas has already been initiated by Chatman and Jahn, accompanied by quite a few other proposals of modification, extension, and refinement of the Genettean model in the wake of Bal's classifications: Brau and Lavergne (1992), Edmiston (1989), Nelles (1990), Nieragden (1996), and by Nünning (chap. 12 of this vol.) and Shen (chap. 9 of this vol.). We seem to stand on the threshold of decisive narratological reorientations, of a paradigm shift that is anticipated by the pervasive discontent with the classic model, an epistemological crisis that promises to herald an imminent breakthrough into new and luscious narratological pastures.

Notes

1. On the reflector mode, see Stanzel (1984: 59–60, 141–50). The identification of internal focalization with the reflector mode in terms of Banfield's deictic center is discussed in Fludernik (1993a: 64, 68 n.39).

2. See the excellent survey of these various remodelings of Genette in Jahn (1996).

3. I do not treat these narratives in this chapter. See Fludernik (1996; chap. 6).

4. For a definition of the term, see Fludernik (1996, chap. 1).

5. See Cohn (1993) and Fludernik (1996: chap. 6) on present-tense narratives.

6. I have not encountered any we-texts of internal focalization so far.

7. For details on second-person narratives, compare Richardson (1991), Fludernik (1993b, 1994) and Margolin (1994).

8. Compare the discussion of this in Fludernik (1995b: 103–4, 113; 1995a: 284–87).

9. Since I deal with this at length elsewhere, the reader is referred to the examples I quote in Fludernik (1994c: 452–53).

10. Again I refer the reader to Fludernik (1993b: 230–39) for examples and for additional uses of "you" that help interpret the second-person pronoun as a SELF.

11. For examples, see Fludernik (1995b: 103–4; 1995a: 284–87).

12. For a full discussion of these texts, see Fludernik (1995a, 1995b).

13. See his *Der schnurgerade Kanal* (1977) as well as his trilogy *Toteninsel* (1979), *Borodino* (1982), and *Die Ballade vom Schneien* (1985).

14. Marge Piercey's *He, She and It* (1991), where the "it" also refers to a robot, never has the narrative adopt internal focalization.

15. Thanks are here due to Manfred Jahn for mentioning the text to me.

16. See my discussion of Ishiguro's "one" in Fludernik (1995b: 103–4).

17. Multiple viewpoint, which I have neglected to treat in the present chapter, functions as a deictic center only when the plurality of persons (observers and protagonists) display a unitary intention, reaction, emotion, and so forth. Since a single linguistic form (diversified only by a succession of contradictory expressions) needs to characterize the crowd's sentiments, this unitary linguistic shape conceptualizes the crowd as one deictic center evincing a succession of, say, inconsistent thoughts and emotions.

Part III

Applications and Case Studies

7

Ironic Perspective: Conrad's Secret Agent

Seymour Chatman

Narratology argues that narrative structure can be analyzed separately from media, that not only words but the appearances and physical movements of actors on a stage, moving shadows projected onto a screen, drawings, puppets, and so on may actualize plot events and character traits. But Rimmon-Kenan has observed that this insistence on narrative's abstract structure neglects its fundamental embodiment in natural language. In principle, the point is not unfair. But the medium of print has not been ignored. A great deal has been written about aspects of the linguistic surface, about indirect free speech or stream of consciousness, for example, as well as about other kinds of features that have special purposes or effects in narrative.

No narratologist would seriously propose that the "story" component of narrative exists independently of the actualized text. *Story* and *discourse* and similar analytical terms are only hypothetical components of what in the real world is an indivisible whole. But it seems both possible and profitable to separate narrative from its materiality, if only as an analytical exercise, and thereby to investigate the structures of narratives that have appeared in the various media.

Film has been of particular interest, and books by Kawin (1978), Branigan (1984, 1992), Bordwell (1985), Kozloff (1987), and others have considerably advanced our knowledge of cinematic narrative. Most narratologists would agree with Rimmon-Kenan (1983, 1990) that the "same" narrative (whatever same might mean in this context) cannot present identical meanings in two different media. I certainly do. Novels and their film adaptations inspire a consideration of differences as much as of similarities. In the process of comparison we learn a great deal not only about the narrative structure of the different versions, but also about the constraints that a given medium imposes on a narrative text.

Studying the functioning of language in narrative is important, but I do not believe that language is narrative's privileged medium. A smaller percentage of the population today read novels than in the nineteenth century, and I suspect that audiovisual narratives will become even more dominant in the future. That may be regrettable, but it seems to be a fact of life. Research on how media other than print actualize narrative helps us understand more about the text-type itself. And the relation between literary and nonliterary narratives remains a topic of considerable interest.

Elsewhere I have written about aspects of literary narrative that prove to be challenging to film or television adaptation (see, e.g., my discussion of *The French Lieutenant's Woman,* in Chatman 1990). Here I shall focus on a single effect, namely, the representation of the character's inner life—of thoughts, perceptions, and emotions—and in particular, the ironization of that inner life, whether by quoting the words that ostensibly pass through the character's mind, or by paraphrasing them. In the first case, the case of quotation or direct imitation, the irony often turns on discrepancies between the character's situation and her inner voice; in the latter, the case of paraphrase, on differences between how the character *might* have expressed the thought or feeling in her own diction, as we know it from direct dialogue, and how the well-spoken narrator actually expresses it. This irony sometimes rests on social and cultural differences between character and narrator, differences that are especially marked in societies (like that of Great Britain) where class distinctions are strong. But I am less concerned with sociological or political implications than with describing the phenomenon itself. I am particularly intrigued by this ironic effect in Joseph Conrad's novels, for instance, *The Secret Agent.*

Irony is blessed by a wealth of precise theoretical discussion, and though not all of its aspects are fully understood, there is general agreement about certain of them. Traditionally, the most basic distinction is between verbal irony and so-called irony of circumstance or fate. Verbal irony is purposefully generated by a human speaker, intentionally communicated to an audience as a subtext at odds with the ostensible message. The success of the ironic communication depends entirely on the audience's capacity to read between the lines. What is said is quite different from what is meant. If speaker A says of a burly three-hundred-pound wrestler: "Butch is a gazelle, an airy sprite," listener B is likely to understand that the comparison is meant ironically, and that the athlete is quite the opposite of such a delicate creature. Irony of circumstance or fate, on the other hand, is not humanly generated, not a covert message (unless you believe in deities) but a "funny" coincidence—"funny" in the sense of odd rather than humorous, for example, a man tries to protect himself from a thunderstorm by standing under a tree but gets killed when lightning strikes the tree, which then falls on him. *Irony* in this sense, as Booth points out, risks self-implosion and ultimate meaninglessness, since people are increasingly using the term with only minimal linkage to coincidence. For instance, for me to say that it is *ironic* to see you simply because I hadn't expected to is to push the term far beyond its traditional meaning.

In verbal irony, the speaker depends on her interlocutor's ability first to understand that the spoken message is not seriously meant; and second, to grasp the covert message, the one that *is* intended. To cite one of Booth's examples, when the narrator of *Tom Jones* refers to Mrs. Partridge as "a professed follower of that noble sect founded by Xanthippe of old," a competent reader understands that the word *noble* is not being offered at face value, since "Xanthippe" is an eponym for "virago" or "shrew," a notion not ordinarily associated with nobility.

Such irony occurs in ordinary conversation, and in other text-types like description or argument. The kind of irony that is the subject of this chapter, however, is peculiar to narrative. A narrator can ironize a character's opinions, attitudes, or feelings by phrasing them in diction more lofty than they deserve. Imagine an encounter between Pat and Mike. Pat might have said something crude, like "Mike, you're just a jerk," but the narrator could paraphrase Pat's remark in his own more genteel terms, for example, "Pat assigned to Mike's inadequacies a mark of the lowest possible esteem." In that version, we would understand not only that Pat felt disdain for Mike, but that we were being asked to look for reasons for the "elevation" of the diction. We immediately begin to search for *why* the narrator might choose to distance us from Pat's actual utterance.

My concern is not characters' speeches, however, but what is usually called their "inner views," as revealed by perspective, or to use the term I prefer, their *filter*, that is, the screened report of thoughts and feelings usually known only to the characters themselves. In the best book on the subject, *Transparent Minds*, Cohn distinguishes three basic techniques for representing a character's consciousness: (1) the narrator's own diction—a form that she calls "psychonarration," and two forms of quotation of words purportedly streaming through the characters' minds; (2) direct thought (in her term *quoted monologue*); and (3) indirect thought (in her term *narrated monologue*) (1978; 11–12). What distinguishes the latter two are well-known features like pronoun-choice ("I" for the direct form and "he" or "she" for the indirect form), present versus past tense of verbs, and the like.

As the European novel negotiated its sharp psychological turn at the end of the nineteenth century, writers like Flaubert developed exquisite techniques for ironizing the mental life of characters. In *Madame Bovary*, for example, the narrator continuously contrasts Emma's fantasies with the tedious circumstances of her daily life. One of the finest moments presents the conflicting thoughts of Emma and Charles as they lie in bed together: Charles dreams of the day when his daughter is old enough to knit socks; Emma fantasizes a whirlwind elopement with a lover in a coach-and-four. The nuptial bodies are together, but the minds couldn't be further apart.

Conrad is no less a master of this technique, especially in *The Secret Agent* (1907). He observed in his 1920 preface that the novel's "purely artistic purpose" was to apply "an ironic method" to a story of political intrigue, in the belief that that "alone would enable me to say all I felt I would have to say in scorn as well as in pity." The balance falls more heavily on the former than the latter. (Conrad's scorn for revolutionaries of every stripe is amply attested in autobiographical writings and in novels like *Under Western Eyes*, [1911].) As in *Madame Bovary*, one of the ironies turns on a couple's profound misunderstanding of each other, for all their physical contact in kitchen, parlor, and bedroom. This misunderstanding derives from both protagonists. Verloc's psychological as well as professional commitment to secrecy—he is a double agent, working at once for the Russian Embassy and Scotland Yard—and Mrs. Verloc's profound need, both economic and psychological, to let sleeping dogs lie. Thoroughly bourgeois in his desire for peace and comfort, Verloc is a good provider, not only to his wife Winnie, but to her slow-witted brother Stevie and her mother. He does so ostensibly through the rubber goods shop he runs but actually through his earnings as a double agent. Winnie did not marry Verloc out of love but out of poverty and concern that her brother be taken care of. Verloc's life is suddenly thrown into turmoil when a new secretary at the Russian Embassy orders him to arrange a provocation, a public outrage, by blowing up the Greenwich Observatory. An indolent man whose career has been devoted to minimizing risks, Verloc is shocked at the need to take action. He persuades the mad professor to manufacture a bomb, but can find no one stupid enough to undertake the outrage. In desperation, he turns to his brother-in-law Stevie. But before reaching the observatory, Stevie stumbles and blows himself up. His scattered remains are identified by a label sewn in his overcoat, and Verloc's hand is quickly discovered by the police. But he has less to fear from them than from the radicals whom he has made a career of betraying. A quiet stint in jail for two years, he feels, will be the safest place for him. Winnie overhears his confession to the police and in a fit of hysterical rage sticks a carving knife into him.

The whole denouement, in the eleventh and penultimate chapter, depends on Verloc's colossal and ultimately fatal incomprehension of his wife's feelings. Her lack of curiosity—voiced frequently in the sentiment that "things don't bear looking into too closely"—suited Verloc's purposes well enough when he was an active spy, but once he is unmasked and in need of comfort and cooperation, it becomes a source of torment. At the moment that he most requires her sympathy for the outrage perpetrated on him by the Russian attaché, she is too engrossed in her grief to even understand what he is talking about. Her brother's death brews a veritable earthquake of rage that proves deadly to Verloc.

In the first third of the chapter, the narrator stays inside Verloc's perspective, then gives a few paragraphs to Winnie's rage, and then mixes the two in what would be a comic misunderstanding if the results were not so deadly. The narrator nuances both characters' thoughts by switching between their diction (in dialogue and in direct and free indirect thought) and his own cooler and more elegant phraseology. The latter is particularly necessary for Winnie, since her state of mind is so profoundly inarticulate and disordered. The narrator precisely fashions the total incompatibility of the couple's patterns of thinking, an incompatibility so severe that it leads to murder and suicide.

Cohn's discussion of psychonarration is highly useful for explaining these effects, especially her distinction between "dissonance"—where the narrator, as in *Death in Venice*, markedly separates himself from the character whose thinking he represents—

and "consonance," where the narrator's slant is little distinguished from the character's filter, as in Joyce's *Portrait of the Artist as a Young Man*. The relation of narrator to characters in *The Secret Agent* is dissonant indeed, but in a way that differs considerably from Mann's novella. Whereas Mann's narrator separates himself through lofty ex cathedra moralizations and a "highly abstract analytical vocabulary," discussing Aschenbach's problems in almost psychiatric terms, Conrad's narrator ironizes his characters by paraphrasing their thoughts in diction that they could not themselves use because it is beyond their competence.

The narrator also uses direct and indirect quotation, but it is psychonarration that scores the most brilliant ironic effects. Often the techniques shade into each other, as in the very opening of chapter 11. The narrator first quotes Verloc's thought directly: "She knows all about it [i.e., Stevie's grisly death]," he thought to himself . . ." but then adds in his own language a description of Verloc's attendant feeling: ". . . with commiseration for her sorrow and with some satisfaction as regarded himself," a passage that shrewdly captures Verloc's shallow sympathy for Winnie's shock and grief but also his private capacity to find redeeming consequences in the boy's death. A few paragraphs later, Verloc's faint compassion reemerges, again in psychonarration: "Mr. Verloc never meant Stevie to perish with such abrupt violence. He did not mean him to perish at all. Stevie dead was a much greater nuisance than ever he had been when alive." In context, the word *nuisance* clearly subverts the more humane sentiment. The order as well as the content of these sentences implies much: his innate sloth and a life devoted to conspiracy has blinded Verloc to any consideration except saving his own skin, so his grief for his brother-in-law's death remains nominal. He didn't mean Stevie to perish with abrupt violence—he didn't *mean* him to perish at all; the concession sounds almost like an afterthought. Verloc's inveterate scheming is reinforced by a psychonarrated passage that occurs slightly later: Verloc *had* recognized that Stevie might be arrested, and was prepared to risk it: "he was not afraid," says the narrator. But this lack of fear, we quickly learn, is not for Stevie's potential incarceration, but for Verloc's own risk of arrest. He has obviated that eventuality by "carefully indoctrinating [Stevie] with the necessity of silence in the course of many walks." The ironic balance tips even more in the psychonarration that immediately follows: Stevie's demise "had appalled him as a humane man and a fond husband. From every other point of view it was rather advantageous. Nothing can equal the everlasting discretion of death." The last sentence elegantly conveys an ex cathedra moral pronouncement, but of a very different sort from those made by the narrator of *Death in Venice*. Though *expressed* in the narrator's tony prose, we are quite certain that this is Verloc's sentiment, the cynical credo of the professional spy. The narrator lets Verloc's values speak for themselves but uses his own elegant prose to flesh them out. Thus both Verloc and the stock-in-trade of the double agent are ironized.

Psychonarration is the perfect medium for conveying the complexity of Verloc's character. A variety of phrases—all true in their way—convey his concern for Winnie, for instance, he withdraws from her "on [a] delicate impulse"; he is "capable of tender sentiments"; "a humane man"; and he has come home "prepared to allow every latitude to his wife's affection for her brother." Superficially, these suggest a certain generosity of soul, but that generosity is laughably dwarfed by the enormity of what Verloc has in fact done to Stevie and his sister. This subtext is communicated not through direct narratorial judgments but through the self-serving opinions of Verloc himself. It is by such means, I think, that Conrad achieves the "dryness" and "coldness" often attributed to the novel.

About a third of the way through the chapter, the narrator switches to Winnie's perspective. Interestingly—and usefully for the cinematic adapter—these take the form of "visions," scenes of her devotion to Stevie's welfare that she visually recalls: "She saw herself putting the boy to bed by the light of a single candle," ". . . brushing the boy's hair and tying his pinafores," "blows intercepted" that were meant by her brutal father for Stevie, and, more recently, images of Verloc and Stevie walking up Brett Street, prompting her observation that they "might have been father and son."

Thereafter, to the chapter's—and Verloc's—end, there is a shuttling back and forth between the two perspectives: as Verloc wonders why she does not support his rage at the Russian Embassy, she expresses, in a rare verbalization, her own rage at *him*: "This man took the boy away to murder him. He took the boy away from his home to murder him. He took the boy away from me to murder him." The narrator tells us that this becomes her fixed idea. What she does mutter aloud, Verloc misinterprets as concern for himself:

> "And I thought he had caught a cold."
> Mr. Verloc heard these words and appropriated them.
> "It was nothing," he said moodily.

Verloc understands "he" as Adolph Verloc, not as Stevie. And so on through a litany of the "extreme disaccord," as the narrator phrases it, of what Verloc says "with her mental condition."

Even when Winnie finally expresses her outrage, screaming that she doesn't want to look at him ever again, Verloc's complacency puts its own precarious interpretation on the outburst, in a sophisticated metaphor that can only be the narrator's: "It was obviously unreasonable, the mere cry of exaggerated grief. He threw over it the mantle of his marital indulgence." To which the narrator adds his own opinion, perhaps to ensure that his attitudes are not identified with Verloc's: "The mind of Mr. Verloc lacked profundity. Under the mistaken impression that the value of individuals consists in what they are in themselves, he could not possibly comprehend the value of Stevie in the eyes of Mrs. Verloc." By Verloc's standards, a dimwit like Stevie could not be worth all that concern, even to his own sister; the narrator must intercede to explain what the character *cannot* think.

Verloc responds to Winnie's outburst with a clumsy line that exemplifies the tragicomic gulf between them:

> "Come. This won't bring him back," he said, gently, feeling ready to take her in his arms and press her to his breast, where impatience and compassion dwelt side by side. But except for a short shudder Mrs. Verloc remained apparently unaffected by the force of that terrible truism. It was Mr. Verloc himself who was moved. He was moved in his simplicity to urge moderation by asserting the claims of his own personality. "Do be reasonable, Winnie. What would it have been if you had lost me?"

Winnie's thoughts are so tumultuous that chaos engulfs her soul, a chaos that only psychonarration could capture. Cohn keenly observes about psychonarration that it is verbally independent "from self-articulation. Not only can it order and explain a character's conscious thoughts better than the character himself, it can also effectively articulate a psychic life that remains unverbalized, penumbral, or obscure. Accordingly psychonarration often renders, in a narrator's knowing words, what a character 'knows,' without knowing how to put it into words" (46). "Unverbalized, penumbral, or obscure" certainly characterize Winnie's train of thought. When Verloc, following the "general consent of mankind," suggests she have a good cry, the narrator explains:

> . . . the lamentable circumstances of Stevie's end, which to Mr. Verloc's mind had only an episodic character, as part of a greater disaster, dried her tears at their very source. It was the effect of a white-hot iron drawn across her eyes; at the same time her heart, hardened and chilled into a lump of ice, kept her body in an inward shudder, set her features into a frozen, contemplative immobility addressed to a whitewashed wall with no writing on it.

Indeed, argues Cohn, the deeper into a character's psyche we go, the fewer *words* we find there. Cohn stands the conventional view on its head: really deep mental plunges cannot be made by interior monologue, since that technique relies on the convention that there really are words—the character's very words—to convey her most intimate thoughts. But the deepest of all internal experiences seem as vaguely formed as creatures at the bottom of the sea. Only a narrator can provide language to shine a submarine light on them. One recourse is to figurative language, which Cohn illustrates with examples from D. H. Lawrence—"electromagnetic, igneous, and meteorological hyperboles" for erotic attraction. Winnie's passion is rather expressed in thermal figures: the eyes seared by a white-hot iron; the heart like a lump of ice. But she mentally articulates few words. Defending against a potential technical objection, the narrator explains that

> These thoughts were rather imagined than expressed. Mrs. Verloc was a woman of singularly few words, either for public or private use. With the rage and dismay of a betrayed woman, she reviewed the tenor of her life in visions concerned mostly with Stevie's difficult existence from its earliest days.
>
> . . . It was a crushing memory, an exhausting vision of countless breakfast trays carried up and down innumerable stairs, of endless haggling over pence, of the endless drudgery of sweeping, dusting, cleaning, from basement to attics.

Since she cannot articulate these feelings even to herself, it is only through iterative psychonarration that the narrator can communicate Winnie's passion and resultant impulse to murder, encapsulating, in a moment of discourse time, the years of mental burden that she suffered for the sake of the brother to whose death this man so callously contributed.

Three filmed versions of *The Secret Agent* have appeared in the last sixty years—Hitchcock's *Sabotage* (1936), the 1992 BBC TV Masterpiece Theater miniseries version directed by David Drury, and the 1996 film directed by Christopher Frampton. Though all are interesting productions, they capture little of the ironic voice of the novel mostly because none employs a narrator. All three are straightforward dramatic pieces. Where irony does occur, it is that of circumstance, not of words.

The filmmakers could have used voice-over narration to convey the narrator's language as well as the thoughts of characters.[1] This technique has existed since the advent of sound, and was especially popular in the forties and fifties. However, it no longer seems aesthetically desirable. Most current filmmakers (at least in America and England[2]) appear reluctant to use voice-over narration in fiction films, usually on grounds that it is unfaithful to the medium and hence less realistic.[3] Of course, they still rely heavily on commentative or "nondiegetic" music-over, music with no visible source in the story-world but added to the sound track to comment editorially on actions and characters.[4]

My discussion of the three adaptations of *The Secret Agent* is not meant to suggest that voice-over narration and representation of characters' thoughts *should* have been used. As dramatic pieces, each has its own merits and each does convey something of the flavor of the book. I simply mean to illustrate how the ironic treatment of the characters' inner lives, so intrinsic to Conrad's novel, was inevitably lost once directors decided not to utilize such a narrator.

Drury's TV version and Frampton's film version stick closest to Conrad's novel. Both capture the physical details of the characters, major and minor, and do the murder scene quite effectively. But they contain little more of the irony of cross-purpose between husband and wife than can be divined from the actors' dialogue or facial expression. David Suchet (well-known for his TV performances as Hercule Poirot) plays Verloc in the BBC version with suitable heavy torpidity; Bob Haskins is less successful, I think, in the film (too bouncily Cockney for my taste). The actresses who play Winnie—Cheryl Campbell in the teleplay and Patricia Arquette in the film—remain silent, even cataleptic. They must have found it difficult to communicate Winnie's thoughts and feelings through face and body alone. Campbell keeps her veil on throughout the scene, maximizing the inexpressiveness of her face. She, I think, does a better job than Arquette, who goes a bit too quickly from tears to stoneface and feverish plunging.

Otherwise, the representation of Winnie's mind is achieved through "mindscreens," and subjective camera movements. Mindscreens are visual imagings of events, whether of flashbacked memories or of imagined happenings. As just noted, this approach was already strongly suggested by the novel itself through reference to Winnie's "visions." Both films repeat shots of the original reality later as flashback memories; Winnie remembers her husband and brother walking off on an errand hand in hand, or hearing Stevie at the bus-stop in the rain say "Verloc is a good man," and the line about the pair being like father and son gets repeated bitterly. In Frampton's film, as Inspector Heat tells Verloc the details of Stevie's grisly end and Winnie eavesdrops on their conversation, shots illustrative of what Heat saw are mixed indiscriminately with Winnie's mindscreen imagining of the horrendous details (e.g., Stevie's head lodged by itself on a branch of the tree whose root he stumbled on).

The other effect used to show Arquette's distress is an erratic camera movement: the camera angle is tilted (horizontals become diagonals), then the camera swings around the shop unevenly and also zooms in and out, suggesting that her perspective has become vertiginous as she tries to digest (without vomiting) the bad news. She is suffering temporary vertigo in three dimensions.

These effects do invoke irony, but it is irony of circumstance, not of words; the meaning of the image of Verloc and Stevie walking off "like father and son" changes drastically after the former is responsible for the latter's death.

The effects are not very refined: neither version even tries to capture the novel's precise details of Winnie's state of mind. How do you photograph "a white-hot iron drawn across her eyes" or a "heart, hardened and chilled into a lump of ice"? Nor can the audience know exactly the kinds of ironic difference between what Winnie feels and what Verloc imagines her feelings to be. Absent the vocal authority of a voice-over narrator, we can only guess. Even the most brilliant actress would find it difficult to convey through face and body alone such complexities as these: In response to Verloc's promise to take her abroad when he gets out of prison, Winnie momentarily forgets that Stevie would not join them:

> This shaking piece of forgetfulness stimulated Mrs. Verloc's intelligence. She began to perceive certain consequences which would have surprised Mr. Verloc. There was no need for her now to stay there, in that kitchen, in that house, with that man—since the boy was gone for ever. No need

> whatever. And on that Mrs. Verloc rose as if raised by a spring. But neither could she see what there was to keep her in the world at all. And this inability arrested her.

And how could the actor (however abetted by the camera) convey Verloc's state of mind in response?

> Had this view become in some way perceptible to Mr. Verloc he would have been extremely shocked. In his affairs of the heart Mr. Verloc had been always carelessly generous, yet always with no other idea than that of being loved for himself. Upon this matter, his ethical notions being in agreement with his vanity, he was completley incorrigible. That this should be so in the case of his virtuous and legal connection he was perfectly certain.

Hitchcock's film is the loosest adaptation, a thriller with an unlikely (and certainly un-Conradian) romantic twist at the end, in which Winnie gets away with the killing and goes off with the handsome investigating detective. Verloc (played by Oscar Homolka) is a villainous, burly Middle European who behaves loutishly toward his wife (Sylvia Sidney). In the typical Hitchcockian way, the movie's emphasis is not on psychological depth but on suspense and perilous action. The characters are more or less one-dimensional. Neither is the film concerned with anarchism, nor with the "complicated personal and political factors that influence government decision-making" (Goodwin, 1981: 218). The motif is rather us versus them, where the "them" are shadowy sinister forces vaguely identifiable with Nazi Germany. (Someone mutters something about foreign elements attempting through sabotage to distract the British public from foreign threats.) The object of the bomb attack is the Piccadilly underground station; the idea is thus bloodier from the outset—even Conrad's Russian secretary was not out to kill a lot of innocent people, but simply to throw a scare by attacking the current "fetish" of science. Hitchcock, as one might expect, goes for broad public hysteria and relates the attack to growing apprehension about war in Europe. But he so little trusted the public's political sophistication that his opening frame shows a close-up of a printed dictionary definition of "sabotage."

Again, without a narrative voice or access to characters' consciousness, the film conveys none of Conrad's narrator's ironies, but it manages some ironies of its own. These turn on visual images, and so, again, are ironies of fate or circumstance, rather than the explicit satiric irony conveyed by Conrad's narrator, for example, there is a complex of ironic references to birds. Canaries and robins become icons of apparent innocence behind which is concealed indiscriminate violence. Stevie's affection for birds is early established with a view of him fondling a pigeon. Conrad's bomb-supplying professor is turned into a bird-shop owner named Chatman (no relation) who has retired from "frontline" espionage and now continues the fight making bombs behind the lines. The bomb is delivered to Verloc in the secret bottom of a bird-cage containing two canaries. The package includes a note reading "The birds will sing at 1:45." Homolka, somewhat braver than Conrad's Verloc, is prepared to deliver the bomb to the Piccadilly station, but he can't do so because he's under heavy police surveillance. Watching Stevie play with his new birds, he decides to send the boy instead, explaining to Stevie that the package is a film to be left at the underground station cloakroom for pickup by the distributor. Stevie never gets to Piccadilly because he is delayed by a huckster and then by a parade, so he is killed on a bus with other innocent passengers. Loder finds the film can label and a newspaper reporter picks up on the news. When she sees the paper, Sidney faints. Homolka coolly urges her to pull herself together in words very close to what Conrad wrote (e.g., "What if it had happened to *me?*"). She is paralyzed, does not respond. When he mentions the future and maybe having kids of their own, she gets up and walks into the movie house; the Disney cartoon *Who Killed Cock Robin?* is on the screen. Forgetting her grief for a moment, she laughs along with the children. Then, when Cock Robin is slain, she remembers, her face grows somber and she returns immediately to the apartment to prepare Homolka's dinner. The song "Who Killed Cock Robin" follows her into her dining room.

The murder scene is a magisterial piece of silent cinema. Sidney's guilt is rendered ambiguous by a series of very brief shots in Hitchcock's characteristic manner.[5] Sidney cuts the roast and spears a potato for Homolka's plate as he grumbles about the way in which the greens are cooked; he suggests sending out for some fresh ones. Out of habit she glances at Stevie's chair, since he would be the one to normally run the errand. The chair, of course, is empty. Cut to a shot of the two canaries in their cage. Three times she looks at the carving knife in her hand and drops it quickly, obviously appalled by her own thought. Finally she pushes the knife away and folds her hands together as if to keep them from picking up the knife. Homolka grows suspicious, gets up and stands next to her, to remove the knife from her grasp. As he reaches for it, she grabs it almost instinctively. They both cry out. We cut to a shot of the knife already handle-deep in Homolka's belly, then cut to the pair looking at each other, Homolka with his mouth open. There is the suggestion that Homolka has walked into the knife, rather than been stabbed. Hitchcock staged the scene this way to vindicate Sidney, since he wanted her rescued from her fate, not by Tom Ossipon, but by the handsome detective, Ted (no relation to either Inspector Heat or to the assistant commissioner).[6] Ted has fallen in love with her and is avidly prepared to sacrifice his career (not to mention his honesty) by running off with her to the Continent.[7]

Although I believe that the voice-over representation of characters' thoughts and narrators' interpretations and comments are underused in contemporary practice (at least in American films), I am not arguing that they become standard techniques for the adaptation of novels. On the contrary: great filmmakers like Hitchcock are able to capture a great deal of the inner life of characters without recourse to voice-over introspection or narration.

Film and TV are independent media, and artists working in these media have every right to their own aesthetic, including restrictions on how the different information tracks are to be used. "Faithfulness" to the novel is not my concern; I don't find it an interesting critical issue. Even if the film or TV version uses the original only as a point of departure—as *Apocalypse Now* used *Heart of Darkness*—it should be assessed on its own merits, as an independent work of art. And being true to the medium is perhaps ultimately as important as being faithful to the original. Still, the disinclination to use voice-over narration deprives modern films of an interesting source of irony.

Notes

1. "Over" means that the voice is not connected to any lips visible onscreen nor within earshot, as, for example, coming from another room "offscreen" but adjacent to the one in the frame.

2. French cinema, however, is more comfortable with voice-over representation of characters' thoughts and narrators' commentaries. Excellent recent examples are Eric Rohmer's *L'Amour L'Après-Midi* (1972, Englished as *Chloe in the Afternoon)* and Bernard Tavernier's *Un Dimanche à la*

Compagne (or "A Sunday in the Country " 1984). For a discussion, see my article "New Directions in Voice-Narrated Cinema" (in press).

3. For instance, there was some criticism (to my mind unwarranted) of the use of Joann Woodward's voice-over narration in Martin Scorsese's adaptation of *The Age of Innocence* (1993).

4. See my *Coming to Terms* (Ithaca, NY: Cornell University Press, (1990, chap. 9).

5. The film is readily available on videotape, and a sequence of frame reproductions is printed in Truffaut, (1967: 78–79).

6. We are fortunate to have clear statements of Hitchcock's intentions in his interview with Truffaut. Truffaut first observed that the

> scene almost suggests suicide rather than murder. It's as if Homolka were allowing himself to be killed by Sylvia Sidney. Prosper Mérimée staged Carmen's death on the same dramatic principle, with the victim thrusting her body forward to meet the slayer's fatal stab. (Ibid., 77–80)

To which Hitchcock responded:

> . . . to maintain the public's sympathy for Sylvia Sidney her husband's death had to be accidental. And to bring this off, it was absolutely essential that the audience identify itself with Sylvia Sidney. Here we were not trying to frighten anyone; we had to make the viewer feel like killing a man, and that's a good deal tougher . . . When Sylvia Sidney brings the vegetable platter to the table, the knife acts as a magnet; it's almost as if her hand, against her will, is compelled to grab it . . . The wrong way to go about this scene would have been to have the heroine convey her inner feelings to the audience by her facial expression. I'm against that. In real life, people's faces don't reveal what they think or feel. (ibid.)

7. Truffaut told Hitchcock "Wherever you have a romantic relationship between the heroine and the policeman, I find the situation rather hard to swallow—it's contrived." Hitchcock blamed it on weak acting.

8

Point of View and Viewer Empathy in Film

Els Andringa, Petra van Horssen, Astrid Jacobs, and Ed Tan

In their description of narrative structures, most theories suppose that the way in which a story is presented by a narrator influences the audience's understanding and emotional involvement. Stam, Burgoyne, and Flitterman-Lewis write: "The category of point-of-view is one of the most important means of structuring narrative discourse and one of the most powerful mechanisms for audience manipulation" (1992: 84). However, empirical evidence for the effects of narrative devices is still rare. A few experiments have used manipulated text versions and integrated reader variables. As yet, these studies have not shown dramatic effects (see, e.g., Millis 1995 and Andringa 1996). In film research, empirical evidence of the effects of narrative devices is practically nonexistent. We know of only one study in which a film's narration was manipulated: Böhm (1990) reports the results of an experiment in which four different versions of the exposition phase were presented, followed by an identical middle part and ending. The expositions varied as to the relative prominence of the film's two protagonists, a man and a woman. Pronounced effects were found on the perceived importance of the protagonists in the film's middle part.

Psychologists studying empathy have successfully manipulated viewers' perspective and emotion by giving different instructions before showing them a film (e.g., Davis et al. 1987 and Zillmann & Cantor 1977). None of these studies, however, manipulated or even identified a well-defined narrative device. The purpose of the present chapter is to empirically establish the effects of film perspective on viewers' character perception and emotional involvement.

Point of View in Film

Though the "point of view" originally refers to the point in space from where a spectator perceives (Bordwell 1985), it also means the observational attitudes (Tan 1996) that people bring to look upon states of things, events, or other people. In theories of narratives the concept relates to a set of narrative strategies and devices used to convey information or a story to the audience. First, there are modes of narration based on the position of the narrating agent. Narrators can be invisible respectively inaudible, in terms of Chatman (1978) "covert," in language or images. However, they become manifest in all devices of presentation that select, construct, or organize information. Such is mostly the case in conventional third-person stories and films. The narrator can also be audibly present without participating in the story. Such an "overt" narrator may, for example, comment on what is told or shown. Because overt narrators are not an element of the story or "diegesis" they are telling, they are called "extradiegetic." There are, however, also narrators who are characters in the story that is told as well. Such is the case in an embedded narrative, where a character presented by the extradiegetic narrator tells a story. This narrator is called "intradiegetic."

A second aspect, called "focalization," is the more literal "point-of-seeing"; it concerns the question who is the subject who does the seeing, feeling, and thinking. In case of *external* focalization it is the narrator's observation that is mediated: characters are shown through the gaze and interpretation of the narrator. In case of *internal* focalization things and events are presented from the consciousness of a character within the story. In the former case readers-viewers seem to look at the characters from the outside, in the latter to look with them from the inside.

Most of these concepts have originally been developed for literary texts. Gradually, they have been modified for and extended to film. Recently, Chatman (1990, chap. 8) has suggested that one must distinguish for the medium of film the *cinematic narrator*, the agent who actually *shows* a film in its visual (and audio) arrangement by all filmic devices used, like, for example, mise-en-scène, editing, lighting, and camera-angle and -movement and sound. The cinematic narrator can be distinguished from a narrator who *verbally* tells the story by means of voice-over (VO). This distinction clearly shows that film has various "channels" for presenting information and also various devices for implying points of view. Points of view can even be doubled. The "cinematic narrator" may show a piece of scenery from a certain angle, eventually focalize a character, while an off-screen extra- or intra-diegetic overt narrator relates or comments by means of a VO. An example is Kubrick's *The Killing* (1956) in which a voice-over in the style of early newsreels informs us about the state of affairs (for a more detailed discussion of VO narrators, see Kozloff 1987).

In addition to distinguishing narrators and narrative levels, recent film theory has identified the filmic devices of focalization. Branigan (1984, 1992) defined subjectivity "as a specific instance or level of narration where the telling is *attributed* to a character in the narrative and received by us *as if* we were in the situation of a character" (73), thus linking narrative strategies directly to effects on the audience. Branigan has developed a theory of subjectivity in classical film referring to a whole range of narrative techniques that offer viewers access to a character's mind. One of them is the P(oint)O(f)V(iew) shot, in which (by means of editing or mise-en-scène) a character is shown while perceiving something or somebody: the viewer sees the character's gaze match the object. The character's emotional states can be expressed by acting, but also by lighting or music. Characters' thoughts, memories, or dreams can, for example, be shown in image sequences that interrupt the ongoing sequence of action or, simultaneously, by means of a VO.

An assumption often taken for granted is that the degree of access to a character's mind determines the degree to which viewers sympathize with a character. However, such intuitions that are often vaguely expressed in analyses and interpretations, lack empirical evidence. It is our aim here to investigate how different modes of focalization influence the way in which viewers perceive and empathize with a character. In an experiment, focalization was systematically varied from external to internal by means of a VO, while the cinematic narrator was kept constant. The VO-versions implied the addition of an *overt*, in one version extradiegetic, in the other version intradiegetic narrator. Table 1 presents an overview of the manipulations. We expect that internal focalization (with viewers having maximal access to what and how a character sees, feels, and thinks) will produce in the audience a clearer image of that character's personality and state of mind, as well as a higher sensitivity to the character's emotions. As a consequence, it will be easier for spectators to infer what a character does or plans to do.

Table 8.1
Principles of Manipulation

Version Narrator Level 1 (covert)	*Narrator Level 2* (overt)	*Focalization*
1. cinematic	—	external
2. cinematic	extradiegetic (off-screen VO in the third person)	shifting between external and internal
3. cinematic	intradiegetic (off-screen VO in the first person)	internal

Materials Used: The Film Emma Zunz

Emma Zunz (Peter Delpeut, dir.; the Netherlands, 1984) is a black-and-white, 16-mm, short feature film of thirty minutes, directed by Peter Delpeut, a Dutch director. A two-minute scene showing Emma slowly undressing was cut out, leaving a total length of twenty-eight minutes; for the credits, see the short filmography in the next section. The film is an adaptation of Borges's famous 1949 story, which derives its complexity and ambiguity from shifts in the narrator's role. Borges's narrative is initially presented by an extradiegetic narrator who sometimes adopts a more prominent authorial role, but shifts to a self-reflective narrator at other places, showing consciousness of his limits of presentation and questioning his own reliability.

The Borges story has been used in studies by Dixon and his colleagues (1993) and Andringa (1996). In both studies the text was manipulated by removing the self-reflective passages from the original text. Both studies established effects on readers' aesthetic appreciation. However, no clear effects were found either on readers' emotional involvement or the way in which they perceived the protagonist's emotions and character traits. This led us to suppose that perception of a character is perhaps more readily affected by focalization. Delpeut's film seemed eminently suited to investigate such effects.

The film is not completely faithful to the story, in that the geographic and historical setting has been changed; several details in the sequence of actions are also different. However, the overall plot construction has been maintained:

Synopsis of the Film's Main Action

Emma Zunz is a reserved young woman. She lives alone in a small appartment and works in a factory. One day she receives a letter from abroad, containing the message that her father has died; he apparently committed suicide. That night Emma rereads her father's affectionate letters she has received over the years. She also rereads some newspaper clippings. These show that Emma's father has once been charged with the misappropriation of funds belonging to the factory where Emma now works. Her father, who has fled to South-America, has written to her that not he was guilty, but the present owner of the factory, a man named Loewenthal.

Arriving at the factory next morning, Emma learns that the employees are planning a strike. Emma makes up her mind; she says she feels ill and goes home. There she calls Loewenthal. She says she can inform him about the strike and promises to visit him at his office at night. First, she burns her father's letters. Then she goes to a pub by the docks and offers herself to a sailor. After the man has gone she goes to Loewenthal's office at the factory. She starts telling him names of people organizing the strike, then simulates to collapse. Loewenthal goes out of the room to get her a glass of water. Emma quickly searches his desk and finds a gun. When Loewenthal returns she shoots him while telling she is taking revenge for her father. Next she calls the police and tells them that she has shot Loewenthal because he has tried to abuse her (adapted from: Borges, *Labyrinths, Selected Stories and Other Writings* [1970: 164–69).

In Delpeut's film, no overt narrator is present. There are no comments that could be compared with the narrator's text in the story, with one exception: at the very end of the film the final sentences of the original story are shown in a title:

> Actually, the story *was* incredible, but it impressed everyone because substantially it was true. True was Emma Zunz's tone, true was her shame, true was her hate. True also was the outrage she had suffered: only the circumstances were false, the time and one or two proper names. (ibid.)

If the cinematic narrator's reliability is questioned at all, it is only at the very end of the film. Unlike the story, the other parts of the film do not show self-reflective elements. On the contrary, the film is consequently reduced to the principle of "telling by showing." The camera registers in a highly objective, almost behavioristic way the main character's doings. Every piece of information is completely integrated in the course of action. The viewer is forced to observe Emma's actions meticulously, but is only able to guess at her plans, feelings, and motives during most of the film, and her actions can only be interpreted retrospectively, after the viewer has seen the whole film.

Event sequences are strictly chronologically ordered. The film can be divided into two parts, separated by Emma's phone call to Loewenthal. The first part has a kind of mystery structure; expositional information about the past that might help interpret Emma's actions, is withheld until after Emma has learned that her father has died. This scene occurs only late in the film, about halfway. In the first half of the film, action sequences develop extremely slowly. Emma's activities after she has read the letter are depicted in almost teasingly long-lasting, static, and narrowly framed shots, showing her just sitting and doing trivial things like drinking a glass of milk. The film thus contains a rare combination of objective narration with restricted plot information. The range as well as the depth of information is very limited throughout: the viewer knows less than the main character, and does not have any additional knowledge.

The second part of the film rather has a suspense structure, rounded off by surprise. From the moment Emma calls Loewenthal, some prospect is created, and suspense sets in. The action speeds up considerably, sequences are shorter, there is more movement in mise-en-scène and framing. The prostitution scene is so elliptic that it is hard to understand for someone viewing the film for the first time. The film clearly works toward the climax at the end. When Emma enters the plant, suspense is intensified. Nevertheless, the denouement, the shooting of Loewenthal, comes as a surprise.

"Restricted narration" in this film is enhanced by the lack of "subjective techniques" (Branigan 1984, 1992). There is no internal focalization; POV-shots are explicitly avoided; when we expect to see an emotional expression, Emma's face is obscured by heavy shadows, or she just looks away from the camera; in some shots we only see her back. The scene that reveals Emma's past is typical for the film's restrictive style. She produces old letters from her father and newspaper articles about his disappearance. The viewer reads them while looking over Emma's shoulder, seeing her hands holding and sorting out the papers; the film does not afford any view of her emotional expression. Following Bordwell's (1985) and Burch's (1973) terminology, this mode of narration could be called "parametric": narration is organized in terms of repetition and variation that is partly independent of the temporal and causal sequence of events organizing the plot (for a representative shot, see p. 140–1). Shot transitions coincide mostly with discontinuity in the action. Shots are repeated with slight variation, and the development of the mise-en-scène within shots often follows a rigid ABA pattern, for instance, in one shot, a view of a telephone on the wall (A) is followed by Emma's entering the frame (B), making her phone call and then leaving the frame again. There is no camera motion in the shot. We are left with exactly the same view of the phone as offered at the beginning of the shot (A). Light-shadow effects and the narrow framing of space additionally intensify the sense of self-contained closedness. Also, the film deviates from more traditional film, in that a music track is lacking, adding to the silence that dominates most scenes.

The Viewing Process

Following Carroll's conceptual analysis (chap. 1 of this vol.), and in line with empirical research, causal connections (in particular such that have to do with goals, plans, and intentions of the protagonists) have a strong impact on processing and recalling narrative. If a narrative does not provide the causal links, readers and viewers will be induced to make inferences or more elaborated constructions (for an overview of research on inferences during comprehending narration see Graesser, Singer, & Trabasso 1994). In *Emma Zunz*, the range of information is so limited that during the first half of the film viewers are hardly capable of framing expectations about what might happen. Also, they can hardly explain what they see by linking it to antecedent events. Causal connections between the scenes are not indicated. Viewers have to guess what is shown and why it is shown. Answers to evaluating questions in a pilot study indicated that the informants found the film rather uncommunicative indeed. However, from the moment Emma calls Loewenthal, suspense is intensified: the viewer senses that Emma plans to do something, and a decisive event seems nearby, although

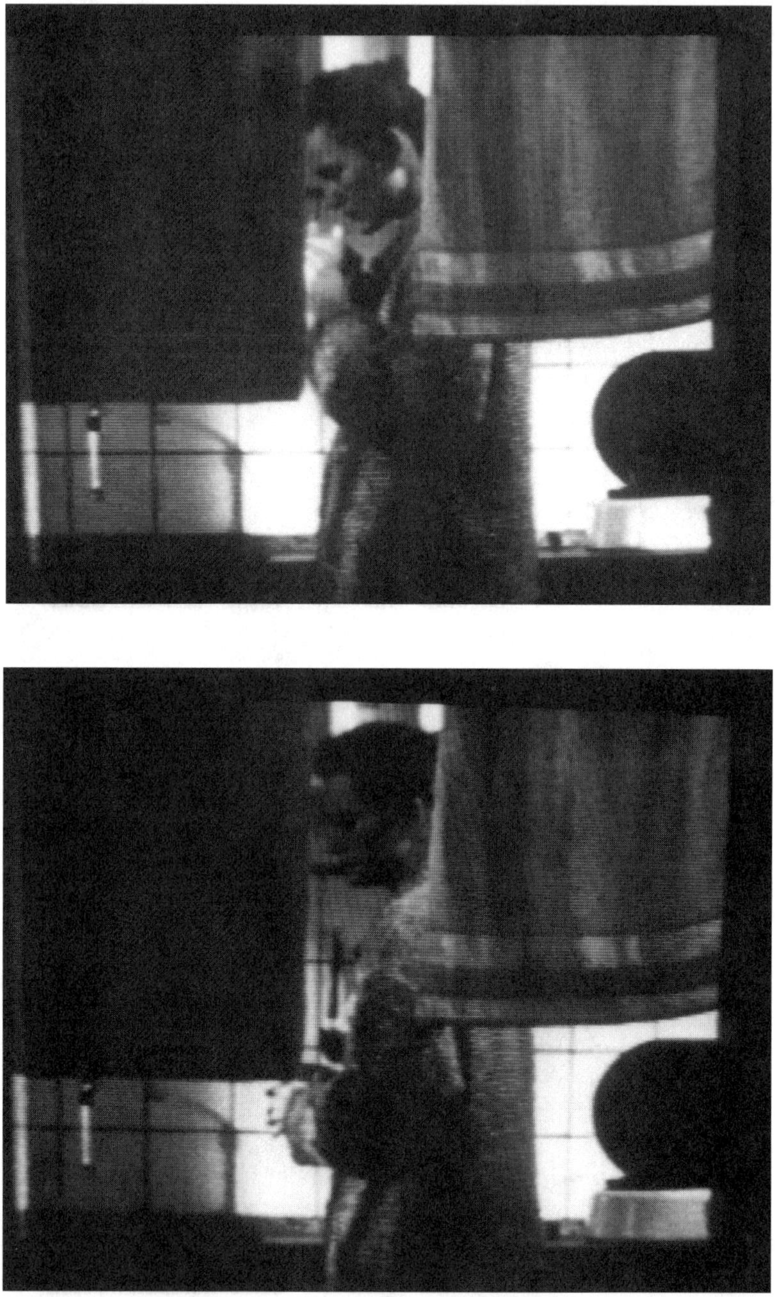

Light-shadow effects and narrow framing in shot 35: Emma in the kitchen after she has read the letter.

there is no clue as to what it might be. As a consequence, the end must have an effect of surprise. Even if the viewer would have some idea of what might happen, the insight in the full causal coherence triggered by Emma's explanation of her motive will be surprising. Moreover, only at the very end of the film is the viewer able to reconstruct what Emma might have felt and thought, what her plans and goals were, and how her motives and intentions are to be causally connected with her action. The film's strength lies in it's "postdictable" surprise structure (Kintsch 1980). The viewer is forced to think over the whole film again and to reconsider Emma's character and emotions in the light of the final outcome.

We expected that, after viewers had seen the film, a post-reception process will be set in motion under the influence of the complete plot information. We predicted that viewers would review the protagonist's character, goals, and motives, as well as the causal coherence of the events. These expectations were confirmed in a pilot study in which the film was interrupted at the moment Emma decides to call Loewenthal. The informants rated emotions and character features attributed to Emma on five-point scales at the interruption and at the end of the film. Additionally, they had to answer questions about their appreciation of the film. The differences between the first and the second measurement showed a shift from neutral to more extreme ratings; in the viewers' perception, Emma had gained in strength and effectiveness. The film's structure evoked an abrupt change in viewers' perception of character and plot. We expected that manipulation of the focalization would further influence the strength of this change depending on the degree of access to Emma's mind. This will be explained in the following sections.

Manipulations

In order to test the effects of focalization on how viewers perceive the main character and how they develop empathic feelings, we sought to supply information about Emma that could be presented from an external, but also from an internal point of view. As the film itself was so restricted and uncommunicative, there were many shots offering space for the supplementation of sound. We constructed VO-texts containing some background information about Emma, revealing some of her emotional reactions. The following principles underlay the construction:

1. The texts should be as natural as possible, and fit in with the film as a whole. Several ideas were derived from the original Borges story.

2. It should be possible to present the information from the outside and from the inside with slightly different emotional tones, however, without differing in substantial information.

3. In order to enhance the accessibility of Emma's mind, a crucial change was made. The VO-versions started with a brief introduction revealing the final outcome of the film (for the text, see table 2). The introduction enables the viewers to interpret Emma's motives and plans in the light of the final outcome. The uncertainty of *what* finally happens changes to how the story develops and *how* the end will take place. Consequently, we suppose that the effects of surprise, and postprocessing will decrease, whereas viewers will be able to understand Emma's plans and goals better; empathy, therefore, will increase.

Most films using the VO of an intradiegetic first-person narrator have a kind of frame-construction allowing a retrospective way of narrating. Examples that come to mind are Hitchcock's *Rebecca*, Wilder's *Sunset Boulevard* and *Double Indemnity*, Eastwood's *White Hunter, Black Heart*, and Bresson's *Pickpocket*. The parallel construction for an extradiegetic narrator is less usual in film tradition. Although there are examples of an extradiegetic VO at the beginning of a film (Curtiz's *Casablanca*), a continuation of such VO is rather rare. However, there are a few examples, like Kubrick's *Killing*, or Dassin's *Naked City* (which has been analyzed by Kozloff 1987: 82–98). In such cases, the VO gives the film a semi-documentary character.

To compensate for the addition of the introduction, a fourth version of the film was added in the design. In this condition, viewers received a short introductory text before they saw the film. It contained the same information presented by the initial VO-text. Additionally, this offered the opportunity to compare the effect of the plot information, as one group of viewers saw the original film without any changes. Consequently, four film conditions were used. Table 2 gives an overview of the film versions. The following sequence illustrates the manipulation:

> Shots 29 and 30: Coming home, Emma sees the letter and picks it up; she goes upstairs to her appartment and starts reading when she is inside.
>
> *Version 1* (O–) *and 2* (O+): No VO (diegetic sound only)
>
> *Version 3* (Ve): [Male VO] Coming home, she saw the letter. The stamp and the envelope looked familiar to her, but the strange handwriting alarmed her. She hesistated to open the letter.
>
> *Version 4* (Vi): [Emma's VO] Coming home, I saw the letter I had hoped for. It was the familiar envelope, but the strange handwriting alarmed me. Suspiciously, I opened the letter.[1]

Hypotheses

Three hypotheses bear on the perception of the protagonist. As the original versions leave more uncertainty in the viewer about the history of the protagonist and about her current goals and plans,

Table 8.2
Film Versions Used

	Original (O-)	*Original + Intro (O+)*	*Male VO (Ve)*	*Female VO (Vi)*
Narrator level 1 (covert)	Cinematic	Cinematic	Cinematic	Cinematic
Narrator level 2 (overt)	—	—	Extradiegetic (male VO, third person)	Intradiegetic (Emma's VO, first person)
Intro	—	Written text: EMMA ZUNZ deals with a woman who works in a factory. Her father had flown to South America because he was charged with malversation. One day she received the message of her father's death. He had committed suicide. Emma decides to take revenge. She kills the man she holds responsible for her father's suicide.	VO: "A murder is hard to imagine when it is committed by somebody whom nobody would think is able to do it. Even if the motive is clear, the improbability makes that the truth not always is revealed. Emma Zunz committed a murder."	VO: "Never I had thought that I would be able to commit a murder. Perhaps that was the reason why nobody suspected me, even though I had a clear motive."
Focalization	External	External	Shifting between external and internal	Internal
Consequences for the viewer	No cue as to what Emma thinks or experiences.	—Plot information —No further information about what Emma thinks or experiences.	—Plot information —Continuous background information about what Emma thinks and feels.	—Plot information —Continuous background information about what Emma thinks and feels.

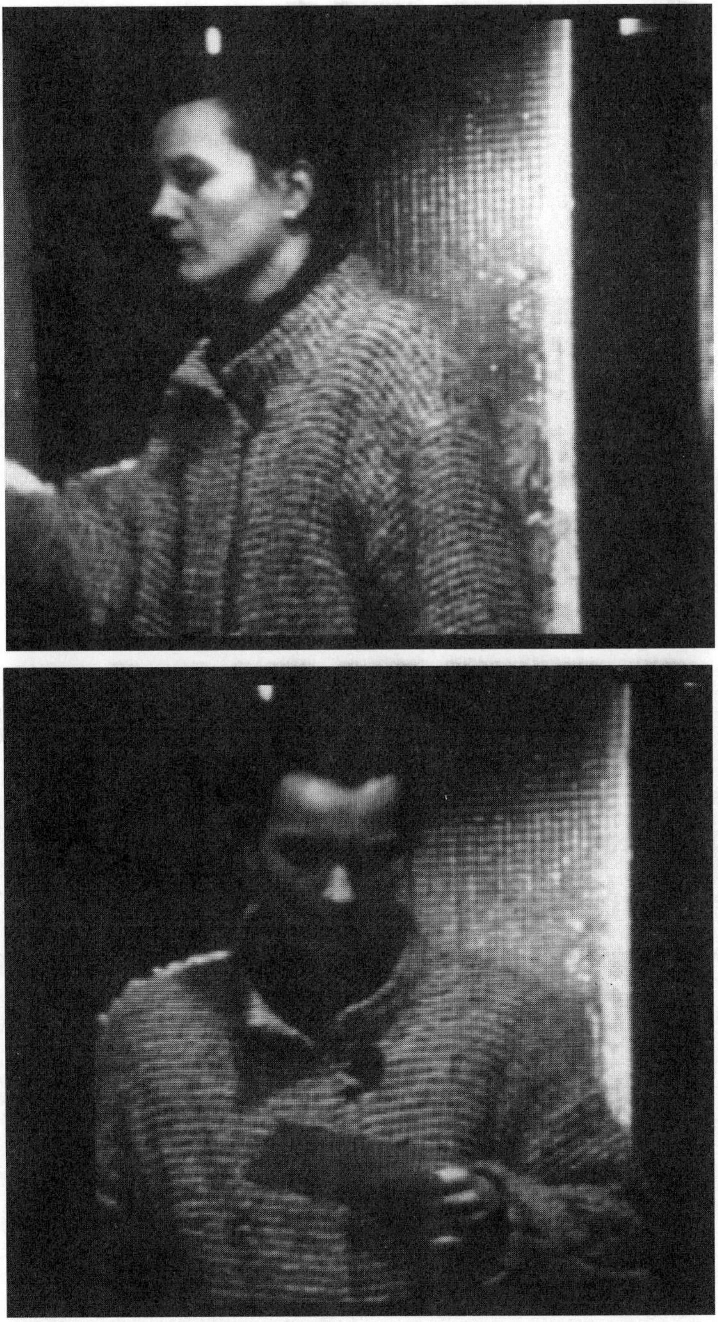

Shots 29 and 30: Emma sees and reads the letter.

we expected that in these versions she would be perceived as weak and odd, in comparison with the VO-versions. In the original version presented without written plot, the viewer does not have any information about Emma's background and current feelings, and her behavior seems to be irrational and strange. Hence, in this version the protagonist should be perceived as weak and odd, and more so than in all other versions. In the VO-versions we expected her to be perceived as less weak and odd, but as more goal-directed and good. The amount of plot information was kept as similar as possible across the two VO-versions. They differed only as to focalization. We assumed that internal focalization would result in a better understanding of the protagonist, in terms of goals and plans, compared to external focalization. Furthermore, we assumed that the effects of information and focalization are additive. Goal-directedness and goodness were expected to be highest in the internal version. In summary, our hypothesis contained the following assumptions: For *Goal-directedness* and *Goodness*: Vi > Ve > O+ > O–; For *Weakness* and *Oddity*: O– > O+ > Ve > Vi (*Hypothesis 1*).

For the same reason (a relative lack of information about the protagonist's goals and plans in the original versions, combined with the fact that most of the information concerned is only given after the interval) we expected that the two original versions would show more pronounced changes in the perception of the protagonist from the first measurement to the second, the original version having the strongest effect: For the *Shift between interval and end*: O– > O+ > Ve > Vi (*Hypothesis 2*).

We also assumed that understanding Emma's history and her current goals and plans would increase empathy. To the degree that a version affords access to Emma's inner life, it should enable the viewer to empathize with her. We expected that viewer empathy is stronger in the two VO-versions than in the two original ones, with internal focalization resulting in strongest empathy, while the original version without summary should give rise to minimal levels of empathy only. In short: For *Empathy*: Vi > Ve > O+ > O– (*Hypothesis 3*).

We also expected perspective to have an effect on the appreciation of the film. Delight in any feature film is in large part dependent on understanding the action and the opportunity this affords the viewer to empathize with the protagonist. However, some degree of uncertainty is necessary for this. Narrative procedures such as mystery, suspense, and surprise are conventional means for regulating an appropriate measure of uncertainty. The original versions of *Emma Zunz* may be expected to offer an unusual high degree of uncertainty, but this is compensated for by the end of the film. At this point, individual differences may be decisive. Preferences for such a radical solution may vary according to film taste. The lovers of art cinema—let us call these "cinephiliacs"—can be expected to favor the radical shift, whereas for other viewers, the end will not sufficiently compensate for the extreme uncertainty that was borne all along. We expected, then, that viewers who are not cinephiliacs will like the VO-versions more than the originals, with internal focalization as the best-liked version, whereas cinephiliacs should like the original versions better than the VO ones, with the original without summary liked best, and the internal focalization version liked least (*Hypothesis 4*).

Design

How do we observe these presumed effects? Participants responded to three groups of measures:

1. the perception of protagonist features
2. empathy with the protagonist
3. appreciation of the film

These measures were taken both at the interval and after the film and they consisted of 5-point rating scales. Protagonist features rated by our subjects included *good* (good); *goal-directed* (determined, efficient, wily, ambitious, passive, cool, and daring); *weak* (boring, weak, vulnerable, and sensitive); and *odd* (impulsive, rancorous, disturbed, prim, unworldly, and isolated). Empathy induced by the film was measured by three items: "I empathized with Emily," "I felt a distance toward the events," and "I imagined how it feels to be in Emily's position." Participants expressed their evaluation of the film by giving a *mark* between 1 and 10, corresponding to the usual grading for school exams in the Netherlands, where 10 is "excellent," and 1 is "extremely bad." More importantly, the cutting score is between 5 and 6, where 5 means "fail" and 6 means "low pass." They furthermore rated the film on a 5-point-rating scale for *appreciation* (good, irritating, and valuable); *comprehensibility* (comprehensible), *aesthetic value* (beautiful and poetic); *originality* (original and surprising); *admiration* (crafty and in style); and *interest* (enthralling and exciting). Thus, for each of the dependent variables we have a 4 (Versions) × 2 (Time of measurement) factorial design, with Versions as a between-subjects and (Point of) Measurement as a within-subjects factor.

Control measures were *cinephilia* (Tan, Eggermont, & Joosten 1989), and *empathetic ability* (Stotland et al. 1978). Cinephilia refers to stable preferences for films deviating from mainstream modes of film narration in favor of a more self-conscious style (see Bordwell 1985). Empathic ability is a stable disposition to imagine how other persons feel. These control variables were registered, because they are assumed to influence viewers' responses along with the experimental manipulations. They were recorded after the film, and immediately followed the perception and appreciation items in the questionnaire.

As participants, 200 college freshmen in psychology (61 male, 139 female) participated in the experiment as part of introductory course obligations. They were randomly assigned to conditions and tested in groups. The four experimental sessions were held in lecture rooms. The film was played from a videorecorder with large screen projection. Subjects were seated at distances from the screen varying from two to ten meters. Subjects said they were satisfied with the technical quality of the filmshow, except for the external VO-version, which suffered from considerable sound amplification problems. In all conditions, the show was interrupted for a five-minute interval during which subjects filled in the first questionnaire. Immediately after the film they filled in the second questionnaire.

Results

Before examining the data in order to test the hypotheses, it may be instructive to take a look at the pattern of perceived traits of Emma in each of the conditions. Figure 1 offers an overview of the

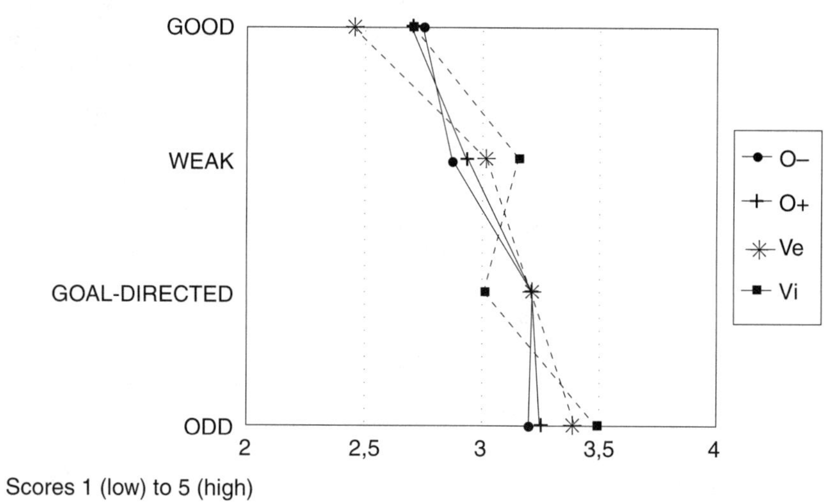

Fig. 8.1. Perceived traits of the protagonist. Means per condition for the final measurement.

mean scores on the separate items. A closer look at the scale scores[2] reveals the following: Emma was perceived as equally *good* across the versions of the film, with a mean score of 2.95 at the interval and 2.72 at the end, the decrease being significant (F = 17.63, df = 1, p = .000), with no interaction effects. Significant main effects of both version and measurement factors were found on perceived *goal-directedness*: Emma was seen as more goal-directed in the VO-conditions than in the original versions (F = 3.59, df = 3, p = .015) and more goal-directed at the end of the film than at the interval (F = 408.99, df = 1, p = .000). At the interval, Emma was perceived as more goal-directed in the VO versions, with the external version scoring highest, but by the end the differences among the versions have disappeared; the interaction between the factors is significant (F = 12,79, df = 3, p = .000). Perceived weakness showed a similar pattern. Weakness decreases from the interval to the end (main effect of measurement, F = 107.57, df = 1, p = .000), and though there is no overall effect of versions, the decrease is more pronounced in the original versions than in the VO-conditions (significant interaction, F = 4.22, df = 3, p = .007). Finally, significant main effects for both factors (and no interaction) suggest that Emma is seen as more odd after the film than at the interval, while she is perceived as more odd in the VO-versions as compared to the original versions (F = 9.37, df = 1, p = .003; F = 4.54, df = 3, p = .004, respectively).

Hypothesis 1 found only partial support. Emma was perceived as more goal-directed in the VO-versions, as predicted, but, contrary to our hypothesis, most goal-directed in the external VO-condition. However, neither did VO-versions add to Emma's goodness, nor was she perceived as weaker in the original versions. Also, the protagonist appeared as more odd in the VO-conditions than in the originals, contrary to our expectations. As can be seen in figure 2, *Hypothesis 2* was partially supported. As predicted, goal-directedness and weakness showed more pronounced changes over the film in the original conditions, resulting in significant interactions, whereas goodness and oddness did not.

The general level of empathy with Emma was extremely low. Contrary to *Hypothesis 3*, no differences between the versions were observed (F = 1.69, df = 3, p = .17), as can be seen in figure 3. Surprisingly, empathy with Emma decreased from the interval to the end of the film (F = 11.73, df = 1, p = .001). The decrease was uniform over the versions, that is, no significant interaction was

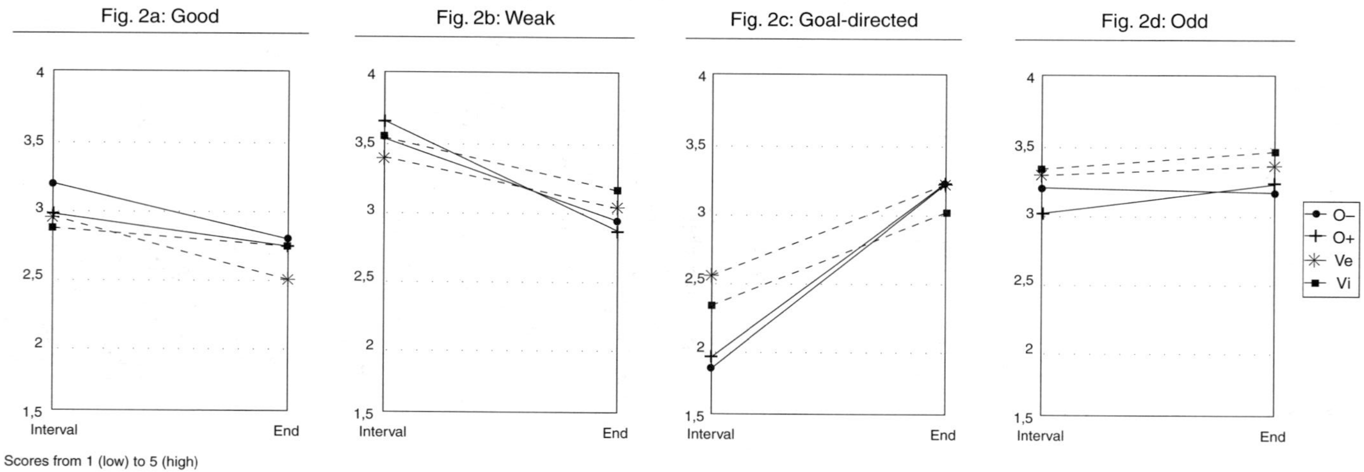

Fig. 8.2. Perception of the protagonist at two measurement points and as a function of the film version.

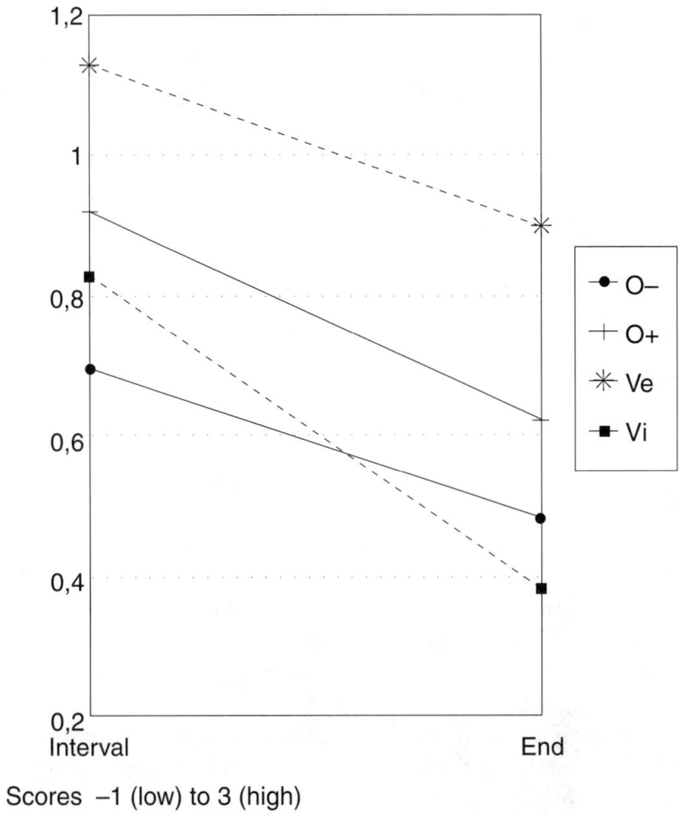

Fig. 8.3. Empathy with the protagonist at two measurement points and as a function of the film version.

found. The experimental manipulations did not exceed the effect of individual differences: empathetic ability did influence empathy; its regression weight was significant and of considerable size (*beta* = .34, t = 2.17, p = .000). Table 3 shows the evaluation marks assigned. The film was not well appreciated, as had been found already in the pilot studies. At the interval, the mean rating was 4.99 (standard deviation = 1.44). At this point, the film was evaluated as a failure. After showing the entire film, evaluation rose to a mean of 5.56 (*sd* = 1.40), which corresponds to a "just pass," but still a "near-failure." Analysis of variance yielded the following outcomes: The evaluation marks for the film versions did not differ significantly (F = 1.29, df = 3, p = .28 across factors). The versions

Table 8.3
Distribution of Evaluation Marks as a Function of Point of Measurement, Cinephilia, and Film Versions

	INTERV			END		
Film	Cin. Lo (n = 99)	Cin. Hi (n = 95)	Lo + Hi	Cin. Lo (n = 96)	Cin. Hi (n = 91)	Lo + Hi
O–	4.60	4.80	4.72	5.71	5.64	5.66
O+	4.75	5.50	5.21	5.50	6.32	5.93
Ve	4.54	5.31	4.97	5.24	5.56	5.35
Vi	5.00	5.14	5.03	5.24	5.17	5.18
Total	4.75	5.26	4.99	5.38	5.74	5.56

interacted with measurement (F = 5.40, df = 3, p = .001), which seemed to be due to the stronger increase of the original versions relative to the VO-versions.

Cinephilia had a marginally significant main effect on evaluation marks (m = 5.66 for the high-cinephiliacs, and m = 5.41 for the low-cinephiliacs, F = 1.09, df = 1, p = .058). No interaction was found between cinephilia and version, so there was no support for *Hypothesis 4* that cinephiliacs like the original versions better than the other participants. Furthermore, the main effect of cinephilia was small compared to that of measurement. This factor had a significant effect (F = 54.31, df = 1, p = .000). The interaction of cinephilia by measurement approached significance (F = 3.47, df = 1, p = .064). This is because the difference in evaluation between high and low cinephilia was larger at the interval than after the film.[3]

Conclusions and Discussion

The experiment produced a number of unexpected results. First, the differences among the versions were smaller than expected. Second, the fact that Emma was seen as more odd in the VO-conditions is conspicuous. Perhaps a lack of insight into the meaning of the events for the protagonist renders her merely unaccessible, whereas her motives and plans, if known, may strike the viewer as unusual to the point of bordering on the insane.

Third, and most strikingly, the manipulations did not result in more empathy with Emma than the originals. To be sure, the VO-versions were judged more comprehensible than the original versions ($F = 6.14$, $df = 3$, $p = .001$), so it would seem that the information about Emma's motives and plans did strike a point. For a more detailed insight into the effect on empathy, we looked at the three individual items measuring empathy. "I empathized with Emma" did not show any significant main or interaction effect. For "I felt a distance toward the events" we found a main effect of condition ($F = 2.86$, $df = 3$, $p < .038$) and a significant interaction between point of measurement and condition ($F = 4.64$, $df = 3$, $p = .004$): the original (O–) and the external version (Ve) showed a decrease of distance at the end, the original + introduction (O+) and the internal version (Vi) showed an increase; these effects are hard to explain. A strong effect of point of measurement, however, was found for the item "I imagined how it feels to be in Emma's position" ($F = 37.66$, $df = 1$, $p = .000$), that is, a decrease. Condition and interaction were not significant. Thus, the overall decline of empathy at the end is a consequence of a consistent decrease of viewers' ability to imagine themselves in Emma's position. Apparently, the ending of the film is so hard to imagine that access to Emma's mind, neither from the outside nor from the inside, does make any difference. Knowing what Emma is up to and what has happened to her does not stimulate the viewer to assume her perspective and to take side with her. Two complementary explanations can be given for these results. One is that the manipulative force of the overt narrator was not strong enough to interfere with the filmic devices used by the covert cinematic narrator. The other is that a moral judgment intervenes: possibly, viewers disapprove of the surprising murder in cold blood, impeding them to imagine how it feels to be in the murderer's place.

Finally, as to the film's evaluation, the outcome was only partly in accordance with the hypothesis. We had expected that high cinephiliacs would have a clear preference for the original versions, but the differences observed were only weakly significant. However, this difference might become more impressive if viewer groups differing in film expertise would be selected a priori. Our general hypothesis that appreciation would rise after the film's end was confirmed both for the original and for the manipulated versions. The rise was almost equal for high and low cinephiliacs. No significant effects of the manipulations were found. This means that the VO-manipulation did not affect the film's attractiveness. The rise in appreciation is independent of the supply of information and the kind of focalization, and therefore must be a result of the film's structure.

In sum, then, our conclusion must be that the effects of the manipulations were not as strong as we had expected. The strongest effects were found for shifts in perception, empathy and appreciation between the interval and the end. These effects, however, have to be attributed to the filmic structure and *not* to the VOs. The addition of information does not seem to have fundamentally affected viewers' way of how they see the character, nor their inclination to share her thoughts and emotions. However, some of the expected differences between the conditions become visible at the interval most clearly. In the original condition, the perception of Emma's character received the highest score for "good" and "weak," and the lowest for "goal-directed." The weak effects at the film's end could be a consequence of general lack of interest, as the film was not very much appreciated. Perhaps the film's "artistic" character deviated too strongly from viewers' expectations to allow much involvement with the main character. Alternatively, it may be that the film's structure was simply too hermetic for the manipulations to override the lack of information and the unexpected denouement. The way in which action sequences are arranged and depicted, the cinematic style and mise-en-scène might guide viewers so strongly that VOs (as were constructed here) are not able to bring about a real change in their empathic and aesthetic involvement. Although it might be technically difficult to carry out, a follow-up experiment should investigate the manipulative force of the cinematic ways of perspectivation—camera position and angle, point of view shots. Meanwhile, we regard the results of this single experiment as demonstrating the power of the cinematic narrator over his subordinate voices.

Notes

The authors are greatly indebted to Peter Delpeut and the Netherlands Film Museum for their cooperation.

1. O– = Original version; O+ = Original Version + Introduction; Ve = extradiegetic male voice-over; Vi = intradiegetic (Emma's) voice-over.

2. Scales were composed by summing the appropriate item scores. Some of the items were negatively associated with the scale, and scores on these were subtracted. The range of scores varies from one scale to the other, depending on the number of items involved, for instance, a state empathy scale consisted of the sum of the scores on two items "I empathized with E" and "I imagined how it feels to be in E's position," minus the score on the negatively

worded item “I felt a distance toward events.” In the analysis, they were indexed to the effect that reported scale scores ranged from 1 to 5. The scale scores were subjected to two-way analyses of variance, with version as a between subjects factor and measurement as within subject factor, and empathic ability and cinephilia as covariates.

3. With measurement as a within-subject factor and cinephilia (low vs. high) and film version as a between-subject factor.

9

Breaking Conventional Barriers: Transgressions of Modes of Focalization

Dan Shen

Introduction

The twentieth century has witnessed a surging theoretical interest in the issue of point of view, narrative perspective, or focalization, with numerous distinctions having been made or modes/types classified (see, e.g., Lubbock [1921], Brooks & Warren [1943], Friedman [1967], Booth [1973], Chatman [1978, 1990], Rimmon-Kenan [1983, 1989], Stanzel [1984], Bal [1977, 1985], and Toolan [1988]). Theorists in this line of inquiry seem on the whole to have operated on the assumption that a narrator or focalizer, when adopting a given mode of focalization, will not transgress its boundary. Scarcely ever has any critical attention been directed toward transgressions of modes of focalization, a kind of phenomenon that is not infrequently found in narrative texts and which, as I will argue, is distinguishable and should be distinguished in nature from variable focalization, as well as from the shift in point of view within a given mode. The present chapter is devoted to an investigation of transgressions as such, so as to shed fresh light on their nature and function; the text chosen for exemplification is Sherwood Anderson's short story "The Egg" (1978).

Sherwood Anderson's Short Story "The Egg"

The story in question is conveyed chiefly through the retrospective point of view of a first-person adolescent-narrator, thus as internal focalization. The present study adopts Genette's tripartite classification: (a) nonfocalization (i.e., omniscience); (b) internal focalization; and (c) external focalization (1980: 189–94). In "The Egg," although the narrating self is better informed than the experiencing self in some respects ("In later life I have seen how a literature has been built up on the subject of fortunes to be made out of the raising of chickens"), he is subject to restrictions of field in others (in such expressions like "It may have been that. . . . She had, I presume,. . . . she may have dreamed that. . . .") If we take the narrator's retrospective viewpoint as external because of the given gap between the narrating and experiencing self, it becomes difficult to account for the similarity between the two—not only in terms of restrictions of field but also in terms of emotive stance (see the next section). Assuming an external viewpoint conceals the differences between the limited, involved first-person narrator/focalizer and a godlike, detached third-person narrator-focalizer. What is called for seems to be a distinction between two different kinds of external focalization: first-person versus third-person, with the former occupying an intermediary position between internal focalization and third-person external focalization. But to avoid complications here, we may still take the mode in "The Egg" as internal focalization.

According to the narrator, the tale focuses "on the egg" (2), but in fact it also centers on the related tragedy of the narrator's father. The climax of the story comes when the ambitious yet inept father tries to do some tricks with eggs to entertain a guest one night in their family restaurant. Despite the father's desperate effort, the tricks do not work, and he ends up having his clothes smeared with egg and himself laughed at by the guest. Flying into a rage from frustration and humiliation, he throws an egg at the guest, an action that marks the total failure of his plan to entertain guests as a means of realizing his American dream, and that drives him further into his lonely isolation.

When this climactic event takes place, the narrator is fast asleep upstairs. He and his mother are awakened by his father's roar of anger, and a few minutes later his father comes upstairs and tells his mother tearfully what has happened. Ordinarily, the narrator would report, in one way or another, his father's words. But this convention is not followed by the present narrator, who makes the claim that "I have forgotten what mother said to him [father] and how she induced him to tell her of what had happened downstairs. His explanation also has gone out of my mind. . . . As to what happened downstairs. For some unexplainable reason I know the story as well as though I had been a witness to my father's discomfiture. One in time gets to know many unexplainable things" (6). With this assertion paving the way, the narrator goes on to tell, in the capacity of an eyewitness, what happened downstairs:

> On that evening . . . Joe was left alone in the restaurant with father. From the moment he came into our place the Bidwell young man must have been puzzled by my father's actions. It was his notion that father was angry at him for hanging around. He noticed that the restaurant-keeper was apparently disturbed by his presence and he thought of going out. . . . For a long time father, whom Joe Kane had never seen before, remained silently gazing at his visitor. He was no doubt suffering from an attack of stage fright. . . . For one thing, he did not know what to do with his hands. He thrust one of them nervously over the counter and shook hands with Joe Kane. "How-de-do," he said. Joe Kane put his newspaper down and stared at him. Father's eyes lighted on the basket of eggs that sat on the counter and he began to talk. "Well," he began hesitatingly, "well, you have heard of Christopher Columbus, eh?" He seemed to be angry. "That Christopher Columbus was a cheat," he declared emphatically. . . . My father seemed to his visitor to be beside himself at the duplicity of Christopher Columbus. He muttered and swore. . . . Afire with the showman's passion and at the same time a good deal disconcerted by the failure of his first effort, father now took the bottles containing the poultry monstrosities down. . . . "How would you like to have seven legs and two heads like this fellow?" he asked, exhibiting the most remarkable of his treasures. A cheerful smile played over his face. . . . His visitor was made a little ill by the sight of the body of the terribly deformed bird floating in the alcohol in the bottle. . . . Father grinned and winked at his visitor. Joe Kane decided that the man who confronted him was mildly insane but harmless. . . . Father made a last desperate effort to conquer the egg and make it do the thing that would establish his reputation as one who knew how to entertain guests

> who came into his restaurant. He worried the egg. He attempted to be somewhat rough with it. He swore and the sweat stood out on his forehead. . . . A roar of anger rose from my father's throat. He danced and shouted a string of inarticulate words. Grabbing another egg from the basket on the counter, he threw it, just missing the head of the young man. . . . (6–8)

In spite of the frequent use of ellipses in this quotation, it is clear that what we have here is a tragi-comedy, with the comic effects arising from the detached narrator-focalizer's satiric humor and, more significantly, from the misunderstanding between the two persons involved: the restaurant-keeper who is extremely anxious to please his guest but who continuously acts in the wrong way, and the guest who always misinterprets the restaurant-keeper's intentions. The point is that if the narrator had presented the scene only by reporting the restaurant-keeper's own tearful words, all of the comic effects in this climactic scene, which contribute greatly to the success of the text, would have been lost, for the restaurant-keeper himself is totally unconscious of his own absurdity. The guest's misunderstandings could not have been expressed, and we can imagine what a dull scene would have emerged.

To avoid such a failure, the narrator acts as an eyewitness. Nevertheless, this witness position is far from sufficient for conveying the comic effects, because the internal focalizer's profound sympathy for his father would make it difficult to maintain the detached perspective necessary for producing such effects. Moreover, the witness position does not permit the focalizer to penetrate into the mind of the focalized, thus being unable to make known the misunderstandings involved, misunderstandings that function to enhance greatly the comic effects concerned. What is needed here is omniscience, a mode through which the narrator-focalizer can keep a detached, objective stance and can effectively gain inside-views of the focalized. But the internal focalizer has no way to shift legitimately to omniscience; the only means available to him is to transgress the boundary of internal focalization, a transgression that he "secretly" practices in this passage, where what we have is in effect superficial internal focalization and essential omniscience. This point may be illustrated by the following diagram:

Internal Focalization	Omniscience
In Terms of Referring Expressions	
"my father"	"the restaurant-keeper"
In Terms of Restrictions of Field	
". . . the Bidwell young man must have been puzzled by. . . ." "Joe Kane decided that the man who confronted him was mildly insane but harmless."	"It was his notion that Father was. . . . He noticed that . . . and he thought of. . . ."
In Terms of Detachment	
	"suffering from an attack of stage fright" "afire with the showman's passion" "the poultry monstrosities" "the body of the terribly deformed bird" etc.

Under the mode of omniscience is listed the referring expression "the restaurant-keeper," which shows itself in "He noticed that the restaurant-keeper was apparently disturbed by his presence." Clearly, it appears like a phrase narrated from the point of view of an omniscient narrator rather than that of the first-person narrator who is expected to use "my father" instead. In this diagram, another omniscient phrase is "the poultry monstrosities." Why is it omniscient? Because a contrast is seen between the different ways of viewing the same thing before and after the transgression takes place. In the father's eyes, the misshaped chicken bodies are valuable artistic treasures, which he "carefully put into a box, and on our journey into town it was carried on the wagon seat beside him. He drove the horses with one hand and with the other clung to the box" (3). As a loving son, the adolescent-narrator-focalizer is much affected by his father's feelings. Before the transgression occurs, he regards the deformed chickens as "the poor little things" and "the little monstrous things" (ibid.), both exhibiting the narrator-focalizer's tender feeling toward the focalized object. In addition, the focalizer reiterates the expression "the grotesques" to refer to the object in question. The grotesque is one of the major themes of Anderson's work, particularly his *Winesburg Ohio*. Anderson's grotesques are deformed persons. To Anderson, "the sources or natures of their deformities are unimportant when compared to their intrinsic worth as human beings needing and deserving of understanding" (see David Anderson: 159–60). In "The Egg," the physical deformity in the chickens is apparently treated as a symbol of the spiritual deformity of the inept father. It is, I believe, no coincidence that, before the transgression comes about, the symbolic and nonderogatory "grotesques" is used three times in succession, while the term "monstrosities" is not employed at all. It is true that the adjective "monstrous" does appear in the phrase "the little monstrous things," but its bad connotations are significantly played down by its neighboring words. By contrast, in the passage marked by transgression, the phrases "the poultry monstrosities" and "the body of the terribly deformed bird," which exhibit the view of the detached narrator-focalizer, are notably out of harmony with the father's view as reflected in the expression "the most remarkable of his treasures," an expression clearly made in this context to take on a strong ring of irony.

Some critics have noticed the change in the narrator-focalizer's emotive stance in the episode concerned, but none has interpreted it as a result of a point of view transgression. Cassill accounts for it in terms of Anderson's insistence "*on the primacy of the imagination* in coming at the truth of the events," since

> The imagined scene has a *concreteness* and *objectivity* that the hypothetically real present (in which the story is being told) has not. . . . The invented, or imagined, scene also has the comic force required to prepare the reader for the pathos to come. (2, my italics)

This interpretation seems to me somewhat misleading for the following reasons: First, the concreteness, in effect, has to do primarily with the temporal aspect of "duration" (see Genette 1980: 86ff.). The text of "The Egg" has a length of less than nine pages, while the story has a time span of more than ten years. On average, that is to say, more than one year in the story takes up just one page in the text. This, however, does not hold true for the episode in question, which lasts merely three hours but occupies more than two pages, amounting to a quarter of the whole textual space. This remarkable slowing down of the narrative speed is due to the fact that, while the rest of the story is mainly narrated in the mode of "summary," the episode is depicted throughout in the mode of scene. This choice is not in the least surprising since narrators usually present climactic events in the mode of "scene." As concrete details such as direct dialogue are expected in this mode, it is only natural for us to find these concrete elements in the present scene.

Second, it is misleading to ascribe the objectivity in the imagined scene to the "primacy of the imagination." The scene is actually no more objective than most "hypothetically real" scenes presented in the mode of omniscience, where we usually find a detached narrator-focalizer. The contrast between emotional detachment and involvement is better seen as an aspect of the contrast between omniscience and internal focalization, since it sounds quite implausible to claim that the internal narrator-focalizer is emotionally detached from his father in his imagination, while being emotionally involved with him in "reality."

Third, Cassill's (1977) interpretation fails to account for the internal focalizer's penetration into Joe Kane's mind. If he had claimed that in the imagined scene the internal focalizer could become omniscient, the claim would perhaps have bordered on absurdity. Clearly, the contrast between this scene and other parts of the story is in essence one between internal focalization and omniscience, rather than that between what is hypothetically real and what is imagined.

The resort to imagination seems to be a convenient device employed by Anderson to get round the restrictions of the field of internal focalization. In the present case, it is adopted, as just discussed, to enable the absent internal narrator-focalizer to function as a witness, so as to convey the comic effects. Earlier in the text, the narrator-focalizer, after giving a detailed account of the father's plan to entertain his guests, hastily adds the explanation: "I do not mean to give the impression that father spoke so elaborately of the matter. He was, as I have said, an uncommunicative man. 'They want some place to go. I tell you they want some place to go,' he said over and over. That was as far as he got. My own imagination has filled in the blanks" (5). Apparently, imagination has to be brought in here, otherwise the inept father would seem to be undesirably articulate. Such a problem, though, would not exist in the omniscient mode, where the omniscient narrator-focalizer can both make known the father's elaborate plan and maintain his inarticulateness by simply presenting his inner thoughts. The point is that, if one fails to get at the difficulty that necessitates Anderson's eliciting support from imagination, one may easily take his act as an insistence on "the primacy of the imagination."

Unlike Cassill, Howe makes no reference to imagination in his discussion of the "imagined" scene: ". . . one night his [the father's] dream bursts; an egg in hand, he comes upstairs from the store with 'a half insane light in his eyes,' and falling on his knees begins to weep. The narrator, deliberately avoiding a direct dramatic line, then *quietly* tells what happened in the store below" (1968: 169, my emphasis). Howe seems well aware of the change in the narrator-focalizer's emotive stance, but like other critics, he does not seem to have noticed the transgression under discussion, which, in fact, constitutes the very key to the narrator's shifting to an objective tone. This regrettable neglect may well be attributed to the fact that twentieth-century narrative theory, while setting great store by the classification of various modes of focalization, has paid very little attention to infractions of such modes.

Other Examples

It is understood that each mode of focalization has its advantages and limitations. If one wants to make use of the former and, when necessary, to get free of the latter, one is quite likely to transgress the boundary of an adopted mode of focalization. Insofar as first-person narration is concerned (no matter whether the "first person" is a protagonist or a peripheral observer, and no matter whether the focalizer is the experiencing self or the narrating self), transgressions of modes of focalization typically take the shape of going beyond the restricted field of the focalizer. In Proust's *Remembrance of Things Past*, there are several instances of such transgression. A most striking case occurs in Marcel's narration of the circumstances of Bergotte's death:

> . . . At last he came to the Vermeer which he remembered as more striking, more different from anything else that he knew, but in which, thanks to the critic's article, he remarked for the first time some small figures in blue, . . . Meanwhile he was not unconscious of the gravity of his condition. . . . at once he ceased to think that his life was in jeopardy and, reverting to his natural optimism, told himself: "It is just an ordinary indigestion from those potatoes; they weren't properly cooked; it is nothing." A fresh attack beat him down. . . . (1932: 509)

Marcel, the first-person narrator-protagonist, is absent from the scene, but he narrates the scene not only as a witness, but also as if he were omniscient, able to penetrate into the inner life of the dying man. If such a case forms an unequivocal transgression, sometimes there occur more ambiguous instances, with the ambiguity characteristically arising from the mode of presentation adopted, for example:

> How was she going to get everything fed?—that was her problem. The dogs had to be fed. There wasn't enough hay in the barn for the horse and the cow. If she didn't feed the chickens how could they lay eggs? Without eggs to sell how could she get things in town, things she had to have to keep the life of the farm going? . . .

This passage is taken from Anderson's short story "Death in the Woods," which is narrated by a first-person observer-narrator. What is presented here is subject to two different interpretations: the protagonist's inner thoughts represented in free indirect style, and empathetic comments made on the protagonist's situation by the first-person narrator, who tends to use the interrogative and the exclamatory form in his narration. While the former undoubtedly constitutes transgression of the mode of focalization adopted, the latter case clearly does not. The ambiguity between the two not only gives rise to subtlety and textual density, but also enables the focalizer to get free from any charge of infraction of the mode.

Regarding the transgression of (third-person) external focalization, it is of interest to cite an example from Hemingway's "Hills Like White Elephants," a narrative widely regarded as a paragon of external focalization. The contravention occurs briefly in "He drank an Anis at the bar and looked at the people. *They were all waiting reasonably for the train.* He went out through the bead curtain" (1986: 464, my emphasis). If it were to appear in some other narrative contexts, "They were all waiting reasonably for the train" might well be a comment by the narrator-focalizer. In the present context of external focalization, however, the narrator-focalizer functions only as a camera and recorder, refraining from making any comment on the characters. We draw the inference that the sentence presents in free indirect style the male protagonist's inner thoughts and thus a transgression of external focalization.

In *Classic Short Fiction*, Bohner raises the following question: "As the man drinks his Anis, he thinks to himself, 'They were all waiting reasonably for the train.' What is the force of the word 'reasonably'? " (464). It seems that Bohner takes this inside-view as a natural occurrence and fails to consider the possibility that it is an infraction of external focalization. But he rightly draws attention to the adverb *reasonably*, which carries the emphasis of the brief infraction. The term, coming out of the male protagonist's mind toward the end of the narrative, seems to carry his implicit criticism of what he takes to be his lover's unreasonableness. However, readers at this point may be well aware of the man's own selfishness and incapability of understanding his lover, and may therefore treat the term as pointing ironically to the man's own egoism. It is significant that this brief inside-view, as a solitary infringement of, or deviation from, the norm, is seen to take on much more weight and prominence than that in a context where inside-view is frequent or commonplace.

As for the transgression of omniscience, the following is a case in point:

> *I hardly know* whether it was the analogies or the differences that were uppermost in the mind of a young American, who, two or three years ago, sat in the garden of the "Trois Couronnes," looking about him rather idly at some of the graceful objects I have mentioned. It was a beautiful summer morning, and in whatever fashion the young American looked at things, *they must have* seemed to him charming. (1979: 339, my emphasis)

This passage is taken from the beginning of James' novella "Daisy Miller." The two expressions "I hardly know" and "they must have" are very characteristic of the restricted field of internal focalization. But further reading will soon bring out that the "I" is in effect an omniscient narrator-focalizer, who has full access to the mental activities of the young American. An omniscient narrator-focalizer is, by convention, omniscient throughout the text and we are justified in taking the claimed perceptual limitation as false information, as an infringement on the mode of omniscience.

Issues of Legitimacy

It is, in my view, both necessary and important to distinguish the transgression of a focalizing mode, which is "illegitimate" from the perfectly legitimate variable focalization (i.e., the shift from one type of focalization to another). An omniscient narrator-focalizer has no conventional right to tell a lie that she has no knowledge of characters' inner thoughts; and if she does so, it will constitute an "unlawful" infraction of the mode of omniscience and the reader may cast doubt on the narrator's reliability. But an omniscient narrator-focalizer has a perfect right to restrict her perspective to that of a character and thus to shift lawfully to internal focalization. In *Daisy Miller*, for instance, the omniscient narrator-focalizer legitimately restricts his vision to that of the protagonist Winterbourne for most of the time, thereby bringing about an alternation between omniscience and fixed internal focalization, with the latter playing a predominant role.

Genette offers a significant and valuable discussion of variations in point of view, but the discussion tends to equate variable focalization with the infraction of a given mode, as reflected in the following statement:

> The variations in "point of view" that occur in the course of a narrative can be analyzed as changes in focalization, like those we have already met in *Madame Bovary*: in such a case we can speak of variable focalization, of omniscience with partial restrictions of field, etc. . . . But a change in focalization, especially if it is isolated within a coherent context, *can also* be analyzed as a momentary infraction of the code which governs that context without thereby calling into question the existence of the code. . . . (1980: 195, my emphasis)

Genette seems either to take to be interchangeable "variable focalization" and the "infraction of a code," or to use the length of the change involved as the sole criterion for differentiation. But in effect, the infraction of a mode, as we have seen, can be most effectively distinguished from variable focalization by the criterion of legitimacy, which concerns the nature or quality rather than just the quantity of the change in question. In the case of "The Egg," the change in focalization takes up a quarter of the text, but since the first-person narrator-focalizer has no "lawful" way to shift to omniscience, we can only regard this long passage as an illegitimate infraction of the code.

As to the momentary change in focalization in *Daisy Miller*, if the omniscient narrator-focalizer did not "lie" to the narratee that he has no knowledge of the focalized character's consciousness but merely observed the character from the outside (still referring to him as "a young American" instead of "Winterbourne"), this would only form a legitimate shift to external focalization rather than to an illegitimate infraction of omniscience. Although both the "legitimate" and the illegitimate change could create similar effects of suspense, the illegitimate one would probably give rise to stronger suspense and would, when the narrator's claimed restrictions of field is found to be false, bear on the narrator's reliability whereas the legitimate case would not.

The criterion of legitimacy might, nevertheless, be called into question in the mode of (third-person) external focalization. If we take the external narrator-focalizer to be really ignorant of the focalized characters' inner thoughts, any inside-view can be regarded as an illegitimate transgression of the mode. But if, as an alternative, we take the narrator-focalizer as essentially omniscient who only chooses to observe characters from the outside, the focalizer's momentary penetration into a character's mind may not be regarded as illegitimate. In this mode, that is to say, the focalizer's unexpected access to a character's consciousness can be interpreted either way, depending on one's understanding of the nature of the focalizer.

It is understood that modes of focalization are very much based on convention. In texts marked by omniscience, for instance, the narrator-focalizer often refrains from penetrating into certain characters' minds, particularly in the case of minor and/or unsympathetic characters. Since many omniscient narrator-focalizers act in this way, we can treat this as a feature pertaining to the mode itself. In this mode, more significantly, shifts to the viewpoints of characters are quite common. That is why "the division between variable focalization and nonfocalization is sometimes very difficult to establish, for the nonfocalized narrative can most often be analyzed as a narrative that is multifocalized *ad libitum*" (Genette 1980:192).

Insofar as the mode of omniscience is concerned, the length of a change in focalization may serve, where applicable, as a criterion to distinguish a shift in viewpoint within the mode itself from a change from this mode to another type of focalization. Stanzel says: "Passages which present an inside view, the thoughts and emotions of characters in free indirect style, can appear within the framework of an authorial narrative situation. The *extended* appearance of such passages can temporarily give rise to an internal perspective" (1984: 112, my emphasis). Stanzel's observation points to the fact that in the mode of omniscience, momentary shifts to characters' viewpoints are quite common and can thus be regarded as a feature pertaining to the mode itself, whereas extended uses of characters' viewpoints are not frequently seen, which may therefore involve the change to internal focalization.

It is worth noting that a shift in point of view within a mode is not peculiar to omniscience. It also occurs in the mode of variable or multiple internal focalization (Genette 1980:189–90), for the mode itself necessarily contains the change from the viewpoint of one character to that of another. Both a shift in point of view within a mode and variable focalization are perfectly legitimate, and can thus be clearly marked off from the illegitimate infraction of a mode.

In Genette's opinion, infractions of modes of focalization fall into two categories: *paralipsis* and *paralepsis* (1972 [1980]: 195–97; in *Narrative Discourse Revisited* published ten years later, Genette still firmly sticks to this distinction). The former consists of giving less information than is necessary in principle, whose classical type takes the shape of the omission, in internal focalization, "of some important action or thought of the focal hero, which neither the hero or the narrator can be ignorant of but which *the narrator chooses* to conceal from the reader" (196, my emphasis). The solid example that Genette offers is Stendhal's dissimulation, in *Armance*, of the hero's central thought: his sexual impotence, through the quotation of many of his pseudomonologues, of the hero's central thought: his sexual impotence in *Armance*. Some of Agatha Christie's detective narratives also provide examples: although the narrative is focalized through the murderer, his memory of the murder is omitted from his thoughts (ibid.).

Genette's discussion of "paralipsis" involves, in my view, confusion between narration and focalization. Paralipsis is carried out exclusively by the narrator who chooses to present the focal character's irrelevant, rather than his relevant, thoughts or who, in other words, presents the focal character's inner thoughts while omitting a most relevant part of it. Such an omission does not in any way bear on the code of focalization, for what remains to be presented is still the focal character's consciousness, and the focalizing position still stays internal.

The other category of Genette's classification is "paralepsis" that takes the form of giving *more* information "than is authorized in principle in the code of focalization governing the whole" (195). It consists either "of an inroad into the consciousness of a character in the course of a narrative generally conducted in external focalization" or "of incidental information about the thoughts of a character other than the focal character, or about a scene that the latter is not able to see" in internal focalization (197).

The transgressions occurring in "The Egg," in "Death in the Woods," and in *Remembrance of Things Past* just discussed may be taken as examples of paralepsis in internal focalization (or first-person external focalization); and the infraction in "Hills Like White Elephants" an example in (third-person) external focalization. It should be noted that cases of paralepsis can be either purposeful devices or just unintentional "mistakes." The interesting point is that, no matter whether they take the shape of devices or mistakes, such cases of paralepsis, which are illegitimate and therefore often foregrounded, tend to draw attention not only to the limitation of the violated modes of focalization, but also to the fact that the barriers between modes of focalization are very much conventional. Furthermore, in cases like those in "The Egg" and in *Remembrance of Things Past*, where a first-person narrator-focalizer is unconventionally given the godlike power to penetrate into somebody else's consciousness, attention tends to be diverted to the fictitious nature of the narrative, and the illusion of verisimilitude is likely to be shattered. In this sense, such cases seem to create, implicitly and perhaps quite unintentionally, a kind of "metanarrative" function.

Apart from such general functions, transgressions of modes of focalization may produce, as indicated in the present analysis, diversified specific contextual effects, which await and invite further critical attention.

10

Holding onto Established Viewpoints during Processing News Reports

Herre van Oostendorp

Introduction

An important but neglected aspect in the study of narrative perspective is the construction of a "situation model" by the reader. A *situation model* is a mental representation of the situation described by the text (Johnson-Laird 1983; Van Dijk & Kintsch 1983). Categories that populate such a situation are agents, actions, space, time, events, and causal relations. In order to properly understand a narrative, a reader has to identify who are the narrative's protagonists, where they are, what they do, and what their relationship is with their surroundings and with each other. Typically texts will offer such information in the opening scenes of a story. Here, for instance, is one such scene from Dickens's *Great Expectations*:

> Ours was the marsh country, down by the river, within, as the river wound, twenty miles of the sea. My first vivid and broad impression of the identity of things, seems to me to have been gained on a memorable raw afternoon towards evening. At such a time I found out for certain, that this bleak place overgrown with nettles was the churchyard. (1861: 35)

Elements that allow the reader to build a situation model are a general location ("marsh country" down by an estuary) and a particular spot (a "churchyard"), and a protagonist ("I"). As Morrow shows (chap. 13 of this vol.), processing narrative events is centered on the actions of a protagonist within a specific spatial location. In the Dickens passage, this location is linked to the past of the first-person narrator with the clause "my first vivid and broad impression of the identity of things" suggesting childhood. The situation model is further embedded in a superstructure (Van Dijk & Kintsch 1983), that of the 'autobiographical' narration, in which an older I-narrator recalls earlier experiences in life. Scores of literary works in the Western tradition attest to the vitality of this superstructure, from Augustine's *Confessions* and Caesar's *De Bello Gallico* to Goethe's *Dichtung und Wahrheit* and Collingwood's *Autobiography*. Dickens also describes the relationship of the narrator to his past: the recollections are "most vivid," "memorable," and—perhaps most important of all—"raw." After having read only a few sentences, readers already possess fairly elaborate information on the protagonist's location and on his relation to his environment, although other things are still open: whether the protagonist is male or female, for example, is still in the air. Thus, the reader's situation model contains elements that focus attention on a particular agent in a specific environment, but also elements that direct the reader's attention toward events to come.

While in general the construction of a situation model may proceed smoothly as the text unfolds, it is also typical of literary texts to contain abrupt shifts in perspective. Such shifts may create special difficulties for readers, who have to infer the reasons and consequences relating to the shift. Readers have to fit the new information into the situation model they have previously constructed, which establishes a qualitatively new perspective. Consider, for example, the clauses following this description:

> [I found out for certain] that the low leaden line beyond, was the river; and that the distant savage lair from which the wind was rushing, was the sea; and that the small bundle of shivers growing afraid of it all and beginning to cry, was Pip. "Hold your noise!" cried a terrible voice, as a man started up from among the graves at the side of the church porch. "Keep still, you little devil, or I'll cut your throat!" (Dickens: 135–36)

While the metaphors ("leaden line," and "savage lair") certainly add to the complexity of information, they also give flavor to the child's perceptions of the overwhelming and threatening landscape.

Similarly, the ungrammatical "small bundle of shivers" may tax readers' comprehension strategies. Yet the most difficult part is formed by the dramatic shift in perspective. Initially, the point of view rests with the older I-narrator recalling his experiences as a child, looking at his surroundings, following some kind of cameralike movement over the marsh, along the river, and up to the sea. The "small bundle of shivers," however, radically changes that perspective. Now the "camera" (and hence the reader) is looking at the narrator himself, describing the small child as a shivering bundle of limbs, confronted with a stranger who suddenly emerges from among the graves and who threatens the child in a coarse and terrible voice. While previously readers perceived "with" the protagonist, they now find themselves "outside" this character.

Obviously, they have to adapt to the new perspective, in order to understand what is happening. Since their situation model clashes with the previously established generic convention of autobiographical narration, updating the model becomes inevitable. The example shows that a situation model is not something static, but a mental representation that is in constant flow, adapting itself dynamically to new, incoming information. I will call this process of adaptation "updating." While it is clear that readers must do such updating during their reading, it is generally not known how precisely they do so, or how circumstances enhance or impede such updating. This chapter studies the way in which readers update new points of view in reading *news reports*. Newspapers are presumably more widely read than novels. It could also be argued that literary texts present more complex cases, as they regularly deviate from generic conventions, as the above example from Dickens illustrates, thus violating readers' expectations (Van Peer, 1992).

Actualizing a situation model is supposed to play an important role in the comprehension of news reports. If we construe the primary goals of reading newpapers as attempts to understand (part of) the world, then accommodating this understanding to changes that happened in the world seems to be a necessary part of the interaction with the text itself (Kintsch et al. 1990; Zwaan 1994). However, one of the main findings of media research is that audiences tend to hear what they want to hear, interpreting content in terms of their own established perspectives (Bell 1991). Similarly, studies have found that readers have difficulty eliminating incorrect or obsolete information bearing on the situation models that they have constructed, even when new, discrediting information prompts them to do so (Johnson & Seifert 1993, 1994; Wilkes &

Leatherbarrow 1988; Van Oostendorp 1996; Van Oostendorp & Bonebakker, 1999).

Various explanations of this phenomenon are possible, for instance, that readers take in the new information more superficially; in other words, that they "skip" the new information because they (erroneously) think that they already possess the relevant information. I will call this the "skipping hypothesis." Alternatively, it may be that readers "reject" these modifications, for instance, because information that constitutes their situation model is hard to change even if the text requires this change; in other words, readers may actively hold onto a first perspective once it is established. I will refer to this explanation as the "rejection hypothesis." The study reported in this chapter tries to get direct evidence about these two explanations. First, however, I will briefly review some experimental work concerning the resistance to the modification of situation models and describe some previous work on updating situation models during reading news reports.

Resistance to Modification of Situation Models

Difficulties in updating situation models were the focus of a series of experiments by Wilkes and Leatherbarrow and by Johnson and Seifert. Both research teams made use of (fictional) news events, constructed as series of short, single messages. In one version of the text (the so-called experimental version) a correction was inserted, which denied a fact reported earlier. Ideally, readers should not only process these corrections into their situation models, but also retrospectiveley reinterpret all intermediate messages—which were given *after* the misinformation and *before* the correction. The central question of the experiments was which conditions result in an optimal updating process.

To give an example here, Van Oostendorp (1996) and Van Oostendorp and Bonebakker (1999) presented readers with a story on a fire in a warehouse. Readers with the experimental version read that "inflammable materials were carelessly stored in a side room." Later in the story they read that "the side room happened to be empty." The most conspicuous conclusion was that the influence of old (discredited) information—like "inflammable, carelessly stored material in a room"—could not be fully eradicated by new (discrediting) information that was provided later. Answers to questions (e.g., What was the cause of the explosion? or For what reason might an insurance claim be refused?) were frequently based on the old information. Even when subjects were aware of the fact that some information had been discredited, they continued to use the obsolete information in making inferences, as appeared from answers such as "carelessness combined with inflammable materials was the cause of the explosion" or "owner's own fault due to his careless behavior" as the basis of the refusal.

Wilkes and Leatherbarrow examined the role of the *relevance* of the information. If initially relevant information about the cause of an event was given, which was discredited subsequently, the influence of the (old) discredited information remained clearly perceptible. If, on the other hand, the initial information was of little relevance to the cause of the event, while the (new) discrediting information was highly relevant, readers successfully updated their situation model. Thus, readers tend to hold on to old, discredited information if that information happens to be highly relevant to the cause of the event being narrated. In this example, the mentioned cause "inflammable, carelessly stored material" is here highly relevant to the fire in the warehouse.

Johnson and Seifert focused on the importance of information with regard to the causal structure as well. Their experiments showed that updating proceeded more successfully if the correction that was provided contained an alternative causal explanation of the event. Nevertheless, some influence of the discredited information remained noticeable. In a similar experiment with comparable materials and procedures, Van Oostendorp and Van Oostendorp and Bonebakker found that even presenting a correction in the text repeatedly did not improve performance. The conclusion of these experiments must be that it is difficult for readers to fully eradicate from memory information that is important to understanding the event in question.

A recurrent finding of studies investigating the way in which readers process news stories is the fact that these readers process these texts rather sloppily and that memory of their content is poor (Findahl & Höijer 1981; Graber 1988; Gunter 1987; Höijer & Findahl 1984). However, we do not know whether readers update their situation model when they read a news text, and more importantly what factors affect this process of updating (Larsen 1980, 1983; Van Dijk 1988).

Though the exact structure of situation models is hard to define precisely, it is clear that they should include schematic categories like time, location, circumstances, participants, actions, and events

(Van Dijk 1988). Causal, temporal, and spatial relations are also involved. And, of course, the relevance of information to the causal chain of events is important as well (Van den Broek 1990).

In a series of experiments Van Oostendorp explored which factors are responsible for an effective updating of situation models derived from newspaper articles. Subjects read a text about the situation in Somalia at the time of the U.S. operation "Restore Hope," followed by a second text some time later, which contained *transformations* of facts mentioned in the first text. These were modifications of parts of the original information following developments in the real world, for example, the first text mentioned "*. . . operation Restore Hope began under the supreme command of the United States.*" In the second text the command structure of the operation had been changed into "*. . . the United Nations took over command in Somalia.*" A correct updating of the situation model implies that the old information is replaced by new information, and that the old information is removed from the situation model or put more into the background. After reading each text subjects received a judgment inference task, for instance, a test item was "*The USA troops operate under the UN-flag*" (True/False) in the previous example. This task was used because the interest was in the subjects' situational representation: in order to make correct judgments, readers cannot rely solely on the surface structure of the text, but must use the situation model they have built (see Fletcher & Chrysler 1990; and Schmalhofer & Glavanov 1986).

The main questions probed by these experiments were whether the transformations are incorporated into the reader's situation model after reading the second text, and which factors were involved. To investigate these questions, several factors were systematically varied. First, the instruction was varied: readers were instructed to read "carefully" or to read "normally." Second, the delay of the presentation of the second text was varied: immediately, or one day after reading the first text. A third factor was the strength of the original situation model. The strength of the model established after reading the first text was measured by an inference judgment task. On the basis of the score on this test, readers with a "weak" or "strong" (original situation) model were distinguished. Fourth, interest in the situation in Somalia was measured on the basis of rating scales that resulted in groups of readers with "low" versus "high" interest. Fifth, the relevance of items on the inference judgment task was assessed. The information involved in the items of this task are not equal in their relevance to the situation described by the text. Some verify details of the situation, while others are highly relevant. Readers rated the relevance of the items to the situation, which were subsequently divided into items of "low" versus "high" relevance.

The main results were that the reading instruction, readers' interest in Somalia, and the delay after reading the first text did not play a significant role in updating the situation model. However, the strength of the original situation model did have a strong influence on a strict form of updating, that is, updating is facilitated when the old, to-be-modified information is correctly represented in memory. Readers who correctly knew what the original situation was—as appeared from their above median performance on the first test—also performed significantly better on the second test than readers who did not know exactly how it originally was. This indicates that the availability of a good situation model is important for correctly actualizing present knowledge.

Finally, the relevance of the information also influenced readers' updating. Remarkably, low-relevance transformations were much better updated than transformations that were of high relevance. This effect of relevance is more or less similar to effects reported by Johnson and Seifert (1993, 1994) with other types of materials and other informational contexts. They found that information previously encoded in memory can influence inferences and judgments, even when more recent information *discredits* it. Furthermore, they suggest that a central and important piece of information in a report will be harder to eradicate from memory if incorrect than less important information. In the fire-example just mentioned, it would mean that a central piece of information that later in a text appears to be wrong is harder to neutralize than a more peripheral piece of information. In the current context this could mean that the (old) information of high relevance continues to exert its influence while reading the second text with new correcting information, and more so than (old) information of low relevance. The next experiment tried to get evidence about the exact cause of the poor updating that takes place while reading the second text.

A Thinking-Aloud Experiment on Updating a Situation Model

As just said, updating situation models, that is, changing your viewpoint when confronted with new information, is supposed to play an important role in reading. However, several studies show that incorrect or obsolete information is hard to eradicate from memory. I have already referred to the *skipping* and *rejecting* hypotheses as alternative explanations for this phenomenon. The present study attempts to get direct evidence about the occurrence of skipping or rejection processes by a method in which readers "think-aloud" while reading. (For more information on the method, see Trabasso and Suh [1993].) The focus was on the way in which readers process the transformations occurring in the second text of the two Somalia reports described before.

The texts used were composed on the basis of different background articles that appeared in several newspapers. Each text contained approximately a thousand words. The second text contained sixteen transformations of facts that were mentioned in the first text. These transformations described changes in the situation (because of developments in the field) rather than because of inconsistencies or contradictions. For each of these sixteen transformations a test item was constructed. After having read each text, readers had to indicate whether the statements could be true or not true, given the text.

The texts were presented in fragments of one to three sentences on separate pages in a booklet. Twenty-four undergraduates from Utrecht University read the texts; they did so at their own reading speed. They were requested to talk aloud about their understanding of each page in the booklet. The instruction given was that they should read each sentence of the text and to tell the experimenter what their understanding of the sentence was in the context of the story; whatever came to their minds could be talked about. They were then asked to turn the page, and to continue the procedure of talking aloud until the end of the text. After each text, readers rated the sixteen test items as either true or false. Readers were tape-recorded and the resulting protocols were analyzed, basically with the same method of analysis as that used by Trabasso and Suh (1993), though I included some finer subcategories within the same main categories. Table 1 lists all the (sub)categories that were developed in the analysis of the protocols collected in this way. Only those categories that are important to the rejecting and skipping hypotheses will be discussed here.

In table 2 I have presented some brief examples of utterances of readers indicating skipping or rejection while processing the transformative information contained in the second text. All of the protocols of subjects were judged on the presence of these six types of utterances.

Table 10.1
Categories of Inferences in the Thinking-Aloud Protocols

1. Repeat Text
A restatement or paraphrase of the main propositions of the focal sentence of the text. Repetitions function to maintain information in working memory.
RPC correct and complete repetition of text
RPI incomplete repetition of text
RPF incorrect repetition of text

2. Repeat Thought
A restatement or paraphrase of a thought that occurred while reading the focal sentence. Repetitions of thought may serve maintenance or explanatory functions.
ROC correct and complete repetition of thought
ROI incomplete repetition of thought
ROF incorrect repetition of thought

3. Retrieve Text
A reinstatement of the main propositions of a sentence that was read previous to the focal one. Retrieval of prior text information reflects a search of long-term memory or maintenance of information in working memory from prior sentences. Retrieval of prior text serves primarily to explain focal sentences and thoughts.
REC correct and complete retrieval of text
REI incomplete retrieval of text
REF incorrect retrieval of text
REP retrieval from previous text

4. Retrieve Thought
A reinstatement of the main propositions of a thought to the current focal sentence. Retrieving thoughts serve primarily to explain focal sentences and thoughts.
RTC correct and complete retrieval of thought
RTI incomplete retrieval of thought
RTF incorrect retrieval of thought

5. Elaborate Consequences of Text (ELC)
Drawing implications or causal consequences of the text. Generating information not present in text, but inferable from it. They serve to continue the event sequence in the text and/or to enrich comprehension of the text.

6. Elaborate Associate of Text (ELA)
Drawing noncausal inferences, adding background knowledge.

7. Explanation
An inference to explain or provide reasons for the information in the focal sentence or in a thought. These inferences answer why and how questions.
EXP posing these questions, instigated by text or thought
EXA answering these questions, instigated by text or thought

8. Prediction (PRD)
A thought that correctly forecasted a future occurrence in the text.

9. Meta-Comments
Evaluative remarks on the content of the text or about the ease or difficulty of understanding the focal sentence.
MCS stating an opinion about the content
MCA stating careless metacomments about the content
MCR comments rejecting the correctness of facts mentioned in the text
MCC comments confirming the correctness of sentences
MCQ expressing doubts whether what has been read was adequately understood.

Table 10.2
Examples of the Skipping and Rejection Categories

Skipping Category
- Incomplete Repetition
  "One year after the invasion on the beach of Mogadishu. . . ." (The text mentions here "More than a year after the invasion of American soldiers on the beach of Mogadishu. . . .")
- Incorrect Repetition
  "After the invasion of the international force on the beach. . . ." (The text mentions here "More than a year after the invasion of American soldiers on the beach of Mogadishu. . . .")
- Careless Metacomment
  "I don't care," etc.

Rejection Category
- Rejecting Comment
  "That is not true," etc.
- Questioning Own Understanding
  "Did I see that right?"
- Retrieval from Previous Text
  "Before it was mentioned that the operation was under American command. . . ." (Information from the first text.)

The main question of this study was whether the low degree of updating is caused by superficial reading (skipping) or by a refusal to change the model in rejecting the transformative information of the second text (rejecting). If superficial processing (*skipping*) is the cause of a poor updating, then we might expect that the following think-aloud activities are of great importance in relation to processing of the transformative information and—negatively—related to the judgment performance: "incomplete repetition," "incorrect repetition," and "careless metacomment." If skipping is plausible, we might expect that a high frequency on these categories is related with low test performance. In other words, the more often subjects make incomplete or incorrect repetitions or utter careless metacomments while processing the new (transformative) information, the lower their judgment test performance should be.

If, however, active refusal (*rejecting*) is the cause of poor updating, then one might expect that the following categories in relation to the transformative information are negatively related to test performance: "rejecting comment," "questioning own understanding," and "retrieval from previous text." In other words, the more often subjects reject current information, the more they question their own understanding, and the more they retrieve corresponding information from the previous text while processing the transformations, the lower their judgment test performance should be. The point of these two hypotheses is whether we can understand test performance by examining what occurred during reading. More specifically, the purpose is to examine whether test performance can be better explained (predicted) by thinking activities classified as skipping rather than by rejection activities.

It could be objected that the method of thinking-aloud is not a reliable indicator of readers' processing activities. I therefore compared readers' performance on the judgment test with the one obtained in the previous experiment. The results happened to be largely the same, both for readers' actual performance as well as for the general pattern of results. On the basis of these results we may conclude that thinking-aloud is not an important disturbing influence in text processing or in building and updating a situation model; see Trabasso and Suh (1993) and Trabasso, Suh, and Payton (1994) for similar conclusions concerning the role of thinking-aloud during discourse understanding.

The most important results concern the frequencies of utterances in relation to the sixteen locations in the text where transformative information was provided, in particular with respect to the think-aloud categories that are important to the two hypotheses: the categories incomplete repetition, incorrect repetition, careless metacomment, rejecting comment, questioning own understanding and retrieval from previous text. As suggested by the hypotheses, the activities in these categories have to be related to the performance on the (transformative) inference questions. In table 3 the mean frequencies and standard deviations of activities in the categories are presented. (The latter figures express how much variation in frequency there is in that specific category.)

Table 10.3
Mean Frequencies of Think-Aloud Categories and Standard Deviations

	Mean	*Standard Deviation*
Skipping Variables		
RPI (incomplete repetition)	4.96	2.07
RPF (incorrect repetition)	.50	.83
MCA (careless metacomment)	.54	.78
Rejection Variables		
MCR (rejecting comment)	0	0
MCQ (questioning own understanding)	2.46	2.65
REP (retrieval from previous text)	.29	.69

As can be seen, all of the categories occur with a reasonable amount of variance, except for rejecting comment. No utterance of subjects was scored as a rejecting comment.

Next, linear multiple regression analyses have been conducted. This is a statistical technique that allows one to assess the extent to which the think-aloud activities (individually and collectively) predict the performance on the judgment test. Very briefly, with this technique of analysis it is possible to examine whether readers' test performance depends on think-aloud activities, for instance, whether the think-aloud activities falling under the skipping category predict test performance, or—opposed to this—whether the reject activities better predict test performance; see also Graesser, Magliano, and Haberlandt (1994) for a clear exposition of the validity and usefulness of the regression methodology to investigate text comprehension.

The first analysis only included the *skipping* variables, that is, in this analysis the (predictor) variables incomplete repetition, incorrect repetition, and careless metacomment were used to examine how much variance in the criterion variable (test performance) is explained. The resulting figure is the (multiple) correlation coefficient. This correlation squared (R^2) is an index of the amount of variance explained by the variables in the analysis (in principle ranging from 0 percent to 100 percent explained variance). The multiple correlation coefficient R is .52 ($F[3,20] = 2.43$, $p < .10$). Skipping as operationalized in this study thus explains 27 percent of the variance on the judgment test. The partial and raw correlations with the criterion variable (judgment test) and beta-coefficients, together with their significance, are presented in table 4.

For convenience the zero-order correlations between predictor variables and the criterion variable are also included (in the first column). A partial correlation coefficient indicates the correlation with the criterion variable when the other variables have been removed from the independent variable as well as from the dependent variable. A beta-coefficient that is statistically different from zero indicates that a predictor variable significantly contributes to the performance on the judgment test. The main variable that significantly contributes to the test performance here is careless metacomment, and also the direction (the sign) is as expected: The more often subjects make careless metacomments during processing transformations, the lower their test performance is.

The multiple correlation coefficient R of the *rejection* variables is .51 ($F[2,21] = 3.75$, $p < .05$), thus explaining 26 percent of the variance on the judgment test. The main contributing variable here is retrieval from previous text, but notice that the direction (the sign) of the correlation is opposite to the expectation: retrieval from previous text corresponds to *higher* test performance. Both multiple correlation coefficients are, thus, substantial, though only the rejection category was (really) statistically significant ($p < .05$) but the sign in this case was not according to expectation.

Next to the separate analyses, I also conducted a regression analysis in which both groups of variables *together*, skipping as well as rejection, were included. In this analysis five variables are, thus, simultaneously used to predict test performance. This analysis was performed because it is interesting to see whether both categories together explain more variance than each category separately. The right-hand columns in table 4 summarize the results. The multiple correlation coefficient is .76 ($F[5,18] = 4.78$, $p < .01$). The proportion of variance now explained rises to 57 percent. This indicates that the overlap between skipping and rejection is minimal and that both kinds of activities contribute to explain the performance on the inference judgment task. As we can see from table 4, there are now four variables significantly or almost significantly ($p < .05$) related to test performance: careless metacomment, incomplete repetition, questioning own understanding, and retrieval from previous text. All of these variables have (almost) significant beta weights. Two observations are in order

Table 10.4
(Partial) Correlations and Beta-Coefficients for the Predictor Variables

		Separately			*Together*		
	corr.	partial corr.	beta coeff.	sign.	partial corr.	beta coeff.	sign.
Skipping Variables							
RPI (incomplete repetition)	.25	.23	.21	ns	.51	.44	p < .05
RPF (incorrect repetition)	.08	.09	.08	ns	.25	.19	ns
MCA (careless metacomment)	–.46	–.47	–.45	p < .05	–.52	–.46	p < .05
		Multiple R = .52					
Rejection Variables							
MCR (rejecting comment)	—	—	—	—	—	—	—
MCQ (questioning own understanding)	.12	.01	.01	ns	.46	.44	p < .05
REP (retrieval from previous text)	.51	.50	.51	p < .05	.43	.35	p < .06
		Multiple R = .51			Multiple R = .76		

here. First, the partial correlations and beta weights of incomplete repetition and questioning own understanding are significant. There is now a significant positive influence of incomplete repetition and questioning own understanding on test performance. Second, careless metacomment significantly correlates in the expected direction. The other variables incomplete repetition, questioning own understanding, and retrieval from previous text also have a significant or almost significant influence, but in a direction that was not expected. A higher frequency of these mental operations corresponds to a better performance. I will interpret these results in the following section.

The analyses with skipping and rejection as independent variables explain an approximately equal (and substantial) amount of variance, each about 26 percent, though only rejection was significant at a conventional level (but in the wrong direction). The main variables in the context of skipping were careless metacomment, and in the context of rejection retrieval from previous text. It seems that careless processing of information—expressed by careless metacomments—corresponds to a lower updating performance. Retrieval from previous text, as a presumed indicator of rejection, seems to indicate something else than rejection. It could be better interpreted as "comparing and contrasting present information with previous information," which—in view of the positive beta-coefficient—contributes to the quality of updating.

Careless processing, as indicated by careless metacomment, again correlates negatively with test performance in this overall equation, incomplete repetition now correlates significantly (and positively). The mental operations behind it should probably be conceived as some kind of "chunking or abbreviating information." In the same way, the positive influence of retrieval from previous text and questioning one's own understanding should be better interpreted as "actively trying to integrate" the transformative information into the situation model constructed during the first text rather than simply rejecting the new information.

Conclusions and Discussion

The results indicate that skipping of transformations indeed leads to a low performance on the judgment test. The mental operations falling under the presumed rejection category (questioning own understanding and retrieval from previous text), however, should be evaluated positively, just as incomplete repetition (incomplete repetition): these operations point to active processing (questioning own understanding), chunking (incomplete repetition) and integrating new information (retrieval from previous text). These activities contribute to the updating of a situation model and enhance readers' performance on the judgment test. Taken together, these results suggest that skipping could be the main cause of failing to update, maybe because readers erroneously think they already know the information that is being communicated.

The results of this experiment, together with the previous ones (Van Oostendorp 1996; Van Oostendorp & Bonebakker, 1999), may have implications for theories of text comprehension, not only of news reports, but also of other types of discourse, for instance, literature. Several perspectives may be distinguished in a text or series of related texts (see, e.g., Andringa & Davis 1994). However, that does not mean that readers also distinguish among or succeed in maintaining several perspectives. The present results suggest that it is very difficult to completely discredit an old perspective, and to exchange that for a new perspective. Readers seem to prefer to skip the information that is needed in order to update their old model or perspective.

However, it remains to be seen to what extent these findings could be generalized across text types. A major question is, of course, whether readers will similarly fail to integrate new perspectives when reading literary texts. Zwaan (1994) demonstrated that readers of literary texts build weaker situation models than readers of news reports. Miall and Kuiken (chap. 17 of this vol.) even argue that processing models that have been developed for "factual" texts are ill-suited to describe readers' processing of literary texts, and they provide concrete evidence for such a difference. And Graesser and his colleagues (chap. 15 of this vol.) provide evidence that readers are quite good at keeping track of different sorts of information during their reading (of stories). Literary texts may also differ from news texts in not deleting old information entirely. Old meanings may remain relevant even as new ones are incorporated. One reason for this is that literary texts sometimes contain "parallelism," for example, at the end of *Great Expectations,* after almost five hundred pages of adventures, countless encounters with other characters, and innumerable inner broodings, we find Pip—now a mature adult—going back to the home of his foster parents, Joe and Biddy. When he surreptitiously opens the old kitchen door and looks in unseen, this is what he perceives:

> There, smoking his pipe in the old place by the kitchen firelight, as hale and as strong as ever though a little grey, sat Joe; and there, fenced into the corner with Joe's leg, and sitting on my own little stool looking at the fire, was—I again! (1861: 490)

By now, the reader is sufficiently familiar with Joe's wooden leg so as not to be surprised by its description. But he must be surprised to see Pip looking at himself, seated in the kitchen as a child. Next day Pip takes the boy for a walk to the village churchyard, where he places him in the almost identical spot that he occupied in the opening scene of the novel. A "vivid" impression of "the identity of things" indeed! A reader who has updated the point of view in such a way that the old information has been completely replaced by new information will have difficulty in perceiving the parallelism involved, and thus miss an important piece of information. Such a reader might also fail to experience the novel's beautiful symmetry and the aesthetic delight it provides. We would judge such a reader to have an inadequate understanding of the novel, perhaps because of sloppy reading comparable to that evidenced in the failed news updatings that I have discussed earlier in this chapter. Ultimately this leads to the question as to how to view the conflicts that may emerge between an analysis of a text and readers' responses to that text (an issue that will be returned to in Short, chap. 20 of this vol.). If narratology is to progress, it will have to continue on the road taken by the kind of interdisciplinary cooperation advanced here.

Notes

I would like to thank Professor Will van Peer (University of Munich), dr. Joost Meijer (University of Amsterdam) and members of the HOGCOG for their helpful comments on an earlier draft of this chapter.

11

Actor-Role Analysis: Ideology, Point of View, and the News

Warren Sack

Introduction

This chapter describes a computational technique for text analysis, specifically, for the analysis of news texts. It improves upon existing work in artificial intelligence (AI) natural language processing (NLP) by extending several key concepts from semiotics and narrative theory (e.g., Jameson's 1987 use of Greimasian semiotics to represent ideological limits). Previous work in AI news story understanding has largely been used to build tools that can summarize stories and categorize them according to the events they describe (e.g., the technologies developed for the Message Understanding Conferences [MUC]).[1] These sorts of technologies are built around the assumptions that (1) events reported as facts in news stories should be "understood" as facts; (2) the style of a story, that is, the way in which the story is told, is not of interest; and, (3) the source of a story should not influence its analysis.These assumptions are obviously unrealistic. By making these simplifying assumptions most existing story understanding systems function as gullible "readers."[2] Everyone knows that one should not believe everything in the news. Reading more selectively requires one to determine not only what events are being reported in a story, but also whose story, whose *point of view*, is expressed in a news article. To build a less gullible story understander it will be necessary to encode in it a means to recognize point of view. By point of view I mean *ideological* point of view as opposed to, for example, *psychological* point of view. Ideological point of view characterizes the political slant of an entire story while psychological point of view (e.g., as it is used by Wiebe 1994) characterizes the source of a given sentence or statement contained within a story.

This chapter describes *SpinDoctor*, a computer program designed to detect ideological point of view in news stories.[3] To detect point of view, SpinDoctor implements a critical reading strategy called "actor-role analysis" (Sack 1994b). Actor-role analysis was developed around the following observation: one means of detecting point of view is to examine how certain people, who appear again and again in the news (i.e., news *actors*), are described or portrayed (i.e., are assigned *roles)*. Thus, for example, if one is given a news story that mentions Oliver North—(in)famous for his role in the Iran-Contra affair and in recent senatorial campaign—and the story assigns North the role of *patriot* (via the use of certain adjectives and verbs), one can be quite certain that the point of view expressed in the story is significantly to the right (in the spectrum of U.S. politics) than that expressed by another news story that assigns North the role of *villain* or *criminal.*

Two aspects of actor-role analysis, as it is implemented in the SpinDoctor system, might be of especial interest to researchers concerned with textual analysis: *A representation for ideological point of view*: Although practically all, contemporary, AI systems for NLP are capable of finding actors and roles in texts to fill in scripts, frames, or templates (e.g., Jacobs & Rau 1993), none of these systems assign any political significance to the pairing of certain actors with certain roles (e.g., North as patriot vs. North as criminal). By contrast, we maintain that sets of actor-role pairs are an interesting and implementable representation for differing ideological points of view. The proposed actor-role representation of ideological point of view accords with some recent work by Lakoff (1991) and generalizes and improves upon previous AI work on representation of ideology (e.g., Abelson & Carroll 1966; and Carbonell 1978). Actor-role analysis can also be seen as a computational analogue of the Greimasian *actor-network* method employed by sociologists to study controversies in the literatures of technoscience (e.g., Latour 1987).

An algorithm for anaphoric resolution: Actor-role analysis incorporates an anaphoric resolution algorithm. It is shown how careful attention to actor-role pairings assists in the resolution of anaphoric reference. By noting, for example, that an instance of the pronoun "he" is cast in the role of *victim* and that, earlier in the same story, "Lieutenant Rodriguez" is also cast in the role of *victim*,

SpinDoctor postulates the resolution of the instance of the pronoun he to the proper name Lieutenant Rodriguez.

This chapter contains three main sections:

Data structures: First, the actor, role, and point of view data structures employed in SpinDoctor are described. An example of the use of sets of actor-role pairs to represent ideological point of view is given and then actor-role pairs are briefly compared to other AI work on the representation of ideology.

Analysis process: SpinDoctor's analysis process is presented and several interesting subroutines are isolated for discussion. In particular, the subroutine *coreference-actors* is described in detail to show how anaphoric resolution is handled by SpinDoctor.

Performance test: Finally, results obtained by testing SpinDoctor on one hundred news stories from the MUC3 corpus are reported.

Data Structures

The abstract data structures used by the SpinDoctor system are described in this section. Particular examples of the data structures are taken from a database created to test SpinDoctor's performance on news stories from El Salvador (from the MUC3 corpus). Results of that test are given in a later section.

Actors

The actor data structures have three properties associated with them:

Names: Each actor can be recognized according to one or more names. Usually the names listed are proper names or titles.

Pronouns: Declared pronouns assist SpinDoctor in its search for anaphoric referents. Certain actors might refer to groups of people and so each such actor could be referred to as "it." Alternatively, an actor (e.g., the actor *army-officer*, which is meant to refer to anyone with a military title (e.g., Gen., Col., and Lieut.) could be referred to as "he" or "she"; while an actor defined to represent a specific individual (e.g., *bishop-romero*) would have pronouns of only one gender associated with it (e.g., he, him, etc.).

Member-of: Almost all actors are declared to be a *member-of* a larger set of actors. Thus, for example, *bishop-romero* is declared to be a member-of the actor called *clergyman* who, in turn, is declared to be a member-of the *Catholic Church*. Those actors who are not a member-of any other actor (e.g., the *Catholic Church*) are called *top-level actors*.

Here is an example definition for the actor Bishop Romero:

de factor	*bishop-romero*
:member-of	clergyman
:names	(monsignor romero) (msgr romero) (bishop romero) (oscar arnulfo romero)
:pronouns	(*he*)

government	*democratic-convergence*	*guerrillas*
police	mpsc	fmln
army	social-demo-party	radio venceremos
soldier	mnr	
army-officer		
coprefa	*catholic-church*	
government-official	clergyman	
president-cristiani	bishop-romero	
ministry		

Fig. 11.1. Actors and member-of relations between actors in a database for the analysis of Salvadoran news stories. This figure lists the actors defined for a database created for the analysis of Salvadoran news stories. The member-of relations between actors are denoted by indentations. The four top-level actors (government, democratic-convergence, catholic-church, and guerrillas) are shown in italics.

Roles

In the SpinDoctor system, roles are defined as sets of simple patterns that are lists of words and variables. Variables are role names and are prefixed with a question mark, for example, here is part of (about one-fourth of) the definition of the *criminal* role used in SpinDoctor:

> (defrole *criminal* ?criminal murdered ?victim)
> (defrole *criminal* ?criminal commit genocide)
> (defrole *criminal* ?criminal participated in the crime)
> (defrole *criminal* ?criminal is responsible for this crime)
> (defrole *criminal* ?criminal was responsible for the massacre)
> (defrole *criminal* ?criminal staged this assassination)
> (defrole *criminal* the arrest of ?criminal)
> (defrole *criminal* ?victim was abducted by ?criminal)
> (defrole *criminal* ?judge decides to punish ?criminal)

Note that one pattern can help define two roles; for instance, the first pattern mentions both the *?criminal* and *?victim* roles.

SpinDoctor's analysis process attempts to match each of the variables to a noun phrase. The following section on SpinDoctor's analysis process will explain how these patterns are matched. However, no claim is made that either this representation of roles or the means by which they are matched is especially interesting, since most AI-NLP systems do some matching of this sort, in a more or less sophisticated manner, to fill in the roles of templates. SpinDoctor's roles work simply because news stories contain a large number of idiomatic phrases that are frequently repeated word-for-word in many stories.

Points of View

Figure 11.2 shows the definitions for the four points of view used to analyze Salvadoran news. A point of view corresponding to each of the top-level actors was defined. However, nothing about the architecture of the system requires the names of the points of view to be related to the names of the top-level actors. Points of view are represented as pairings of top-level actors and roles.

The news corpus used to test the system (the MUC3 corpus) was gathered in the late-eighties/early-nineties when El Salvador was in the midst of a civil war between the *government* and the *guerrillas* (the FMLN-FDR). Caught in the middle of the fighting were both the Catholic Church and the Democratic Convergence (a coalition of center-left political groups).

The government's point of view can be detected by looking for news articles in which the government was the source (i.e., played

---

defpov
government

(government ?source)
(government ?military)
(guerrillas ?terrorist)
(guerrillas ?criminal)

defpov
democratic-convergence

(democratic-convergence ?source)
(democratic-convergence ?victim)

defpov
guerrillas

(guerrillas ?source?)
(guerrillas ?military)
(government ?criminal)

defpov
catholic-church

(catholic-church ?source)
(catholic-church ?victim)

Fig. 11.2. Definitions of four points of view useful for the analysis of Salvadoran news stories

the role of source) of the story, the guerrillas were characterized as criminals and terrorists, and, in which, the violent actions of the government and military were characterized as legitimate military actions (rather than criminal actions).

The stories that represented the guerrilla's point of view often had the guerrillas as the source of the story and characterized the guerrilla's violent actions as legitimate military actions while assigning the role of criminal to the Salvadoran government and to the armed forces. In other words, the government, in these news stories, called the guerrillas "terrorists" and "criminals" while the guerrillas reciprocated by calling the government "criminals." Displays of complementary epideictic rhetoric of this sort were the means by which the points of view could be readily discerned.

Priests of the Catholic Church and leading politicians in the Democratic Convergence (a center-left organization) were murdered. Neither the Catholic Church nor the Democratic Convergence had any military presence. It is not surprising then that neither of these parties engaged in the sort of name-calling that characterizes the stories representing the government and the guerrillas. Stories representing the Catholic Church tended to avoid blaming anyone for the deaths of its members. The Democratic Convergence also tended to not to cast anyone in the role of criminal when discussing the death of one of its members. Instead, these stories can be recognized by, for example, the use of the Catholic Church as the source of a story and the assignment of one or more members of the Catholic Church as *victim(s)*.

One might think that all points of view are simply determined by the source of the story. Although the source of a story is important it is not definitive of the point of view because, for example, more than one source can be represented in a story and the "top-level source," that is, the broadcaster or publisher of the story, is not necessarily in agreement with the point of view represented in the story (e.g., when the Catholic Church broadcasts its point of view on the Salvadoran government radio station). Also, although the source is a powerful way of categorizing radio, TV, or newspaper stories, it is less effective in the electronic environments for which SpinDoctor is being developed, for example, in looking through news stories posted to electronic bulletin boards or sent as email, potentially millions of individuals could be a source and so the recipient of a story may be familiar with the point of view expressed, but not necessarily with the source who sent the story.

Related Work in Artificial Intelligence and Cognitive Science

During the Gulf War, Lakoff (1991) wrote an essay on the metaphors used by journalists to justify the war. In the essay he points out how the war has been cast by the American media in a fairy talelike format where the United States plays the role of hero, Iraq the role of villain, and Kuwait is the maiden in distress. Actor-role analysis can be seen as an attempt to create a computational model of, and elaborate the insights sketched out by, Lakoff in his short essay.

Actor-role analysis can also be seen as a generalization of some early AI work on the representation of ideology. For example, Carbonell's work (1978) attempted to represent ideologies as pairings of actors with goal trees. Thus, a "conservative" American ideology was represented as a description of a set of plans and goals that the actor Russia could take to achieve domination of the world, and a set of plans and goals that the United States could take to prevent Russia from doing so. Contrasting ideologies assigned different actors different goal trees. Goals and plans (i.e., goal trees) can be seen as a limited form of the roles used in SpinDoctor. However, to equate roles with goal trees would be tantamount to making Carbonell's mistake of equating ideology with teleology when, in fact, ideology can encompass more than just plans and goals. Although one might want to argue that goal trees are a good representation for everything, when the issues at stake are more ones of, for example, description, rather than actions (e.g., when the Salvadoran government radio broadcasts call the FMLN "terrorists"), then something like SpinDoctor's role data structures are certainly more flexible and, thus, more appropriate than Carbonell's goal trees. Carbonell's goal trees were incapable of representing subtle differences in style and description because his parser was built to coerce natural language text into Schankian conceptual dependency primitives which, by design, wiped out any interesting differences in wording in the original texts. To avoid this problem SpinDoctor has been designed to use multiple idiomatic phrases in its role definitions rather than some set of language "primitives."

Interestingly enough earlier work by one of Carbonell's teachers, Abelson, did not confuse ideology and teleology and did not crucially depend up language primitives (e.g., Abelson & Carroll 1965, before the beginning of Abelson's collaborations with Schank). However, while Carbonell's system, POLITICS, was capable of handling natural language texts, Abelson's earlier systems accepted only logical propositions. Nevertheless, Carbonell's system only handled a few small example texts while SpinDoctor has been applied to hundreds of stories that are each hundreds of words long.

Analysis Process

Analyze-Story

Analyze-story is the top-level routine of the SpinDoctor system. Given a news story, *analyze-story* processes it and returns the name of the point of view that is represented by the story. The analysis process followed by *analyze-story* is as follows: (1) Given a news story *analyze-story* calls the subroutine "find-actor-role-bindings" to find which noun phrases (i.e., actors) play which roles in the story. (2) Then, it determines which actors are of a similar group or are identical to other actors. The subroutine that performs this task is called "coreference-actors." Coreference-actors does both (a) anaphoric resolution (e.g., determining who or what is being referenced when pronouns like "he," "she," and "it" are used); and, (b) actor grouping (e.g., inferring that "an army spokesperson," "Major Rodriguez," and "General Bustillo" are all a part of the same group (e.g., the armed forces). (3) After coreferencing the actors into groups, *analyze-story* uses the subroutine *construct-high-level-weighted-actor-role-bindings* to construct a profile of the analyzed story that describes how often (within the given story) top-level actors were assigned different roles. (4) Using weighted actor-role bindings allows the final subroutine, *identify-pov*, to distinguish, for example, stories in which the government is cited as a source once and the guerrillas are cited ten times from stories in which the guerrillas are cited as a source less often than the government. *Identify-pov* matches the weighted actor-role bindings against the point of view definitions, determines which point(s) of view match(es) best, and outputs the name of the one (or more) best-matching point(s) of view.

Find-Actor-Role-Bindings

The purpose of the find-actor-role-bindings function is to determine which noun phrases (i.e., actors) that occur in a story fill variables in the role patterns matched to the same story. Thus, the input to *find-actor-role-bindings* is a news story and the output is a set of actor-role bindings. *Find-actor-role-bindings* first calls the subroutine "find-noun-phrases" (to identify the noun phrases in the story) and then calls the subroutine "find-roles" (to match all of the defined role patterns against the text of the story).

Given the text of a story *find-noun-phrases* first employs the Xerox part-of-speech tagger (Cutting et al., 1993) to tag the words of the story. After tagging the text of the story, *find-noun-phrases* attempts to group together words into noun phrases. Thus, after processing, a sentence like "Bill went to the movies" would become (noun-phrase "Bill") "went to" (noun-phrase "the movies").

For each role pattern, *find-roles* outputs a list of bindings between the pattern and possible positions in the text of the story. The role variables, like *?victim* and *?criminal*, are assumed to be filled by noun phrases. *Find-roles* returns a range of positions within the text in which the actor that fills a role might occur.

Find-actor-role-bindings combines the output of find-roles with the output of *find-noun-phrases* to create extended actor-role bindings. Extended-bindings are a data structure with four slots:

> a *noun-phrase* slot that is filled by a list of words and their start and end positions in the text; this slot represents the actor
>
> a *role-variable* slot that names the role against which the actor was matched by find-actor-role-bindings
>
> a *coreferents* slot which, at this point in the analysis of the story is empty
>
> an *actor-groups* slot that is also empty but that will later be filled by a list of groups (social, political, and economic) that the actor might belong to; thus, for example, President Cristiani might be grouped together with other government officials

Coreference-Actors

The function *coreference-actors* starts with the output of *find-actor-role-bindings* and begins by matching a set of actor "name" patterns against the noun phrases identified as actors by *find-actor-role-bindings;* for example, Major Rodriguez can be categorized as member of the army by noting that his title "Major" is a rank that army officers have. The lists in the names slot of the actor definitions are the patterns that are used to group actors.

Coreference-actors then applies a set of constraints in order to try to resolve pronoun references and in order to partition all of the actors into mutually exclusive sets. It thereby identifies that, for example, a reference to "Major Rodriguez," a reference to "Rodriguez," and an instance of "he" might all represent the same actor and, furthermore, that references to "Rodriguez" and "General Bustillo" are both instances that represent the more inclusive actor named the "army."

The following constraints are used by *coreference-actors:*

1. The "member-of" relations that detail which groups of actors include other groups; for instance, "army-officers" is contained in the more inclusive actor group army.

2. The positions of the actors in the text of a story; the control structure of *coreference-actors* has been designed to apply this constraint by first searching through all of the other actors that are positioned above the current actor (i.e., toward the beginning of the story) in its search for a coreferent for the current actor before it searches through all of the actors positioned below the current actor.

3. The role(s) assigned to an actor; for instance, if "Major Rodriguez" is determined to play the role of *?source* in an article, then it is expected that other noun phrases representing unknown actors (e.g., "the spokesperson" or the "interviewee") which are also identified as *?sources* would be more likely to be matched to "Major Rodriguez" than unknown actors who play other roles (e.g., the role of *?victim*).

4. The pronouns associated with certain known actors, for instance, President Cristiani is defined in the database of SpinDoctor to have a list of appropriate pronouns that include "he" and "him" but not "she" or "it."

5. The words in the noun phrases that constitute the actors, for instance, "Major Rene Rodriguez Hurtado" matches the actor "Major Rene Rodriguez" better than it matches "General Bustillo."

Coreference-actors has been written to use all of these constraints to coreferences-actors. However, if a coreferent for an actor cannot be found, then the constraints are dropped one-by-one until only a subset of the constraints remain and either a coreferent is found, or no coreferent is found even with the smallest allowable set of constraints.

Coreference-actors applies the constraints in a slightly different manner depending upon the form of the current actor. If the current actor is a pronoun, constraint (5) is not applied, for instance, an earlier occurrence of "he" is considered a poor coreferent for the pronoun he even though the words of the noun phrases match exactly. For both pronouns and nonpronouns, nonpronoun coreferents are sought. A further specialization exists for the pronouns "I" and "we." "I" and "we" are assumed to refer to actors who fill the role of *?source*. Consequently, in the case of "I" and "we," pronouns constraint (3) is dropped in favor of constraint (3a) which favors coreferents that fill the role of *?source*. Constraint (3a) is the role of the actor is assumed to be *?source*.

The program uses the following "derefinement operators" to slowly relax the constraints if no coreferent can be found for an actor. The derefinement operators are lists of conjuncts of constraints. If the first conjunct of constraints in a list cannot be fulfilled, then the *coreference-actors* picks the next conjunct in the list and tries again, until the end of the list. Here, the conjuncts are represented by lists of numbers that refer to the numbered constraints just cited:

derefinement operator for nonpronouns:
[(3 1 5) (1 5) (3 5) (3 1) (5) (1) (3)]
derefinement operator for "I" and "we" pronouns:
[(3a 1) (3a) (1)]
derefinement operator for other pronouns:
[(3 1) (3) (1)]

Constraints 2 and 4 are not listed as they are members of all of the conjuncts of constraints shown. The procedure *coreference-actors* propagates the relationships that it finds between actors and so, in the end, actors may be found to have several groups and several coreferents. The effect of *coreference-actors* is to fill in the "coreferents" and "actor-groups" slots of the extended-binding structures output by the find-actor-role-bindings routine.

Construct-High-Level-Weighted-Actor-Role-Pairs

Given the extended-binding structures output by *coreference-actors*, the routine *construct-high-level-weighted-actor-role-pairs* further abstracts the actors into their most inclusive actor groups and then counts the number of times actors from each of the top-level actor-groups play each role matched in the text of the story under analysis.

Each list of groups in an extended-binding structure is a list of actors. So, for example, a binding that contains the noun phrase "President Cristiani" in its actor slot might also contain the list of actors (President Cristiani government-official government) in its actor-groups slot. *Construct-high-level-weighted-actor-role-pairs* finds the most inclusive group in each of the actor-groups slots; it uses the member-of declarations in the actor definitions to determine the most inclusive group. In this example, President Cristiani is a member-of government-officials who is a member-of the government and so the government is the most inclusive group in this case. Right now the system does not support multiple member-of declarations for an actor. Obviously this would be a worthwhile and interesting extension.

After *construct-high-level-weighted-actor-role-pairs* has determined the most inclusive group for each binding it then goes through and counts the number of times each most inclusive actor group is bound to a particular role, for instance, if "President Cristiani" appeared in the role of *?source* once, then *construct-high-level-weighted-actor-role-pairs* would create a weighted actor-role pair like this (assuming that no other government official appeared as a *?source* in the story): (government *?source* 1).

The output of *construct-high-level-weighted-actor-role-pairs* is a list of weighted actor-role pairs.

Identify Point of View

The routine *identify-point-of-view* performs the final stage of analysis. Given a list of weighted actor-role pairs, *identify-point-of-view* compares them with each of the points of view defined in the database to determine which point of view matches best to the actor-role pairs found in the story. If one of the actor-role pairs matches an actor-role pair in the point of view (see fig. 2 for a list of point-of-view definitions), then the weight associated with the pair is added to the score for the point of view. The point of view that has the largest score—after the weighted actor-role pairs have been matched against all of the points of view—is output as the point of view that matches the story. If two or more points of view have the same score then they are all output. Thus, at its most discriminating *identify-point-of-view* returns one point of view, while at its least discriminating, that is, when it cannot determine the point of view for the story, *identify-point-of-view* outputs the list of all of the points of view defined in the database.

Performance Test

To build up the actor, role, and point of view representations the first twenty-five stories about El Salvador in the MUC3 corpus were scrutinized. Characteristic textual patterns were noted and then coded into the actor and role definitions. The point of view definitions were then defined by trying to articulate the strongest ideological differences that seemed to be represented in the stories (e.g., that the guerrillas call the government "criminals" and vice versa).

After coding the databases using the first twenty-five stories about El Salvador, SpinDoctor was then run on the first one hundred stories in the MUC3 corpus. Tables 1, 2, 3, and 4 summarize the results of that test. The columns labeled *right* contain the number of times in which SpinDoctor was able to pick which one of the four points of view was represented by a given story. The columns labeled *wrong* contain the number of times in which SpinDoctor picked a subset of the points of view (often a subset of one point of view) for the story and none of the elements of the subset were actually represented in the story. This was the case, for example, when the story was written from the point of view of the El Salvadoran government and when SpinDoctor incorrectly deduced that the story either represented the Catholic Church or the Democratic Convergence. The columns labeled *vague* count the number of times in which SpinDoctor selected a superset of the points of view actually represented in the story. In such a case, SpinDoctor was not actually wrong; the stories did indeed represent a subset of the points of view selected by SpinDoctor. However, this was the case when, for example, SpinDoctor reported that a story represented both the Catholic Church and the government when, indeed, perhaps it only represented the government's points of view.

As one can see in table 11.1, unsurprisingly, SpinDoctor did best with the subcorpus of stories that were used to create the databases (i.e., the first twenty-five stories about El Salvador). What is more interesting to see is table 11.2 that shows how well SpinDoctor did on stories about El Salvador that were not a part of the twenty-five used to create the databases of actors, roles, and points of view. This test result indicates that SpinDoctor could provide a user with at least a partially effective, news filter to detect point of view. It is important to note that SpinDoctor was often overly vague, but rarely completely wrong in its assessment of point of view.

Table 11.1
The Training Set: Twenty-Five Stories about El Salvador

	Right	*Wrong*	*Vague*	*Totals*
Number of Stories	19	2	4	25
Percentage	76	8	16	100

Table 11.2
Test Set Number 1: Seventeen Unseen Stories about El Salvador

	Right	*Wrong*	*Vague*	*Totals*
Number of Stories	6	1	10	17
Percentage	35	6	59	100

Table 11.3
Test Set Number 2: Fifty-Eight Unseen Stories about Other Countries

	Right	*Wrong*	*Vague*	*Totals*
Number of Stories	17	0	41	58
Percentage	29	0	71	100

Table 11.4
Totals: One Hundred Stories Seen and Unseen

	Right	*Wrong*	*Vague*	*Totals*
Number of Stories	42	3	55	100
Percentage	42	3	55	100

Perhaps what is the most surprising of the test results is that SpinDoctor behaved reasonable well with news stories that were neither from nor about El Salvador, but were rather descriptive of events in other countries in Central and South America (see table 11.3). To a certain degree many of the other countries represented in the MUC3 corpus had, like El Salvador, serious internal, civil disputes. Consequently, some of the parties in these disputes are called "the government" and other parties are called "the guerrillas." These structural similarities in the news discourses about various civil disputes in different countries allowed SpinDoctor to sometimes correctly detect the point of view represented by a news story about something that had no direct relation to the politics of El Salvador. Table 11.4 shows the totals for all 100 hundred stories analyzed: 42 right, 3 wrong, and 55 overly vague.

Conclusions and Future Work

This chapter has shown how ideological point of view can be represented by sets of actor-role pairs. Differing ideological points of view are represented by different actor-role pairs (e.g., Oliver North as patriot vs. North as criminal). The computer program, SpinDoctor, can recognize the point of view represented by a news story by matching actor and role patterns to the text of the story and then by comparing the actor-role pairings matched in the story with a set of predefined ideological points of view. The *actor-role analysis* method employed by SpinDoctor was compared to earlier AI work on the representation of ideology. SpinDoctor was tested on a portion of the MUC3 corpus and the results of that test showed that SpinDoctor could be used as a news filter to detect point of view.

In future work we will expand SpinDoctor's actor, role, and point of view databases and combine its abilities to recognize point of view with conventional techniques from information retrieval and NLP (e.g., those techniques employed in systems built for the MUC competitions) to create a news filter capable of examining stories according to both events described and the point of view from which the events are described.

Notes

1. The Message Understanding Conferences are sponsored by the Defense Advanced Research Projects Agency (DARPA) to test leading artificial intelligence natural language processing programs against one another. In this chapter some of the MUC3 (1991) test corpus will be examined.

2. There are some early exceptions (e.g., Abelson & Carroll 1966) and this neglect has not been complete in closely related areas (in dialogue and argument understanding, e.g., Allen Perrault 1980; Birnbaum, Flowers, & McGuire 1980; and Alvarado 1990; in intelligent tutoring systems, e.g., Farrell & Bloch 1988; and, in the field of language generation, e.g., Hovy 1988).

3. An earlier version of SpinDoctor (Sack 1994a) used a more sophisticated version of role matching that included a syntactic parse and morphological analysis of the text of the stories and which, therefore, allowed the

word order and, for example, verb tenses in the role patterns to be automatically varied. This extra level of sophistication was found to be unnecessary in demonstrating the central features of actor-role analysis: the determination of whose point of view is represented by a news story and by the representation of ideological points of view.

Part IV

Comprehension

12

On the Perspective Structure of Narrative Texts: Steps toward a Constructivist Narratology

Ansgar Nünning

If there is one thing that narratology does not seem to need it is more suggestions for the introduction of new concepts. Yet this is exactly what I will try to do. What I wish to do, however, is to propose a different perspective on perspectives. It is not the problem of narrative perspectives in the sense of Stanzel's (1965, 1966, 1984) narrative situations, Chatman's (1978, 1986, 1990, 1995) structure of narrative transmission, or Gérard Genette (1980, 1988) and Mieke Bal's (1977, 1985) focalization theories (for a survey, cf. Jahn 1995) that the present chapter is concerned with. It will argue that the prevailing sense in which the term *perspective* is used in narratology is neither the only nor even the most useful way in which the concept of perspective can be applied in the study of narrative. Specifically, I will take up and modify the concepts of "character-perspective" and "perspective structure" that Pfister (1988) introduced in his influential book so that they can be fruitfully applied in narratology.[1]

In what follows I wish to propose that the notion of perspective is applicable not only to the rhetorical structure of narrative transmission, but, in a more literal manner, to the description of the semantic content of narratives, namely to the world-models of the fictional individuals that populate the represented universe projected by narrative texts. By perspective, I do not mean the acts of narration and focalization, but more generally a character's or a narrator's subjective worldview. Such character-perspectives and narrator-perspectives are conditioned by the individuals' knowledge, mental traits, attitudes, and system of values. What my deliberations will try to show is that the concepts of character-perspective, narrator-perspective, and "perspective structure of a text" can be useful analytical tools in the analysis of narrative.

After a preliminary discussion of the concept of perspective, the first part of the chapter gives an outline of a constructivist narratology. The second part presents a set of categories for the description of character-perspectives and narrator-perspectives. The third part will be devoted to introducing criteria for the distinction between different types of perspective structure. A discussion of some of the uses of the framework delineated concludes the chapter.

The Concept of Perspective in a Constructivist Narratology

A look at the concept of perspectives may help to distinguish the notions of character-perspective, narrator-perspective, and perspective structures argued for in this chapter from the prevalent use of the term *perspective* in narratology in the collocation *narrative perspective*.[2] Chatman's (1986) critique of the importation of the term *point of view* into narratology and of the metaphoric transfers that make even such a neologism as "focalization" a problematic term can also be applied to the narratological use of the term *perspective*. Suffice it to say that the concept of narrative perspective fails to distinguish between different functions in the structure of narrative transmission, and that *perspective* has had an even longer and more complex career than the term *point of view*. Guillén's excellent reconstruction of "the itinerary of the metaphor of perspective in its progress from optics to philosophy" (1971: 287) may serve as a reminder that the use of the term *narrative perspective* in narratology is by no means the only possible way of applying the concept of perspective in the study of narrative.

There is another sense of the term *perspective* that would be useful for narratology, one informed by the philosophical theory of perspectivism. According to the OED, perspectivism is the "theory that knowledge of a subject is inevitably partial and limited by the individual perspective from which it is viewed." A "cognitive theory of perspectivity" (Graumann & Sommer 1989: 35) emphasizes the "inevitable relativity of human knowledge" (ibid.) and the wide-ranging influence of personal perspective on the individual's view of the world. According to Graumann and Sommer, who have developed such a cognitive theory of perspectivity and experimentally demonstrated the influence of perspective on text production and comprehension, in phenomenology and in the philosophy of mind, *perspective* is mainly used "as a term for the structure of the inner representation of the outer world or, more generally, of the mental (or cognitive) representation of the human world" (36). In contrast to their use of the term *perspective structure* to describe the internal structure of mental representations of the outer world, I will use the term to refer to the relationships between the various individual perspectives projected in a text.

Following a route pioneered by Pfister, Ryan (1985, 1986, 1991), and some others, I propose to apply such a cognitive conceptualization of perspective to the study of the subjective worldviews of characters and narrators. The individual perspectives projected in a narrative text can be adequately described in the framework of a constructivist narratology. What has been labeled *radical constructivism* (for an introduction, cf. von Glasersfeld 1984; Rusch 1987; Schmidt 1987, 1992; and Watzlawick 1984) explores the cognitive activity through which observers create subjective models of the world they regard as actual. Constructivism proceeds from the radical and somewhat counterintuitive assumption that human beings do not have access to an objective reality and that they cannot know anything that lies outside their subjective cognitive domains. Their processes of cognition therefore do not objectively copy features of the external reality; instead individuals generate subject-dependent constructs of their world through their mental representations and verbal descriptions.

What bearing do these theoretical reflections, then, have on the study of narrative perspective? The application of constructivist insights in literary criticism is rooted in the assumption that literature, as Schmidt puts it, is "the only place where the construction of world-models as such becomes thematic" (1984: 265). Narrative fiction, in particular, thematizes and structurally reflects the problems attached to the construction of world-models. The insights of constructivism can potentially be applied to every level of narrative communication. The cognitive processes through which an individual (or collectivity) actively constructs a model of the world are not only represented on the story level in the perspectives of the characters but also reflected on the discourse level. Constructivist interpretation (cf. Herring 1985) and constructivist narratology explore what proponents of narrative semantics have called "the world-making activity" (Ryan 1991: 110) through which characters or narrators shape the subjective world-models that constitute their individual perspectives. Constructivist narratology specifically tries to describe those features of narrative texts that have a bearing on wider epistemological issues (for applications of constructivism to an analysis of fiction, see von Glasersfeld 1979; and Nünning 1989b, 1994). More specifically, a constructivist approach to the problem of perspective focuses on the structural devices used in narrative texts for foregrounding the subjectivity, perspectivity, and constructivity of experience, recollection, cognition, and emotion.

On the Concepts of Character-Perspective and Narrator-Perspective

Given the foregoing constructivist underpinnings, let me now turn to outlining a set of categories for the description of character-perspectives and narrator-perspectives. A character-perspective can be defined as a fictional agent's subjective worldview. According to Pfister, the perspective from which a character observes the world is defined by three factors: by "the level of advance information the figure has access to," by the "psychological disposition," and by the "ideological orientation" (1988: 58) of the character. Just as a character can "only articulate what corresponds plausibly to his or her particular . . . situation and psychological disposition" (ibid.), each verbal utterance and each physical or mental act of a character provides insight into his or her perspective. Despite their vagueness, these parameters provide a rough-and-ready account of what conditions a character's worldview.

If one attempts to further specify the features that make up the semantic content of a character-perspective, one can resort to models devised by empirical personality theories. What Ryan has termed the "pseudoreality that characters have for the reader" (1991: 21) invites the reader to project upon a fictional world everything he or she knows about real persons and the factors that influence their subjective worldviews. Even at the risk of incurring the displeasure of those who will immediately be suspicious of mimetic and referential fallacies, I would like to maintain that there is no reason why narratology should not avail itself of empirical personality theories in the study of literary character. Compare what Ryan refers to as "a law of primary importance in the phenomenology of reading," namely "the principle of minimal departure": "This law . . . states that we reconstrue the central world of a textual universe in the same way we reconstrue the alternate possible worlds of nonfactual statements: as conforming as far as possible to our representation of AW [the actual world]. We will project upon these worlds everything we know about reality, and we will make only the adjustments dictated by the text" (51). Literary characters can thus be said to be endowed with perspectives comparable to those of real human beings, a point developed empirically (see Dixon and Bortolussi, chap. 16 of this vol.).

An obvious possibility for defining the contents of a character-perspective would be to apply the notion of a "communicative system of preconditions" proposed by exponents of what has come to be known as the "Empirical Theory of Literature." According to Schmidt, one of its chief proponents, these preconditions include a person's knowledge, abilities, motivations, needs, intentions, expectations, psychological and physical states, as well as the general economic, political, social, and cultural conditions under which he or she lives (cf. 1982: 30f.). Yet another way of refining the concept of character-perspective is provided by the sophisticated work on literary character that has been done in recent years, especially in the framework of possible world semantics. Since Margolin has not only described the state of the art in an exemplary fashion in several articles, but also developed a viable and comprehensive theory of literary character, I shall simply call attention to his work here (cf. 1983, 1987, 1989, 1990a, and 1990b).

A character-perspective could thus be defined as an individual's fictional system of preconditions or subjective worldview—the sum of all the models he or she has constructed of the world, of others, and of herself. A character-perspective is governed by the totality of an individual's knowledge and belief sets, intentions, psychological traits, attitudes, ideological stance, and system of values and norms that have been internalized (for a more detailed definition of the term *character-perspective,* see Nünning 1989a: 69–74). In short, it embraces everything that exists in the mind of a character.

The notion of character-perspective provides an analytical tool for accounting for the fact that the semantic domain projected in a narrative text consists not just of one fictional world, but of a range of subjective perspectives, each organizing its constituents into a different world-model. The narrative universe of a text contains what Ryan calls "a number of subworlds, created by the mental activity of characters" (1991: 4), a "plurality of represented worlds" (20).

Such a notion of character-perspective thus has an obvious affinity to other concepts recently proposed in narratology. It is compatible with, for example, Ryan's concept of "the private domains of the characters" (1986: 324), "the private worlds of the characters' mental constructs" (1991: 40), and with what Margolin terms the "subjective belief worlds" (1990: 850) or subdomains of the characters and of the narrative agents. The relationship between Ryan's model and my concept of character-perspective is one of only partial overlap, however, since, according to Ryan, the "possible worlds of a character's domain are built out of truth-functional propositions; they are collections of facts which can be compared to the facts of the actual world" (1991: 111). In contrast to Ryan, I would argue that subjective judgments, opinions, emotions, and beliefs, irrespective of whether they are erroneous or not, are an integral part of a character-perspective and should not be left out in an account of the perspectives or private domains of characters.

The distinction between subjective character-perspectives and the actual textual world as construed by the reader makes allowance for the possibility that the world of fictional facts need not be accurately reflected in the mental representations constructed by a character: "the concept of factual domain, or actual world, . . . is made up of what exists absolutely in the semantic universe of the text, as opposed to what exists in the minds of characters" (112). The concept of character-perspective and the hypothesis that a narrative text projects a range of subjective private world-models is illustrated graphically in figure 1.

Figure 1 is a highly simplified representation of the actual textual world narrative fictions typically project, represented by a disproportionately small circle, and of the naive iconic models of two characters. The very large heads of the two gentlemen with bowler-hats, figures I have taken from an article on constructivism by von Foerster (1984), represent their individual character-perspectives. The fact that these private worlds are inhabited by yet other anthropomorphic phantoms may serve to illustrate that the cognitive domains of characters contain not just a general world-model, but also models of others and of themselves.

Any attempt to apply the concept of perspective structure to the theory and analysis of narrative texts would, of course, be incomplete if it did not take into consideration the existence of an additional communicative level of narrative transmission. It can be argued that the proposed concept of perspective can also be applied to narrators, because narrators may also be endowed with a range of individuating features (cf. Margolin 1990a: 457–58). By analogy to the term *character-perspective,* the concept of narrator-perspective can be defined as the system of preconditions or the subjective worldview of a narrating instance (cf. Nünning 1989a: 74–76). Just

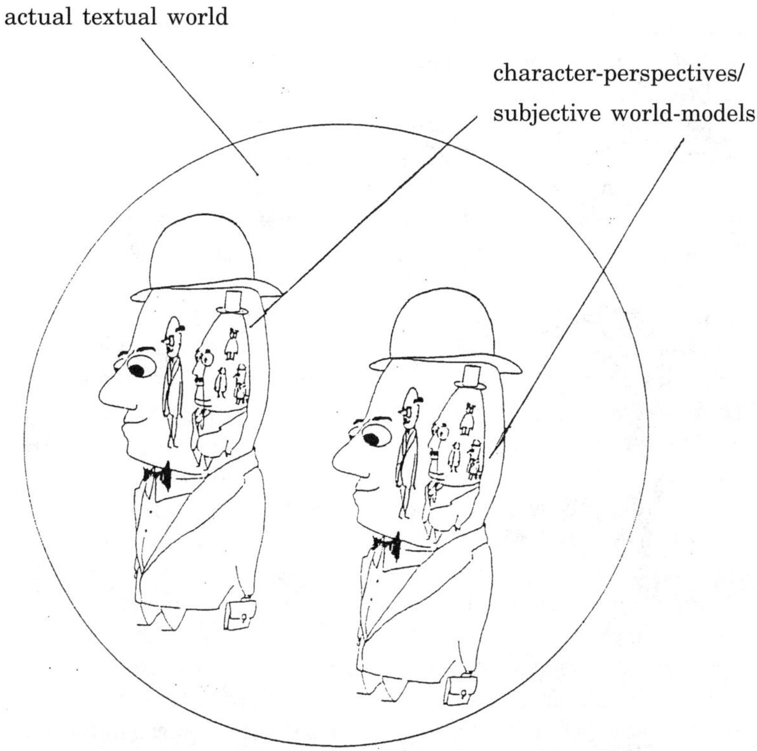

Fig. 12.1. The actual textual world, characters, and their private world-models or character-perspectives.

as for each character, the reader can construe an individual perspective for the narrator, by attributing to the voice that utters the discourse psychological idiosyncrasies, attitudes, norms and values, a set of mental properties, and a world-model.

One should add, however, that the concept of a narrator-perspective is relevant only for what Chatman calls "overt narrators," not for "covert" (1978: 33, 197–262) narratorial instances or impersonal voices: "Since anonymous speakers are deprived of human dimension, and cannot express subjective opinions divorced from those of the implied author, the reader may dispense with the reconstruction of their personality, beliefs, and judgments as an autonomous private domain" (Ryan 1991: 71). Since overt narrators are characterized as individuated subjects clearly recognizable as speakers or writers, they invite the reader to project onto them realist frames of cognition associated with the category "person" and to construct for them a subjective mental domain. With respect to personal or individuated narrators, Ryan also argues that the "worlds of their private domain form an integral part of the textual universe: the reader treats their beliefs, projections, wishes, and opinions as existing on a par with those of characters. The apprehension of the textual universe would remain incomplete without an assessment of the narrator's private domain" (70). Therefore it seems sensible to postulate for overt narrators an individual perspective or worldview similar to those private domains of the participants in the story that I have defined as character-perspectives. There are, however, obvious differences in the processes involved in the reader's construal of a character-perspective and in his or her reconstruction of a narrator's attitudes, beliefs, and system of values. While the reader constructs the perspectives of the various characters on the basis of what the narrator tells him or her about the characters' physical, verbal, and mental acts, a narrator-perspective manifests itself solely in what he or she says, that is, in the discourse that "reflects the contents of his or her mind" (113). In both cases, however, the pieces of information provided by the text are supplemented by inferences on the part of the reader.

Supplementing the concept of character-perspective with that of narrator-perspective provides a basis for applying the notion of perspective structure to an analysis of narrative texts. The semantic domain projected by a narrative text consists of a plurality of subjective world-models (cf. 4). The term *perspective structure* can be defined as the general system formed by all the character-perspectives and narrator-perspectives as well as by the patterns of relationships between them. It embraces the collection of all the character-perspectives and narrator-perspectives, whose relationships form what Margolin has called "larger designs or patterns of interrelations, be they actantial, ideological or formal-compositional" (1987: 109).

Before I incur the displeasure of those to whom all of this sounds suspiciously like some old hat from the paleostructuralist period, I should like to remove at least one possible source of misunderstanding. I hasten to add that from a constructivist point of view there is a clear answer to the intriguing question of whether a perspective structure as just defined is an objective reality or an operational hypothesis: such a structure is not inherent in a narrative text, but rather construed by the individual reader. By establishing relationships between the individual character-perspectives and narrator-perspective, he or she assigns not only meaning to a text but also a perspective structure. The perspective structure of a text is thus realized in the reading process.

On the Selection and Arrangement of Perspectives: Toward a Typology of Perspective Structures

After these definitions I will now turn to the question of how the reader's constitution of the perspective structure is influenced by the structural properties of the narrative text. The reader's construal of the relationships between the various perspectives is not hit or miss, but follows from certain techniques used to coordinate and to assess the individual perspectives. Since the form of the perspective structure depends on the selection and arrangement of the perspectives, it has both paradigmatic and syntagmatic dimensions (for the following, cf. Pfister 1988: 60ff.).

The paradigmatic aspect of the construction of a perspective structure consists in the selection of the individual perspectives. One can distinguish between the mere quantitative criterion of the number of perspectives that are established and the quality of the scope or diversification of a given perspective structure. A quantitative increase in the number of perspectives contributes to the complexity of the resulting perspective structure. This is even more true of the qualitative diversification of the perspectives. The greater the spectrum of social, moral, and/or ideological differences between the various character-perspectives, the more diversified and complex is the perspective structure that emerges.

Even more important for the construction of a perspective structure than selection is the way in which the individual perspectives are combined and coordinated syntagmatically. The contrasts and similarities between the characters can be used as a basis for analyzing the structural correlations of perspectives. There are a number of parameters that are relevant in most cases; Pfister calls them "suprahistorically relevant features" (1988: 167). These include gender, generational differences, social class, and race. In addition to these, the construction of the perspective structure of a text usually involves a wide range of psychological, moral, and ideological features. On the basis of the relevant semantic axes (cf. Bal 1985: 86–87; and Margolin 1987: 109) it is possible to construe the main opposing features between the character-perspectives and to establish a pattern of contrasts and correspondences. The perspective structure that results may therefore be represented as a matrix of distinguishing features, in which each character-perspective is assigned a specific set of traits (cf. Bal 1985: 86–88; and Pfister 1988: 169).

These categories for describing the selection and arrangement of perspectives allow us to analyze the scope, distribution, and configuration of perspectives in a given work. Moreover, they provide a basis for distinguishing between different types of perspective structure. A convenient place to begin for developing a typology of perspective structure is Pfister's distinction between "three idealised models for the perspective structure of dramatic texts," namely "a-perspectival structure," a "closed perspective structure," and an "open perspective structure" (65–68). Whereas in texts with an a-perspectival and closed perspective structure a "line of convergence that might draw all of the perspectives together" (67) is either explicitly stated or just implied, texts with an open perspective structure are characterized by unresolvable ideological discrepancies between the individual perspectives.

Useful though this typology is, I would like to propose three modifications. First, I suggest that one should dispense with what Pfister calls "the reception-perspective intended by the author" (58–64). As the self-betraying term already reveals, this not only lets the author, be it the implied-author (for a critique of this concept, cf. Nünning 1993) or the real author, in through the back door, but it also suggests that there is one correct interpretation, namely that which conforms to the authorially intended reception-perspective. Second, instead of distinguishing a limited number of ideal types, it is perhaps more rewarding to think of open and closed perspective structure, not as binary categories, but as poles of a continuum or the end points on a graded scale. Third, instead of using such a normative and problematic notion as authorially intended reception-perspective as the sole basis for the typological classification of a given text, I would briefly like to suggest four descriptive criteria for distinguishing between different types of perspective structure.

First of all, what needs to be taken into consideration is what Pfister calls "the degree of 'emphasis' given to each individual figure-perspective" (1988: 63). The term he uses to describe the differing degrees of emphasis applied to perspectives is *focus* (ibid.), which bears more than just terminological resemblance to Chatman's "interest-focus" (1986: 197–98). Focus here refers to the question of the degree to which the various character-perspectives are highlighted.

Second, there is the question of whether or not there is a hierarchy of perspectives. There may be a hierarchy either involving only the character-perspectives, or there may be a hierarchical relationship between them and a superordinate and all-encompassing narrator-perspective. Third, a question especially pertinent to the arrangement of perspectives in a narrative text is to what degree the narrator-perspective is individualized, and whether the narrative instance coordinates the various perspectives and integrates them into a unified worldview.

Fourth, since a broad scope of perspectives does not in itself result in an open perspective structure, the degree of homogeneity or intersubjectivity that the various perspectives display must be taken into consideration. Different types of perspective structure can be classified typologically according to the degree to which the individual perspectives overlap and converge toward a single dominating worldview or the degree to which they represent a plurality of conflicting moral and ideological stances. A highly diversified spectrum of character- and narrator-perspectives makes greater demands on the reader for coordinating the individual perspectives than a text with a more limited and less diversified set of perspectives. The broader and more differentiated the perspective structure of a text is, the more difficult it becomes, argues Pfister "to determine the focal point of all these diverging perspectives" (1988: 63).

This last criterion could serve as a basis for assigning to texts a place on a graded scale between what—following Bakhtin (1981)—one could call a monologic and a dialogic or polyphonic form of perspective structure.[3] In the case of the extreme monologic structure, perspectives are identical or complementary and converge in a single normative worldview. A dialogic perspective structure, by contrast, is characterized by unresolved conflicts between discrepant world-models. Since each of them has its own subjective validity, they typically challenge and relativize one another and thus undermine the notion of an authoritative worldview: "The dialogic relationship confronts unresolved contrary ideologies, opposing voices in which conflicting world-views resist submersion or cancellation" (Fowler 1983: 93).

The application of these criteria yields similar, but more flexible and differentiated possibilities of typological classifications than those achieved using Pfister's three ideal types of perspective structure. To explain the advantanges involved, I would like to illustrate what I have said with some examples and to apply the categories outlined to a description of the different perspective structures of

Stanzel's three typical narrative situations. At the risk of some oversimplification, they may be summed up briefly as follows (cf. Jahn & Nünning 1994: 290–92).

First-person narratives usually involve two main perspectives: the narrator-perspective represents the private domain of the homodiegetic narrator, whose worldview is conditioned by the knowledge, psychological dispositions, attitudes, and values of the narrating "I." Telling the story in retrospect and knowing its outcome, the narrating I has a wider perspective than the narrated or experiencing I, who previously inhabited the time and space of the story level (cf. Chatman 1986: 194). Since the first-person narrator remembers what the narrated I knew, experienced, thought, and felt, the character-perspective of the experiencing I is embedded in the cognitive domain of the narrating I. Figure 2 offers a simplified model of the perspective structure in first-person narrative.

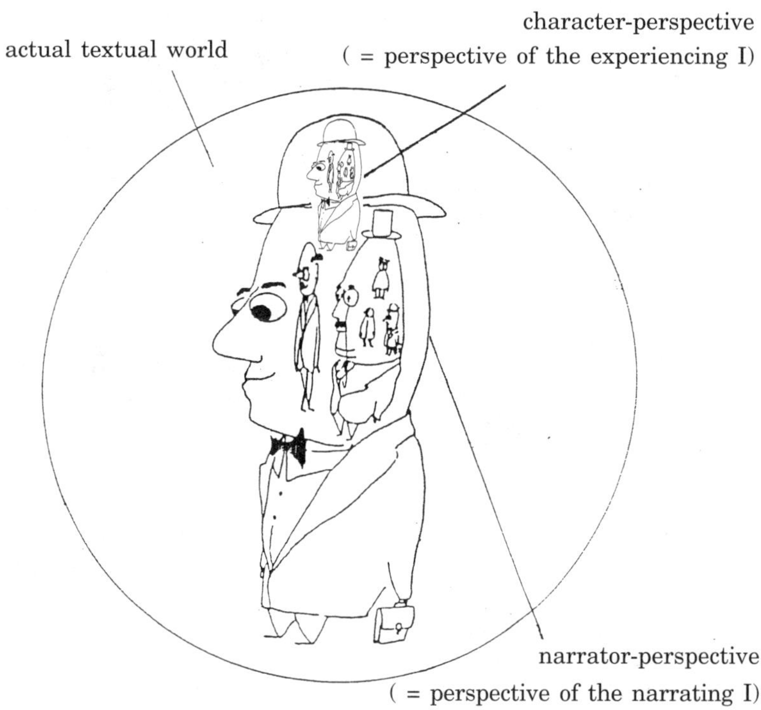

Fig. 12.2. Perspective structure in first-person narrative/texts with a homodiegetic narrator.

The format of the perspective structure in first-person narrative tends to highlight the discrepancy between the actual textual world and the subjective world-model of the experiencing I and the often equally partial recollections of the homodiegetic narrator. The degree to which subjective distortion is involved in a given work may vary from text to text, ranging all the way from the comparatively reliable accounts given by Defoe's *Robinson Crusoe* or Brontë's *Jane Eyre* to the mad monologuists one encounters in many of the fictions of Poe or Ian McEwan. Despite the advantages of hindsight, the narrating I is never omniscient: his or her perspective tends to be highly partial, biased, or even distorted as a result of the cognitive limitations and inherent subjectivity of the human mind.

By contrast, in what Stanzel calls "authorial narration," one does encounter an omniscient and usually omnipresent narrator endowed with an individuated perspective. Such a heterodiegetic, overt, and personalized narrator surveys the whole of the action, he conventionally knows everything, and the values he propounds provide a normative standard according to which all the character-perspectives are judged. The conventional perspective structure in authorial narration is represented graphically in figure 3.

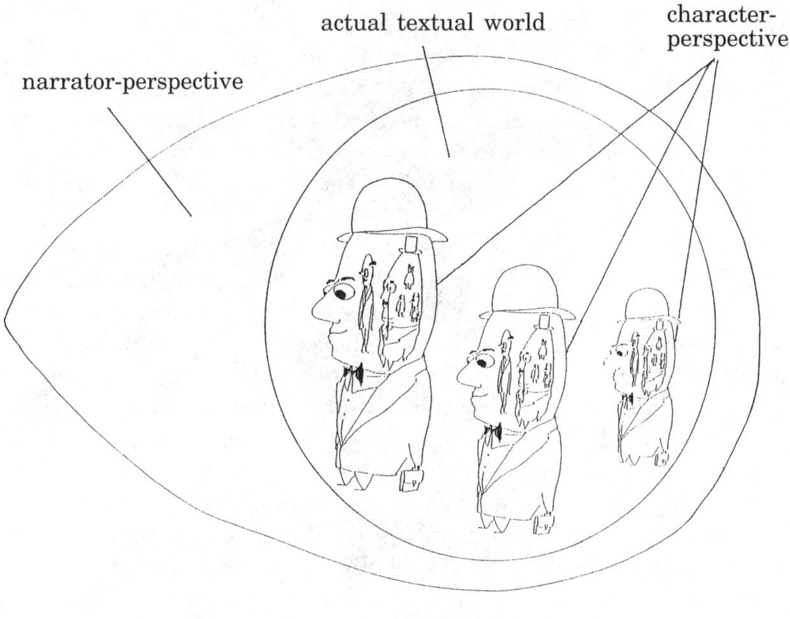

Fig. 12.3. Perspective structure in authorial narration/texts with a heterodiegetic and overt or personal narrator.

The narrator-perspective is represented by a cone-shaped field-of-vision in order to indicate what distinguishes it from the perspectives of full-fledged characters, which tend to be more anthropomorphized than the narrator. I have tried to illustrate that the authorial narrative situation usually involves a hierarchical arrangement of perspectives, with the character-perspectives being embedded in the narrator-perspective and with the narrator functioning as a controlling, coordinating, and integrating instance. Often, an authorial narrator is particularly interested in (and amused by) what the characters think, feel, believe they know, or do not know, Henry James's novel *What Maisie Knew* being an obvious case in point. Moreover, the character-perspectives are often evaluated by the authorial narrator, who explicitly comments on the cognitive limitations deriving from human subjectivity. A classical example of this is the role the narrative instance plays in many of George Eliot's novels. The individual's isolation and the distortions that a limited perspective gives rise to are the subject of many of the observations the narrator in *Middlemarch* makes. Anticipating later research into perspectivity, Eliot's narrator has the insight that each character is "the centre of his own world" (111) and thus accounts for the alienation that occurs between Lydgate and Rosamond: "Poor Lydgate! or shall I say, Poor Rosamond! Each lived in a world of which the other knew nothing" (195). From the subordinate perspectives of the characters, the reasons for the conflicts are only partially understandable, whereas from the superordinate perspective of the narrator the reader is made to understand that their respective views of one another are completely distorted.

In contrast to authorial narration, in the "figural narrative situation" the various character-perspectives tend to be coordinated on equal terms. The narrator withdraws or becomes covert, sometimes to the point of seeming to vanish altogether. The fact that there is no individuated narrator-perspective in figural narration is indicated in figure 4 by the dissolving contour of the narratorial field-of-vision.

In figural narration, the subjective perceptions, thoughts, feelings, and recollections that make up the various character-perspectives are not coördinated and controlled by a superordinate narrator-perspective. In multiperspectival novels, several character-perspectives may even be juxtaposed without a narrator acting as a mediator, and the different perspectives may qualify and relativize one another. Woolf's later novels, particularly *The Years* and *Between the Acts*, come to mind as typical examples of such a perspective structure.

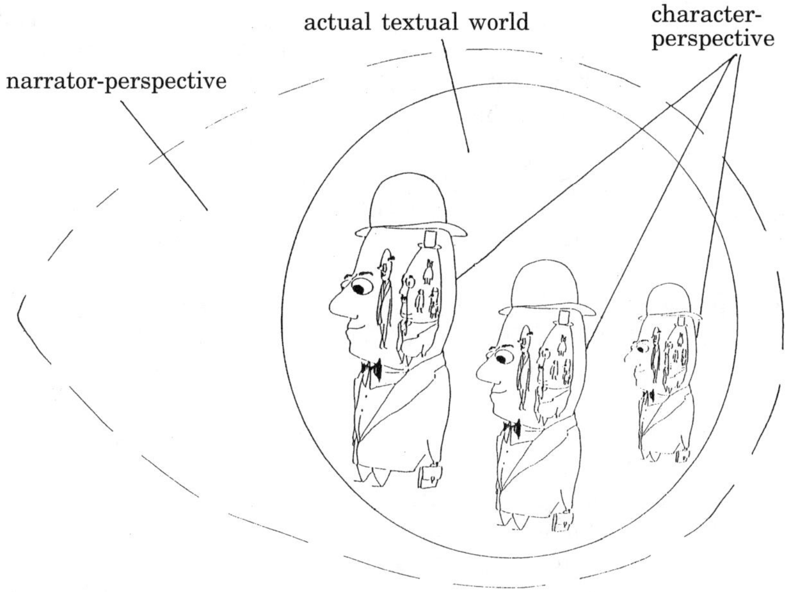

Fig. 12.4. Perspective structure in figural narration/texts with a heterodiegetic and covert or impersonal narrator.

Some Further Uses of the Conceptual Framework Delineated

Now that we have seen some simplified models and concrete examples of different types of perspective structures, let me conclude with a few brief indications of some of the new territories to be explored that such a framework for the analysis of perspective structure in narrative texts may open up. First, the proposed framework of distinctions provides a basis for describing the unique configuration of perspectives in specific novels. The study of perspective structure is the most rewarding in texts with a broad scope and great diversification of character-perspectives and with no superordinate overt narrator to control them and to evaluate their individual validity. Second, the notion of perspective structure can also be usefully applied in the as yet unwritten narratological history of the development of narrative techniques (cf. Fludernik 1996), for example, a study of the changes that occurred in the English novel between the late Victorian period and modernism could very well demonstrate the importance that alterations in perspective structure have had.

Third, such a theory of perspective structure may provide a basis for incorporating Bakhtin's (1981) challenging theory of the dialogic or polyphonic novel into narratology, something that is perhaps hovering in the back of the minds of many narratologists. Fourth, the framework delineated may provide an as yet missing conceptual bridge between narrators and characters as speakers in the process of narrative transmission and as the semantic focus to which sets of traits are ascribed (cf. Margolin 1983: 4). Fifth, another advantage of the approach outlined is that it supplies a convenient analytical tool for applying the notion of discrepant awareness to the study of perspective in narrative and for refining current theories of unreliable narration, because the concept of character-perspective accounts for discrepancies between the actual circumstances in the textual world and the characters' subjective interpretations. Sixth, the concept and typology of perspective structure may provide a basis for determining correlations between the structural properties of narrative texts and their cognitive, emotional, epistemological, and ideological implications. Lastly, a cognitive theory of perspectivity and a typology of perspective structures may be useful for determining which perspective a reader is likely to take and for understanding how readers make sense of a narrative as a whole.

Even if the proposed notions of character-perspective, narrator-perspective, and perspective structure do not meet with general approval, I would still argue that careful consideration should be be given to exploring configurations of cognitive perspectives, for at least three reasons: the concept of perspective structure draws attention to a hitherto neglected aspect of the impact of perspective on narratives, it offers a wide range of possible applications, and it may provide a way of demonstrating both the relevance of narrative structure for the meaning of texts and the usefulness of narratology for thematic and ideological criticism and for the writing of literary history.

Notes

1. The term *perspective structure* was coined by Pfister (1974, 1977: 91; 1988: 57). So far as I know there has never been any sustained attempt to apply Pfister's model to narrative texts except for Nünning (1989a: 64–83).

2. Compare Pfister, who specifies three idealized "models of this kind of implicit, evaluative ordering of figure-perspectives":

> 1) the symmetrical grouping of falsely orientated and diametrically opposed figure-perspectives around a central figure-perspective whose orientation coincides with the intended reception-perspective and only needs to be recognised as such by the receiver; 2) the contrasting of a correct figure-perspective and a false one, leaving the receiver to choose between them; 3) the contrasting of two opposite and extreme types of falsely orientated figure-perspectives in such a way as to persuade the audience to choose the "golden mean" as the intended reception-perspective. (1988: 65)

3. For an example of the application of Bakhtin's (1981) theory of the "polyphonic" novel to a narratological analysis of a novel, see Fowler (1983).

13

Situation Models and Point of View in Narrative Understanding

Daniel Morrow

Introduction

The present volume attests to a growing interest in bridging literary and cognitive approaches to understanding fiction. These approaches tend to have complementary goals and methods: Literary theorists often analyze the experience of understanding narrative worlds, using descriptive tools such as taxonomies of narrative perspective. Cognitive psychologists often start with similar observations about understanding narratives, and then empirically test theories of the mental processes underlying this phenomenology. Combining these approaches should lead to a more complete theory that relates phenomenology to cognitive processes involved in understanding fictional worlds (e.g., Dixon et al., 1993; van den Broek, Rohleder, & Narvaez 1994; and Gerrig 1993). In the present chapter, I start with some observations about the experience of reading narratives and then analyze several cognitive processes underlying this experience.

Readers are often said to "imagine" an unfolding world, guided by the narrative and by their knowledge and experience. This observation is elegantly put by Birkerts, who emphasizes the role of the reader's attention in this process: "If we are told in the early pages of a story that it is a rainy night, and if the descriptions have set us inside a drafty old house, then we naturally inhabit that context. Having brought a setting to life in our imaginations, and having invested it with the tones and shadings that are uniquely our own, we sustain it. . . . We work hard to establish the image, and then move our attention elsewhere; the image becomes part of the context through which we filter what we read" (1994: 97).

My colleagues and I have investigated how reader point of view relates to focus of attention during the process of "imagining" narrative worlds. Because comprehension depends on an interaction between the text and the reader, we analyze point of view both as a part of the narrative and as a reader response to the narrative (Dixon et al. 1993; Gerrig 1993).

Literary theory generally analyzes point of view as part of the narrative. An important distinction is between narrator and character point of view (e.g., Chatman 1990). The narrator's point of view (or *slant*) is anchored at the time of telling the story, while the character's point of view (or *filter*) is part of the "here and now" within the story world. Relations between narrator and character point of view are often complex. For example, narrators may be omniscient, presenting the inner lives of one or more characters, or they may have a more restricted point of view with limited access to characters' thoughts. Point of view is indicated by a variety of devices in narratives, for example, deictic expressions presuppose a point of view: In conversation, expressions such as "this" or "there" are used to refer to objects or places relative to the speaker's location. Similar devices occur in written narratives, where "extended deixis" indicates narrator or character point of view (Bühler 1982). Another pervasive device for indicating point of view is reporting or describing a character's thoughts and emotions (Leech & Short 1981). Thus, literary research has produced many insights about how point of view organizes narratives, and how it is signaled by a range of devices.

Cognitive psychologists are interested in how point of view helps organize the reader's mental processes during comprehension. Cognitive psychology provides a general account of the mental processes and representations involved in understanding narrative, which can help explain the role of point of view and focus of attention in comprehension. According to this approach, information is mentally represented in long-term memory in some form, such as a network of interconnected conceptual nodes. Perceiving a scene or understanding a description of this scene involves activation of the relevant nodes (e.g., Anderson 1980). At any moment, the amount of activation is limited; that is, we can only attend to, or think about, a limited amount of information (James 1950). This limitation on cognitive resources is conceptualized in different ways, such as a limited capacity mental workspace or working memory. A key issue for language comprehension is how we understand extended text such as narrative despite limitations in cognitive resources—how do we keep appropriate information active, or in focus, as we read (e.g., van Dijk & Kintsch, 1983; and Garrod & Sanford 1988)? One answer to this complex question is that the point of view adopted by a reader influences what information is focused in their representation of the narrative. The cognitive approach also suggests that comprehension depends on the amount of cognitive resources, which varies with age, reading ability, and other reader factors (Perfetti 1985; Stine 1995). Thus, reader point of view should depend both on how point of view is signaled in the narrative (as suggested by literary theory) and on these reader factors. Readers may take one or another point of view depending on the amount of available cognitive resources, what they already know about the narrative topic, or their interests (e.g., Gerrig 1993).

We have investigated the influence of narrative and reader factors on reader point of view within the framework of situation model theory, a cognitive approach to language comprehension that relates language to perception, where point of view plays an obvious role. According to this framework, readers understand narratives by creating a situation-model, which represents the narrative world described by the text rather than the text itself (Johnson-Laird 1983; van Dijk and Kintsch 1983). This assumption is echoed in many observations about understanding literary narrative, such as the following: "We read a few words at the beginning of the book or the particular story, and suddenly we find ourselves seeing not words on a page but a train moving through Russia. . . ." (Gardner 1984: 30–31). The situation model construct accommodates the complexity of narrative worlds since it represents character goals and emotions, temporal and causal coherence, and other aspects of the narrative world (e.g., Zwaan, Magliano, & Graesser 1995). The narrative world can be distinguished from the discourse context, because writers can present the same events in different orders or describe them at different levels of detail. However, the construct of situation model has primarily been used to represent the narrative world rather than the discourse context (but see Andringa & Davis 1994; and van Dijk 1995).

An important claim of the situation model approach is that models created from language, like those created from perception, are created from a point of view, with parts of the situation focused from this vantage point (e.g., Bryant, Tversky, & Franklin 1991).

In narratives, this point of view is associated with a "here/now" point (Morrow, Greenspan, & Bower 1987) or "deictic center" (Duchan, Bruder, & Hewitt 1995). This point is the location of the observer at the current moment of the narrative. It can be associated with a character, often the protagonist (Morrow 1985a; Garrod & Sanford 1988), or it can be associated with the narrator and thus external to the character. While point of view often shifts between character and narrator in the same narrative (Gerrig 1993; Millis 1995), we assume that readers tend to interpret each sentence in a narrative from a single point of view (Banfield 1982). By doing so, they establish a "focus space" in their situation model that is organized around a point of view (Sanders & Redeker, 1996). This is similar to the construct of explicit focus in cognitive theories of text processing, which contains the subset of highly activated information at any point during comprehension (e.g., Garrod & Sanford 1988).

Adopting a point of view should have a number of consequences for comprehension. First, adopting the protagonist's point of view should activate information about this character's thoughts, emotions, or goals, making it highly accessible from the situation model during comprehension. Taken to an extreme, this would mean that readers ignore information that is not relevant to the protagonist (Albrecht et. al., 1995). More likely, adopting a point of view will change relative levels of information accessibility. Second, switching point of view, or the changing focus of attention from the same point of view, may take time and slow comprehension (Black, Turner, & Bower 1979). Third, point of view should influence a variety of reader responses to the narrative, such as causal inferences or emotional reactions to events (Gerrig 1993; Tan 1994).

I will describe several empirical studies that examine how narrative cues influence reader focus of attention by indicating the narrative here/now point during comprehension. Because the here/now point depends in part on character location and on how this location changes as the narrative world unfolds, we examined cues such as verbs and prepositions, which express spatial and temporal information (Morrow 1986). The first study primarily examined relationships between reader focus and the here/now point associated with the physical location of the protagonist, which constrains the character's perceptual point of view. The second study examined how focus depends on the here/now point associated with the character's mental location, reflecting a more conceptual point of view. The third study directly examined the influence of reader as well as narrative factors, investigating if focus depends on how readers allocate cognitive resources such as working memory capacity during comprehension. These studies, like much of the situation model research, focuses on spatial aspects of narrative worlds such as the setting (see Morrow 1994, for a review), although we will see that reader focus of attention also depends on nonspatial aspects of narrative worlds, such as character goals.

Study 1: Point of View, Focus, and Protagonist Location

To investigate focus of attention in situation models, Bower, Greenspan, and I developed a technique to probe these representations during comprehension. We started with the assumption that readers are most likely to create situation models when the discourse relates to a well-established domain of knowledge. Thus, participants in our studies first learned about the layout of a building (a research center) that served as the setting for the narratives they would later read. This laboratory situation is similar to reading or listening to narratives that take place in familiar settings, such as when your sister calls and tells you that the old family house has just been flooded. Understanding such narratives requires creating a situation model from information in the narrative and from what is already known about the setting.

The first study examined if, when building a situation model, readers focus on information that is relevant to the protagonist's point of view (see Morrow, Greenspan, & Bower 1987 for more detail). We assumed that the protagonist's current location defines the narrative here/now point, and tested if objects close to the character were part of the reader's focus of attention and thus readily accessible from the situation model. After learning about the research center, participants read narratives such as the ones cited in Table 13.1. This narrative established Judy as the protagonist (e.g., by frequently mentioning the character as the subject of the main clauses) and encouraged readers to take her point of view, in part by describing her thoughts and emotions. Thus, the narrative here/now point was associated with this character, and her actions advanced this reference point within the narrative world. After introducing the protagonist's goal, the rest of the narrative described the character moving through the building in order to accomplish the goal.

Critical sentences described the protagonist moving from one room to another. This action was described in one of two ways,

Table 13.1
Example of Narratives in Study 1

[Introduction]

Judy had received several threatening notes in her mailbox at the research center, but she dismissed them as a joke.

She was trying to finish up a project so she worked late one night in the laboratory.

Her concentration was broken by the sound of a slamming door.

Then she heard footsteps in the distance.

She looked around the laboratory but didn't see anyone.

Suddenly she remembered the threatening notes and became frightened.

[Protagonist goal]

She decided to see if anyone else was in the building.

[Critical sentence]

While she was walking through the storage area toward the washroom, she glanced nervously behind the crates.

which was expected to influence the narrative here/now point and thus what readers focus on as they update their model (see fig. 1). In goal sentences (e.g., "Judy walked through the storage area into the washroom"), the action was described as completed, so that the character's current location was inside the goal room. In path sentences (e.g., "While Judy was walking through the storage area toward the washroom"), the action was described as in progress, with the character still on the path heading toward the goal. If readers update (see van Oostendorp, chap. 10 of this vol.) their situation model from the protagonist's point of view, they should understand the goal sentences by advancing the here/now point to the goal, so that the character's current location is focused. In addition, if focus depends on protagonist point of view, readers will focus on objects that the protagonist is thinking about even if these objects are not near the character. Therefore, readers should understand path sentences by establishing a here/now point that encompasses both the path room (the character's current location) and the goal room (the intended location). Presumably, the protagonist is thinking about objects in the goal as well as path rooms.

To test these predictions, after each critical sentence readers were presented a probe that named two objects from the research center (see fig. 1). Their task was to decide if the objects were from the same room or from different rooms of the building. As shown

Path Sentences

While she was walking through the storage area toward the washroom. . . .

Probe Type	Probed Room
1. Location Room (Path)	Storage Area (Dock, Lifter)
2. Mentioned Room (Goal)	Washroom (Sink, Lockers)
3. Other Room*	Experiment Room (Clock, Speakers)

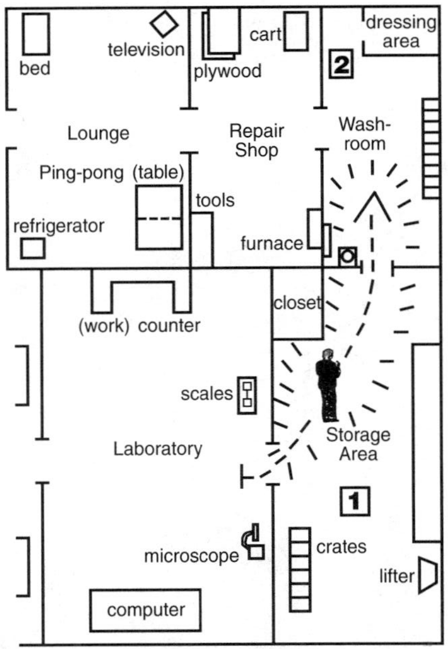

Goal Sentences

She walked through the storage area into the washroom.

Probe Type	Probed Room
1. Location Room (Goal)	Washroom (Sink, Lockers)
2. Mentioned Room (Path)	Storage Area (Dock, Lifter)
3. Other Room*	Experiment Room (Clock, Speakers)

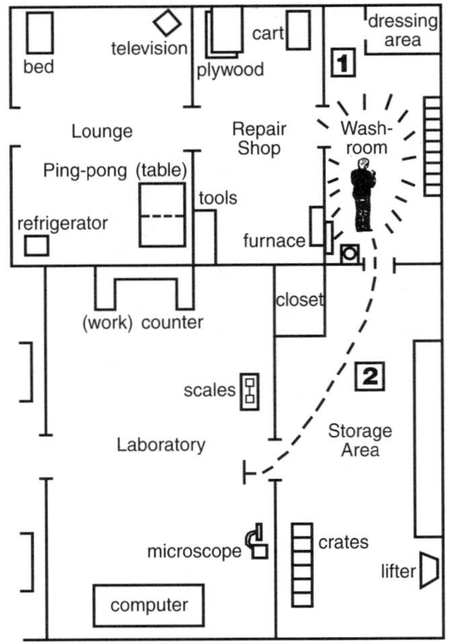

Fig. 13.1. Example of probe types for goal and path sentences in Study 1.

---

* The other room is in part of the layout not depicted in this figure.

in figure 1, we probed the character's current location, the other room mentioned in the critical sentence, and an unmentioned room that is out of the presumed focus of attention. For goal sentences, the location was the goal room and the mentioned room was the source of motion, while for path sentences the protagonist's location was the path room and the mentioned room was now the goal. If probe time reflects focus of attention in the situation model, readers should answer location (goal) probes faster than the other probes after goal sentences, but the location (path) and mentioned room (goal) probes should be equally fast after path sentences, and faster than unmentioned room probes.

Figure 2 presents the response times for location, mentioned, and other (unmentioned) room probes after goal and path sentences. As expected, the two sentences produced a different pattern of focus in readers' situation models. After goal sentences, readers

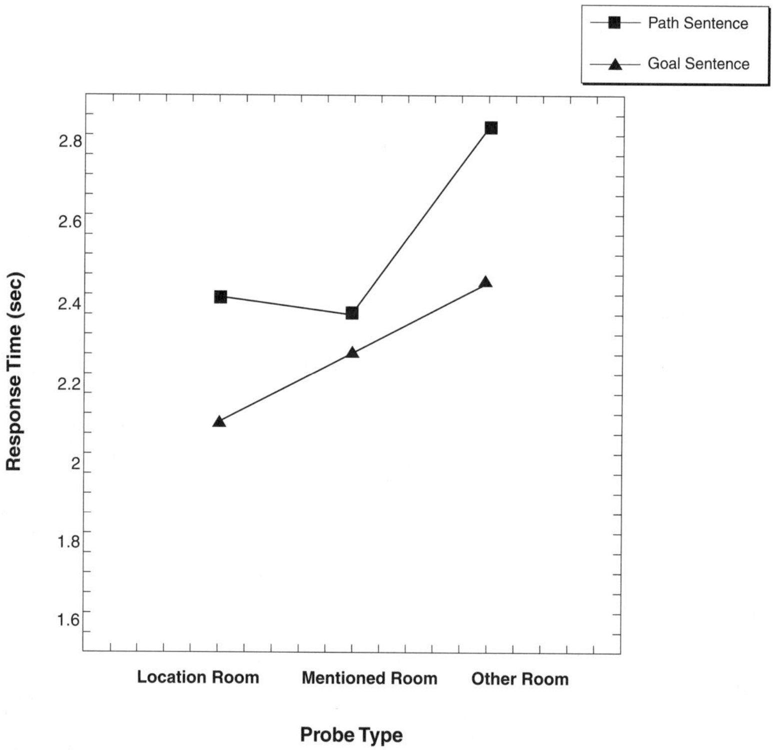

Fig. 12.2. Response time for probe types after goal and path sentences in Study 1 (from Morrow, Greenspan, & Bower 1987).

focused on the protagonist's current location (the goal room) more than on distant locations. After path sentences, however, they focused on the current location (the path in this case), but in addition they focused on the protagonist's intended location (the goal room). Morrow (1985b) also contrasted narratives that either described the protagonist as on the path or as inside the goal room. In this study, the critical sentence was followed by a sentence that referred to an object from the character's point of view, as in the following example: "Sally walked through the living room toward [into] the bedroom. The chair in this room needs to be fixed, she thought." When the protagonist was on the path, readers indicated that she was thinking about goal as well as path objects (e.g., chair in the bedroom or living room). When the character had reached the goal room, readers indicated that the protagonist was only thinking of objects in this room. Both in the earlier described probe study and in this study, the narrative here/now expands to include the protagonist's intended goal as well as the current location when the character is on the path. Thus, readers tend to focus on information that is relevant to the protagonist's perceptual point of view (also see Bryant, Tversky, & Franklin, 1991). In addition, the fact that the protagonist's intended as well as current location is focused suggests that point of view is conceptual as well as perceptual.

While the first study suggests that readers construct situation models from the protagonist's point of view, it is also possible that readers in our study adopted the point of view of an audience, viewing the described situation from a stance external to the character (Albrecht et al. 1995). An external point of view is consistent with a focus on protagonist locations because readers can focus on this location from an audience point of view. However, the external point of view explanation has a tougher time explaining why the intended as well as current location is focused when the protagonist is on the path. With a character-external point of view, focus should not be influenced by the protagonist's thoughts and goals.

Study 2: Focus and Protagonist Mental Location

The second study provides stronger evidence that readers can adopt a protagonist point of view by linking reader focus of attention to the protagonist's mental location (see Morrow, Bower, & Greenspan 1989 for detail). In the situation investigated in this study, the protagonist was in one room of the research center, but was thinking about a different room (e.g., "Wilbur [in the laboratory] thought the office should be rearranged to make room for a display of current research"). In this case, the narrative here/now point is projected from the character's physical location to the mental location, so that the situation is more clearly "filtered" through the character's experience than in the first study. According to the situation model approach, the mental verb in the critical sentence (e.g., "think" and "wonder") specifies an embedded focus space in the model that is organized around the protagonist's point of view (Sanders & Redeker, 1996). To test if readers shifted their focus to the character's mental location when reading the critical sentence, we used the same technique as before and probed both the protagonist's physical and mental locations (as well as an unmentioned room) after the critical "thought" sentences in the narratives.

Mental location probe times were faster (mean *RT* = 2.18 sec.) than either the physical location (*RT* = 2.36 sec.) or the unmentioned room (*RT* = 2.35 sec.), showing that readers focused on the protagonist's mental location more than on the physical location. Moreover, control conditions showed that readers did not focus on the mental location simply because it was last mentioned before the probe.

Both of these studies suggest that readers sometimes create situation models by focusing on information relevant to the protagonist's perceptual or conceptual point of view. My recent work has investigated if the focus of attention is influenced by reader as well as by narrative factors. This research has used reading time rather than probe time to measure focus, because this measure is part of reading and thus eliminates the possibility that the probe task itself shapes focus strategies (Wilson et al. 1993).

Study 3: Focus and Reader Age

The third as well as the second study examined if readers shift their focus of attention in order to keep track of the protagonist's mental location (viz., Graesser et al., chap. 15 of this vol. to this end). If the process of shifting focus requires a certain level of cognitive resources, readers who are able to devote these resources are more likely to successfully update their situation model from the protagonist's point of view. Therefore, we examined the influence of reader age and level of cognitive resources on point of view and focus of attention (see Morrow et al., 1997, for more detail).

While the previous study examined reader focus of attention after the protagonist was already thinking about a location, we now examined the process of shifting focus to this mental location in the first place. Participants read narratives with critical sentences that described the protagonist walking from one room (the source) through an unmentioned path room into a goal room (e.g., "Maria walked from the office" [through the conference room] into the library). The critical sentence was followed by a target sentence that described the protagonist thinking about an object either in the goal, path, source, or some other unrelated room ("She remembered that she had seen a package beside the copier [in the library]/table [in the conference room]/picture [in the office]/loading dock" [in the storage area]). As in the previous study, readers should establish a focus space in their situation model that is organized around the protagonist's point of view, shifting the narrative here/now point from the goal room (the current location) to this mental location. If readers update their model from the protagonist's point of view, they should read more slowly those sentences that require a shift of attention in order to follow the protagonist's mental location. We also varied whether the target sentence explicitly mentioned the room containing the object. Mentioning this location should help readers shift their focus in the situation model.

Focus of attention may also depend on reader age as well as on narrative factors. We examined the influence of aging because older and younger readers tend to differ in ways that are relevant to narrative understanding. Because older readers generally have fewer cognitive resources (Salthouse 1991), comparing older and younger readers may provide insights into the role of cognitive resources in updating situation models. Although older adults may have fewer cognitive resources than younger adults, they often bring a broader context of knowledge and experience to reading, which may compensate for resource declines, for example, they may maintain the protagonist's point of view as a way to remain engaged in the narrative world despite resource declines. To examine the success of focus strategies during comprehension, we compared readers who were more or less accurate in answering questions after each narrative.

The study involved older adults (60–80 years of age) and younger adults (20–30 years of age). Older participants had a lower mean score on a sentence span task, which measured verbal working memory capacity. The procedure was the same as before, except that participants read target sentences rather than responding to probes after the critical sentences.

Figure 3 shows that readers took longer to read sentences that described the protagonist thinking about more distant locations, suggesting that they needed additional time to shift the narrative here/now point associated with the protagonist's mental location. Rinck and Bower (1995) have found the same pattern for younger adults under a variety of layout learning and narrative conditions. Older adults in our study slowed more dramatically than younger adults when reading sentences about distant mental locations. An earlier study found a similar pattern when we probed locations that were near to or far from the protagonist (Morrow et al., 1994). Both findings are consistent with theories of age-related resource declines (Salthouse 1991). In addition, the fact that older readers showed the same pattern as younger readers suggests that both age groups updated their situation model from the protagonist's point of view.

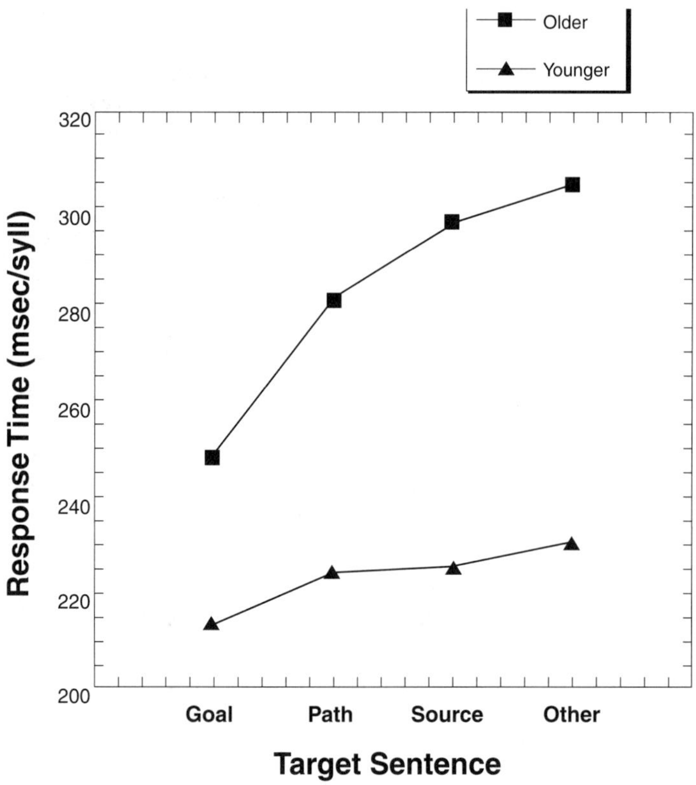

Fig. 12.3. Target sentence reading time for goal, path, source, and other room sentences in Study 3 (from Morrow et al. 1997).

Readers in the present study also slowed down for sentences that did not mention the room containing the target object. Older readers who understood the narrative most accurately especially slowed down when the room was not mentioned, suggesting that they used a different strategy than younger readers in order to maintain an accurate situation model. Successful readers in both groups were especially likely to slow down when reading sentences that described the protagonist thinking about objects in distant rooms that were not mentioned in the sentence. These readers also had more cognitive resources than the less accurate readers: They had higher sentence span scores. Thus, tracking the narrative here/now point during reading places demands on cognitive resources, and readers who can devote these resources are more likely to successfully update their situation model.

Our analysis assumes that maintaining the protagonist's point of view is a component of updating an accurate situation model. More phenomenologically, maintaining a point of view may help the reader remain involved in the narrative world. Miall and Kuiken (1994) found that readers slow down at those points in narratives that invite involvement, for example, by interpreting the described situations in terms of past experiences. While this study differs from our studies in many ways, both lines of research suggest that a slower reading pace indicates greater engagement with the narrative world rather than, or in addition to, difficulty in understanding the text. In future studies, my colleagues and I hope to understand the focus of attention both as a cognitive process and as a means of maintaining involvement in the narrative world. Our study also suggests that examining readers who vary in cognitive resources, background knowledge, or on other dimensions provides a tool for investigating the ability to create situation models of narrative worlds.

Conclusions

I conclude by suggesting how the situation model approach can help explain the comprehension of more complex narratives, and how this approach can be enriched by considering how readers interpret literary forms of narrative. First, the technique in our studies can be used to explore cognitive mechanisms underlying a variety of phenomena related to point of view. The narratives in our studies simplified relationships between character and narrator point of view in order to explore protagonist point of view. Yet many narratives require readers to shift between character and narrator perspective (Millis 1995), or require readers to keep track of information known by the narrator but not by the character, for example, in a narrative that describes a bomb located near an unsuspecting protagonist, our technique might reveal if readers focus on both the protagonist and bomb locations. If so, this "dual focus" may influence other aspects of narrative understanding, such as the reader's emotional responses to the narrative, for example, the reader's suspense may increase as the distance between character and danger closes (Gerrig 1993). The ability to maintain a dual focus may depend on reader factors such as the level of available cognitive resources, as well as on the narrative (Lee-Samson & Whitney 1991). Such studies would not only show that situation models are multidimensional representations (e.g., Zwaan, Magliano, & Graesser 1995), but help analyze how readers integrate spatial, emotional, and other aspects of the narrative world in order to create a situation model (Tan 1994). Research on point of view would also help expand the construct of situation model to include the discourse context as well as the narrative world (van Dijk 1995).

Finally, the situation model approach may help explain how readers understand more literary forms of narrative. To illustrate, I close with a few suggestions about the role of point of view and focus of attention in how readers might understand a passage from *The Road to Wellville*. Charlie, the protagonist of the passage, is a young man with high hopes of breaking into the lucrative but fiercely competitive breakfast food industry at the beginning of this century. In this passage, Charlie is investigating an abandoned factory as a possible site for his new enterprise:

> ... he kicked his way through the debris to the big open back room to have a look at the ovens. A bird shot across the room and out into the gathering dark as he came through the open doorway, and something—rats?—stirred in the far corner.
>
> Then it was quiet. Eerily still.
>
> Two of the great three-story ovens remained, rising up out of the ruins and into the sky, rusted, battered, strewn with swallow's nests.... For a long moment he stood there in awe of the machinery before him, and in that moment he was an archaeologist, a treasure hunter come upon the undreamed of temple, the rare find, the jewel. He was

> stunned. This was the source, the fount; this was where all those cereal flakes had come from. . . . (Boyle 1993: 128)

Several devices in this passage invite readers to adopt Charlie's point of view on the scene, both perceptually (deictic expressions such as "this," "before him," and "the far corner") and more conceptually (reporting the character's thoughts and feelings). Thus, the narrative here/now point is associated with Charlie as he explores the ruined building, and information about the factory should be more focused in the reader's situation model than other information, such as Charlie's taxi ride from his hotel to the factory. The here/now point may also influence how the reader connects the currently described situation to previous situations in the book. Because readers "see" the scene from Charlie's point of view, they not only focus on salient parts of the scene such as the ovens, but may retrieve relevant information that was mentioned earlier, which elaborates their interpretation of the current situation, for example, Charlie's excited reaction to the ovens may remind readers of his ambition to succeed in the breakfast food industry, as well as his gullibility (readers may thus adopt both Charlie's point of view and an ironic narrator's point of view—another example of dual focus). Finally, the spatial/visual structure of the situation may help connect this situation with more global aspects of the situation model by conveying larger narrative themes. The image of Charlie looking up at the ruined roaster also deftly foreshadows his doomed aspirations in the breakfast food industry. In this way, readers are prepared for larger themes by constructing a situation model of this scene early in the book.

These observations are meant to illustrate possible cognitive mechanisms underlying the comprehension of literary narrative as well as the simpler narratives investigated in our studies. Hopefully, they hint at how phenomenological analysis and empirical testing of mechanisms underlying the experience of reading provide complementary tools for exploring narrative worlds.

Notes

1. Preparation of this chapter was supported by NIA grant R01 AG12163. I am grateful to Elizabeth Stine-Morrow for many thoughtful comments on the chapter. Correspondence should be addressed to Daniel Morrow, Department of Psychology, Conant Hall, University of New Hampshire, Durham, NH 03824 (email: dgm@hopper.unh.edu).

14

Collective Perspective, Individual Perspective, and the Speaker in Between: On "We" Literary Narratives

Uri Margolin

"We" and Narration

The Range of "We" Discourses

A literary narrative is always someone's story, this someone being defined relative to the superordinate textual voice. The vast majority of literary narratives has always been narrated in the first-person singular or the third person. Standard narratological models have accordingly restricted themselves to these so-called "Ich" and "Er" forms. Nevertheless, several innovative writers, especially in our own age, have opted for the highly marked "you" (see also Fludernik, chap. 6 of this vol.) and "we" forms, forms that necessitate a corresponding enlargement and/or modification of traditional models, as well as raising the question of their possible aesthetic and cognitive motivation. In the present chapter, I shall seek to outline some of the salient features of the narrative "we" as speech position/role or narrative-voice indicator, as focalizer-experiencer, and as a narrated entity, a collectivity defined by some kind of internal relations, and engaged in a series of activities.

The "We" Pronoun and the Communicative Situation

A natural point of departure for the study of "we" discourses in general is an examination of the nature of "we," or the first-person plural pronoun, in terms of its function and reference. One might be tempted to understand "we" as a simple multiplication, replication, or extension of the "I," at least in its role as speaker, functioning as an indicator of the multiple or shared origin of the ongoing discourse. A closer examination will reveal, though, that this is usually not the case, and that "we" occupies in fact an intermediate position between the sender role (I), and those of the second and third persons (not-I). The reference class of any token of "we" must indeed by definition consist of at least two individuals, at least one of whom is the utterer of the current token of "we," hence *we* = *I* + *other(s)*, or speaker + augmentation. But these additional persons may not be co-utterers of the current piece of discourse, oral or written, and may not even be participants in the ongoing communicative transaction. In other words, their roles may be restricted to those of receiver or topic entity, and "we," unlike "I," can thus be wider in its scope than the "we" sayer(s). Moving from communicative role to reference class, we can see that unlike "I," and like all other pronouns, a token of "we" uttered by someone cannot, in and by itself, uniquely identify its reference class. While any I + you (singular or plural) conjunction generates a "we," the reverse is not true, since "we" can also generate "I" + "she" or "he," and so forth. Furthermore, while each token of "I," picks out uniquely its utterer, different tokens of "we," uttered by different speakers or groups of speakers, may still pick out exactly the same reference class. Conversely, different tokens of "we," uttered by the same speaker on different occasions, may pick out classes whose shared membership is limited to this speaker alone. Once more, unlike "I" but like "you" (singular or plural), readers or overhearers may appropriate tokens of "we" as applying to them even if they are not part of the initial or intended reference group. The intermediate position of "we" extends from reference to intensional contexts as well. Every "I" sayer has by definition immediate epistemic access to his or her own sensations, mental states, and episodes. On the other hand, any "we" sayer who makes assertions such as "we felt that" or "our current state of mind is" combines in fact immediate inside knowledge regarding his or her own internal states with beliefs (second- or third-person attributions), based upon inference from external data, concerning the internal states of the other individuals in the "we" reference class.

"We" Utterances and Speaker Empowerment

As we have just seen, the relation between the "we" utterer and the reference class denoted by this token of "we" is not unique, but rather allows for a whole range of possibilities. In principle, four cases are conceivable. (1) All members of the reference class utter jointly as one speaking entity this token of "we," making them joint simultaneous originators of the current discourse. Good examples are collective prayers and hymns, such as those found in the book of Psalms or the prayer books of church and synagogue. (2) A proper subset (at least two individuals) of a wider class utters a token of "we" in unison to refer to the whole class. Such a subgroup speaking collectively about, and possibly also for, its larger reference group is best illustrated by the delegation or group of representatives making representations or reporting to an outside recipient(s). The prime literary example is probably the chorus of twenty-five to thirty people on stage in Greek tragedy, addressing their king/queen or the gods on behalf of the citizenry as a whole (cf. Van Peer, chap. 19 of this vol.) (3) Several or all members of the class utter tokens of "we" individually, in succession, or alternately, to refer to the whole class. This is exemplified by John Barth's novel *Sabbatical* (1982), in which the two members of a couple alternate in their oral accounts of their joint sabbatical adventures. (4) A single member of the class utters all tokens of "we" in a given stretch of discourse to refer to the whole class. The most common example is the speaker who provides nongroup members with an account of what befell his group or what they did, such as the convener or chairperson who signs a "we did" report.

In cases (2)–(4), but most acutely in case (4), the question immediately arises whether or not the speaker(s) are empowered to speak on behalf of the reference class as a whole, thus conveying a joint/common communicative intent. If they do, they are speaking *for* the group, not only *about* it, and their utterances possess the status of group or collective speech acts. If they are not so empowered, the tokens of "we" in their discourse cannot designate the originators of this discourse, but only its topic entity. The "we" sayer(s) can indeed speak about their group as a whole, but the authority and illocutionary force of their "we" speech acts rest with them individually.

Specific Features of Literary "We" Narration

Having surveyed the major speech situations that can be associated with "we" utterances, one is now in a better position to enumerate the distinctive features of literary "we" narration. The list of eleven points that follows is in part inductive, based on the examination of a limited corpus (see references), and in part deductive, inferred from the foregoing theoretical considerations. Like all models, it is tentative and open to revisions motivated by either the occurrence of new literary texts or by a change in the theoretical perspective adopted.

1. There is always a single "we" sayer on the highest level of textual embedding. In most cases, this sayer/narrator stays the same throughout the text, while in a few there are two "we" sayers who alternate (Barth, Brechon & Brechon, possibly Faulkner 1930). In almost all cases this "we" sayer explicitly refers to himself/herself as speech participant and as participant in the narrated events by means of "I." Only in three texts (Armah 1973; Faulkner and Silvain 1971) is there a total absence of "I" on the levels of narration and narrated alike, turning the speaker into an unspecified voice emanating from somewhere within the group. An interesting complication in this respect is presented by Brechon and Brechon (1974). Within the fiction, the husband and wife, Nicolas and Anne, express to each other their views on their past joint life through an exchange of letters, so that each token of "we" in the text stems from a single speaker. But since the actual text is jointly produced and signed by both Arlette and Robert Brechon, all tokens of "we" in the discourse originate literally and actually from a joint or collective writing activity.

2. There are numerous instances of "we" in the narrator's discourse and the majority of them refer to the narrated rather than to narrational sphere. The speech acts of the narrator concerning this "we" are primarily constative (reporting) rather than expressive or performative, as opposed to the lyrical "we."

3. The nature or identity of the "we" group spoken of is defined by features belonging to the narrated domain: a system of roles, institutional structures, and relations that transcends and usually also precedes the current communicative transaction.

4. Consequently, what the "we" sayer asserts about her group concerns its identity, relations, states, and activities in the narrated sphere, which is usually in the past with respect to the time of narration, but sometimes contemporaneous with it (Helprin 1981; parts of Silvain).

5. The "we" sayer is not a designated spokesperson for G, the group referred to by "we," and of which s/he is a member. The "we" sayer thus speaks about this group, not for it, unlike the lyrical persona, where, for example, the lover in "we" discourses speaks for the couple. The literary narrative "we" speech act is hence not

a group speech act, because its content is neither negotiated nor consensual.

6. The addressee of the narrator may be other member(s) of the "we" group or the anonymous multiple narratees of most fiction, but not a specific named outside individual or group. Even when the addressee is another member of G (Brechon & Brechon, White 1978, Wohmann 1975), s/he is not in the present sender's immediate deictic field and is hence an addressee at a distance, again unlike the lyrical lovers' discourse, where the beloved is often there to listen to the lover's pronouncements.

7. Since the narrator is not speaking on behalf of any G, the reference group designated by tokens of "we" in her discourse may shift in identity, scope, size, and temporal location in the course of the narration. In *A Rose for Emily* (1930), for example, most "we" references are to the townspeople, a community that encompasses three different generations, not all of whom could be alive together at any given moment. And in one place at least the "we" is narrowed down to the town's administration, the "we" who sent Emily a tax notice every December. In Armah's *Two Thousand Seasons* (1973), no less than half a dozen reference groups with complex relations of inclusion or partial overlap can be distinguished. These include contemporary African writers and political activists ("the people of the way"); all Africans who fought actively against colonialism; all those who possess an African identity or self-consciousness; all contemporary Africans; specific past generations of Africans, such as the first victims of slavery; and, finally all Africans of the past one thousand years (= two thousand seasons).

8. Since the "we" narrator is not speaking as *pars pro toto* but only as an individual member of G, s/he can on occasion dissociate him/herself from the other members of G, thus subdividing the we group into an I + you or I + s/he, two subgroups that may differ regarding both certain narrated events and their current evaluation (Brechon & Brechon, White, Wohmann). In a later text segment, though, the individual "we" sayer may return to the common/general "we" stance and perspective regarding some other past events and their current significance. In this precise sense, a "we" narrative is the only narrative mode that can alternately be homo- or autodiegetic (= about the speaker) and heterodiegetic (= about others) without change of speaker. This too is ultimately rooted in general linguistic possibilities. It is not contradictory to say, for example, "We accepted their offer, but I voted against it."

9. Not speaking on behalf of G, the "we" narrator has no access to the current communicative intentions or expectations of any of its other members, since his/her speech act is not preceded by group deliberations. By the same token, the narrator is not under any communicative obligations to the group, except self-imposed ones, and the perspective and evaluative stance s/he adopts toward the narrated events may be his/her specific individual one.

10. As in first-person singular narratives, the "we" sayer's perspective on the narrated events is from within this system. After all, the story s/he is telling, the actions and states s/he is recounting, are at least in part his/her own. But whenever mental factors, such as the beliefs, attitudes, internal states, and episodes of other members of the narrated we group are concerned, the "we" sayer's only knowledge of them is indirect, based on his/her inferences from the others' behavior and claims in interpersonal space. Any "we felt," "we thought," "it occurred to us" statement in a first-person plural narrative, unlike "we ran" or "we found ourselves at," is internally heterogeneous, based as it is on the individual speaker's immediate knowledge of his/her own psyche, and on (defeasible) hypotheses formed by this "we" sayer regarding his/her coagents. Once again, "we" turns out to be I + other(s), not I + I.

11. "We" assertions made by a single teller, and narrating the perceiving or focalizing activities of the "we" sayer + one or more other(s) are every bit as problematic and heterogeneous, and for the very same reason. There are some "we" narratives (Faulkner and Mann 1930) in which the collectivity in question acts primarily as witness, observer, or mediating instance of the narrated system rather than as its main agent. But collective observation statements of the "we saw" or "we noticed" variety are once again a hybrid of the "we" sayer's own immediate sense experiences and of the presumed experiences ascribed to the cofocalizers by the speaker on the basis of their public actions and statements. After all, one can no more directly know what and how much someone else sees or hears than one can know what they think or feel.

"We" and the Narrated

The Nature of Narrated "We" Groups

Whenever a reference to a "we" in the narrated domain is made in a discourse, a group of some sort is immediately evoked. Three fundamental dimensions for the description of any group phenomenon are: its identity, structure, and properties—both collective and distributive—(2.0), its activities (2.1), and its self-awareness or self-image (2.2). At one extreme, any random collection of individuals could be regarded as an ad hoc group. At the other extreme, when a group is defined solely through a transpersonal, institutional aspect, such as a role or function it performs collectively (the military or the judiciary), sight is lost of the specific individuals who embody it at any given point in time. The literary "we" narratives examined follow a middle course in this respect. On the one hand, the groups involved are definitely more than mere aggregates: they are collectives, and are so described. On the other hand, some specific individual members are always singled out and presented as essential to the very identity of the group.

Issues helpful in drawing up the profile of any literary "we" group along the individual/collective axis, might include the following:

a. Size of the group and its extension in space and time. Quite a number of the texts surveyed focus on the smallest possible group: the couple (including the homosexual one in White's novel). Mann chose a family (parents and children) as his focalizers, and for Silvain it is a small isolated task group of technicians charged with the maintenance of a windmill and water reservoirs in the desert. Helprin and Senesi have larger groups of undefined size: the boys, the soldiers, but all of them are copresent in the narrated actions and events. The same cannot be said of Faulkner and Armah's narratives, where the collectivities stretch out over several, or even many generations. In these two cases, the groups tend indeed toward the institutional, the southern townspeople and the people of Africa respectively.

b. Number and nature of the aspects that go into the definition of the group. Some examples are a marital relation, a family bond, age, shared social role, geographic location, nation, and race. A closely related issue is the number and dimensional diversity of the additional collective, nondistributive predicates possessed by the group as a higher order unit.

c. Degree of individual diversity among members of the group. Do they merge into collective anonymity, looking and acting like exact replicas of the same mould, or do they rather stand out as distinct, relatively autonomous agents? There are, for example, sharp contrasts among different members of the African "we" (Armah), whereas Silvain's technicians are often indistinguishable regarding their mannerisms, daily actions, ways of speaking, thinking, and even dreaming[!].

d. Division into subgroups. The dynamics of a group as a whole and its action or failure to act often stem from the existence within it of subgroups. For each "we" group it is therefore important to determine the number, if any, of its subgroups, the lines along which they are divided (e.g., age in Mann, Helprin, Faulkner, and Senesi or ideology in Armah), and the nature of the interactions among them (cooperation, indifference, and antagonism). Divisions inside a group inevitably thematize and problematize the possibility of ultimate integration being achieved. In Helprin's story, for example, old and young soldiers, initially divided by experience and attitude, manage to achieve a commonality of goals and action, while the source of Africa's tragedy, according to Armah, is the unbridgeable gap between the People of the Way and the rest. Finally, since a social group is minimally composed of two persons who form its singleton subgroups, one could well regard "we" stories about the interaction between members of a couple (Brechon & Brechon, Barth, and Wohmann) as a limit case of stories portraying collective entities and their inner dynamics from the unique internal plural perspective.

Collective "We" Actions

Not all actions undertaken by members of a collective, whether simultaneously or in succession, are joint actions, but it is precisely joint actions that form the core of several-as-one or plural agency, and that define the specificity of the "we" agential situation. In the absence of joint action, the group cannot tell a sustained "we" or shared narrative, and its collective aspect may remain confined to the bare minimum: the group defining properties together with unactualized potentialities of joint action. At the same time, the actions that do take place may remain separate individual ones. A prime example is Wohmann's story, where the couple fail to act jointly, possibly due to failure of communication and disparity of attitudes and wishes. In Armah's novel, joint action does take place within the subgroup of People of the Way, but, due to total disparity of goals and values between it and other African subgroups, the people as a whole (i.e., the widest group) are not able to carry out any joint actions. On the other hand, the boys (Senesi), the technicians (Silvain), the soldiers (Helprin), and members of the two couples (Barth and Brechon) manage to perform joint actions, either from the very outset or as a result of joint striving. To be more precise, the two couples are engaged in an ongoing joint communicative enterprise of recollecting, recording, or inventing their own joint actions (past or present, real or invented) with the common goal of producing the very texts we are actually reading.

But what does such multiperson joint action consist of, and what makes it possible in the first place? Several components seem to be indispensable for bringing about such a complex phenomenon. One is a view of the other(s) as potentially cooperative agent(s), and the at least partial success of interpersonal communication. Second comes the formulation and endorsement of shared goals by several members of the group. Third, and of crucial importance, is a joint commitment by members of the group to act as a body in order to achieve the shared goals ("Let us do X") and a readiness to place such shared goals, and their attendant plans and interests, above individual goals. Helprin's story is an excellent illustration of these different stages of preparation for joint action, in this case, going into battle.

The Individual's Sense of Being Part of a "We" Group

Whoever says "we," as in "we shall do X" or "we are thus and so," seems to acknowledge the existence of a collective plural subject, an I + other(s), of which the speakers feel themselves part and parcel, of a group of people linked by some tie, each of whom sharing with the "we" sayer some beliefs, attitudes, values, and propensities for action. At issue is not whether such a group may or may not be said to exist when examined by an impartial external observer, but rather that speakers have a sense of "'us" or "we-ness" with respect to a certain group, and that this sense forms a central component of their self-awareness, self-consciousness, or self-image. If such a belief with respect to oneself, several other individuals, and the same collectivity as a whole is shared by several individuals, then this group exists as a fact of social psychology, and forms indeed a collective subject.

The general feeling of "we-ness" or "us" and its specific content for members of a given group can in principle be described from the outside in the third-person plural, especially in literature, where unrestricted access by the narrator to the minds of others is a constitutive convention. But a more effective, immediate, and convincing manner of expressing this reflexive dimension is to let its possessors speak for themselves "from within," so to speak, as members of their chosen reference group. This may indeed be one of the main reasons why creative writers choose this mode when portraying a collective plural subject, especially in lyrical poetry. One can distinguish several ever stronger strands of which the individual subjects' sense of we-ness may be woven:

1. The individuals think of themselves and define their public or social identity primarily on the basis of their membership in a larger, transindividual group defined intensionally, that is, according to some underlying common properties. The community thus precedes the individual subject, who has the ability to speak and act only by virtue of being its member, and who cannot exist without it. This is the profound reason why the narrator in Armah's *Two Thousand Seasons* (1973), a novel about the African identity, speaks exclusively in the "we" mode and never refers to himself by means of an "I" or a proper name.

2. Most members of the group G believe that they are members of a collectivity whose members share a significant number of views, attitudes, values, goals, and so forth, and also impute such a belief to most other members of G.

3. "Us" versus a specific s/he (Faulkner's townspeople vs. Miss Emily); us versus them, another group (Armah's Africans vs. colonists and slave traders, and Senesi's boys and children against the adults); or us versus all others (Silvain's isolated technicians and the rest of humanity) defines in a relative contrastive manner the distinctness or the uniqueness of the group and its members as conceived of by these members. Members of G thus believe that they, qua members of G, are markedly distinct from some/all other groups and that this distinctness is an essential part of their group identity.

4. A sense of inner solidarity, unity, homogeneity and cohesion is complementary to a sense of group distinctness or separateness. Members of G thus often entertain a cluster of beliefs to the effect that what unites them, what they have in common, is far stronger than whatever differences may exist among them, that they have more in common with one another than with any outside individual or group and that their shared distinctness from outsiders is stronger than their internal diversity.

Specific Features of Literary "We" Groups as Narrated Entities

It is now time to move to the "we" as the collective agent in the narrated domain. As we all know, "we" narratives are not unique to literature. Yet, it seems that on the level of the narrated, not less than on that of narration, the literary ones manifest certain peculiarities that set them apart from their nonliterary counterparts. As in most things literary, the distinction is not absolute, but resides rather in a different proportion of some elements or in a different functional hierarchy of elements and patterns. In what follows, I shall try to sketch out briefly and tentatively some of these peculiarities on the level of the narrated as they seem to emerge from my limited corpus:

1. No literary "we" narrative moves entirely on the global institutional level of, for example, "our party" or "our university," with its nondistributive properties and actions. Rather, it always singles out and names certain specific individuals or subgroups of the collectivity in question. Consequently, not all state and action descriptions are in the universal "we" mode. Some of them have such singled out individuals and subgroups as their topic entities, and refer to them minimally as "some of us," but more often as "she," "he," "they," or even "you" (singular or plural), depending on the presence or absence of an "I" in the narratorial system. Singling out takes place mostly when one member of the group engages in an activity that the others cannot or will not share, as, for example, when Brazier leaves the group in Silvain's (1971) *Les Eoliennes*, or when different subgroups, such as the young and the older soldiers in Helprin's story, display different attitudes and expectations in a shared situation.

2. While joint actions may be crucial to the narrated, they are never portrayed exclusively from the group or global perspective. Even if the collective action is made up entirely of tokens of the same action type, say, marching together, individual variations in the manner of execution are still noted. This is even stronger when complex actions are at stake, for here the joint action of the group consists by definition of individual subactions that are different from one another as well as from the complex action as a whole. In all cases, some of these subactions get described in addition to the collective ones.

3. Describing complex verbal action, such as a speech event as a whole, from the group or global perspective exclusively will yield statements such as "we had a debate" or "we reached a decision," where constituent individual utterances are not singled out, and where it is impossible to quote any participant either directly or indirectly. But while debate is collective, the speech acts that make it up are individual. The particular flatness and uniformity, including typographic, of Silvain's novel, for example, is to a large degree

a consequence of the refusal to subdivide a collective speech event into its constituent utterances, unlike all of the other works examined.

4. Also, one should not forget that narrative, especially modern, is not only a record of actions and states, but also of the reflection or image of such actions and states in the minds of their individual participants, and of their associated images of themselves, of others, and of the group to which they belong. "We" narratives would also want to portray the formation, change, and possible dissolution of a sense of "we-ness" in members of a group. In the first case, individual mental contents and events will have to be portrayed, and, in the second, processes of interpersonal communication and negotiation consisting essentially of individual verbal gestures. The married couples in Barth and Brechon and Brechon's novels portray this process through the use of "I" and "you" statements. The rejected homosexual lover in White's (1978) *Nocturnes for the King of Naples* contemplates the past process of "I" and "you" forming an unstable temporary "we" and the subsequent drifting apart into an "I" versus "you." Once again Silvain's novel provides a stark contrast. The technicians feel and think as one from the beginning of the story, so that it is enough for the anonymous "we" sayer (who never self-refers as "I") to report in summary fashion the gist of their mental acts, deliberately depriving the narrative of any psychological variety or dynamism.

5. Since the group's story is told, sometimes in the present tense, by a group member who is not its spokesperson, most "we" narratives contain at least passing references to this I as narrator, and sometimes also as participant in the narrated events. We are thus reminded that while the protagonist of the narrative is a collectivity, the image we get of it is filtered through individual center(s) of awareness. The authorial and authoritative "we" of scientific articles or joint reports, based on the coming together of all members through a public process of negotiation, is not to be found here.

To conclude: in spite of their distinguishing linguistic marker, literary "we" narratives, unlike histories of an institution, for example, are not exclusively, and sometimes not even mostly, accounts of collectivities of and their irreducible properties and actions. They may portray the emergence of such collectivities through individual acts of communication, and always portray actions, both physical and verbal, of individual group members. The proportion between the story of the group as a whole and the substories of individual members will vary from text to text, primarily according to the group's function in the narrative: protagonist or observer/

focalizer, and the group's status as already established from the outset or in the process of coming into being or dissolving. If the inevitable mix of collective and individual propositions is what distinguishes literary "we" narratives from nonliterary ones, it is the perspective through which both groups and individuals are seen that sets them apart from "I," "you," "she," "he," and "they" literary modes of narration. The specificity of this perspective is twofold. In the first place, individual agents are seen, presented, or defined first and foremost as members of a collectivity, from married couple to nation. Second, the one who adopts and conveys this collective mode of presentation is himself/herself a member of this very collective, a stakeholder in the plural subject, so that the story of the other narrative agent(s) is indissolubly also his/her own story, both parties being united by the overarching, encompassing "we."

Literary "We" Narrative: An Unstable Form

One last question remains, Why are literary "we" narratives so rare, even in comparison with "you" ones? My own feeling is that the reason may well lie in what Roman Jakobson has called "the semantic instability and internal contradiction, [two] inherent properties of the first person plural" (1973: 454). Whenever more than two agents are involved in a "we" state, or action description, the exact scope of "we" may remain ambiguous, since it may cover most, but not all members of G, since it may or may not include the speaker, and since its reference group may consist of somewhat different subsets of G on different occasions of use. Second, the mental access issue remains inherently unresolved in "we" narratives, inevitably combining in any "we" mental action description immediate first person inside knowledge with a second- or third-person inferential one. The fact that the "we" narrator is not an authorized spokesperson for G makes this problem even more acute. But even a narrative of external actions and events cannot for long be sustained entirely on the global "we" level, so that a partial division into subgroups or individuals and their distinct activities always takes place. Finally, the intense sense of collective subject, of "us" or "we-ness," so central to any "we" discourse (solidarity, unity, distinctness, and sharing) is probably easier to convey directly in lyrical or meditative texts than to embody in a description of situations and courses of events. In plain English, the payoff may simply not be worth the effort, with the drawbacks outweighing the specific potentialities of the form.

15

Who Said What? Who Knows What? Tracking Speakers and Knowledge in Narratives

Arthur C. Graesser, Cheryl Bowers, Ute J. Bayen, and Xiangen Hu

Characters, Narrators, and Readers

When a literary narrative is comprehended, such as a novel or a short story, the readers ideally construct multiple agents in their cognitive representations. Each agent is a human entity that is normally capable of speaking, perceiving, believing, knowing, wanting, acting, and experiencing emotions. One ensemble of agents consists of the characters in the story. *Character* agents are very salient in the text and in the minds of the readers as they construct their mental story worlds. The protagonists, antagonists, and other main characters are more salient than the minor characters and those characters that are functionally props. A second ensemble of agents consists of the narrator, narratee, writer, and imaginary reader. These agents will be called "pragmatic" agents because they address the communicative exchange between the narrator and narratee, or between the writer and reader. Pragmatic agents are frequently invisible to the reader, particularly those readers who have not received formal training on how to read literature.

What are the virtues in viewing literary stories as linguistic products of multiple agents? The multiple agent view encourages researchers in relevant fields (e.g., literary scholars, cognitive psychologists, text linguists, and writers) to identify, track, and dissect the various agents that are associated with a literary text. The researcher can track the "life" of each agent as the story unfolds and as sentences are interpreted: What is the total set of agents associated with a story? What are the properties of each agent? What is the intended audience for each agent? What agents are relevant to the interpretation of sentence S? How is the wording of statement S constrained by the ensemble of relevant agents? The multiple agent view prevents the researcher from adopting a simplistic picture of the structure and content of a literary story, for example, cognitive psychologists once believed that text comprehension involves little more than a single speaker/writer, a comprehender, and a structured sequence of sentences. This simple analysis is inadequate from the perspective of multiple agent architectures. The multiple agent view is also compatible with the theories of cognition that are currently popular in the fields of discourse processing, cognitive science, and artificial intelligence. According to many cognitive theories, intelligence emerges from the recruitment of multiple intelligent agents that interact in parallel (Franklin 1995; Minsky 1989). According to contemporary theories of conversation, speakers frequently articulate speech acts in a fashion that caters to the constraints of multiple audiences, even when only two parties are in a conversation (Clark 1993). In a recent analysis of conversations in call-in radio, for example, Hutchby (1995) identified four agents that constrained the course of the broadcasted conversations: (1) the caller, (2) the expert advice giver, (3) the studio host, and (4) the overhearing audience. A single speech act is shaped by the knowledge states of multiple agents.

The multiple agent view is hardly a revolutionary idea. The general idea is adopted, either explicitly or implicitly, in virtually all accounts of narrative in narratology, literature, and literary criticism (Bakhtin 1981; Banfield 1982; Chafe 1994; Chatman 1978; Fludernik 1993; Leech & Short 1981; Prince 1982). Among other things, these analyses specify frequent configurations of agents and how particular agents may be amalgamated with other agents, for example, when the story has an omniscient, third-person narrator, the narrator sits above the story world and tells the story to the narratee, having a privileged access to the mental states of all of the characters. When the story has a first-person narrator, the narrator-agent is amalgamated with one of the character agents; the narrator sees the world from the point of view of the character and does not necessarily have access to the mental states of other characters. When the story has a second-person narrator, there may be an amalgamation of three agents (narrator, narratee, and character) in an effort to involve the reader. The three narrator configurations are illustrated as follows:

First-person narrator. "I woke up and had the sinking flash that I was pregnant."

Second-person narrator. "You wake up and have the sinking flash that you are pregnant."

Third-person narrator. "She woke up and had the sinking flash that she was pregnant."

Of course, there are yet other configurations of agents that involve the narrator. Whatever narrator configuration is adopted, the narrator portrays a particular interpretation of the events and states in the story world.

Some writers have invented stories with unusual configurations of agents. In some forms of postmodern literature, for example, the narrator perspective may change throughout the story rather than remaining constant. Yet there is no guarantee that readers will detect and appreciate these unusual multiagent inventions. For those writers who care about the impact of literature on actual readers, there needs to be some understanding on what the human mind can handle, that is, to what extent is it feasible to expect a human mind to construct particular mental representations and to perform particular cognitive processes during story comprehension? There needs to be an interdisciplinary field that lies at the intersection between psychology and literary studies. This is precisely the direction that some researchers have pursued in the relatively new paradigm known as the "empirical studies of literature" (Dixon et al. 1993; Kreuz & MacNealy 1995; Miall & Kuiken 1994; Zwaan 1993), and what Dixon and Bortolussi (chap. 16 of this vol.) have called "psychonarratology."

Psychonarratologists have already discovered a number of limitations of the human mind that apply to readers when they comprehend stories, for example, readers are not able to generate several alternative future plots as they comprehend story episodes in real time (Graesser, Singer, & Trabasso 1994). Readers can accommodate and explain the immediate episode being comprehended and how it relates to past episodes. But it is extremely difficult for the reader to forecast lengthy chains of episodes that extend into the future. It is much easier for readers to comprehend stories that report events in a canonical chronological order than stories that have flashbacks, reversed ordering of episodes, and embedded story sequences (Ohtsuka & Brewer 1992). It takes additional time and effort to comprehend sentences in literary stories that involve continuity breaks at the level of causality, temporality, or spatiality

(Zwaan, Magliano, & Graesser 1995). Literature is known to have a comparatively high density of literary devices (Gibbs 1994; van Peer 1986), such as metaphor, hyperbole, and irony, but some of these devices are too subtle to be detected by the average reader (Graesser, Mio, & Millis 1987). These and other empirical findings underscore the importance of exploring the cognitive mechanisms that underlie the comprehension of literary stories.

The present study investigates whether adult readers are capable of monitoring the various agents that exist in literary short stories. More specifically, we explored two questions. The first question addresses whether readers are able to remember who expressed particular speech acts in the stories, that is, are readers able to keep track of who said what? The possible speakers include the character agents and the pragmatic agents (viz., the narrator). In most stories, there are shifts between the narrator as the speaker and particular characters as speakers. It is conceivable that readers will have difficulty keeping track of the speakers of speech acts, given that there are several agents in most stories and that there are shifts among the agents who speak. However, it is also conceivable that readers will have very little difficulty tracking the *sources* of speech acts because of the substantial conceptual constraints that exist in the story world.

The second question addresses whether readers are able to keep track of who knows what? Given that some proposition is expressed in the literary story (e.g., "Glenda is pregnant"), can readers discriminate which of the characters know about the proposition? The ability to comprehend and appreciate some stories critically depends on the ability of readers to accurately track the knowledge of agents. For example, consider *Oedipus Rex*, the Greek drama by Sophocles. At one point in the story, Oedipus is ignorant of his own identity, of the fact that he murdered his father, and of the fact that he married his mother. However, these facts are known by other agents, such as the sightless prophet Teresias and the audience. Thus, our second research question explores whether adult readers can track the knowledge states of the various agents in a literary story. It is conceivable that this would be a difficult achievement for most readers. As each proposition is comprehended, the reader would need to update whether each agent knows about it. If there were 10 agents associated with a story and there were 1,000 propositions expressed in the story, then the reader would need to evaluate 10 x 1000 = 10,000 expressions about knowledge (i.e., "X knows proposition P"). Alternatively, it is conceivable that this would be an easy achievement for most readers, especially if the story world had substantial conceptual constraints.

The field of cognitive psychology provides little theoretical and empirical guidance as to whether readers are capable of tracking who said what and who knows what. However, the field does offer the methodological tools for investigating the phenomena. In this study, college students read literary short stories and subsequently completed a test that assessed their memories for who said what and their beliefs about who knows what. The tests permitted us to explore specific hypotheses about the readers' *source memory* (i.e., memory for who said particular speech acts) and about the readers' *knowledge judgments* (i.e., beliefs about what characters know about particular propositions). The test items that were included in our sample were selected judiciously, that is, the items in the source memory test were speech acts that could have been spoken by the narrator and by several of the characters. Similarly, the items in the knowledge judgment test were propositions that could have been known by several of the characters. It would not be informative to select test sentences that adults could accurately or systematically handle without ever having read the story.

Although cognitive psychologists offer little theoretical guidance on what patterns of data to expect, it is tempting to propose some feasible alternatives. One possibility is that the reader constructs a "stripped down," concrete representation of the story world that includes the physical actions, events, and states that were explicitly expressed in the story and the propositional content of the speech acts expressed in the story. In essence, this *concrete* reader would remember only what happened and what was said. This reader would entirely lose track of the voices, knowledge states, and perspectives of the various agents associated with the story. The resulting data would show poor source memory scores because the reader would remember what was said, but not who said it. The reader would be unable to differentiate which of the characters knew about particular propositions. A second possibility is that the reader carefully monitors the activities and knowledge of all agents associated with the story. If there were ten agents associated with a story, then this *multiagent* reader would simultaneously and independently construct ten tracks of meaning. The source memory scores would be very accurate because the reader would remember both what was said and who said it. The reader would have a sensitive palate when attempting to differentiate who knows what. Aside from these two extreme possibilities, there are a host of intermediate positions that we will not address at this point.

Who Said What?

Events in narrative can be portrayed from different perspectives. At one extreme, there is an *objective* perspective because an event is described from the perspective of an impersonal, objective, omniscient, third-person narrator, for example, if a character became pregnant in the story world, then the third-person narrator would directly assert: "Glenda became pregnant." An omniscient, third-person narrator is "all-knowing" in the sense that the narrator has complete knowledge about the physical actions, speech acts, mental states of characters (including beliefs, knowledge, desires, emotions, and sentiments), and facts about the culture of the story world. At the other extreme, there is a *subjective* perspective because the event is portrayed from the point of view of a particular character. A first-person narrator is one way of providing a subjective perspective, for example, if Glenda were the narrator, then the narrator would assert: "I was pregnant." In this case, the narrator would not be all-knowing because the narrator would be limited to Glenda's perspective. First-person narration is not the only way of establishing a subjective perspective and of magnifying the consciousness of a character agent, however. Literary scholars have documented the various linguistic, stylistic, and rhetorical devices that set up subjective perspectives in literary stories (Banfield 1982; Chafe 1994; Chatman 1978; Leech & Short 1981). Psychonarratologists have recently begun to explore the impact of perspective and points of view on readers (Bruner 1986; Duchan, Bruder, & Hewitt 1995; Gerrig 1993; Sanders 1994).

As just discussed, a multiagent reader would need to keep track of the narrator perspective and of the speakers of speech acts in the story world. In contrast, the concrete reader would gloss over such details. The concrete reader would not remember which of the following ways a story conveyed that Glenda was pregnant:

1. Glenda was pregnant. (assertion by third-person omniscient narrator)
2. Glenda said, "I'm pregnant." (assertion in direct speech)

3. Glenda said that she was pregnant. (assertion in indirect speech)
4. The family never accepted Glenda's pregnancy (presupposition by third-person narrator)
5. Glenda said, "My family has never accepted my pregnancy" (presupposition in direct speech)
6. Glenda said that her family never accepted her pregnancy (presupposition in indirect speech)
7. Betty said, "Glenda is pregnant." (assertion in direct speech)
8. Betty said that Glenda was pregnant. (assertion in indirect speech)
9. I was pregnant. (assertion by first-person narrator)
10. My family never accepted my pregnancy. (presupposition by first-person narrator)

These different ways of conveying that Glenda was pregnant have important pragmatic repercussions, and therefore are sometimes detected by readers (Clark & Gerrig 1991; Wade & Clark 1993). For example, direct speech has a demonstrative function in the sense that it vividly re-creates the experience of Glenda's pregnancy being revealed to listeners. The function of indirect speech is more informational than demonstrative; the function of presuppositions is more referential than informational or demonstrative. These linguistic and stylistic variations would need to be monitored by the multiagent reader, but not by the concrete reader.

In these ten variations, there are different voices expressing that Glenda was pregnant. Stated differently, there are different agents speaking. In sentence 1, the speaker is a third-person narrator. In sentence 9, the speaker is Glenda, who serves as the first-person narrator. The speaker is also Glenda in sentence 2, but in this case Glenda is not the narrator. The speaker is another character, Betty, in sentence 7. The speaker status is either uncertain or vague in the case of presuppositions, as in sentence 4. These variations illustrate how a particular proposition can potentially be asserted or presupposed by multiple-agents.

The central question in the present study was whether adult readers can keep track of the speakers of sentences after they finish reading literary stories. In order to investigate this question, we employed a *source memory* paradigm (Johnson, Hashtroudi, & Lindsay 1993). After reading a short story, college students were presented test items that consisted of sentence excerpts from the story. There were four categories of test sentences: (1) sentences spoken by the narrator, (2) sentences spoken by character A, (3) sentences spoken by character B, and (4) false sentences that were not expressed by any agent associated with the story. For each test sentence, the college students made a decision about the source of the test sentence by selecting one of four response options: narrator, character A, character B, and "neither" (i.e., neither the narrator, A nor B). This procedure permitted us to use a mathematical modeling approach for the quantitative analysis of the data (Bayen, Murnane, & Erdfelder, in press; Riefer, Hu, & Batchelder 1994). The mathematical model segregates three classes of parameters, with values that range from 0 to 1:

> *Sentence detection.* To what extent does the reader detect a sentence (S) as being a true sentence with respect to the story world?
>
> *Source discrimination.* To what extent does the reader remember that an agent said sentence S?
>
> *Bias.* To what extent is the reader guessing that sentence S is detected or that an agent said S?

The sentence detection and source discrimination parameters were the critical parameters from the standpoint of the present study.

Stories

Two literary stories were selected in this investigation of who said what. The first story was "Almost Her," by Bridget Mazur. The story is nine printed pages in length, and involves a sexual-romantic intrigue with three main characters: Vicky, David (Vicky's husband), and Jim (David's brother). Although Vicky is married to David, there is a mutual attraction between Vicky and Jim. The story is written from the point of view of Vicky, who is the first-person narrator of the story. Most of the episodes in the story involve conversations among characters in various settings, such as a bar and a living room.

The second story was "The Conscience of the Cop," by William Fay. The story is fourteen printed pages in length, and is about a police officer who kills a robber while the latter is attempting to rob a clerk in a store. The police officer's conscience suffers from the episode so he has a series of conversations with the robber's friends and family in an effort to learn about the life of the robber. For most of the story, the police officer learns that the robber is a good person and an upstanding citizen. It is only at he end that the officer finds out from the robber's family that the robber was truly a rogue, much to the police officer's relief. The story had an impersonal omniscient narrator. The three agents under consideration in the study were the narrator, the police officer, and a friend of the robber.

Test Sentences

We selected 72 sentence excerpts from each of the two stories. The narrator was the speaker in 24 sentences, whereas character A was the speaker in 24 sentences and character B was the speaker in the remaining 24 sentences. We purposely selected sentences that conceivably could have been spoken by all three agents (i.e., the narrator, character A, and character B). Potential test sentences were eliminated from consideration if the reader could accurately reconstruct the speaker (i.e., the source) on the basis of the intrinsic meaning of the sentence. Some example test sentences are: "Michele is photogenic" (speaker is Dave), "Michele decided that stars were not enough from a man" (speaker is Jim), and "Michele would never sleep on anybody's couch" (speaker is Vicky, the narrator).

We created a yoked false sentence for each of the 72 true test sentences in each story. The yoked false sentence had the same wording as the original true test sentence, except for a word or phrase that altered its meaning, for example, "Michele would never sleep in a hotel" was the yoked false sentence for the original sentence "Michele would never sleep on anybody's couch." The sentence "Michele decided that diamonds were not enough from a man" was the yoked false sentence for "Michele decided that stars were not enough from a man." These false sentences were needed in order to get a sample of test sentences that were spoken by neither the narrator, character A, nor character B.

Four different versions of the test booklet were prepared in order to distribute the false items among the test sentences. In any given version of the test booklet, there were 18 original sentences spoken by the narrator, 18 sentences spoken by character A, 18 sentences spoken by character B, and 18 yoked false sentences (yoked from 6 narrator sentences, 6 character A sentences, and 6 character B sentences). The other versions of the test booklets had a different sample of the 18 original narrator sentences, 18 original character A sentences, 18 original character B sentences, and 18 yoked false sentences. We counterbalanced the four test versions across readers so that each test sentence was in the original form 75 percent of the time (and the yoked false form 25 percent of the time). The test sentences were randomly ordered in the test booklets.

Procedure

The readers consisted of sixteen college students enrolled in introductory psychology classes who participated in order to receive extra credit in the course. They were instructed to read the story carefully and slowly enough to enjoy the story. They were told that they would later be asked some questions. Half of the readers were randomly assigned to each of the two stories. The subjects were also instructed to time their reading by recording the clock times when they started and finished reading the story.

After the readers finished reading the story, they completed the source memory test. They were instructed to select one of four response options for each of the 72 test sentences in the booklet: narrator, character A, character B, and neither. While completing this test, the readers were reminded about the identity of each of the characters, including the fact that Vicky was the narrator in "Almost Her." The readers completed the source memory test at their own pace.

After the readers completed the first story, they read the other story and completed the source memory test in the same manner as they did for the first story. It should be noted that the subjects were aware of the nature of the source memory test when they read the second story. We were curious whether they would be more sensitive to monitoring the speakers of the sentences after they had been exposed to the test.

Results

The basic, raw data in this study consisted of the proportion of decisions within each of the four response options (i.e., narrator, character A, character B, and neither), segregated by the categories of test sentences. For example, consider the test sentences in which the speaker was the narrator (Vicky) in "Almost Her." The proportion of responses were .69, .11, .04, and .15 for the narrator, David, Jim, and neither, respectively. Therefore, the correct response was given 69 percent of the time. When the speaker was David, the proportions were .15, .61, .12, and .12 for the narrator, Dave, Jim, and neither, respectively. Similarly, the distributions of proportions were (.05, .12, .74, and .09) for sentences spoken by Jim and (.18, .11, .09, and .62) for the yoked false sentences.

These distributions of proportions are only moderately informative, however. Researchers in the source memory paradigm have gone a giant step further by performing mathematical models that simulate these proportions (Bayen, Murname, & Erdfelder, in press; Riefer, Hu, & Batchelder 1994). It is beyond the scope of this chapter to discuss these mathematical models, however. It suffices to say that these models estimate values for three classes of parameters when fitting the data to the mathematical model: sentence detection, source discrimination, and bias (see the earlier discussion in this chap.). We will focus on the sentence detection and source discrimination parameters in this chapter. Moreover, it is important to mention that the data had an excellent fit to Riefer, Hu, & Batchelder's (1994) mathematical model of source memory.

The sentence detection parameters are estimates of the extent to which the readers' memories could discriminate between true original sentences and the yoked false sentences, that is, to what extent could the readers discriminate true versus false sentences about the story world? The parameter values could vary between zero (absolutely no ability to discriminate) to 1 (perfect ability to discriminate). If the readers were perfect, they would never decide "neither" for the original true sentences and would always decide "neither" for the yoked false sentences. The sentence detection parameters were found to be fairly high and had little variability among stories and speakers. There were 12 estimated parameters when considering 2 stories, 2 orders of reading, and 3 speakers per stories. The sentence detection parameters varied from .51 to .86, with a mean of .70. Sentence detection was about the same for "Almost Her" and the "Cop" story (.72 vs. .68), and for the first versus the second story read (.73 vs. .67). The parameters were not appreciably different for the narrators (.66) and the other, character agents (.73). In most of the statistical tests, we did not find significant differences among the sentence detection parameters.

The source discrimination parameters were particularly interesting. They fluctuated substantially, ranging from .00 to .86, with a mean of .58. The mean source discrimination parameters were .00, .85, and .46 for the omniscient third-person narrator, the first-person narrator, and the nonnarrator characters, respectively. Statistical tests revealed that the parameters were significantly lower for the third-person narrator than for the characters and the parameters were significantly higher for the first-person narrator than for the characters. The impersonal, omniscient, third-person narrator was indeed an invisible agent because the source discrimination parameters were zero both for the first and second stories read. In contrast, the first-person narrator was a visible and salient agent because the source discrimination parameters were extremely high.

Major Conclusions

So what have we learned from this initial study of memory for who said what? We have learned that some agents are more salient than others when readers track the speakers of speech acts. More specifically, we can offer four general conclusions:

1. The impersonal, omniscient, third-person narrator is an invisible agent to the reader. The reader is entirely unable to discriminate exactly what was said by the third-person narrator.

2. The first-person narrator is a very salient agent. Readers have an excellent source memory for the speech acts expressed by the first-person narrator.

3. The nonnarrator characters are moderately visible agents. Source memory is intermediate for these agents.

4. Multiagent readers are more prevalent than concrete readers. Otherwise, readers would not be able to keep track of the sources of speech acts.

Although our data strongly support these claims, it is important to hedge and point out that additional source memory experiments need to be conducted on a larger sample of stories.

Who Knows What?

When events and speech acts occur in the story world, they are normally perceived by character agents. The characters who witness these episodes acquire this knowledge and sometimes disseminate it to other characters. Thus, knowledge about a proposition P is propagated among the ensemble of character agents in the story world. In this section, we report a study that assesses whether this propagation of knowledge is accomplished systematically.

It is conceivable that readers are not very good at tracking the knowledge of character agents. For example, readers might sometimes mistakenly project their own knowledge onto the knowledge states of characters. That is, if the reader knows proposition P, then the reader assumes that a character knows proposition P (unless there is salient information in the story that suggests otherwise). This *reader knowledge projection* principle is a very parsimonious principle for the reader to adopt. The reader does not have to go through the laborious task of determining who knows P and who doesn't. It should also be noted that knowledge tracking is frequently a challenge in everyday two-party conversations. The speaker often sustains the illusion that the addressee knows what the speaker knows rather than taking into account the perspective of the addressee (Schober 1995). Speakers are frequently egocentric rather than being sensitive to the knowledge of the addressee.

It is also conceivable that readers are quite good at tracking the knowledge states of characters. Indeed, that is expected for readers of *Oedipus Rex*. Throughout most of this drama, Oedipus does not know that he has killed his father and married his mother. A reader who fails to realize the knowledge deficits of Oedipus would miss an essential feature of the tragedy. The *multiagent* reader is capable of tracking the different knowledge states of characters.

Keysar (1994) has reported mixed support for the reader knowledge projection principle, as just articulated, in his studies of how readers and audiences interpret sarcastic utterances. Readers do not have any difficulty separating their factual privileged knowledge from a protagonist's knowledge, such as when the readers know P and it is clear that the protagonist does not know P. However, readers do mistakenly assume, inferentially, that the protagonist knows P when the reader interprets a sarcastic message from the protagonist's perspective. Thus, readers can discriminate between "reader knows P" and "character knows P" when asked to make such discriminations directly. This outcome is compatible with the multiagent position, and incompatible with the reader knowledge projection principle, as just stated. However, readers sometimes use the information in P (and inferentially assume that P is true) when they interpret an utterance from the perspective of the character. This incorrect inference is compatible with the reader knowledge projection principle, but not the multiagent position.

When a character performs a speech act in a story, there are potentially five classes of character agents, as defined in the following section.

> *Speaker* (*S*). The character who performs the speech act;
>
> *Addressee* (*A*). The character to whom the speaker is speaking;
>
> *Onhearer* (*O*). A character who is not involved in the conversation, but who is spatially close enough to hear the conversation;
>
> *Friend* (*F*). An intimate friend or relative of the speaker, but not in the scene of the speech act;
>
> *Nonfriend* (*N*). A character who is not an intimate friend or relative of the speaker, and who is not in the scene of the speech act.

If readers are multiagent readers, then these five classes of characters would not have equivalent knowledge of the information expressed in a speech act. The speaker should of course know proposition P because it was spoken by the speaker. The nonfriend should not know proposition P because the nonfriend was not a party of the conversation, was not within hearing distance of the conversation, was not in the same scene as the conversation, and probably did not have conversations with the speaker prior to the speech act. The other classes should have intermediate degrees of knowledge of proposition P, as discussed in the next section. If, however, the "reader knowledge projection principle" is correct, then all five classes of characters should have equivalent degrees of knowledge of proposition P.

We performed an experiment that assessed the knowledge that characters had about speech acts expressed in literary stories. College students first read a literary story. They subsequently rated the extent to which particular characters had knowledge of particular propositions expressed in speech acts. There was a 6-point knowledge rating scale, varying from 1 (character definitely does not know proposition P) to 6 (character definitely does know proposition P). Mean ratings were computed for the five classes of characters just specified. The pattern of mean ratings was scrutinized in order to evaluate the following hypotheses.

Reader Knowledge Projection

The reader assumes that the characters know what the reader knows. The predicted pattern of knowledge ratings is: $S = A = O = F = N$.

> *Speaker primacy*. The speaker has the most knowledge of the information expressed by the speaker. The predicted pattern is: S > maximum (A, O, F, N), that is, the mean for the speakers should be higher than the highest mean among the characters in classes A, O, F, and N.
>
> *Conversational unit*. The parties of a conversation have more knowledge of the information expressed in the conversation than characters who are not part of the conversation. The predicted pattern is minimum (S, A) > maximum (O, F, N), that is, the lowest mean of S and A should be higher than the highest mean of O, F, and N.
>
> *Spatial proximity*. Characters who are spatially near a conversation should have more knowledge of the information in the conversation than characters who are distant from the conversation. The predicted pattern is minimum (S, A, O) > maximum (F, N).
>
> *Affiliation*. Friends of the speaker in a conversation should have more knowledge of the information in the conversation than should nonfriends. Thus, intimate friends and relatives are assumed to share information with each other. The prediction is: F > N.

Clearly, there are several ways in which knowledge can be propagated among the character agents in a story world. Our goal was to evaluate different hypotheses about knowledge propagation.

Stories and Methods

With one exception, the stories and methods were exactly the same in this who-knows-what study and in the previous who-said-what study. Instead of completing the source memory task, the forty college students in the present study completed a knowledge rating task. After reading a story, the college students were presented eleven test sentences that had been spoken by characters in the story. For each test sentence, there was a list of all of the characters in the story, together with a 6-point rating scale. The readers were instructed to rate the extent to which each character had knowledge of the information in the test sentence, for example, two of the test sentences were: "One thing Jim can't give up is a cigarette after sex" and "Jim is now a baker." The readers rated the extent to which each character had knowledge of this sentence. The knowledge ratings were made on the following 6-point scale: (1) character definitely does not know; (2) character probably does not know; (3) undecided, but guess character does not know; (4) undecided, but guess character knows; (5) character probably knows; and (6) character definitely knows.

Results

Mean knowledge ratings were computed for the five classes of characters. The mean ratings were 5.90, 5.42, 3.36, 3.22, and 1.65 for the speakers, addressees, onhearers, friends, and nonfriends, respectively. When an analysis of variance and planned comparisons were performed on these data, the following pattern of means was uncovered: Speaker > Addressee > Onhearer = Friend > Nonfriend. These results clearly did not support the reader knowledge projection hypothesis. Instead, readers were quite sensitive to the different knowledge states of the various character agents. Moreover, their knowledge ratings were quite systematic. The data supported the speaker primacy, conversation unit, and affinity hypotheses.

Follow-up analyses were needed to adequately evaluate the status of the spatial proximity hypothesis. Specifically, we needed to segregate those Onhearers who were friends versus nonfriends. The mean knowledge ratings for Onhearer-friends (3.78) was significantly higher than Onhearer-nonfriends (3.21); this difference lends further support for the affinity hypothesis. The spatial proximity hypothesis was supported by two comparisons that ended up being statistically significant. First, ratings were higher for the Onhearer-friends than the Friends (who were not onhearers), 3.78 versus 3.22, respectively. Second, ratings were higher for the Onhearer-nonfriends than the Nonfriends (who were not onhearers),

3.21 versus 1.65. Therefore, the data supported the spatial proximity hypothesis.

Major Conclusions

Our study supported two major conclusions about the ability of readers to keep track of who knows what:

1. The readers were multiagent readers in the sense that they were sensitive to the differential knowledge states of the characters. The reader knowledge projection hypothesis was not supported: The readers did not assume that the characters know what the reader knows.
2. The information expressed in characters' speech acts was propagated systematically among the agents in the story world. The propagation followed the principles of speaker primacy, conversational unit, spatial proximity, and affinity.

We suspect that we do not have the final word on how knowledge is propagated among agents in the story world. We would not be surprised if there were more principles and if there were constraints on these four principles, for example, the affinity principle may be violated under specific conditions. A speaker might try to withhold sensitive information from a friend, as in the case where the speaker is having an affair with the wife of the "friend." Additional research is needed to refine the principles of knowledge propagation among agents in a story world.

Final Comments

The multiagent position has clearly been supported in our explorations of who said what and who knows what. It is worthwhile to view literary stories as products of multiple interacting agents. These agents include the pragmatic agents (i.e., the narrator) as well as the characters. Readers are quite good at keeping track of the agents who speak and are sensitive to the knowledge states of the agents. We found that the only agent who was invisible to the reader was the impersonal, omniscient, third-person narrator.

The present study is the first to systematically investigate the speech and knowledge of the various agents in a literary story.

There is no reason to limit ourselves to speech and knowledge. There are many other "propositional attitudes" for psychonarratologists to explore, such as perceiving, wanting, liking, and emoting. It also may be fruitful to examine a number of questions that naturally emerge from the multiple agent architecture. How does the reader dynamically construct the properties of each agent during the course of comprehension? What configurations of character agents provide interesting plots? How can pragmatic agents be effectively amalgamated with character agents? What configuration of agents are confusing to readers? We believe that the multiagent architecture empowers psychonarratologists with a very useful set of conceptual tools—perhaps more useful than some prominent theoretical frameworks of the past.

Part V

Effects and Consequences

16

Prolegomena for a Science of Psychonarratology

Peter Dixon and Marisa Bortolussi

In the present chapter, we propose some parameters for a new field of psychonarratology. The motivation for this proposal is twofold. On one hand, any number of scholars in modern narratology have proposed that a resolution of narratological issues requires some understanding of how actual readers process texts. However, the field of narratology as a whole is ill-equipped in some ways to conduct this kind of investigation. Discourse processing and cognitive psychology, on the other hand, have many of the methodological and interpretive tools for investigating reading processes, but for a number of reasons have been only peripherally concerned with narratorial processing and with narrative perspective in particular. What we are proposing here is a framework in which the best of narratology and discourse processing may come together to make some progress concerning these problems.

The Relationship of Narratology and Discourse Processing

As we see it, one of the major advances in recent work on narratology is an agreement that what the reader does with the text is crucial for an understanding of narratives and how they function. For example, Booth (1961) suggests that readers construct an image of the implied author in the course of understanding a literary work; Prince (1990) notes that modern narratology is concerned with narrative pragmatics, including the way in which readers process the text; and Lanser (1981) has claimed that narratives need to be considered in terms of speech act theory, in which readers construct some representation of authors and their intentions. These views share a common supposition that the process of reading must be considered in understanding the way in which narratives function. Furthermore, it seems that such views entail that the narrator should be thought of as a mental representation in the mind of the reader, rather than as a collection of textual signs. However, there is much less consensus on what exactly readers do with a text, what their representation of the narrator consists of, and what the status of narratorial processing should be. Our view is that what readers do is essentially an empirical question that can only be answered by systematically observing readers as they read. Inevitably the answer to this question will be complex: What readers do will vary with the characteristics of the individual reader, the nature of text, and the context in which the reading takes place. This means that what is required is a large body of empirical evidence on how these variables operate, how they interact, and how they combine to determine readers' processing. Although this is a daunting project, it is essentially tractable and can be addressed with established methodologies and experimental paradigms.

In fact, there is already a great deal of evidence and theorizing on how readers process texts in discourse processing. For example, researchers have investigated the nature of inferences drawn during reading (Graesser, Singer, & Trabasso 1994), how people construct spatial mental models while reading texts (e.g., Morrow, Greenspan, & Bower 1987), and how reading processes vary with the skill and knowledge of the reader (Just & Carpenter 1992). However, this research has been concerned only minimally with narrative perspective and literary processing generally. The reason, we suspect, is that much of discourse processing has been focused on the communicative functions of text. For example, according to the most common theoretical framework for research, the goal of discourse processing is to understand how readers decode the author's intended message. Consequently, it seems that the problem of processing the narrator and narratorial perspective is often not recognized as a separate problem at all. In general, we believe that discourse processing does not have the conceptual distinctions, comparable to those developed in narratology, which are necessary for understanding narrative text.

A Framework for Psychonarratology

In our view, the resolution to the present situation is to foster a new interdisciplinary enterprise that brings together the best of narratology and discourse processing. However, to be successful, such an enterprise must divide up the problem of narratorial processing so as to have the right methods for answering different kinds of questions. Our proposal for such a division is shown in Figure 1. The crucial step on this analysis is to distinguish *text features* from *text effects* (Dixon et al. 1993). We use the term *text feature* to refer to anything that can be objectively identified in the text. Text features include many of the textual distinctions from classical studies of narratology, such as mode, focalization, hetero- versus homodeigetic narration, and absent versus present narrator. We believe that trained observers can reliably agree whether or not such features are present in a given text if they are provided with sufficiently detailed and specific definitions. In contrast, *text effects* refer to events in the mind of reader. These effects include mental representations of various sorts, changes in attitude or belief, and affective reactions. Crucially, effects are subjective, in the sense that they can vary across readers, and contextual, in the sense that they vary with the reading situation and readers' goals and expectations. The important point for our proposal is that although effects are variable, they are knowable in an aggregate sense. That is, one can attach a certain amount of statistical certainty to generalizations as long as they are sufficiently delimited with respect to reading context and to reader population.

We believe a distinction between features and effects is essential for allowing one to bring the right tools to bear on different aspects of the problem of understanding narrative processing. A reasonable model of how this can work can be found in the field of psycholinguistics. Psycholinguistics involves the use of empirical methods from cognitive psychology to investigate how features of language are processed by language comprehenders. In many cases, formal linguistics provides the conceptual distinctions and interesting variables for this investigation, while cognitive psychology contributes the empirical methods and interpretive tools. For example, formal linguistic analyses indicate that the structure of sentences with reduced sentential complements are momentarily ambiguous as they are being read. Following this kind of analysis, psycholinguists have used experimental techniques such as the measurement of the duration of eye fixations in order to understand how

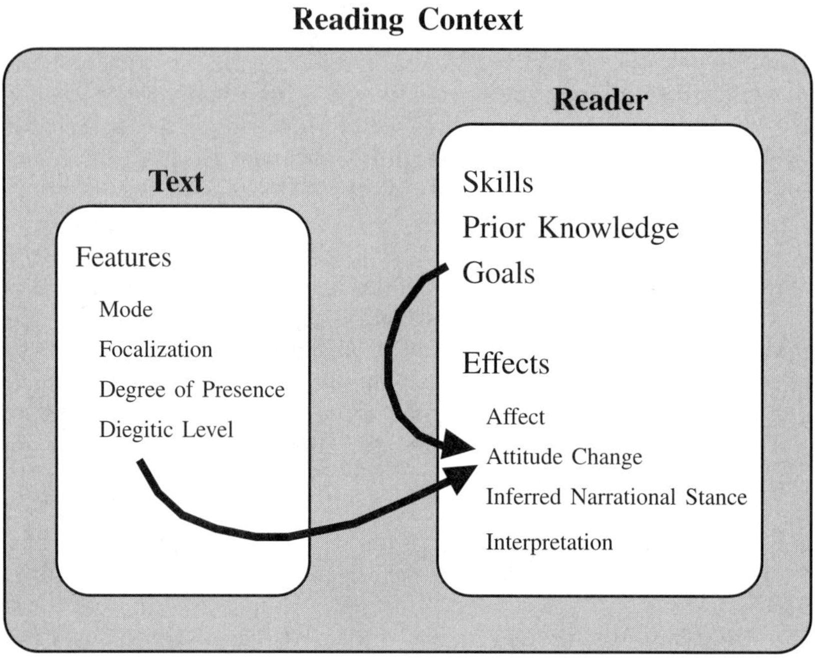

Fig. 16.1. The relationship between text features and text effects.

readers process that ambiguity (e.g., Frazier & Rayner 1982). By analogy, we use the term *psychonarratology* to refer to the interdisciplinary investigation of narratorial processing. In our view, psychonarratology should consist of the empirical investigation of how the distinctions and variables identified by narratologists are processed and how they affect readers.

Narrator as Conversational Participant

As an example of how one can use this framework, we propose a testable hypothesis in psychonarratology: Readers construct a mental representation of the narrator that is parallel to that constructed of the other participant in conversation. This parallel is illustrated in figure 2. In some respects, our proposal is similar to that of Fludernik (1993), who suggested that readers assume that a story is being told and construct some representation of the teller who is doing the telling. However, we suggest further that there is strong analogy between the representations and processes used in conversation and those that are used in understanding narratives. In particular, in conversation each speaker must of necessity maintain a representation of the other participant, together with certain aspects of their mental state in order for communication to proceed. For example, in conversation this representation must include information about the participant's perspective, so that one can understand deictic expressions such as "here" and "there." The representation must also include information about the knowledge and mental state of the participant, so that one can decide what information of one's own would be helpful to provide. The representation must include information about the intentions and goals of the other participant in order to understand the function of speech acts during the conversation. These and other requirements of the representation of the other participant have been discussed extensively in psycholinguistic analyses of conversation (e.g., Clark & Schaefer 1989). Our proposal is that the same kind of representation is constructed in processing narrative and that similar processes are used to maintain it. However, in this case, that representation is a representation of the narrator, not a representation of an actual individual, and it is inferred by the reader from textual features. We propose that, just as in conversation, the representation of the narrator contains information concerning the narrator's knowledge, goals, and perspective.

In many ways, this is similar to arguments of Lanser (1981) and others, who suggest that narrative texts should be considered as analogous to speech acts and must be interpreted in terms of readers' understanding of the goals and intentions of the author. Although Lanser's view has some merits, it has a number of implications that we are reluctant to embrace. For example, it implies that text should be considered as communication, but a literary text is demonstrably not communication in the usual sense. For example, the reader and author do not share common perceptual ground; they cannot engage in communicative processes of confirmation and error correction; the same text can be processed quite differently depending on the context; and the knowledge and goals of the reader; and so on. Lanser's solution to these problems is to describe narrative as communication in a special sense that is not really the same as the usage common in communication theory. We prefer to avoid these issues altogether by adopting a crucially different interpretation: communication and the related assumptions

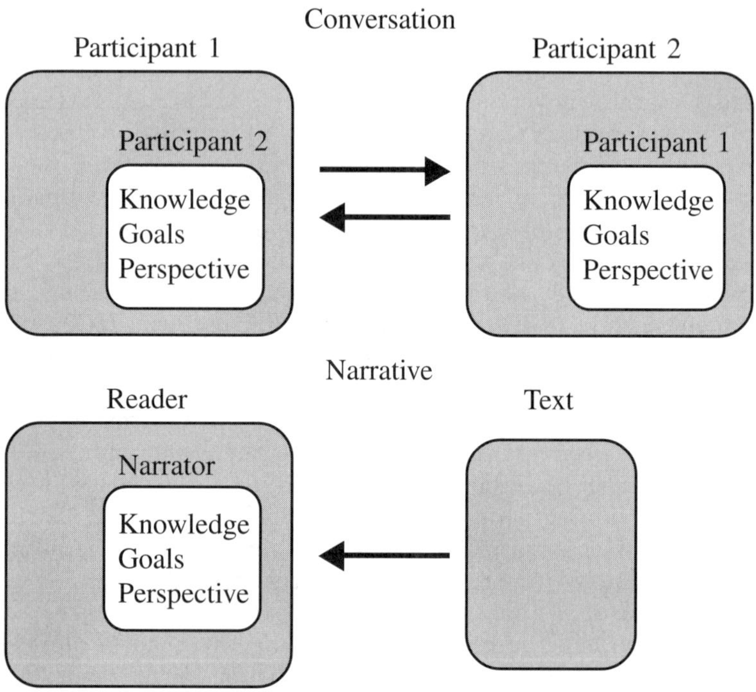

Fig. 16.2. The parallel between the representation of conversational participants and the representational of the narrator.

of speech act theory only exist in mind of the reader. In other words, text is not communication, but it is often treated as if it were by readers. Furthermore, we suspect that this may be a very natural process, and it is possible that people have an almost inevitable tendency to deal with language in this way.

Implications of a Conversational Narrator

The assumption that readers process the narrator as a conversational participant is powerful and easily generates a host of predictions and interpretations. To demonstrate how this proposal can be developed and what kinds of empirical evidence are relevant, we have selected four of the more obvious implications to present here. We will now discuss each of these in turn and provide some relevant data.

First, if the narrator is processed as a conversational participant, the reader must attribute to the narrator those properties that are necessary for conversational communication. In particular, the narrator would be assumed to share perceptual ground, language, and culture with the reader. When this is not case, and there is no explicit indication of that in the text, readers will have trouble understanding and remembering material. A clear demonstration of this prediction can be found in a study by Kintsch and Greene (1978). This study was in part a systematic replication of Bartlett's (1932) classic work on remembering. The authors compared two stories, one based on familiar cultural schemata (a Grimm's fairy tale), and one based on unfamiliar cultural schemata (an Alaskan Indian folktale). Following the procedure of Bartlett, they compared story recall after five retellings from one person to another. The dependent variables included both the number of correctly recalled propositions from the text as well as the proportion of "gist" propositions that refer to the overall structure and point of the story. Their results are shown in figure 3: Stories with familiar cultural schemas were recalled better by both measures, although the difference was particularly notable with the recall of story gist. Further analysis revealed that the poor recall of unfamiliar story gist was caused by systematic distortions of the material to match readers' cultural schemata. Kintsch and Greene's interpretation of this result was essentially the same as Bartlett's (1932): material is easier to remember when readers have an appropriate set of schemata in memory. Our own conclusion goes somewhat further: We believe that the reason why readers attempt to apply inappropriate schemata to the Alaskan folktale is that they expect the narrator to share common cultural schemata. Under other circumstances, readers may be unlikely to apply such schemata inappropriately and the kinds of distortions observed by Kintsch and Greene would not be observed. For example, we suspect that if material were presented as a list to be memorized rather than as narrative, or if the narrator explicitly pointed out how his or her schemas differ from those of the reader, then the results would be quite different (cf. Paul 1959). In our view, the pattern of results observed by Kintsch and Green and Bartlett are directly related to the process of treating the narrator as a conversational participant.

Second, if the narrator is assumed to be a conversational participant communicating about the described world, then the narrator must be part of that world. Logically, this means that the narrator must have a unitary location and focalization in that world,

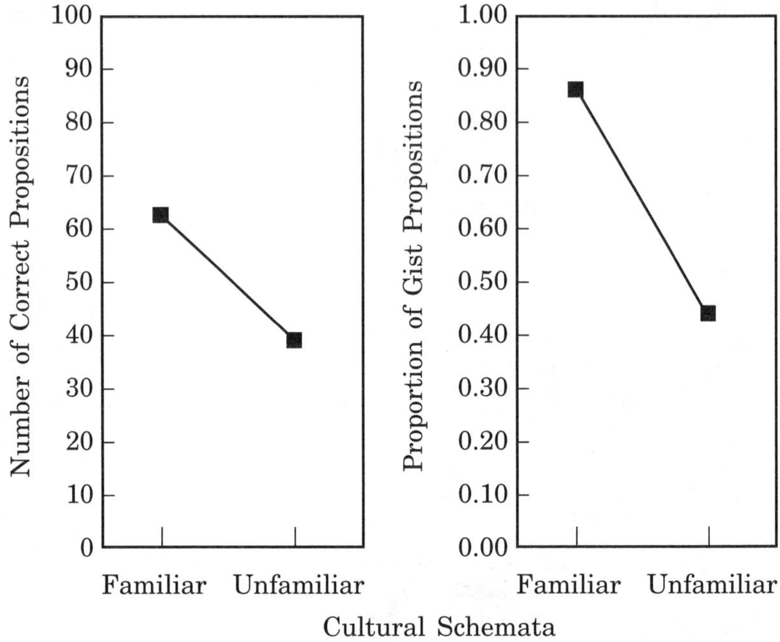

Fig. 16.3. Recall of stories with familiar and unfamiliar cultural schemata. From Kintsch and Greene (1978).

even when the narrator is technically absent from the narration. The implication is that when focalization changes in an arbitrary and unheralded way, comprehension will be disrupted because some extra inference or processing is required. A study by Black, Bower, and Turner (1979) illustrates this point. They compared sentences such as "Bill was sitting in the living room when John *came* into the living room" to slightly different versions with an inconsistent focalization such as "Bill was sitting in the living room when John *went* into the living room." This manipulation was carried out with single, complex sentences (such as the present example) and with pairs of comparable simple sentences as well. Figure 4 shows the reading time per syllable for the final clause in these sentences. The reading time is substantially slower for sentences with an inconsistent focalization. Presumably, the extra time in reading these sentences is related to the extra processing needed to infer how the narrator's position must have changed. In fact, Black, Bower, and Turner's (1979) interpretation was similar to that developed here. They assumed that the narrator is a mental representation on the part of the reader and that people prefer to interpret material from consistent narratorial points of view. The present approach further entails that a unitary focalization and position are the logical consequences of representing the narrator as a conversational participant and as part of the described world.

Third, we predict that readers attempt to cooperate with the narrator and to use their own knowledge and experience to fill in gaps or background as required. In conversation, these kinds of inferences have been termed *implicatures* by Grice (1975); according to his principle of cooperation, a conversational participant is invited to make whatever such inferences are necessary for utterances to make sense. In narrative, if the narrator is processed as a conversational participant, then implicatures would be applied to narratorial perspective. The net result is that readers' knowledge is used to justify the narrator's stance toward characters and events

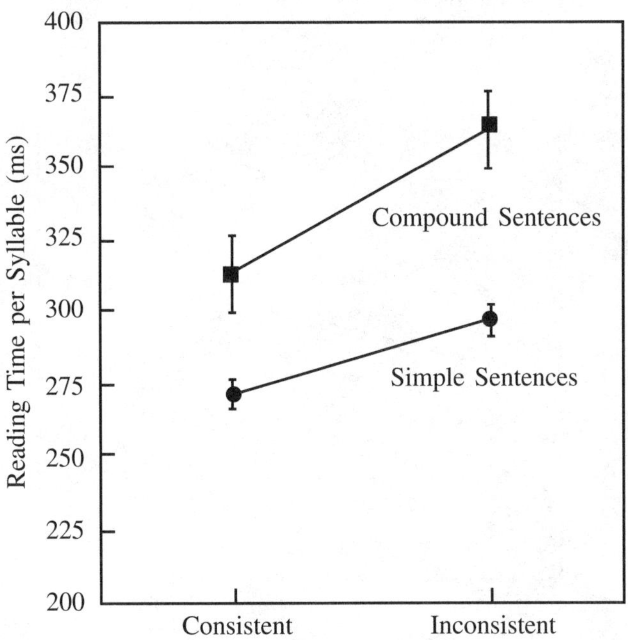

Fig. 16.4. Reading time for sentences with consistent and inconsistent narratorial position. From Black, Turner, and Bower (1979).

in the narrative whenever such justification seems necessary for the narrative to make sense. Some evidence related to this point comes from an earlier study of our own (Dixon & Bortolussi, 1996). Readers were asked to read the story "Rope" by Katherine Porter. The story consists of an argument between a husband and wife, related almost entirely as conversation with minimal intervention of the narrator. However, by manipulating dialogue style, we were able to create the suggestion that the narrator was partisan to either the man or the woman. Figure 5 shows the result of asking readers to rate how rational they thought the characters were. As is apparent, when the narrator is partisan to one character, that character is seen as relatively more rational and justified than when the narrator is partisan to the other character. Our interpretation of this result is that readers cooperate with the narrator and use their own knowledge and experience to justify the narrator's

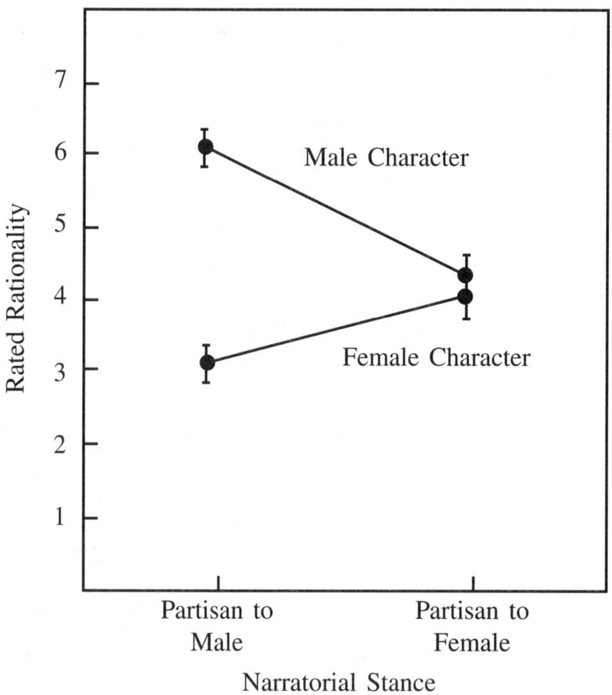

Fig. 16.5. Rating of character rationality for versions of "Rope" with narratorial stance partisan to male and female character.

stance. Thus, the character favored by that stance becomes more justified in the reader's mind.

The fourth prediction is that just as in conversation, readers assume that the narrator is cooperating with them. In particular, readers expect the narrator to provide exactly necessary and sufficient information. This has two implications for processing. First, if the text in fact provides extra, unnecessary information, readers will presume that it is necessary and may spend additional time and effort attempting to ascertain how the additional information is relevant or important. Second, if the text provides insufficient information for comprehension, readers will assume that there is a plausible inference that could be made in order to render the narrative comprehensible, and they are likely to spend time searching for such an inference. Evidence related to these predictions can be found in another study of ours. In this case, readers were asked to read the story "Emma Zunz" by Borges. This story is interesting because the narrator is essentially omniscient, but the text contains language suggesting that the perspective and knowledge of the narrator are limited. This device has a plausible interpretation in terms of the theme of the story, which we suspect is related to the ambiguity of fictional narrative and perhaps to the inadequacies of language generally. In order to evaluate the importance of this device in the context of the story, we created a new version of "Emma Zunz" in which the language suggesting limited narratorial perspective was removed, creating the effect of a more typical omniscient narrator. We also added the same kind of language to another, superficially similar story, "Death Was Her Dowry," taken from *True Detective* magazine. With these additions, the narrator's perspective and knowledge in "Death Was Her Dowry" was presented in essentially the same way as that in original "Emma Zunz." In this case though, the ironically limited narratorial perspective was unrelated to the theme of the story. Average reading times per sentence in this study are shown in Figure 6. These reading times are for the majority of sentences that remained the same across the manipulation of narratorial perspective. Thus, they are uncontaminated by any changes in the number of words or differences in sentence structure that the manipulation may have introduced. As shown in the figure, "Death was her Dowry" was read substantially slower when language suggesting limited narratorial perspective was added. We suspect that this additional time is spent trying to find a coherent representation of the narrative in which that information is relevant. In addition, changing the narratorial perspective in "Emma Zunz" tended to make that story somewhat harder to read as well, perhaps because the theme of the story is somewhat more difficult to determine without this particular narratorial device. However, this effect was unstable, and the language suggesting limited narratorial perspective may not be important for many of the readers in our study.

The studies we have described here serve to illustrate the kind of work that needs to be done in order to test our hypothesis concerning narratorial processing. However, none of these studies were designed as such a test, and we would not argue that they provide incontrovertible evidence in its favor. Instead, our point is simply that the proposal for psychonarratology is not an empty theoretical framework but rather an evolving approach to empirical investigations of narratorial processing. It is straightforward to construct testable hypotheses concerning narratorial processing and to find evidence with which to evaluate the hypotheses.

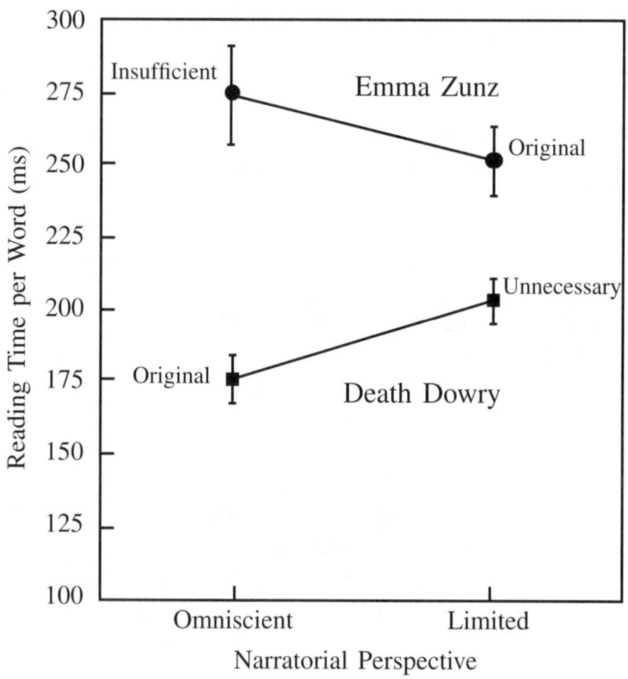

Fig. 16.6. Sentence reading times for story versions with unnecessary and insufficient information.

Conclusions

In conclusion, we suggest that this kind of approach, whether it is called "psychonarratology" or not, has the potential for illuminating a number of difficult problems with respect to the narrator and to how the narrator is processed by the reader. The concept of narratorial perspective is one example. In our terms, narratorial perspective is a complex of ideas that has at least two distinct components: The first component is similar to what has been termed *narratorial focalization* and can be objectively and reliably identified in the text. In our terms this is a text feature. The second component might be termed *narratorial stance.* Although in some cases the stance of the narrator can be found explicitly in the text, more often than not, it must be inferred by the reader. This means that stance is a text effect and should be construed as existing in the mind of the reader, not the text. Moreover, certain elements of narratorial stance, such as the narrator's knowledge, his or her cultural expectations, and the narrator's goals in relating the narrative, are likely to be constructed automatically because they would be required for conversation. In contrast, other elements, such as the attitude of the narrator toward characters, the relation of the narrator to the implied author, and the theme of the story, are likely to require more deliberate, strategic processing that depends on the reader's knowledge and training. Thus, different aspects of narratorial stance are likely to be affected by quite different variables. In sum, we feel that the value of present proposal is that it divides up the work of understanding narratorial perspective into a number of more manageable subproblems. Moreover, some of these subproblems are amenable to systematic and straightforward empirical investigation.

17

Shifting Perspectives: Readers' Feelings and Literary Response

David S. Miall and Don Kuiken

Perspective: Cognitive and Emotional Models

"It is only a novel," exclaims the young lady, in Jane Austen's *Northanger Abbey*, when asked what she is reading. It is only, says Austen,

> some work in which the greatest powers of the mind are displayed, in which the most thorough knowledge of human nature, the happiest delineation of its varieties, the liveliest effusions of wit and humour are conveyed to the world in the best chosen language. (chap. 5)

The richness of narrative and its cultural significance call for an equivalent complexity in our attempts to understand not only how narratives are constructed, but also the role they play in our lives. Here, the concept of perspective is an important one. Already much discussed, particularly since the work of Stanzel (1984), the concept of perspective provides us with a way of bringing order to some of the many questions we wish to explore.

We propose that Austen's young lady experiences a range of feelings as she reads, and that this may prove to be her principle reason for reading the novel. Her response when challenged, which in Austen's account is either pretended indifference or shame, suggests that her reading is self-involving: some special interest or desire is implicated that she is unwilling to have suspected. We are left to wonder what personal perspective she is subtly protecting.

Thus, among other things, an account of narrative response will focus on how readers' feelings and emotions shape their personal perspectives. Our proposal will distinguish several aspects of feeling and several forms of perspective during reading. First, consider some of the ways in which perspective has been discussed and empirically examined at both the local and global levels of text structure. At the local level, where influences on perspective are exerted sentence by sentence or even word by word, three local variations in perspective have been studied: spatiotemporal, experiential, and aesthetic. Each can be assessed objectively (e.g., by identifying shifts from one visuo-spatial perspective to another) so that its influence on readers can be studied using measures such as reading times or reader ratings. On the other hand, at the global level, perspective may be affected by textual features beyond the sentence, including episodes or other complex structures identified in the text, for example, a succession of improbable perspective shifts may prompt the reader to represent the author's more comprehensive perspective. Such global factors have less frequently been the object of empirical study, and at this level of analysis literary texts pose especially challenging difficulties. We will discuss the influences on perspective that can be examined at the local level; then, in the last section of this chapter, we mention one attempt to examine response at the global level.

At the local level, spatiotemporal perspective plays a central role. Delimited in terms of a character, a narrator, or even an author's stance toward fictive time and space, this seems analogous to the use of camera position in film. The point of view given is either that of a character within the story or of an external observer. Correspondingly, shifts in points of view are manifest either as changes in a particular figure's visuo-spatial point of view, or as changes between internal (e.g., character) and external (e.g., narrator) perspectives (cf. Stanzel 1984: 66). Such shifts increase the work required of the reader, who must correspondingly adjust her situation model in spatial and temporal terms. Such adjustments challenge the reader's schema, which must be particularized anew from the propositions available in the text and from the inferences that can be drawn from them. Since this process occurs on-line, one measure of the reconstructive activity required of the reader has been reading time. There is evidence that longer reading times occur when there are shifts in visuo-spatial point of view (Zwaan, Magliano, & Graesser 1995), including shifts between internal and external viewpoints (Millis 1995).

However, variations in perspective can also be understood more broadly. In Rimmon-Kenan's (1983) account, where perspective (following Genette 1980, 1988) is referred to as "focalization," point of view is broadened beyond space-time perception to include variations in a characters' conceptions of, and beliefs about, fictive situations (cf. Bal 1985: 100 ff.). By this account, a character's feelings and attitudes also imply a particular perspective (77–82) and could be analyzed with some objectivity as formal aspects of a given narrative (although a full analysis of these aspects would extend beyond the local level). In our judgment, Rimmon-Kenan's discussion opens the possibility that a change in a character's affective stance within a fictive situation can be regarded as a shift in perspective, as well. As with visuo-spatial point of view, a shift in a character's feelings or attitudes, such as the revelation of previously undisclosed emotions, may challenge readers to reconstruct their representations of that character's feelings or attitudes. Since this, too, occurs on-line, it will complicate reading and increase reading time, as evidence by Cupchik and Laszlo (1994) suggests. For readers who respond empathically to this type of perspective change, distinctions between character and reader feelings begin to blur. Nonetheless, such feelings are manifest as different perspectives within the text, rather than occurring in response to the text. They contrast, for example, with feelings of sympathy in response to a character's distress, as well as with feelings of suspense in response to plot uncertainties (cf. Brewer & Lichtenstein 1983).

However, broadened in this way, perspective variations of another kind become salient in literary texts. In particular, feelings manifest in the text include those embodied by stylistic devices, which we would argue are distinguishing features of literary narratives. We propose that stylistic devices, which are deviations from nonliterary language forms (cf. van Peer 1986), embody subtle shifts in feeling, for example, a metaphoric description of a story setting presents a different "felt sense" of that fictive place; an alliterative expression provides a particular "feeling for" the current textual referent, and so forth. In our studies (Miall & Kuiken 1994b), we have provided evidence that such stylistically induced feeling shifts require readers to reconstruct their understanding of the narrative in a way that prolongs reading time. Although the feelings evoked by stylistic devices are less frequently attributed to a story character and more often attributed to the narrator, these stylistic variations nonetheless "focalize" feelings and constitute a type of perspective shift. And, for readers who respond affectively to these stylistic devices, distinctions between reader and (usually) narrator feelings may blur, although these feelings are embodied by the text and not simply by affective responses to it, for example, the feelings embodied in a metaphoric description contrast with mere enjoyment of its aptness, as well as with simple satisfaction in having understood it. By maintaining these distinctions, feeling focalization in response to stylistic devices may be seen as a type of perspectival adjustment distinctive to literary reading.

We can conceive of perspective, then, as a compound of at least three narrative elements, each amenable in some degree to objective analysis. The first element consists of the spatiotemporal point of view, including internal versus external perspective. The second is focalization of the feeling experience of a character(s). The third element is focalization of the feelings and attitudes embodied in stylistic devices that are a distinctive feature of literary texts. Feelings are directly implicated in the last two of these components, although quite differently. In the focalization of a character's feeling experience, readers are responding to an aspect of narrative content, in particular, the feeling experiences of a character (cf. the model of reflective reading outlined by Cupchik 1995). In focalization of feelings in response to stylistic devices, readers are responding to more distinctly aesthetic qualities embodied in the text (and the related feelings are A-emotions in the terminology of Kneepkens & Zwaan 1995).

It is aesthetic focalization, we argue, that cognitive models of reading have not adequately conceived or studied. Theories of text comprehension devised for expository prose or simple (often experimenter-generated) stories, often fail to consider the importance of shifts in reader perspective occurring in response to stylistic devices (e.g., Kintsch 1988). For the study of literary reading, then, we propose a central question that takes us beyond spatiotemporal point of view and beyond the focalization of character feeling experience. We want to understand how a reader arrives at a felt perspective, often a personal one, which inheres in a literary text's expressively rich aesthetic components.

Our own empirical studies represent an attempt to address this question, and in the next part of the chapter, we will demonstrate that the aesthetic components of perspective construction contributes to the reading process independently of spatiotemporal point of view and focalization of character feelings.

Story Features and Perspective Differences between Readers

Unless a narrative segment is ambiguous or indeterminate, indicators of all three perspective components can be identified. Here are the first four segments of a short story we have employed in several studies, "The Trout," by O'Faolain:

> (A) One of the first places Julia always ran to when they arrived in G—was The Dark Walk. (B) It is a laurel walk, very old, almost gone wild, a lofty midnight tunnel of smooth, sinewy branches. (C) Underfoot the tough brown leaves are never dry enough to crackle: there is always a suggestion of damp and cool trickle. (D) She raced right into it.

The spatiotemporal perspective established is external, and the narrator's point of view is pervasive. In the second and third segments, which elaborate the nature of The Dark Walk, the indications of perception given in "Underfoot" and "a suggestion" appear to be from the point of view of an omniscient observer. This observer's temporal perspective changes, however, in (D). There is a shift from a broadly historical perspective (e.g., "always ran" "are never," "is always") to one that refers to Julia's present activities (e.g., "She raced right into it").

Also, feeling focalization is uniformly missing. These segments lack description that refers to Julia's feelings, attitudes, or motives. Descriptions of The Dark Walk convey what any visitor would experience; they are not given as an indication of Julia's feelings toward The Dark Walk or of the motives for her interest in it. Only inferences from her running and racing (A and D) even hint at the enthusiasm that will become focal in subsequent passages.

Other features of (B) and (C) serve to create aesthetic perspective. This is the array of stylistic features, such as the metaphor of "lofty midnight tunnel," the alliteration of "smooth, sinewy," and the consonance of "damp and cool trickle." We suggest that those features focalize aesthetic feeling. Consistent with this notion, we have found that the concentration of such foregrounded features has three significant correlates in the responses of the readers we have studied: it seems striking, it evokes uncertainty, and it arouses feeling (Miall & Kuiken 1994b).

Aesthetic focalization of feeling complicates any decision a reader might make about perspective. In response to foregrounding, readers consistently find the passage striking or evocative, sense the presence of feelings (however vague), and reflect longer as they engage the openness of the meaning possibilities there. However, their interpretive adjustments in response to foregrounding are anything but consistent from reader to reader. Examining actual responses to these segments reveals a wide range of interpretive adjustments, including adjustments in spatiotemporal perspective and in character feeling focalization. Here are just a few of the comments that readers made to (C), when asked to think aloud about their thoughts and feelings while reading this story.

Reader 16 elaborated the external perspective on the setting: "you can feel how . . . how it's cold there. But not freezing cold, just cool. Nice and dark and lonely, but not alone." Note the use of the impersonal "you," corresponding to the omniscient perspective we identified from the linguistic features of the sentence. Reader 35 elaborated the setting in a slightly more personal way: "The fact that the tough dry leaves are never dry enough to crackle makes . . . me imagine a . . . a musty smell." The personal meaning of the setting for reader 17 was more specific: it evokes a personal memory. "Reminds me of a place you go when you're young just with your friends or just to get away. Reminds me of my backyard." Yet another reader, reader 24, appeared ready to interpret the meaning of The Dark Walk from Julia's perspective: "It seems a place of calm for this girl to go. She seems anxious to get to this area."

The first point to note, in the examples we have cited, is the presence of feeling. Two of the responses are explicitly colored by feeling, as shown by the phrases "Nice and dark and lonely" and "seems anxious." Feeling may also be implicit in the other two, in the "musty smell," or in the reader's memory of her backyard. Regardless of its clarity or locus, feeling consistently is present in response to foregrounding. When asked to rate the segments of this story for feeling, foregrounded passages like these received significantly higher ratings. Also, foregrounded passages were consistently found to be more striking or evocative, which we interpret as evidence of aesthetic feeling focalization.

Second, it is clear that these readers respond to these moments of aesthetic feeling in their own ways. (In a think-aloud study, of course, reading is slowed considerably, enabling readers to elaborate their sense of the implications of a given segment. However, we assume that the different and interestingly complex perspectives revealed here are also likely to occur during normal reading.)

Thus, the acts of focalization vary, often quite markedly, from one reader to another. Although the narrative invites empathy with a central character, the reader may remain distant; or, conversely, a reader might identify closely with a main character, although only an external perspective is offered. Thus, when shifts in interpretation occur in response to foregrounding, the narrative does not predetermine the nature of the adjustment in the reader's perspective. Aesthetic feeling opens rather than closes the possibilities for shifts in spatiotemporal or feeling experience perspectives. This is a critical point to consider in accounting for narrative perspective.

We have obtained evidence that foregrounding and aesthetic feeling contribute to reader perspective independently of spatiotemporal and experiential perspective components. As mentioned earlier, the influence of various features of narrative has often been measured by reading times, on the assumption that certain features place greater demands on the readers' resources. In a recent study, we were able to assess the relative influence of a range of local perspective features on sixty readers of "The Trout," from whom we also collected measures of individual differences, using the Literary Response Questionnaire (LRQ) (Miall & Kuiken 1995), and the Multidimensional Personality Questionnaire (MPQ) (Tellegen 1982).

For this study, we adopted the discourse measures of Zwaan, Magliano, and Graesser (1995), which enable individual segments of a story to be coded for propositional features (new arguments and argument overlap) and for discontinuities in time, space, and causation. We also created an additional measure, experiential perspective: a four-point scale marking the degree to which a given segment indicates an internal or external perspective on the main character, or no perspective on that character; the internal perspective divides into cognitions, on the one hand, or emotions and motives on the other (see table 1). Our view was that the more the narrative invites the reader to experience the internal thoughts or feelings of the main character, the greater the amount of processing required of the reader (cf. Cupchik & Laszlo, who found that segments that provided "insight into the characters' experiences" [1994: 304] were read more slowly). For readers who identified with the main character in particular, the perspective measure should show a positive correlation with reading speed. We also measured the amount of foregrounding present in each segment, as well as segment position and number of syllables per segment.

Table 17.1
Perspective on the Main Character

1. No mention of character.
2. Character's actions or appearance are described, but as though from an external, observer perspective. This includes indirect discourse and most direct discourse (where an observer perspective is assumed).
3. Character's cognitions: perceptions, thoughts, and so forth, where unmarked or only mildly marked by feeling; and direct discourse if this seems to invite the reader's involvement in character's perspective.
4. Feelings of character, where these appear to raise motivational issues for character; motives and emotions; most passages of free indirect discourse; and direct discourse only if it clearly invites the reader to share character's emotions or motives.

Note: Scale for scoring narrative segments, 1 to 4.

First, regression analyses were carried out on the reading factors just described, with mean reading times as the dependent variable. Both standard regression and robust regression (Andrew's Sine) were used; in robust regression the effect of outliers in the data is minimized. In the standard regression analysis, the number of syllables per segment and the number of new arguments both contributed to the prediction of reading time. These may be regarded as separate indices of sentential and propositional complexity (see table 2). Also, readers were influenced by segment position: they tended to speed up as they approached the end of the story. More important, independently of those factors, foregrounding also substantially contributed to the prediction of reading time. The robust regression analyses reflected the preceding relations, as well as indicating the independent contributions of argument overlap, causal discontinuities, and experiential perspective.

Our analysis points to an important conclusion. While the reader must construct—and sometimes reconstruct—a situation model that is mediated by the arguments within each segment, and by relationships in time, space, and cause, this will be constructed by the reader whether the text is literary or not. What is notable here is that foregrounding, which is distinctive to literary texts, appears to exert a strong influence independently of these more general factors. This may indicate that a situation model limited to these factors is insufficient for understanding readers' reactions to this

Table 17.2
Multiple Regression Analyses of Story Factors for "The Trout" with Mean Reading Times (Standard Model, and Robust Regression Analysis)

df 82	standard simple corr.	robust partial corr.	partial corr.
segment position	.083	–.421**	–.712**
syllables	.882**	.826**	.946**
foregrounding	.630**	.358**	.660**
new arguments	.582**	.206*	.311**
argument overlap	.059	.179	.476**
time	.197*	.119	.099
space	.147	–.016	–.083
cause	.253*	.169	.364**
perspective	.202*	.124	.353**

*p < 05 **p < .01 (one tailed)

story. Readers in this study turned to foregrounding (and perhaps to experiential perspective) for additional guidance during construction of their understandings.

Thus there are several sources of perspective in a literary story, including foregrounding and focalization of character feelings, as well as the discourse features employed by Zwaan, Magliano, and Graesser (1995). Moreover, individual readers may vary in how they utilize these various factors. To examine the role of individual differences, we also compared readers' scores on the LRQ and the MPQ with the same set of influences on reading speed. Regression analyses were carried out for each reader, with individual reading times as the dependent variable. The partial correlations for each factor were then transformed to z-scores and correlated with questionnaire scores. While the results are not particularly clear-cut, they show that, even when considering reading speed only, individual differences were apparent, for example, those most responsive to foregrounding scored low on Alienation and low on Traditionalism, a hint that foregrounding may be more engaging for readers who are secure socially but also independent thinkers. Although such findings are suggestive, further interpretation would be speculative: clearly more research must be done to examine the influences and predispositions at the individual level that shape readers' perspectives.

Toward a Phasic Model of Literary Response

If when reading a given segment readers are influenced by feeling in response to foregrounding or experiential perspective, what effect does this have on the course of reading? Our studies of this question have served to take us beyond the model of local perspective effects, toward a complex, phasic structure of response in which feeling plays a central role.

How might feeling evoke perspective? In De Sousa's (1987) account, an emotion sets the salience of the cognitive field; that is, it selects which objects will become the focus of attention. A comparable notion is captured by Frijda's (1988) law of closure, which describes the "control precedence" of emotion, its regulation for the time being of motor and cognitive activity. Both of these accounts involve perspective-setting operations, which we can examine in a range of everyday situations as well as during reading. More distinctive to literary response is the process most often termed *defamiliarization* (other terms used include Brecht's *estrangement,* or Cupchik's 1996 *disorientation*): here, we will suggest, focalization of aesthetic feelings plays an important role in bringing about changes in the reader's current perspective. At its most powerful, the context in which a reader usually experiences a feeling will be challenged and modified. Our analysis of literary reading thus calls for an understanding of the transformations in feeling that readers may experience.

Some initiating event appears to arouse feeling in the reader and to cause longer reading times (e.g., focalization of aesthetic feelings in response to stylistic devices). We surmise that the reader experiences uncertainty at such a moment, and turns to feeling in order to locate an alternative source of meaning. We have found effects that can be traced across a number of succeeding segments. Some effects are apparent within two or three segments of the most highly foregrounded one; others occur at a distance of six or seven segments. The clearest marker we have for this phasic process comes from short-term correlations (measured across six segments) between reading times and affect ratings, which fluctuate in a rather consistent way between negative and positive (cf. Dijkstra et al. 1995: 147: affect and reading speed have a variable relation, dependent on the locus in the story). A positive correlation indicates that when reading time is long, more intense feeling is occurring in response to an experience of defamiliarization, since such peaks in positive correlation tend to occur three segments after a highly foregrounded passage. They are followed at a lag of several further segments by an increase in shifts in story understanding (shown by data derived from a parallel study on story remindings). Some of these features are shown in figure 1.

These data suggest a three-phase structure in response. First is the encounter with a defamiliarizing story event or feature (e.g., a stylistic device), which arouses feeling. A second phase ensues during which feeling directs a search for a context for the local meaning of the story, which has been unsettled. In the third phase a shift in the reader's general story understanding takes place, and what had been defamiliarized is now contextualized. Such a sequence is likely to recur several times during response to a literary text. In the story that was the focus of our study, a cycle of this kind appears to have taken place at least three times, as a graph of the correlations of reading times and affect ratings shows (see fig. 2).

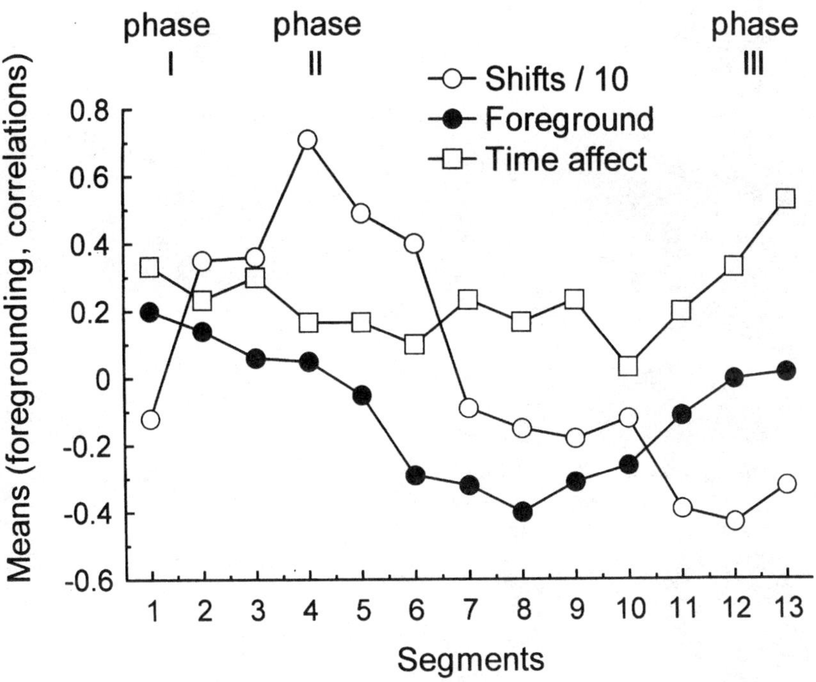

Fig. 17.1. Story phases: indicators derived from mean story and reading data for thirteen segments.

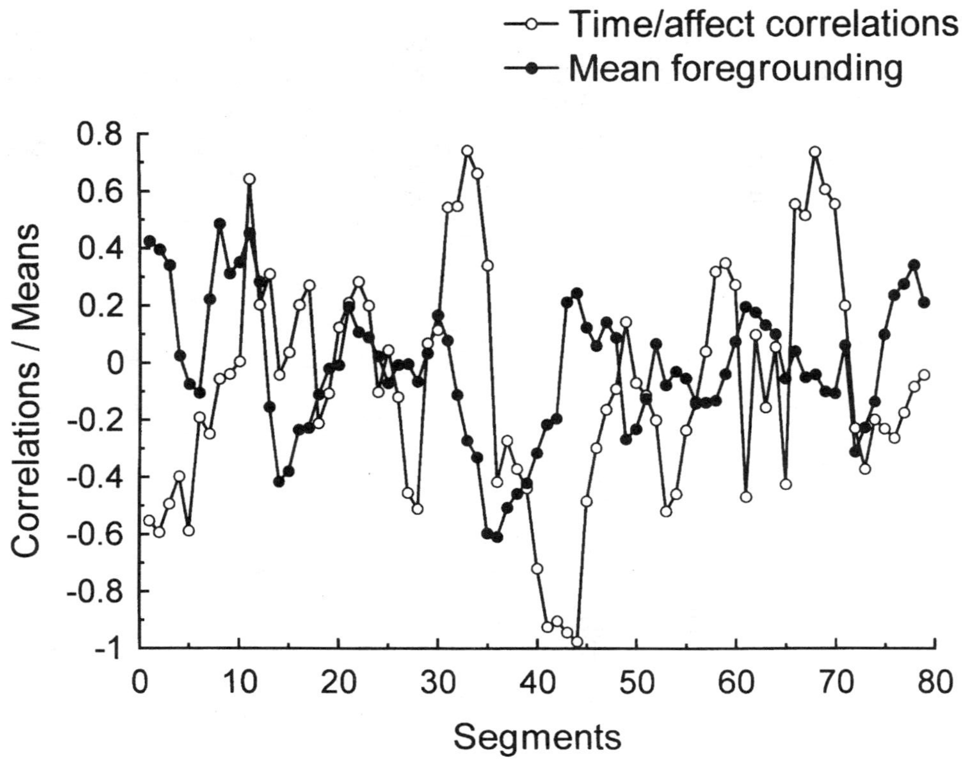

Fig. 17.2. Six-segment correlations of reading times and affect ratings for "The Trout."

A literary narrative thus appears to be made up of a series of episodes, in which the reader's perspective is repeatedly disrupted and reshaped, especially in response to stylistic devices. In this process, it is the feelings available to the reader during the defamiliarizing moment that guide the search for a new perspective.

The concept of phases in narrative has been described before, although with rather different implications. Kneepkens and Zwaan (1995: 135–36), for instance, note the possibility that when the reader "encounters abstract or vague descriptions" in a story, she will experience a decline in empathic emotions until a new episode is reached; in this way reception may be cyclic. Brooks elaborates a Freudian model of plot to explain what he terms *repetition with variation,* or the basic *pulsation* of narrative text (1984: 102). His figure for this is taken from a squiggle made by Balzac at the end of his first novel, which was turned into the emblem of a snake by the novel's first printers. This in turn might remind us that Coleridge described the reader's journey through a literary text as like a snake: "at every step he pauses and half recedes, and from the retrogressive movement collects the force which again carries him onward" (1817/1983: 2.11).

Our contribution to this model, apart from providing some empirical confirmation for it, is to identify the key role of feeling in reshaping the reader's perspective during reading. If feeling is self-referential, as we have previously suggested (Miall 1989; cf. Frijda's [1988] law of concern), literary narrative may be an important instrument in the elaboration and evolution of our feelings. Through the new perspectives it opens up, we contemplate other possible selves, and learn whether to accept or reject them. But if we are to understand better how literary reading creates perspective, and what its implications are for individual readers, other more imaginative and well-designed empirical studies will be needed.

18

Perspective as Participation

Richard J. Gerrig

Imagine you are reading these words for the first time:

> "Call me Ishmael."

What information have you acquired so far? Clearly you now know the narrator's name (or, at least, you believe that you do). You've also learned that the story soon to unfold will be told in the first person, from Ishmael's perspective, and perhaps you've also learned that Ishmael will tell the story in a way that is particularly intended to engage his audience. You may also quickly come to have some hypotheses about exactly what sort of person Ishmael may be:

> Some years ago—never mind how long precisely—having little or no money in my purse, and nothing particular to interest me on shore, I thought I would sail about a little and see the watery part of the world.

Thus, in these first two sentences of Herman Melville's novel *Moby-Dick* (1851) the reader can start to learn about both the perspective from which the story will be told and what some of the ramifications, characterologically speaking, of that perspective might be.

In this chapter, I will provide an account of some ways in which readers participate in the experience of narratives to discover and use perspectives. In my analysis of the opening of *Moby-Dick*, I described patterns of thinking that readers might, or might not, set in motion. I will present here a series of cases in which perspective effects similarly rely on readers' voluntary activities. My goal is not to deny that some types of perspectives may not affect readers without participation, but rather to identify the many circumstances in which participation is required. I begin by briefly setting out a framework for participatory aspects of narrative experiences. I then present case studies and data relevant to particular instances of participation.

Possible Perspectives and Participation

What perspectives are possible in a narrative work? Several classic works of literary analysis (e.g., Booth 1983; Chatman 1978; Cohn 1978; Genette 1980, 1988, and Fludernik, chap. 6 of this vol.) lay out a remarkable number of distinctions that can be made in the way in which narration is accomplished in works of fiction. Such works may have dramatized or undramatized narrators, reliable or unreliable narrators, self-conscious or impersonal narrators, and covert or overt narrators. They may employ psychonarration and quoted or narrated monologue. It is possible to marshal literary evidence for each of these distinctions. However, as a psychologist, the question I wish to ask is, How are readers affected by these distinctions? That is, if all these types of perspectives lie waiting for the adventurous reader, how do those perspectives achieve their effects?

To address this question, I will explore the ways in which readers participate in the construction and use of perspectives. Consider a standard horror movie scenario in which a character approaches a door, behind which the viewers know danger lurks. If a viewer, mentally or literally, calls out "Don't go through the door!" I would count that as a participatory response (p-response) (Allbritton & Gerrig 1991; Gerrig 1993). The important contrast here is to inferences and inference processes. Rather than bridging a gap in the text, p-responses generally reflect a sort of voluntary participation in the narrative world. Most theories of text processing within cognitive psychology have focused solely on the ways in which texts act on readers: They attempt to specify the types of inferences a text requires readers to make (see Graesser, Singer, & Trabasso 1994; and McKoon & Ratcliff 1992). By shifting our attention to p-responses, by contrast, we begin to focus on how readers act on texts. I suggest that this shift in focus will provide a useful starting point for the cognitive psychological study of perspective.

To make this framework more concrete, let's return to the outset of *Moby-Dick*:

> Call me Ishmael.

Suppose, after reading this sentence, an individual thinks, "OK, I'll call you Ishamel." That's a participatory response. If this individual goes on to think "But who is Ishmael?" then we can see how a p-response can direct the construction of a perspective. Immediate contemplation of Ishmael is not required by the text—this is not a necessary inference—but it will begin to allow a reader to develop a perspective on the unfolding story: a perspective that will presumably differ in some important ways from Ishmael's own. I claim that participation, realized by participatory responses, directs readers to discover particular perspectives. (In the sections that follow, I will provide several illustrations of discovery.) Note that discovery will most often involve a complex interweaving of inferencing and p-responding, for example, the p-response "But who is Ishmael?" may initiate contemplation of *Moby-Dick*'s narrator, but inferences ("What kind of person would be broke and take to the sea?") are required to fill out the model. Similarly, in the horror movie scenario, an inference ("That's the door behind which danger lurks") gives rise to a p-response ("Don't go through that door!") which may, in turn, establish a perspective on events ("She deserved to be disemboweled by the monster, because I warned her not to go through that door"). My general claim is that participation often sets in motion the mental activities (i.e., both inferencing and p-responding) that allow readers to discover perspectives.

My first concern, therefore, will be with discovery: How is it that readers begin to apprehend features of the ways in which narratives unfold? Although I will not be trying to confirm particular aspects of the taxonomies I cited earlier (i.e., Booth, Chatman, Cohn, and Genette), I believe that the psychological value of these taxonomic distinctions will rely on readers' ability to discover them. However, I'd also like to demonstrate that the distinctions have consequences. If, for example, readers discover that a story is being told by an unreliable narrator, in what ways does that come to matter? The taxonomic distinctions are much less interesting if we can't establish how they affect the moment-by-moment experience of a narrative. Having sketched out this general framework for examining perspective, I now exemplify the links between the discovery and consequences of those perspectives.

Discovering Perspectives

I have already suggested that readers participate, via p-responses, in the discovery of perspective. I will now work through a series of examples of the way in which readers discover perspective. An important part of this analysis will be to describe why this discovery matters: I will try to identify some of the consequences that perspective has on the way in which readers are affected by the narratives they experience. I begin with the perspectives people bring with them to the stories they read.

External Perspectives

Of the many definitions we might give to "perspective," one of the most straightforward could be "the unique point of view with which each reader approaches a text." By analogy to visual perspective—in which each viewer encounters an object from at least a slightly different vantage point—we can claim that each reader brings at least a slightly different set of prior knowledge, beliefs, and expectations to his or her experience of a narrative. Although it is sometimes the case that readers have an awareness of what that perspective might be (I'll return to that idea shortly), there are still important ways in which readers discover even their external perspectives through interaction with the text.

To illustrate this point, I will use an excerpt from Robertson Davies's novel, *The Lyre of Orpheus*. Maria, who is pregnant, speaks first:

> "I was drinking this [rum and milk] last night when Al and Sweetness were here, and Sweetness was shocked."
>
> "Shocked by rum and milk? . . . What shocked her?"
>
> "She gave me a long, confused talk about what she called the foetal alcohol syndrome; booze in pregnancy can lead to pixie-faced, pin-headed, mentally retarded children.
>
> I knew something about that; you have to drink rather a lot to be in danger. But Sweetness is a zealot, and she's deep into the squalor of pregnancy, poor wretch. . . . She is paying the full price nasty old Mother Nature can exact for Al's baby. I just hope it's a nice baby." (1988: 344–45)

I read this paragraph secure in the knowledge that Maria is incorrect. Although fetal alcohol syndrome is most often associated with heavy drinking, a child's future performance can be impaired when mothers drink even small amounts of alcohol during critical periods of pregnancy (Coles 1994; Jacobson & Jacobson 1994). When I first read Davies's novel, this passage had rather a wrenching effect on me. Had I caught Davies in a lie? Was he misinformed about the facts? Had he purposefully put misinformation into Maria's mouth? Was I supposed to think substantially less well of Maria, but not of Davies? The novel provides additional evidence: As the story continues, Maria delivers a healthy child but Sweetness delivers a stillborn baby. The book, therefore, appears to demonstrate that women can (should?) have a relaxed attitude about drinking during pregnancy—which led me, ultimately, to think poorly of Davies. I had mostly enjoyed his novels, but this discovery changed my perspective. My new perspective required a sort of wariness and scrutiny that had been absent from my previous experiences of his work.

My more general claim is that moments like this one—at which a reader's attention comes to be focused on some aspect of a narrative that is strikingly at odds with prior beliefs, knowledge, or expectations—constitute the discovery of an external perspective. The discovery relies on an initial p-response, "That's not right!" and gives rise to a whole train of participation. To the extent that readers wish to carry their perspectives through, they can begin to examine the text—to focus their attention strategically—to construct a representation of the text that encodes their own unique viewpoints.

When I read *The Lyre of Orpheus*, I did not approach the work with the expectation that an external perspective would deform my experience of the book. In many cases, however, readers are fully aware of the perspectives they bring to narratives. If we consider, for example, the practice of literary criticism, the main motivation a reader might have is to apply a particular perspective to a work: to see how the understanding of a work is enriched by filtering it through a particular perspective. Even in these cases, however, the concept of discovery applies, but in a somewhat different fashion. My anecdotal report on *The Lyre of Orpheus* suggested that ordinary, or initial, acts of discovery are largely passive. I was not reading with an eye toward finding and pursuing a perspective. My perspective emerged because Maria (or Davies's) misinformation catapulted me out of the narrative world. By contrast, discovery is anything but passive when readers purposefully apply systems of theory to narrative works. In these cases, they struggle to discover the moments in a work when the theory best applies. The advisability of giving some plot or character element a Freudian or feminist reading, for example, often becomes a matter of critical debate. The underlying method, however, allows a perspective to shape moments of discovery.

Note that for the ordinary reader, passive discovery often becomes transformed into active discovery. The wary perspective I acquired for *The Lyre of Orpheus* gave rise to a whole new strategy for reading the book, as I tried to determine what Davies's agenda might be. Similarly, we might expect readers who discovered that a particular character harbored views at odds with their own (e.g., by expressing opinions that were too liberal or conservative), would use that perspective to focus particular scrutiny on the character. What would begin as passive discovery ("How could she think that?") would end as active discovery ("Here's more evidence for my case against her").

I have chosen these examples of discovery to make it apparent why I believe that perspectives have consequences. I read the last hundred or so pages of *The Lyre of Orpheus* quite differently than I would have had the subject of alcohol and pregnancy never been broached. Therefore, if we were to examine my representation of the story—the way in which I had committed information from the story to memory—it would almost certainly be different from the representation of a reader who had not been so appalled by Maria's misinformation. This is one straightforward type of consequence. I am interested, however, in consequences beyond memory representations. In particular, I believe it is important to examine how perspectives affect the way in which readers apply the information they acquire from narratives to their judgments about the real world.

To illustrate this point, I will describe an experiment that I conducted with Prentice and Daniel Bailis (Prentice, Gerrig, & Bailis 1997). In our study, participants read a short story that included discussions of a series of topics. Some of these discussions were clearly at odds with the facts of the real world. Consider this excerpt from our story:

> "Do you think it's going to rain?" Brad asked.
>
> "It might," Maureen replied, "and I don't want to get soaked and end up catching a cold."

> In his best pre-med voice, Brad responded, "You shouldn't subscribe to that old wives' tale. You don't get a cold from getting soaked, you get it from a virus."
>
> "I'm sure that's true, but. . . ." said Maureen.
>
> Brad interrupted, "In fact, in some ways, getting totally soaked will help you avoid getting a cold. When you get soaked, your body has to pump itself up to help keep you warm. When you increase your body's internal temperature, that also makes it harder for viruses to live within you. So, by getting soaked you can help kill the virus that might cause a cold—how does that sound? Getting soaked actually helps prevent colds."

Suppose you had read this part of the story. Under what circumstances might you actually come to believe that, contrary to what our mothers taught us, getting soaked is good? Prentice, Bailis, and I looked to the social psychological literature on persuasion to make our predictions. Researchers have demonstrated that readers tend to evaluate more critically information relevant to issues that are of personal importance (for reviews, see Johnson & Eagly 1989; and Petty & Cacioppo 1986). We made the information in the story more or less personally important by carrying out a rather subtle manipulation of perspective. Half of our participants were Yale undergraduates; half were Princeton undergraduates. Half the participants read a story set at Yale; half the participants read a story set at Princeton. We reasoned that participants would discover different perspectives for the matching (home) and mismatching (away) schools. Because participants reading from the home school perspective should find the information more personally relevant, we predicted that they would evaluate our fictional information more critically; critical thinking should lead to a relatively smaller change in beliefs.

Our story recounted a kidnapping (which had taken place at Yale in one version and at Princeton at the other). As the action unfolded, readers encountered discussions of sixteen topics about which most people have strong real-world beliefs (i.e., most people agree that getting soaked in a rainstorm is not a good health strategy). Half of those discussions were at odds with the real world (as in the example given earlier) whereas half supported the real-world belief:

> "Do you think it's going to rain?" Brad asked.
>
> "It might," Maureen replied, "and I don't want to get soaked and end up catching a cold."
>
> In his best pre-med voice, Frank said, "You don't get a cold from getting soaked. You get it from a virus."
>
> "True enough," said Maureen (who was still an active pre-med), "but if you get totally cold and soaked you can provide the virus a much more hospitable place to make itself at home. Mom was doing the right thing when she dragged you in out of the rain."

Our prediction, again, was that participants reading from the home school perspective would evaluate the information in the story more carefully. After reading the story, participants performed a brief filler task. We then assessed their beliefs by asking them to indicate their agreement on a 1- (strongly disagree) to 9- (strongly agree) point scale to statements such as "Getting soaked in a rainstorm decreases your chances of catching a cold."

Table 1 presents a summary of the experiment's results. The figures represent average persuasion in the direction of information in the story. The pattern of data strongly support the prediction that persuasion will be greater when participants read the text from the away school perspective, that is, the amount of persuasion in the nonmatched cells (e.g., Yale readers of the Princeton story) is considerably larger than in the matched cells.

Let me review why these data support the characterization of perspective as participation. Consider the version of the story set at Princeton. Both Yale and Princeton students read exactly the same text, word for word. The differences we found in the amount of persuasion cannot, therefore, be attributed to the text. They can only be attributed to the cognitive activities the students carried out with respect to the text: that is, the way in which they participated in their experience of the text. I suggest that these cognitive

Table 18.1
Average Persuasion in the Direction of Story Information

	Yale students	*Princeton students*
Yale story	0.07	0.49
Princeton story	0.55	–0.31

activities were set in motion by an act of discovery. The very first paragraph of the story sets the scene. Some participants read, "He looked out the window and saw that it was the beginning of another boring and gloomy day in Princeton, New Jersey." For other participants, the sentence established the setting as "New Haven, Connecticut." At this early juncture, readers discovered whether the story was consistent or inconsistent with their own external (Yale or Princeton) perspective. Presumably, this perspective defined the story as more or less personally relevant, and our persuasion effect ensued.

Another strength of this experiment, I believe, is that it makes clear how concrete the effects of perspective can be. Not every story will try to persuade its readers to a new point of view, but what we have demonstrated is that readers' perspectives (in this case defined by the external perspective they bring with them to the experience of the story) can have a strong influence on whether such persuasion is possible. The experiment suggests that perspective affects not just the moment-by-moment experience of a narrative, but also the potential for the narrative to have a long-term impact on its readers.

First-Person versus Third-Person Perspective

The previous section was devoted to the types of perspectives readers discover they have brought with them from their real worlds, external to the narrative. I will now consider the perspectives readers discover within narrative worlds. My starting point will be a distinction that I believe will not actually require much discovery on the part of readers: the distinction between first- and third-person narration. It should be clear, relatively early in a text, on which side of this divide the narration falls. Therefore, my concern in this case is not so much discovery, but the types of consequences that may follow when readers experience a text from a first- versus a third-person perspective.

Note that the distinction I am making between first and third person is too simplistic, and certainly runs afoul of more subtle literary analysis. I am, for example, ignoring the middle ground type of narration that has been called, among other things, "free indirect style" or "narrated monologue" (see, e.g., Cohn 1978). Even then, however, both Booth (1983) and Genette (1980) caution that the global distinction between first and third person is too crude. In search of a more nuanced account, these theorists make a series of what are, ultimately, empirical claims about what readers can notice, or respond to. However, in this section, I demonstrate that even the most coarse-grained rendering of the distinction between first-person and third-person narration can lead to measurable consequences.

Consider this very brief bit of narration in the third person:

> "Ray watched as the mugger made off with the elderly woman's purse."

Now consider the same scene in the first person:

> "I watched as the mugger made off with the elderly woman's purse."

In a formal sense, these sentences are equivalent. That is, if we were to look at, for example, a propositional representation of the content of both sentences we would expect them to be identical in most important respects. Even so, we can wonder whether the simple difference between third and first person might affect readers' judgments about Ray's/the narrator's culpability with respect to the mugging.

There is a strong tradition within the study of text processing to focus on the perception of causality: Research has shown that the search for causal relations guides comprehension and that those causal relations, once recovered, provide much of the global coherence of memory representations (O'Brien & Myers 1987; Trabasso & Sperry 1985; Trabasso & van den Broek 1985; Trabasso, van den Broek, & Suh 1989; van den Broek 1988). I believe, however, that the generalizability of much of this research suffers because the texts used do not include causal ambiguities. Within this tradition, antecedents and consequences of actions are well defined. "Causality" has typically been assessed by reference to a straightforward formula: "To judge whether a causal relationship exists between two events, the criterion of necessity in the circumstances is used (Mackie, 1980). Necessity is tested by the use of a counterfactual argument of the form: If not A then not B, that is, an event A is said to be necessary to event B if it is the case that had A not occurred then, in the circumstances, B would not have occurred" (Trabasso & Sperry 1985: 598). Unfortunately, this cognitive psychological tradition of judging causality by necessity yields few insights into readers' appraisal of the causal ambiguities and complexities that are the backbone of much great literature. If we are going to examine the effects of perspective on causal judgments, we have to move to research outside the text processing tradition that has concerned itself with causal ambiguities.

Consider even the brief scenario I offered earlier:

> "Ray watched as the mugger made off with the elderly woman's purse."

What analysis do we want to give about Ray's behavior? Did he just watch (i.e., rather than coming to the elderly woman's assistance) because he is a coward, or because he takes pleasure in other people's misfortune? Or did he fail to help because the mugger was waving a gun, and would've shot Ray had he tried to be a hero? The contrast here is between a dispositional and a situational attribution, a contrast that has been essential to the social psychological analysis of causal attributions (Heider 1958). Almost all events permit either a person- or situation-based causal explanation.

Social psychologists have demonstrated consistent ways in which individuals prefer one type of explanation over another. A finding that seems particularly germane to the contrast between first- and third-person narratives is the actor/observer difference. Across a range of circumstances, people who observe events tend to make more dispositional attributions than do people who actually act in those events (see Jones & Nisbett 1972; Watson 1982). Moreover, when observers and actors are made to take each other's perspectives, the pattern of attribution shifts. Storms (1973), for example, made two videotapes of the same interaction between two people, one from the perspective of a participant and a second from the perspective of an observer. Replicating the standard effect, observers tended to make more dispositional attributions for the participants' actions than they did for themselves. However, when the participants and observers were shown the videotapes that switched their perspectives, the observers' attributions were now less dispositional than those of the participants. Perspective, quite literally, had a substantial effect on causal assessment.

What forces give rise to this result? First, we can credit perceptual salience: Observers are focused on the actors, but actors are focused on the situation around them (Storms). Second, we have information availability: Actors typically know more about themselves, and their circumstances, than observers do (Jones & Nisbett). Let's now apply these concepts to the circumstances of first- versus third-person narratives. Suppose we read this account:

> "I watched as the mugger made off with the elderly woman's purse."

Although the narrator is reporting an event he observed, he is also an actor in the scene. If we, the readers, are wondering why he didn't come to the elderly woman's assistance, he has ample opportunity to let us know. Our own experience as actors—in which causal attributions have been guided by the forces of perceptual salience and information availability—have generated the expectation that actors can or should explain themselves. When a dispositional attribution is not warranted in our lives, we know why. If we read a first-person narrative in which an actor recounts an event that reflects poorly on him or her, we would expect some alternative explanation. In the absence of such an explanation, we may come to believe that a dispositional attribution is highly justified.

These considerations lead to the prediction that, when first- and third-person narratives provide equal amounts of information, that will have the effect of making a dispositional attribution seem more appropriate for the first-person narrator. In essence, we are predicting that readers will wonder "Why didn't he (i.e., the first-person narrator) have more to say?" or "Why didn't she defend herself against my dispositional attribution?"

To test this prediction, Deborah Prentice and I designed a simple experiment. We wrote third- and first-person versions of a scenario that allowed our readers to make a judgment of causality about a situation that presented reasonable ambiguity. Here is the sports scenario we devised, in its third-person version:

> Washington was watching the baseball game from his position in right field. It was the bottom of the 9th inning, with two outs and two men on base. Washington watched Carl Logan step up to the plate and glare fiercely at the pitcher, Sy Oldes. Oldes wound up and hurtled a fast ball toward home plate. Washington saw Logan take a might swing and connect with the ball. It made a long arc out into deep right field. Washington kept his eye on the ball as he started a long run to try to reach it. He raced toward the right field fence, watching the ball as it neared the ground. The ball bounced out of Washington's glove. The crowd groaned as the winning run crossed home plate.

Suppose now you were asked, as our readers were, "To what extent did Washington cause his team's defeat?" How do your intuitions change when the story is recast in first person?

> I was watching the baseball game from my position in right field. It was the bottom of the 9th inning, with two outs and two men on base. I saw Carl Logan step up to the plate and glare fiercely at our pitcher, Sy Oldes. Oldes wound up and hurtled a fast ball toward home plate. I saw Logan take a mighty swing and connect with the ball. It made a long arc out into deep right field. I kept my eye on the ball as I started a long run to try to reach it. I raced toward the right field fence, watching the ball as it neared the ground. The ball bounced out of my glove. The crowd groaned as the winning run crossed home plate.

In this case, readers were asked, "To what extent did the narrator cause his team's defeat?" Responses were given on a scale that ranged from 1 (Not at all) to 9 (Very much). Ninety-three subjects read either the first- or third-person version of the story.

We predicted that readers would attribute a greater causal role to Washington when the story was presented in the first person. This prediction was confirmed. For the third-person version, the average rating was 4.94; for the first-person version, the average rating was 6.00. This difference is reliable ($F[1,91] = 5.46$, $MSe = 4.822$, $p < .025$). Therefore, although in all important respects the formal causal structures of the two versions are identical, the shift from third- to first-person has a robust effect on readers' causal judgments. Because the texts have formal equivalence, we attribute this difference to reader participation.

This simple experiment serves as an existence proof: A shift in perspective from first to third person can have a measurable effect on the way in which readers think about a story's causal structure. Even so, I don't believe that this main effect—more causality attributed in the first- versus third-person perspective—will obtain in all cases. The basis of the prediction was a general account of the types of participatory responses readers are more likely to produce when they read a story from a first-person perspective. As we develop this account more fully, and apply the weight of more varied data, it is likely that we will also begin to be able to define circumstances in which a third-person perspective will generate a stronger sense of causality. The important point for now is that, by virtue of the types of thought they entail, perspectives have consequences, and we can predict what some of those consequences will be. I turn now to another consequence of perspective for causal analysis.

Perspective and Causality

We were able to predict the consequences for first- versus third-person perspectives by suggesting the types of participation these perspectives are likely to provoke. Research on patterns of attributions allow us to make additional predictions about the way in which perspectives are likely to effect causal analysis. Let's return to the contrast I introduced earlier between dispositional and situational attributions. Another important finding with respect to this contrast is what has been called the "Fundamental Attribution Error" (FAE) (Ross 1977): People show a strong tendency to prefer dispositional attributions rather than situational attributions. (Note that this is apparently true only in Western cultures; see Miller 1984.) The FAE is a close kin to the actor/observer difference because individuals most often commit the FAE when they are observing others' behaviors.

Let us suppose that, given a text that is ambiguous with respect to causality, readers could either adopt a situation- or character-based perspective. If we extend the FAE to circumstances of reading, we might predict that readers would prefer a character-based perspective, that is, we might expect readers to seize on dispositional explanations as they become available. Deborah Prentice and I designed a study to explore this preference. Consider this short, sad tale about Jimmy, who wanted a new bike.

> Once there was a boy named Jimmy. One day, he saw his friend, Tom, riding a new bike. Jimmy wanted to have a new bike. He decided to run home to speak to his mother. He was almost hit by a car. Jimmy always forgot to look both ways before he crossed. Jimmy's mother refused to buy him a bike. His mother told him that he should have his own savings. Jimmy wanted to earn some money. He asked for a job at the grocery store. He made deliveries for the grocery store. After two weeks, he was fired from the job. Jimmy wasn't able to buy a new bike. (adapted from Soli & Trabasso 1993)

The critical sentence here is "Jimmy always forgot to look both ways before he crossed," which we intended to prompt readers to take a dispositional perspective on the events of the story. Our measure, in this case, was participants' thoughts as they read the story. Readers were given these instructions:

> In this experiment, you will be asked to read a series of brief stories and "talk aloud" about the content of the story. Each story will be presented as a packet of cards. You should read the sentence on each card out loud and then tell us what your understanding of the sentence is in the context of the story—no matter how obvious it is to you. You should talk aloud about whatever comes into your mind.

The talk-aloud protocols allow us to determine, first, whether readers make the appropriate dispositional inference and, second, whether they apply their dispositional perspective to the events of the story. Our prediction was that readers would, in fact, seize on the character-based perspective as soon as it became available. Representative data are presented in table 2. In the top portion of the table we see clear evidence that readers put the information in "Jimmy always forgot to look both ways before he crossed" to immediate use to draw general conclusions about Jimmy. Moreover, this perspective has consequences. Now when Jimmy's mother refuses to buy him the bike it's because she doesn't trust Jimmy. Compare these responses to those in the lower portion of the table, which are strictly about the situation. As soon as readers develop a hypothesis about Jimmy—a perspective on his character—that perspective spreads quickly to their causal analysis of other events in the narrative. Note that, once again, this straightforward effect suggests that the tradition in cognitive psychological research of using a strict test for causal necessity will not be adequate. An understanding of perspective effects on causal analysis requires a more flexible and fluid approach to causality.

Although our result is preliminary, it does, once again, support the contention that perspective effects quite often rely on participation. To be sure, the initial discovery of perspective in this case relies on an inference: readers must use the information that Jimmy always fails to check the road before he crosses to infer something about his character. At that point, however, readers can apply the inference or not, according to individual predilections. That is, readers can choose whether they are going to apply their character-based

Table 18.2
Excerpts from the Talk-Aloud Protocols

Dispositional inference condition:

1. Jimmy always forgot to look both ways before he crossed.
   This probably means that Jimmy shouldn't have a bike since he doesn't watch the road even when he's walking.

   Jimmy's mother refused to buy him a bike.

   Probably because she knows that Jimmy doesn't look both ways when he crosses the street.

2. Jimmy always forgot to look both ways before he crossed.

   Jimmy was in a hurry, ah, well he wasn't in a hurry most of the time. Ah, Jimmy was careless and he usually didn't look both ways before crossing the road.

   Jimmy's mother refused to buy him a bike.

   She punished him for being so careless.

Control condition (which excludes, Jimmy always forgot . . .):

1. Jimmy's mother refused to buy him a bike.

   Well, Jimmy wasn't very lucky because his mother . . . I guess she didn't have the money or she thought that a new bike wasn't necessary. She wasn't willing to buy him a new bike.

2. Jimmy's mother refused to buy him a bike.

   I guess Jimmy's mother for some reason or the other, maybe a budget constraint or something of that kind, ya know, told Jimmy that she was not gonna, that they were not gonna get him a new bike.

perspective to make attributions as the story unfolds (this choice need not, of course, be conscious). The text provides a certain range of information; readers opt to interpret that information from a particular perspective. The application of the perspective constitutes participation.

Difference Perspectives

In the previous two sections, we considered cases in which discovery may be rather straightforward. The presence of first- versus third-person narration lies plainly on the surface; dispositional attributions are made with great regularity. In this final section, I will examine circumstances in which readers must sometimes work a bit harder to discover perspectives. We will observe, once again, the type of participation that enables readers to construct these perspectives.

I will begin with a classical example, the final moments of *Hamlet*. The reader (or viewer) knows that Laertes and Claudius have devised two means to bring about Hamlet's death. Laertes will use a poisoned sword in his duel with Hamlet. Should Laertes' swordsmanship fail, Claudius will offer Hamlet poisoned wine. When this latter event transpires, Hamlet responds, "I'll play this bout first; set it by awhile" (5.2.1.285) Shortly thereafter, Hamlet's mother, Queen Gertrude takes up the cup:

> QUEEN. The Queen carouses to thy fortune, Hamlet!
>
> HAMLET. Good madam!
>
> KING. Gertrude, do not drink.
>
> QUEEN. I will, my lord; I pray you pardon me. [*Drinks.*] (5.2.2.290–92)

This scene provides readers a moment of great discovery. When Gertrude lifts the glass of wine, we realize that we know something critical that Gertrude does not: The wine is poisoned. With that knowledge in hand, we have discovered (at least for the brief time it takes the action to play out) that we are viewing events from quite a different perspective than Gertrude is. The discovery of our different perspective contributes, presumably, to the magnitude of our feelings of tragedy (Gerrig 1996). If only we could really participate in the narrative world, to warn Gertrude!

Let us call the type of perspective discovered by this means a "difference perspective." My suspicion is that a large majority of the perspectives most relevant to narrative experiences narratives are difference perspectives: Circumstances in which what readers expect, or predict, or desire, based on their own knowledge diverges noticeably from what narrators or other characters expect, predict, or desire. Difference perspectives require participation, because the difference will matter most when readers work through the consequences of the divergence. As I suggested just earlier, it is, in part, an appreciation of how the reader's perspective differs from Gertrude's that adds depth to the emotionality of the scene.

I carried out a simple experiment to demonstrate the discovery of a difference perspective. Consider this opening paragraph to my own short story, which bore the title "The Eyewitness":

> When I heard the sirens, I carefully tucked the small gun into the deep pocket of my overcoat. Then I ran in the direction of the police car. When the first cop jumped out of the car, I called out, "It happened over here." I then led the pair of cops into the corner of the parking lot where the body lay sprawling.

How might readers interpret the narrator's act of hiding the gun? Given that the story will be told from his perspective, what ideas do readers start to develop about the features of their narrator? The act of hiding the gun becomes even more salient, as the story continues:

> The first cop, whose badge said "Cortez," kneeled down to examine the evidence. "It looks like he took a small caliber bullet right to the heart," Cortez said.
>
> "Let me tell you what happened," I said. Cortez looked up, so I went on. "I was walking toward my car (I pointed at my car, which was at the other end of the lot), when I heard what sounded like a fire cracker going off. Then I saw one guy running like hell away from here. I called 911 as soon as I saw the body, but I think the guy who did this still has a ten minute head start."

Could the narrator's account be true? That is, could the narrator have really witnessed some other assailant producing the body on the ground? Of course—but what makes the narrator's tale to the police less than compelling—or, at least, open to an alternative reading—is the readers' knowledge that the narrator hid a gun. In particular, readers should come to understand—to discover—that their privileged knowledge gives them an immediate perspective on the events that the police officers will not have.

To test this proposal, I prepared a second version of this same excerpt that excluded mention of the narrator's gun. In this case, the opening sentence read, "When I heard the sirens, I ran in the direction of the police car." My prediction was that knowledge of the gun would lead readers to discover the difference between their perspective and the officers' perspective. The "no gun" version provides an appropriate control for that prediction. To measure the effect of perspective, I asked readers a pair of questions after they completed one of the two versions of the opening section to "The Eyewitness":

> How much do you think the cops will believe the narrator's account of the crime? How much do you believe the narrator's account of the crime?

Each question was accompanied by a scale that ranged from 1 (Not at all) to 9 (Completely). Each version of "The Eyewitness" was read by thirty-five students.

Results are given in table 3. The data reveal a large impact of the inclusion of information about the narrators' gun. To begin, readers gave higher belief ratings overall in the absence of the gun ($F[1,68] = 17.962$, $MSe = 3.742$, $p < .001$). Presumably, when the narrator reveals that he is hiding his gun, readers begin to develop a model of him as, in some way, criminal. This general aura of shadiness, which we can count as part of the readers' difference perspective, most likely gives rise to this main effect on belief ratings between the two versions of the story.

Table 3 also reveals a main effect for ratings of the cops' beliefs versus the readers own beliefs ($F[1,68] = 8.381$, $MSe = 4.058$, $p = .005$). On the whole, readers report that they will believe the narrator less themselves than the cops will. However, this main effect must be interpreted in light of the reliable interaction that was the original prediction ($F[1,68] = 4.579$, $MSe = 4.058$, $p < .04$). This interaction provides the strongest evidence that students who read about the narrator's gun came to understand that they and the police officers would have different perspectives on the narrator's account of the crime.

Table 18.3
Results of Perspective Experiment

	Holders of Beliefs		
	Cops	*Self*	*Mean*
Story version			
Narrator has gun	5.09	3.37	4.23
No gun	5.74	5.49	5.61
Mean	5.41	4.43	

Table 18.4
Results of Perspective Experiment
(Readers Made a Single Judgment)

	Holders of Beliefs		
Story version	*Cops*	*Self*	*Mean*
Narrator has gun	4.68	2.59	3.61
No gun	5.62	5.18	5.41
Mean	5.16	3.84	

One problem with this initial experiment is that it is possible the questions themselves may have helped readers to "discover" the difference between their perspective and the police officers' perspective. To allay this concern, I ran another version of the study in which participants rated only their own beliefs or the cops' beliefs. Roughly 28 students read each version of "The Eyewitness."

Results are given in table 18.4. The data reveal the same effects as in the initial version of the study. Readers gave high belief ratings in the absence of the gun ($F[1,109] = 20.802$, $MSe = 3.049$, $p < .001$). Readers also attributed great belief to the cops than to themselves ($F[1,109] = 17.193$, $MSe = 3.049$, $p < .001$). Finally, the predicted interaction obtained: The presence of the gun produced a bigger difference in evaluations of the readers' own beliefs versus the cops' beliefs ($F[1,109] = 4.925$, $MSe = 3.049$, $p < .03$). This second version of "The Eyewitness" experiment suggests that the story, rather than the task, allowed discovery of the perspectives.

Let me review why I believe this experiment demonstrates the importance of reader participation. The initial insight readers must have in the gun version of "The Eyewitness" is that the small gun the narrator tucks away in the opening sentence may very well be the same gun that produced the "small caliber bullet" the corpse received "right to the heart." This is an important inference; should readers fail to draw it, they will have a very different experience of the story than will their peers. With this inference in hand, however, readers must now construct their own perspective, versus the officers' perspective, by producing p-responses. What might we expect from the students when they read, "I was walking toward my car, . . . when I heard what sounded like a fire cracker going off. Then I saw one guy running like hell away from here?" My guess would be that they think to themselves something akin to, "Oh yeah, right." This is the type of p-response that allows them to discover their perspective: "I know enough to disbelieve the narrator; the cops do not."

Suppose "The Eyewitness" had continued. What would I expect? I suspect that the readers would have had many occasions to rediscover their perspective. If, for example, Officer Cortez had taken the narrator's account at face value, readers would be reinforced in their belief in differing perspectives. If Cortez and his partner were to drive off in search of the other "guy" identified by the narrator, readers would have the opportunity to p-respond, "Bad idea." In fact, readers might wonder, from their perspective, what should be done at all. After all, don't they know who the murderer is? These questions show, once again, how questions of discovery shade immediately into questions of consequences. Because "The Eyewitness" is only an excerpt, we don't have room here to examine consequences. The experiments I described in the earlier sections, however, should provide assurance that we could also examine how difference perspectives percolate through the experience of a narrative.

Conclusions

Readers can take many perspectives on an unfolding narrative. Some of those perspectives they bring from the external world; others are, in some sense, present in the text. I have suggested that readers participate in their experiences of narratives to discover those perspectives. I have also demonstrated that those discoveries, have consequences (compare the distinction made in chap. 16 of this vol. between "features" and "effects"). The perspectives that readers discover may recalibrate their analyses of the causal structure of a narrative and they may affect the degree to which the rhetoric of the fictional world affects evaluation of real-world truths. Readers' experiences of narratives are greatly enriched by their own complicity—their own participation—in the construction of perspectives.

19

Justice in Perspective

Willie van Peer

One of the most remarkable capacities is our ability to adopt the point of view of other persons.

—Turner (1991: 74)

Perspective and Society

Perspective influences our sense of justice. The text of Euripides' *Medea* illustrates this by the very different interpretations it has given rise to. If one adopts a misogynist perspective, the play essentially reflects and consolidates sexist stereotypes of women in Athenian society.[1] After all, Medea is portrayed as a witch, a barbarian sorceress, who has murdered her brother and betrayed her father, who has plotted to have Pelias cruelly killed by his own daughters, and who is about to take a horrifying revenge on Jason's new bride and her father, and to subsequently kill her own children. On the other hand, people have interpreted *Medea* as a text that sheds light on the battle of the sexes from a feminine perspective. After all, Jason could very well be seen as a traitor: it is he who has broken his solemn marriage oath, setting in motion the train of tragic events we are about to witness. It is his new marriage that is the cause of all the ensuing suffering. He is also indifferent to the harsh exile Medea will suffer at the hands of Kreon, not even touched for one moment by the fact that he will lose his children through this exile as well. He is arrogant and smug, always and only demanding obedience of his wife, mocking her even in the face of terrible emotional anxiety that tortures her.

What are we to make of these contrasting interpretations? Can we decide who is right? The possibility of answering this question hinges on a prior condition, namely that an interpretation be in correspondence with the text as a whole. While this prior condition is disputed by many, I will work on the assumption that it is essentially a sane one, and that by sacrificing it, unsurmountable problems are created rather than solved. If you agree that an interpretation must be supported by the text as a whole, then differences over interpretation may indeed be solved, if not always, then at least often.

My argument in what follows will be that in order to come up with a convincing interpretation of *Medea* (or most other texts), it is crucial to look at the perspective through which we are given the story, or in this case, the drama. I therefore propose that interpretations should be based on an adequate representation of the perspective and that in order to arrive at such a representation, one has to use the tools that are provided by linguistic and literary analysis. I will come back to these tools shortly.

This issue is not merely an academic one, for it has clear consequences for how we think and feel in the outside world as well. Indeed, if we are given Jason's perspective in the play, then the text is clearly a sexist and imperialistic one: it elevates the Greek view of the world, and it downplays the feminine experience by excluding it from the text of the play. (At face value, one could expect this, since the text was written by a man—not a woman—and a Greek—not a "barbarian.") If, however, the text makes us see the events from Medea's perspective, then it is clearly an emancipatory one, in which a woman (and an outsider) is given a voice at the expense of the native male. In the latter case, Euripides is involved, not in the propagation of a Greek and male superiority complex, but instead in an act of cultural self-critique. It will be evident that we are dealing here with issues of gender and multicultural relations, and Euripides' text is a reminder to us all that such issues are neither new nor simple.

Therefore, the study of perspective may fruitfully lead to the analysis of systems of justice and equity in societies. In the words of Fowler: "Is there a single dominating world view, or a plurality of ideological positions?" (1986: 215). For instance, in our culture all parties in a lawsuit should be represented: plaintiff and defendent both have a right to have their side of the matter presented. The judge or the jury is to listen with equal care to both perspectives. But this institution did not exist in all societies. Is it possible that the circulation of stories with pluralist perspectives contributes to the emergence and/or maintenance of a legal system of impartiality? Or to a political system of proportional representation? Similar questions arise: Are stories with omniscient narrators more frequent (and more valued) in closed societies? Are narratives with unreliable narrators more frequent (and more valued) in open societies? Admittedly, these are major, and not very precisely formulated questions; yet they are questions worth pursuing if we care for a better understanding of how narratives contribute to the organization of societies.

It can hardly be denied that literary texts do play a role in the social arena. Many examples can be provided in which literary texts feed and legitimize particular worldviews. Haynes (1994), for example, has shown how the popular imagination of the scientist still rests on literary models such as *Faust* and *Frankenstein*. There is also good evidence from medieval studies that perspective was sometimes used to represent women unfavorably. Thus the cultural functioning of texts will in part rely on the kind of perspective that the text offers. What I am saying is that a proper understanding of such cultural functioning of texts requires a distanced analysis in which objective textual factors are given the credit they deserve, independently of the analyst's own social, sexual, or ideological preferences.

Determining a Perspective

If divergent interpretations of, say, *Medea*, result from aspects of perspective, then how are we to determine perspective? This is, obviously, akin to Dixon and Bortolussi's (1996) *text features* and to Gerrig's (1993, 1996) "internal" perspective, to distinguish it from the "external" perspective with which each unique reader approaches the text. While the latter is inherent in the reader and may be "activated" by the text, the former has to be "discovered" by the act of reading. Since we are dealing with a play, we cannot fall back on the usual procedures of analysis that have been developed for the study of narratives. However, as de Jong (1991) has convincingly shown, certain parts of (ancient Greek) drama, such as prologues, asides, soliloquies, messenger speeches, or the utterances of the chorus, can be studied fruitfully with the help of narratology; see also Pfister (1988). I propose that one can determine perspective by analyzing its linguistic markers. One of the best inventories of such markers is from Short (1996). Table 1 summarizes this:

Table 19.1
Inventory of Perspective Markers

1. Schema-oriented language
2. Value-laden expressions
3. Given versus new information
4. Thought presentation
5. Character perception
6. Deictic expressions
7. Social deixis
8. Sequencing of actions and events
9. "Ideological Viewpoint"

(From: M.H. Short, *Exploring the Language of Poems, Plays, and Prose*. London: Longman, 1996.)

Admittedly, this list is neither exhaustive nor very systematic. Items such as Chatman's (1990) "slant" or Fowler's (1986) "modality" could be added. I submit that a detailed textual analysis of a broad range of perspective markers allows one to settle some interpretive issues. Let me, by way of an illustration, pick out a category that I think is particularly promising, that is, schema-oriented language. By *schema* is meant here "a structured cluster of concepts; usually it involves generic knowledge and may be used to represent events, sequences of events, precepts, situations, relations, and even objects" (Eysenck & Keane 1990: 275). Protagonist-schemata are, for instance, "hero," "femme fatale," "martyr," "saint," "schemer," and "underdog." In order to create a particular perspective, a writer may portray a protagonist systematically according to a particular schema. Thus Shakespeare makes us watch Katherine in *The Taming of the Shrew* as a shrew indeed: We must infer this when we see (in 2.1: 141) Hortensio, one of her lovers (who acts as her music tutor), stumble on the stage *with his head broke*, telling Baptista and Petruchio that Katherina had broken his lute over his head,

> While she did call me rascal fiddler
> And twangling Jack, with twenty such vile terms,
> As had she had studied to misuse me so.
> (2.1.157–59)

Other events fit in the same scheme: her challenge of her father's authority, her assertion (in 1.1: 61–65) that—if married—she will scratch her husband's face, knock him on the head with a stool, and generally use him as a fool. Very soon, a pattern builds up that leads the audience to interpret Katherine as fitting the "shrew" schema. However, as Culpeper (1994) convincingly demonstrates, later in the play elements occur that disrupt our initial interpretation of Katherina as a shrew, making her a more interesting character, and providing the play with a psychological dynamics. In other words, the initial perspective is later disrupted. Again, however, we are able to provide sound linguistic evidence why, at that moment, the perpective is changed.

An Example: Euripides' Medea

How does Euripides characterize Medea? Does he provide other characters with expressions that facilitate a schematic interpretation of her character? Is she a shrew, a sorceress, a good mother, or a femme fatale? And how do we get to know Jason? As a hero, a dedicated father, a shrewd politician, or a noble friend? Here the detailed textual analysis should begin. I will concentrate here on a central part of the play, the famous verbal duel between Medea and Jason (lines 446–643). The scene depicts the two protagonists as pitted against each other. But whose perspective do we get? Various schemata are referred to in this dialogue:

oath to Zeus binding marriage partners
erotic passion
banishment
love for children
adultery
economic prosperity
sophistry

A close analysis reveals that in none of these cases is language slanted toward Jason's profit. For instance, the language used to refer to the oath-schema reveals Jason as the one who is the perjurer, and his calling the gods to witness (line 619) has a particularly hollow ring to it, given his history of infidelity. We are witnessing a clear example of schema-related language here. As Medea says:

> MEDEA. Respect for your oaths is gone, and I cannot tell whether you think that the gods of old no longer rule or that new ordinances have now been set up for mortals,

> since you are surely aware that you have not kept your oath to me. (lines 491–95)

Oaths were of profound significance to the Greeks, as witnessed by the fact that Zeus himself supervised their execution. There was a special term referring to the consequences of breaking an oath, *exoleia*: "root-and-branch destruction with loss of all progeny" (Kovacs 1994: 289), precisely the punishment given Jason at the end of the play: his children are dead, as well as his future bride, and Medea escapes in her fiery chariot.

Another good illustration of schema-oriented language can be found where Medea recalls a particular incident:

> MEDEA. O right hand of mine, which you often grasped together with my knees! (lines 496–98)

What is the point here? Modern readers may be somewhat puzzled by this reference, and perhaps interpret it as an erotic gesture, Jason's expression of tenderness when still in love with Medea. But to a Greek audience, these words are intimately linked to the ritual of supplication *(hiketeia)*, which provided the possibility of begging for help in extreme situations; see Gold (1973). A suppliant was to kneel in front of a benefactor, grasp his right hand, clasp both his knees, and beg. The religious background of the ritual urged the benefactor to give the response that the suppliancy requires: "respect for the sanctity of the suppliant and acquiescence in what he asks" (Kovacs 1994: 325). The Greeks had special terms to refer to such a schema; the response given by the benefactor, for instance, is designated by the verb *aideomai,* or the noun *aidoos* (see ibid. 1994: 325). The suppliant, on his part, by the very act of supplicating acknowledged his complete dependence on the benefactor. Hence Medea here refers to the fact that she has literally granted Jason his life several times when he acted as a desperate suppliant before her.

Thus if anything, Euripides loads the dice against Jason. It is Jason who does not live by the rules of his own culture (which were, of course, the rules that the audience in the theater would venerate). Note also how the Chorus is on Medea's side:[2]

> CHORUS LEADER. Jason, you have marshalled your arguments very skilfully, but I think, even though it may be imprudent to say so, that in abandoning your wife you are not doing right. (lines 576–78)

The Chorus, by the way, is not just a group of local women, but represents the city of Corinth itself. Although it is difficult to know exactly how Euripides wanted us to think about Medea, there is wide consensus among Graecists that Jason is "portrayed throughout as callous and vain" (Kovacs 1994: 287). His efforts at camouflaging his new marriage as a means to provide for the family (lines 550–) are exposed by Medea as sophistry (lines 584–85).

Thus, although on the whole there is an effort to portray the conflict from both sides, there are indications that the perspective from which the action is portrayed is much more that of Medea.[3] Though we certainly are meant to experience horror at the manner of her revenge, we are also meant to retain a degree of sympathy for her. Jason's perjury and treachery, on the other hand, are so heinous that few spectators can have had much sympathy with his plight.

Social Effects of Perspective

Now that we have seen how the determination of perspective may proceed on a methodological ground, can we now rest assured that the social effects of perspective are sufficiently done justice as well? May we take for granted that perspective increases readers' sense of perceived justice? The idea is certainly plausible and intuitively appealing. The current theory of social effects of perspective is indeed predicated on the assumption that readers will identify with a particular point of view, for instance, Leech and Short argue that "the very exposure . . . to a character's point of view—his thoughts, emotions, experience—tends to establish an identification with that character, and an alignment with his value picture" (1981: 275). Walton similarly operates on this assumption. The reader or spectator, according to Walton, takes part in a game of make-believe "from the inside" (1990: 212) and thereby achieves "a kind of empathy with the characters, an ability to look at things more purely from their points of view" (237).

But this assumption itself needs to be inspected critically. What evidence is there that perspective influences people's empathy? The most obvious way to put the assumption to the test is through empirical research. One such piece, on which I will now report, shows that the assumption is in for a good shake.

This experiment probed some effects of manipulating narrative perspective. As materials we (Henk Pander Maat and myself) used a short story of some two pages in length, in which a conflict between husband and wife erupts in the course of the story.[4] Of this story, two new versions were made, one in which internal focalizations of the female protagonist were inserted in several places, and another in which the same was done for the male protagonist (in italics):

> (A) It is evening. Ted Jones, factory worker, is sitting in front of the television set, watching the sports events, while his wife, Liz, has just finished washing up in the kitchen.
>
> "Turn down the volume," she says, "I want to talk to you."
>
> Ted does as is asked.

> (B) It is evening. Ted Jones, factory worker, is sitting in front of the television set, watching the sports events, while his wife, Liz, has just finished washing up in the kitchen.
>
> "Turn down the volume," she says, "I want to talk to you."
>
> *"Can't she ever leave me alone?" he thinks.*
>
> Ted does as is asked.

> (C) It is evening. Ted Jones, factory worker, is sitting in front of the television set, watching the sports events, while his wife, Liz, has just finished washing up in the kitchen.
>
> "Turn down the volume," she says, "I want to talk to you."
>
> *"Can't he ever think about this himself?" she thinks.*
>
> Ted does as is asked.

As can be seen, the additions in (B) and (C) make the manipulated texts longer, all in all about 10 percent longer than (A). These are, of course, the kind of devices that create perspective, as outlined by Short (1996): value-laden expressions, schema-related language, and the like. For instance, in (B) the inserted thought of Ted creates the schema of the bossy wife, always ordering her husband around, whereas in (C) the schema of the lazy good-for-nothing husband is created through Liz's focalization.

These three texts were used in a reading experiment in which 172 seventeen-year-old students from high schools in Deventer and Oldenzaal (the Netherlands) participated. The three versions were distributed randomly among participants who read the story individually and then answered various questions in writing.[5] Two such questions are relevant for our considerations here:

> Which character do you find most *just*?
> Which character do you find most *considerate*?

If the assumption on which narratologists have been working so far is correct, then readers who were exposed to the female protagonist's thoughts and emotions must find her more just and considerate, other things being equal. The point here is that in such a reading experiment, these other things *are* equal. Figure 19.1 shows the answer to the first question.

As can be seen, the female protagonist is indeed perceived as more "just" by readers who have read the version containing the female internal focalizations when compared to the answers given by readers who had read the version in which the male character had been given such focalizations. The mirror image is true too: the

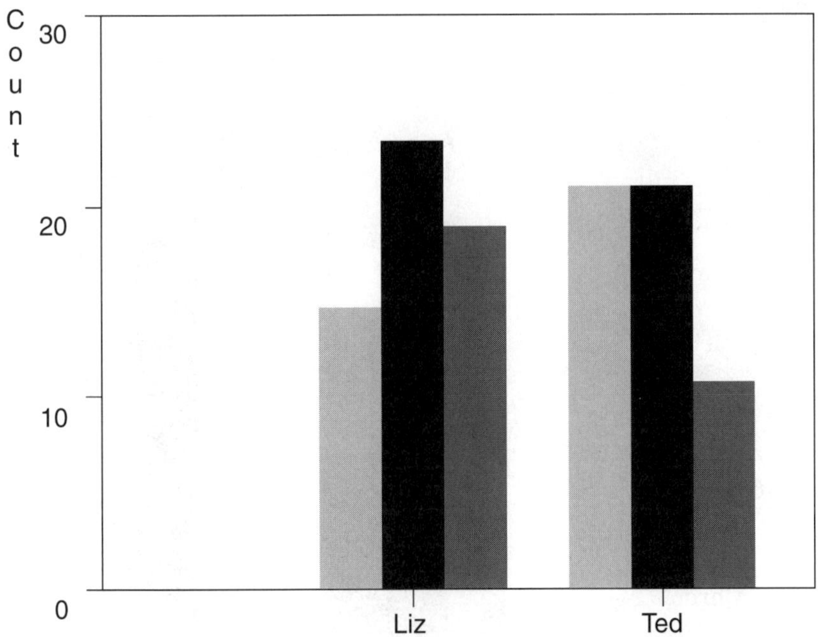

Fig. 19.1. "Just." The black bar (middle) is the neutral version; the light-shaded bar (left) is the male version; the dark-shaded bar (right) is the female version.

male character is seen as more just by readers who read "his" version of the story, or considerably more so than readers who had read the story from the "female angle." These differences are statistically significant: a t-test for independent samples yields a p-value of .03. However, there is an anomaly here: according to the working assumption, the "neutral" version of the story (in which neither protagonist had any internal focalizations) should be perceived as somewhere in the middle between the two "slanted" versions. But this is clearly not the case! It yields responses equal to that of the "male" version, and the female protagonist is seen as much more just in this neutral version than in the "female" version. Such results present a real oddity, and cast a shadow over our working assumption.

Now let us look at the results of the second question, which again is related to matters of social justice and fairness. Is a character judged as more considerate when readers are provided with that character's perspective (see fig. 19.2)?

These results tell us to throw away our working assumption: almost none of the responses given by readers is in line with that

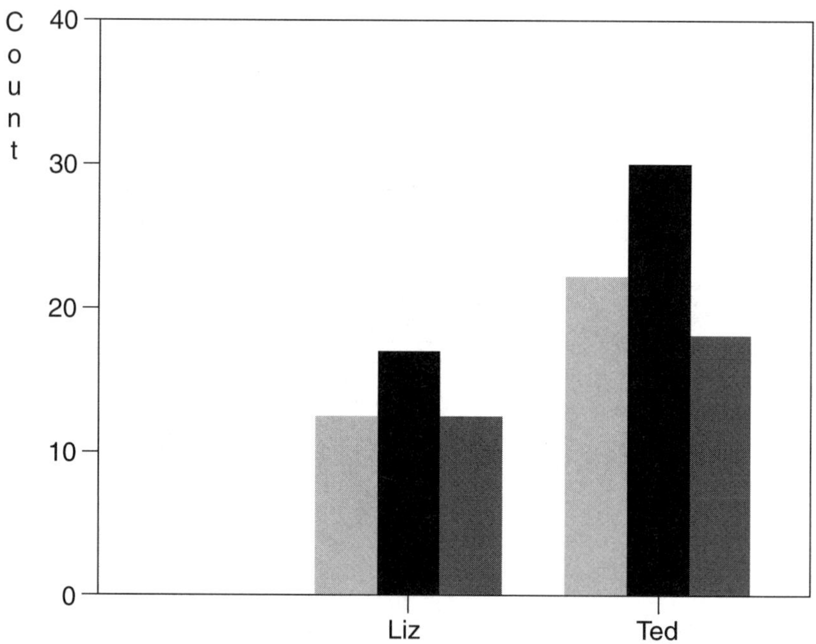

Fig. 19.2. "Considerate." The black bar (middle) is the neutral version; the light-shaded bar (left) is the male version; the dark-shaded bar (right) is the female version.

assumption. First, the female character is judged equally considerate in both slanted versions, while the neutral one yields a higher rating still. On the part of the male character, we notice that he is judged as more considerate on the whole, and again that the neutral version is much more successful in promoting this response. There is a slight effect of perspective with the male character, but the difference is marginal (and statistically not significant). Hence it seems that, contrary to our expectations, narrative perspective does not by itself automatically cause readers to perceive issues of social justice in the direction that our narratological models tell us.

Some Methodological Reflections

To conclude, while perspective effects may be real, and while they may have ideological implications or political effects, we will have to get involved in much more fine-grained linguistic analyses of texts if we wish to localize the source and understand the nature of such effects. I would defend the view that the current emphasis in literary studies on "interpreting" texts should be complemented by analysis, that is, by detailed study of the textual ingredients and their cognitive and motivational processing. This requires a lot more work of an empirical kind. As I have perhaps been able to show, the presumed effects are not that strong, nor that general, so that we must critically question the traditional assumptions of narratology.

Some caveats are in order, though. Of course one could question how competent those readers were. After all, they were only seventeen-year-old kids. Would the results have been different if professional literary critics had been the respondents? And should one not give greater credit to their answers? This announces an important aspect of my conclusion, that is, the fallibility of readers, who—after all—are only human, and therefore apt to err. We also did not ask our readers about their values or norms prior to the reading experiment, so that we do not really know (in Gerrig's words) what external perspective they brought to the reading act. Finally, it is obvious that the short story that was read is discoursally very different from a theater play, and it may well be that effects of perspective work differently in various genres; this is yet another hypothesis that needs testing.

So far, you may have felt that I have been arguing in two opposite directions. On the one hand, I have argued that interpretive issues may often be settled by a detailed analysis of textual perspective. On the other hand, I have provided some evidence that readers do not always behave in accordance with the results of such analysis. The second claim seems to contradict the first one. However, that need not be the case, and I submit that the contrast is the source of much confusion in discussions about literature. All too often they have been pitted *against* each other without properly looking at the *interaction between* them. Another way of formulating this is by asking the following two questions:

—Is a textual analysis invalidated by readers' reactions?
—Are readers' reactions invalidated by a textual analysis?

There is a strong temptation to answer such questions with a simple "yes" or "no," while it may be more profitable not to give in to that temptation. I would answer them with "maybe, but not necessarily so."

Conclusions

Let me, by way of a conclusion devote some attention to the way in which we could investigate the interaction I spoke of. The contrast we observe between textual analysis and reader behavior may be due to at least two factors: human fallibility and constraints on time and resources. Readers are limited in the knowledge required to understand a literary text, or they may have neither the time nor the inclination to devote enough attention to the text's content or structure. These factors make their reactions limited in scope and depth. Under such constraints a detailed textual analysis may reveal precisely where the limitations of such reactions lie. The contrast between both will tell us something about the limits of our cognitive and emotional resources. Second, even the best readers may make mistakes, so that even interpretations of professional literary readers are prone to error as well. Again, textual analysis may bring to light the kind of mistakes that readers, even the best readers, make. This is a promising area of research, in which some work is beginning to emerge. Keysar (1994) has shown how readers systematically (and unjustly) transgress perspective-boundaries in the interpretation of utterances. (This seems to be a processing counterpart to Shen's transgressions of focalization mode [see chap. 9 of this vol.].) Such research will tell us where readers' intuitive strategies are unreliable, in the same way investigations of everyday forms of statistical reasoning inform us about the unreliability of our statistical intuitions.

But the opposite holds too, of course. The theoretical models that we develop also have their limitations, and may contain mistakes. Insofar as these models are based on armchair analyses of texts, a confrontation with concrete readers' reactions may tell us where precisely the incompleteness of our theories and the mistakes in our models are to be found. For instance, the research data that I have provided would seem to indicate that a theoretical model that is based solely on textual analysis is inadequate. One such example is in the fact that schemata may change during the course of history, or they may even disappear. Readers do not then, as in the case of the supplication schema in Greek drama, have access to perspective markers (at least not without the trouble of learning about Greek culture). In sum, if readers may make mistakes, then—by implication—our theoretical models about this reading may contain mistakes as well. What is needed, therefore, is a developed methodology; this means, at the simplest level, that we have to agree on standards and procedures on how to decide which are mistakes, which are not. So far, narratology and empirical studies of literature seem to have worked without the possiblity that someone made a mistake. That, I think, was a mistake.

Notes

I am grateful to James Phelan, Mick Short, and Irene de Jong for insightful comments on an earlier version of this chapter.

1. See, for an overview, Rabinowitz (1993: 125–54).

2. Although in all fairness it should be added that this sympathy of the chorus for *Medea* decreases as the play unfolds and as her cruel revenge takes shape.

3. Obviously, this is not the end of the story, and any conclusion will have to relate to the way in which the play was performed, taking into account such matters as the wearing of masks by Greek actors, and performances taking place in large outdoor theaters; see Rehm (1992) and Taplin (1978). A full analysis of the play would also have to relate the text to the legal status of women and foreigners in the Greek city-states; see Lefkowitz and Fant (1992) and Des Bouvrie (1990).

4. The story was a Dutch translation of “Känsterle” by the German author Rainer Brombach. Other research that made use of this story is Andringa (1987) and Van Peer and Pander Maat (in press).

5. I am limiting myself to some aspects of the experiment only, mainly to keep matters clear.

20

Epilogue: Research Questions, Research Paradigms, and Research Methodologies in the Study of Narrative

Mick Short

Introduction: Research Paradigms in Literary Study, and What Counts as News

The present volume is innovative in drawing together scholars from a wide variety of fields interested in narrative: narratology, the linguistic analysis of literary texts, film studies, psychology, philosophy, empirical literary studies, and computing. What brings these disparate scholars together is an interest in researching narrative structure, and how we understand it, in a careful, reasoned way. But in the past scholars from these areas have tended to work independently, and in this chapter I would like to suggest that we need to agree more clearly on a common research program for investigation, and to begin to explore how we might go about it.

Although these areas of interest do not automatically overlap with each other, they do all intersect, through the concentration on literary texts, with literary criticism and literary theory. Most work on narratology has been on *literary* narrative. This fact causes a difficulty, in that what constitutes news in mainstream literary criticism and literary theory sometimes interferes with more empirical research aims. The easiest way to be newsworthy in literary criticism is to provide a new interpretation of an established text or to bring a new, innovative writer to critical attention. The emphasis is thus on the new—surprising interpretations or new writers who break the mould in some way. But to investigate how readers interact with texts in order to understand them, narratologists, text-analysts, and those involved in informant-based research usually need to start with less outlandish interpretations and texts, precisely because linguistic, perceptual, and interpretative norms need to be established and explained (often using relatively simple texts and constrained perceptual and interpretative contexts) before the more extraordinary can be tackled. This in turn lays such careful work open to the charge of not being "interesting" (i.e., newsworthy in terms of new texts or interpretations examined), a charge that is often coupled with another, namely that empirical work on literary understanding is pointless because it seeks an objectivity that does not exist in the text-interpretative world of literary study.

Leaving aside the oft-debated issue of what exactly objectivity is and whether or not those who strive to be empirical about literary understanding are as objective as they claim to be, we can notice clear differences in approach between the scholars interested in narrative just referred to and the literary critical approach that they are all connected to. Practical Criticism and New Criticism used to be relatively careful about making clear statements about literary texts and giving at least some evidence in favor of whatever view was being promulgated. But much contemporary literary criticism, and in particular so-called literary theory, deals in rather more grand-sounding statements. Such utterances impress the unwary at first glance, but are often also extremely vague, if not unfalsifiable. This is particularly true of the fashionable deconstructionist and poststructuralist movements, and their successors. The connection with literary criticism may often lead the more careful researchers to want to make less accurate, less disprovable statements than they might otherwise utter, in order to establish at least a modicum of "newsworthiness"; but I suspect that none of the contributors to this volume would ever have been tempted to write the following (culled within five minutes and almost at random from the literary theory section of my bookshelf):

> *Glas*, then, is Derrida's own *Journal du voleur*, and reveals the volonto-theology of writing. Writing is always theft or bricolage of the logos. The theft redistributes the logos by a new principle of equity . . . as the volatile seeds of flowers. Property, even in the form of the *nom propre* is *non-propre*, and writing is an act of crossing the line of the text, of making it indeterminate, or revealing the *midi* as *mi-dit*. (Hartman 1980: 205)

This is Hartman discussing Derrida's *Glas* (which incorporates passages from Genet's *Journal du voleur*), and that is quoted, with apparent approval, by Selden and Widdowson (1993: 156). What we see here would seem to be more of an attempt to impress with word-play and apparent erudition than an effort to move forward the human understanding of a particular text or the general process of interpretation. For me there are so many local problems of interpretation that I find it more or less impossible to conclude what it is that Hartman is trying to say, let alone whether I believe it or whether it is worth saying. What exactly is the "volonto-theology of writing"? Why does he use *"logos"* and not *"word"*? Are theft and bricolage the same thing? In what sense, if any, is it possible to talk of writing as theft, and does this really mean any more than saying that when you use a word lots of people will have used before you? And we haven't even gotten to what is involved interpretatively in the word-play Hartman indulges in!

Part of the problem here is that in current literary circles it sometimes doesn't seem to matter what you say as long as others are impressed by it. For example, I have pointed out to two different well-known critics that their applications in their writings of de Saussure's *langue/parole* distinction involves a fundamental misunderstanding of that distinction—only to be told that it doesn't matter. Misunderstanding is not a problem—all you have to do, apparently, is to say something "interesting" (i.e., different? outrageous? Fishy?). But the difficulty for me with this sort of "argumentative" move is that it reduces literary criticism to the status of the fashion statement. To say something interesting becomes not to say something that is carefully thought out and phrased, and for which you have reasonable evidence, but merely to say something that is different or that will attract attention. Such an approach constitutes a disservice not just for empirical scholars of literature, but also for the host of more careful, but less trendy literary critics who strive to provide genuine insights into literary texts.[2]

An important problem with the fashion-statement approach to the description and understanding of literary works is that theories and approaches are being continually cast "in" or "out," usually by being described in extreme and out-of-date ways, for example, the linguistic analysis of literary texts for the purpose of elucidating and supporting textual interpretation—an enterprise that is usually called "stylistics" in England—is currently "out" with the critical fraternity, and stylisticians are often accused of being "formalist," which appears to mean that they study texts and textual structure and pattern as part of their work. But it has been clear for a long time that a rigidly formalist account of textual understanding (e.g., of the sort suggested, by Jakobson & Lévi-Strauss [1962] in their analysis of Baudelaire's "Les Chats") cannot explain how we arrive at textual understanding, because it does not take account of the knowledge and assumptions that the reader brings to the text, or the complex process of inference that takes place when texts are read. I know of no modern stylistician who is "formalist" in the sense that the charge is usually made. But then if you read them carefully you can see that very few of the formalists themselves practised this kind of "formalism" in their work.

Clearly, textual understanding must involve a complex interaction of textual pattern and reader response to that pattern. Different theories have often promoted one, or a few, element(s) of what is involved, and these are empirical matters that can be tested. But within literary criticism this kind of careful, painstaking work is done less and less. Instead the bandwagon rolls on to the next new fashion, and conveniently literature is never subjected to the forms of careful academic inquiry we see in other subjects. Instead, its status as a mystical, magical, unknowable beautiful beast is protected.[3]

What about More Empirical Researchers?

Criticizing the more extreme literary theorists is too easy, however, and we must remember that those who use the kinds of approaches used in this volume can be guilty of other crimes. Empirical work on literature often gets a bad name in literary circles because it can be so careful about saying something that is true that it says very little indeed, or because it says nothing that is *useful* from the critic's point of view.

An article from early stylistics that came in for considerable criticism was Sinclair's account of Larkin's poem "First Sight," where he made a supposed merit out of pointing out a series of linguistic facts associated with the poem so that the critics could take them into account when discussing the text. He studiously did not interpret the poem at all. Here he is discussing the line "Newly stumbling to and fro" describing the newborn lambs in the poem:

> The selection of *newly* deserves a note. Although an adverb, *newly* is not one that is commonly found as an exponent of

> A [Adverbial] in clause structure. Its commonest place is as a verbal modifier; as in *a newly-advertised product, a newly-made dress.* I suppose that the average reader notes that there is something a little odd about the line, but has no difficulty, of course, in understanding it. (78)

The comparisons Sinclair brings in do not seem to help interpretatively at all. He does not make the possible lexical connection with newborn lambs, and in general he does not in any way try to elucidate the foregrounded feature that he has pointed to. It is thus no surprise that this article has proved so unpopular with the critics and has been used more than once to lampoon the entire enterprise that I have referred to as stylistics, the linguistic analysis of literary texts.

An example of psychological research to no apparent critical purpose at all is Simonton (1988). He compared an index of value judgments of the aesthetic merit of certain American short stories with citation counts from anthologies in university libraries and concluded "... we can confirm that objective citation counts from a library shelf of anthologies yields an index in the same league as having judges evaluate the same stimuli" (71). But the establishment of this correlation tells us nothing whatsoever about *how* human beings evaluate literary works, and, indeed, it is difficult to see why this particular research enterprise was embarked upon in the first place. I would have expected in advance that the correlation would hold in academic libraries, but not in popular libraries, because of the differing readerships and their effect on buying policies. To be fair, Simonton does demonstrate good intersubject agreement on the aesthetic rating his informants produced for the stories they were asked to read.[4] This does suggest, as he says, that aesthetic preference is not an arbitrary matter. I, for one, would have been surprised to learn otherwise, but I can see that it is worth demonstrating clearly that those who do think that aesthetic preference is like a preference for carrots over cabbage are mistaken.

I do not, of course, want to decry all work by empirical researchers on literature, anymore than I want to criticize all literary criticism. Far from it. Indeed, I think of myself as both a critic and an empirical researcher. Later in this chapter I will suggest the use of computer corpora work as a research tool, so I will also include a quotation from Oostdijk, which I think, not unreasonably, the critics would also object to:

> The figures . . . seem to confirm Marckworth and Bell's conclusion: for all samples the mean length of a reported utterance is shorter than that of an utterance in indirect speech, so that it holds true that the larger the dialogue content the shorter the overall mean length. However, the statement does not apply across samples. . . . This can be explained through the fact that the mean length of utterances, whether in indirect speech, reported utterances etc., is obviously a characteristic of personal style. (1990: 237)

It is more or less bound to be the case, other things being equal, that Direct Speech (Oostdijk's "reported speech") will be shorter than its Indirect Speech "translations." Compare "He said, 'Mum is ill' " with its indirect version "He said that his mother was ill." The introduction of the subordinating conjunction will add a word whenever it is used, and the disambiguation involved in changing "Mum" to "his mother" adds another. And it is no more surprising to find that one author's direct strings might turn out to be longer than another's direct strings.

I could add more examples, but I hope that the general point is clear. Being careful not to claim more than you legitimately can is important if you are trying to be reasonable and objective, but we must try to answer questions that need asking, and in literary terms, that involves getting rather closer to interpretative news than some text analysts and empirical researchers seem willing to try.

So What Should *We Be Doing Then?*

I see narratology as part of a more general attempt at elucidating how we understand specific texts and texts in general. Narratology can, of course, apply to nontextual objects, like film and mime, as Chatman demonstrates (chap. 9 of this vol.). But textual narratives are by far the dominant mode quantitatively and historically, and, as language texts have been the most intensively studied, we have better developed terminologies and analytical methodologies for language-based narratives than others. Consequently, I will use the term *text* as a general cover term.

If we agree that our general aim should be explaining how we understand texts in the sense that I have just outlined, we arrive at a different conception of what is behind the traditional term *poetics.* The aim becomes not to corral off literature from other texts, but to increase our understanding of how we interpret all texts, literary or nonliterary,[5] and how we are affected by them. And an important by-product of this aim will be to demystify literature, in that the more we understand literary texts, and how they create their meanings and effects, the less literature will appear magical, mystical, and unanalyzable. Much of the work of the contributors to this volume has already supported this general aim, for example, through a better understanding of foregrounding theory and how it relates to textual understanding (see, e.g., van Peer, 1986). Whether there is a magical core at the center of our most revered works of literature will then itself become an empirical question. By chipping away at how we understand and respond to literary texts we will more easily be able to see what is left to be explained, and indeed whether there really is something that remains unexplainable.

The subpart of this grand enterprise that narratology has as its core would seem largely to divide into an understanding of how, when we process narrative texts, we perceive and respond to: (a) fictional worlds and the characters who inhabit them, (b) plot structures, (c) viewpoint and sympathy relations, and (d) how these three factors interact with one another in our understanding and response. There are, of course, other aspects of textual meaning and effect that need to be resolved, and that will also be present in stories, the classic narrative texts—for example, sound patterning and conversational structuring and their effects. But the easiest sites for the examination of these aspects of textual understanding will be poetry and drama, respectively.[6]

A final point needs to be made about what it is to be empirical. Clearly, the kind of work done by many psychologists interested in literature is empirical. We could characterize this enterprise as testing out with informants what actually happens when they interact with texts. But it is also worth noting that textual examination can itself be empirical. In this case, the analyses involved need to be well-argued, performed in considerable analytical detail and with as observable an analytical methodology as can be managed, given the state of the art. This is what the linguistic stylistic analysis of literature, sets out to do. The resulting analyses are not God's "truth" of course. Analysts (and those using informants too, for that matter) can be mistaken because they have not taken particular factors into account. And alternative explanations of the same data may also be valid. But by producing clear and observable analyses in this way, it is easier for others to challenge or to make more precise what is proposed. Moreover, explicit analyses of this sort are more open to informant testing and to other methods of empirical investigation, just because they are detailed and observable. In this way, the text-analyzers and the informant tweakers can usefully come together. I will try to make these sorts of links clear in the rest of my chapter.

Illustrations

A Painting

Just as stories can have sound patterns and dialogues, many poems tell stories and so are amenable to narratological analysis. Even some paintings, which have no obvious narrative form can be analyzed in this way, as, for example, the Dutch seventeenth-century painter Vermeer has shown us. His paintings often capture a moment of possible narrative disequilibrium or complication (see Bremond [1966: 62–63]) which we can then perceive as part of a story, and that imbues the painting pregnant with significance. Take, for example, *Woman in Blue Reading a Letter* in Amsterdam's Rijksmuseum. An apparently pregnant woman is reading a letter in a room with a map of the world on the wall. Her facial expression is fairly neutral, possibly apprehensive. She is certainly not demonstrably happy or sad. The "text" of the painting leads us to infer that the letter could be from the woman's husband or lover, or about him. The painting on the wall suggests that he might be a sailor or explorer. And it is then easy to imagine the painting as representing a moment in a story where she receives a letter from him in which she is about to read that he is not going to return (perhaps he has a lover in another port?), or a letter from one of his friends to say that he has had some misfortune (perhaps has been drowned at sea?). We may well come up with different "explanations" of the story that we see the painting as part of, but the range of stories is severely restricted by the painting. There are an infinite number of things the painting cannot possibly be about, but a relatively small set of things it can be about. We are, for example, are very unlikely to infer that the letter is an invitation to a ball. Already, this kind of example helps us to see the general nature of the text-receiver relationship that is at the base of literary (and indeed all) understanding.

A Poem: Keats's "Song"

Poems are short, and so are very useful for illustrative discussion of narrative. I shall now comment on fictional world creation, plot, and viewpoint in a short poem by Keats called "Song" that alludes to the medieval tradition of courtly love. I have discussed its more poetic features in *Exploring the Language of Poems, Plays and Prose* (60–61) and so will not elaborate on those matters here, except insofar as to illustrate my previous comments about literary "magic." To this end, I would like you to read the poem carefully a couple of times, bearing in mind two at first sight rather unusual questions to which the poem does not explicitly give an answer, but that I think you can infer without too much difficulty. Both questions relate to the last stanza: how fast is the stranger's horse going, and what color is the scarf that the lady's maid is wearing?

The stranger lighted from his steed,
And ere he spake a word,
He seiz'd my lady's lily hand,
And kiss'd it all unheard.

The stranger walk'd into the hall,
And ere he spake a word,
He kiss'd my lady's cherry lips,
And kiss'd 'em all unheard.

The stranger walk'd into the bower—
But my lady first did go,—
Aye hand in hand into the bower,
Where my lord's roses blow.

My lady's maid had a silken scarf,
And a golden ring had she,
And a kiss from the stranger, as off he went
Again on his fair palfrey.

Explaining the Magic of Textual Understanding

Over the years, when I have asked my students the question about the speed of the horse, everyone agrees that it is moving reasonably fast. There is often disagreement about exactly how fast (cantering? galloping?), but it is definitely not moving slowly. How do we know this? There are, I think, three factors that lead us toward this view. First a narratological one: we can infer that the stranger is making love to the lady without the knowledge of the lord, her husband. It is thus reasonable to assume that he will want to depart quickly to avoid being found out. Second, the line in which the horse appears is metrically unusual. The poem's overall stanzaic form has an iambic 4-3-4-3 foot structure often found in ballads. The line in question is a 4-foot line, and so we would predict that it would have roughly 8 syllables, 4 weak, and 4 strong (with the standard leeway of one too many or one too few light syllables). But this line has 11 syllables, that is, 7 weak syllables instead of the standard 4. As a consequence, a performance of this poem will demand a faster rendering of the light syllables in the line to preserve the rough rhythmic equivalence with the other 4-foot lines. This increased speed can then be easily related, via Grice's maxim of relation or Sperber and Wilson's Relevance, to the speed of the horse. Finally, the grammatical and phonetic structure of "off he went" can also be seen to have an appropriate relation to the speed of the horse. As a consequence we have an explanation of what might appear at first sight to be poetic magic, using standard processes of inference in relation to the poem's textual structure and the schematic assumptions that it invokes.

The issue of the color of the lady's scarf is amenable to similar treatment, although among my students the measure of agreement is not normally as high. That said, a majority consistently say that the scarf is silver-colored. The explanation this time is through the device of parallelism. In the lines:

> My lady's maid had a silken scarf,
> And a golden ring had she,

"a silken scarf" is grammatically parallel to "a golden ring," leading us to search for meaning equivalence. Both are expensive gifts given to the maid, presumably to encourage her to keep the secret. Moreover, "silken" has the same initial syllable as "silver," which is connotatively connected with gold, and these two parallelisms together predispose many readers to see the scarf as silver.

These two minor aspects of the poem's interpretation in essence constitute fairly precise predictions, with an associated proposed interpretation, and are therefore open to falsification in a way that Hartman's claims about Derrida's *Glas* that I already quoted are not. They thus represent an interesting way of connecting together textual analysis and empirical literary study involving informant testing.

Fictional World and Plot Structure

Let us now examine some of the more straightforwardly narratological elements of Keats's "Song." The fictional world presented is one in a schematic medieval setting where an anonymous servant tells us that the lady of the castle or hall is cuckolding her husband through an affair with another important man (rich enough to own a fine horse, certainly, and who gives the lady's maid expensive presents). This description raises the issue of how we can infer this sort of fictional-world information from the language of the text. I do not have the space to discuss this general issue in detail here, but proposals as to how we infer fictional worlds from poetic texts using deixis, schematas and possible-world theory can be found, for example, in Semino's "Schema Theory and the Analysis of Text Worlds in Poetry," which builds on the works of Cook (1995), Ryan (1985, 1986, 1991) and others. This sort of work, like the suggestions I make throughout this chapter, are also specific enough to be used in informant-testing work.

In plot terms, we can see that we have a classic state of disequilibrium, which allows us to infer a series of unresolved competing scenarios that add to the resonating texture of he poem. Will the lady's maid keep the secret? Will the lord find out anyway? If so, will he fight the stranger, or give up his wife? And so on. Again, it would be relatively easy to construct informant questionnaires around such issues, allowing us to test out proposals for underlying plot structures for texts, how we infer them and how they relate more generally to textual understanding.

Point of View

The third main area that I suggested as the base of narratological study was viewpoint. And this short poem also has some interesting possibilities for viewpoint study. It would appear that the "song" is produced by a household servant who is relatively intimate with the detailed goings-on in the castle. He or she witnesses the two protagonists kissing, knows about the presents that the lady's maid has received, and sees the stranger and the lady going into the bower. The servant refers to the lady as "my lady," the possessive pronoun suggesting a preformed, but relatively distant social relationship between the lady and the teller of the tale, but the stranger is not referred to by name or role, and so we can infer that he is not recognized by the servant, which suggests a relatively recent liaison between the lady and the stranger. But the stranger must have visited before (otherwise the servant would have used the indefinite article in referring to him). Note that the viewpoint, here controlled in part by choice of referring expressions, thus has consequences for fictional world construction. These aspects of interpretation are also relatively precise and amenable to informant-based testing.

The linguistic instantiation of the viewpoint has been explored extensively in the stylistics and narratological literature (e.g., Fowler 1986: 127-46; Toolan 1988: 67–144; Chatman 1978; 146–253) and Van Peer, chap. 19 of this vol.) discusses my (1996: 263–87) proposed checksheet of linguistic indicators of viewpoint, which I have used to inform my brief discussion of viewpoint in "Song." Others can check their intuitions against the checksheet, and add to, or amend it in other ways. Again, it is relatively easy to use the checksheet to develop testable hypotheses concerning viewpoint in particular texts, and by uncovering its deficiencies to improve our understanding of how viewpoint is encoded in general terms.

Using Computer Corpora in Text Analysis

I have already indicated that I believe that detailed text-interpretative analysis of the sort that I, and analysts like me, perform is empirical. However, there is always the danger, when working in detail with individual texts, of overgeneralizing what one finds in those texts to other circumstances, and so misrepresenting textual features and how they relate to interpretation.

The advent of the computer has provided us with a convenient way of dealing with this problem. Large amounts of text can be stored, tagged for whatever features are under investigation, and then searched and manipulated in a variety of ways for research purposes (see, e.g., Biber 1988 and Butler 1992). To give an example of how computers can be used in the empirical study of texts, I will report briefly on a research project on speech and thought presentation (S&TP) in which I am currently involved with my colleagues Elena Semino and Jonathan Culpeper. The manipulation of S&TP choices (e.g., using Direct Speech vs. Indirect Speech to represent what a character says) is another area of choice, in addition to those mapped out on my point of view checksheet, which writers can use to manipulate viewpoint. We are interested in examining S&TP to see whether the various speech and thought presentation categories and their functions that linguists have proposed are adequate. In this sense, our work is parallel to that of Fludernik (1993), who has made an exhaustive personal search through a wide range of fictional material to validate various theories of discourse representation. However, our approach forces us to be much more systematic than previous researchers as, rather than reading and noting down interesting examples, we have to associate every single stretch of a text we include in the corpus with an annotation, or tag. This means that we cannot "overlook" inconvenient or nonprototypical instances that happen not to fit with our theoretical hypotheses. Reports of our work to date can be found in Short, Semino and Culpeper (1996); and Semino, Short, and Culpeper, (1997).

Most work on discourse presentation has been carried out on fictional narrative, but our approach involves equal amounts of fictional and nonfictional texts. Our current corpus consists of 40 extracts of roughly 2,000 words, 10 extracts from each of four different prose genres: serious fiction, popular fiction, and British broadsheet newspapers and tabloid newspapers. The next phase of our project will involve doubling the number of extracts in each category, and to add parallel data from other fictional and nonfictional genres. But our preliminary results already suggest that some changes will have to be made to our characterization and understanding of discourse representation and how it operates. I will now provide a couple of examples to illustrate the work so that it is possible to see how such an approach might be of interest in the study of texts and how we understand and react to them.

Categories and Clines

In order to relate linguistic choices accurately to meaning and effect it is important to have an accurate and explicit set of descriptive categories. We have based our S&TP categorization on Leech and Short (1981), as it is well-known and arguably the most explicit of the accounts of S&TP. Leech and Short, along with a number of other theorists (see Fludernik, chap. 6 of this vol.) have proposed that discourse representation is best seen not as a series of discrete categories, but as a scale, or cline, of categories that merge into one another. Our work has given general support for the notion of the cline by exposing the large extent of ambiguity between adjacent S&TP categories, and even between some categories that are not adjacent on the scale. However, the research also provides evidence for relatively discrete boundaries at particular places on the cline, in particular at the interface between Free Indirect Speech (FIS) and Direct Speech (DS). Hence the S&TP continuum is not 'even' in its gradations in the way that, for example, the color continuum is.

In "Speech Presentation, the Novel and the Press," I proposed that the long-held distinction between Direct Speech and Free Direct Speech (FDS) was not a category distinction all, but merely a kind of variation within DS. This argument was based on evidence from newspaper headlines and from the fact that although a *formal* distinction could be made between DS and FDS it was not possible to find a *functional* distinction. Our corpus has displayed considerably more ambiguity at the DS/FDS interface than elsewhere, and we have reported a number of fairly arbitrary decisions that had to be made in order to label particular stretches of text as DS or FDS, respectively.

Our more systematic approach has also led us to propose some new categories and variations on categories already established. In Leech and Short (323–24) the category called Narrator's Representation of Speech Act (NRSA) was proposed to account for examples like "He berated her" or "Her mother ordered her to go," where the speech presentation is so minimal that, unlike Indirect Speech (IS), no propositional content is presented. Such representations are often used by novelists to fill in essential information in a minimal form in order to move onto more expanded representations of more important aspects of the speech or thought being presented. In the first of these examples we have only the speech act represented, and in the second the speech act occurs with an indication of the topic that it relates to. But in our newspaper data we have discovered many examples where the representation of the topic is very extensive indeed, while still not being propositional in form (which would be needed for IS):

> Labour called last night for a streamlined Scandinavian style monarchy to banish Britain's class-ridden society. (*The Daily Mirror*, 12 May 1994)

This kind of example, which appears to have a greater summarizing effect than IS versions of the same content, has led us to make a distinction between the more minimal NRSA forms and what we are now calling "NRSAP"[7] (Narrator's Representation of Speech Act with Topic).

Distributions of S&TP Categories

Over the past few years there has been an extensive debate over whether literature can be distinguished from the rest of language in terms of its "linguistic ingredients" and/or the processes of understanding that readers employ when reading literary and nonliterary texts. S&TP is one area where it is possible to look for different categories and distributions, and a corpus approach gives us a methodology for investigating linguistic similarities and differences with a reasonable degree of objectivity.

In terms of *speech* presentation, *all* of the categories we have distinguished occur in the four genres we have examined, and the distributions for serious and popular fiction are close enough across the board to suggest that we cannot use speech presentation distribution to distinguish prized from less prized fictional writing. There are distributional differences between the fictional and newspaper data, particularly in the amount of NRSAP, which is considerably higher in the newspaper data, but this difference appears to have more to do with the different immediate functions or purposes of writing in the texts concerned than the issue of literariness.

Similarly, there is a distributional difference within the newspaper data that is also best explained by reference to function. The tabloids use DS approximately twice as much as the broadsheets and, conversely, the broadsheets use roughly twice as much IS as the tabloids. This pair of related distributional contrasts appears to be explained by the images of themselves that the newspaper types wish to convey: lively and exciting for the tabloids, and objective and considered for the broadsheets.

Arguably, it is in the area of thought presentation that we might expect to find the most interesting differences in relation to the literariness debate. Much serious nineteenth- and twentieth-century fiction has been concerned with exploring the inner worlds of characters (see Chatman, chap. 7 of this vol.), and so it would be a reasonable starting assumption that the more immediate thought presentation modes, free indirect thought (FIT) and (free) direct thought (F)DT) would therefore occur with higher frequencies in serious fiction than elsewhere. But in our data, as for speech presentation, the distribution of categories in serious and popular fiction is remarkable similar. There is a clear distinction between the fictional and newspaper texts. Apart from a very small amount of Indirect Thought (IT), thought presentation does not occur in our newspaper data. Note, however, that we cannot conclude from our data that the presence of thought presentation is a distinguishing feature of literariness, as it may occur with greater frequency in other nonliterary texts (e.g., autobiography or articles on psychotherapy).

Of course the size of our corpus is not yet large enough to be reliable, and it may be that increasing the quantity of data will change the picture (although we suspect that the characterization of fiction and newspaper reports will not change much). We are now involved in increasing the samples in each text-type and also in extending the text-types represented (to check on issues like the one related to thought presentation just mentioned). This next phase of our project will help to make our observations more objective, and provide an explicit account for other scholars to consider.

Conclusions

I have tried to argue that to be successful in persuading others that what we do is of interest, empirical researchers on literature (whether they be text analysts or informant-based researchers) need to address questions that the literary establishment will see as news. These questions are largely related to an elucidation of meaning and effect. However, it is equally important that when text analysts provide interpretations of texts they do so in a form that allows those using reader-informants to test the conclusions arrived at, whether they be related to some specific text or are more general accounts of understanding. I have also tried to show how text analysts can produce accounts of particular works that are detailed and observable, by using explicit replicable analytical methodologies designed to reveal how we interact with texts, understand them, and are affected by them. I hope that other researchers will take up the specific proposals and analyses I have produced in my own work to see if they can be falsified. Such a combined research endeavor related to interpretation has the potential to move literary study away from the impressionism and changes of fashion that have so bedeviled it in recent years.

Notes

1. I would like to thank Will van Peer for his helpful comments on an earlier draft of this chapter.

2. For a critique of the grand-sounding statement used to obfuscate, see Popper (1994).

3. For a critique of the attempt by some literary critics to give literature an unanalyzable status, see Barthes (1957).

4. Actually there are also doubts as to whether Simonton has achieved even this goal. We are not told exactly what instructions he gave to his informants, and so we cannot determine exactly what task they thought they were performing. Moreover, the informants were all undergraduate students, and so there must be an issue as to how representative they were. In addition, the article considers for comparative purposes a set of Hungarian short stories and informants as well as the American stories and students just referred to. But the comparison cannot be straightforward, as Simonton points out, because there is no real equivalent in Hungary of the Western collections of short stories by many authors, and so he uses different correlative measures. The results for the Hungarian data are not statistically significant, and so the discussion tends to disappear in the article's conclusions.

5. Interestingly, although we can easily distinguish between more and less aesthetically successful films, no one seems too bothered about corraling off a "film-literary" set of films from "non-film-literary" films.

6. It is worth remembering, however, that literary criticism, and indeed the linguistic analyses of texts provided by stylisticians, assume a rather idealized reading situation, for example, they "pretend," when providing accounts of understanding and effect, that the text concerned is being read for the first time, in spite of the fact that the critic or analyst will have read it many times. Similarly, they assume that the readers involved are maximally attentive, never make mistakes and can pick up all the allusions that a text makes. This idealization is necessary if criticism is to "get off the ground" in the sense that scholars can be sure that they are talking about the same thing, and are not at cross-purposes. This *necessary* idealization has consequences, still not clearly worked out, for the relationship between criticism and informant-based work, and, similarly, for literary theory in general.

7. Using the second consonant of "Topic" in order to avoid a possible confusion of our use elsewhere of "T" as an abbreviation for "thought." The extension of the corpus referred to above has now taken place and a number of other findings have been reported. Semino, Short, and Wynne (1999) contains a comprehensive set of references to date (2000).

Glossary

autodiegetic narrator: a narration in which an I-person tells a story about him/herself (in the first person).

diegesis: the fictional "world" of events narrated.

discourse: the way in which the content of a narrative is presented, the "how" of a story (in contrast to "story," the "what" of the narrative).

external perspective: see **focalization;** in Gerrig's chapter, the term refers to the set of beliefs and motivations readers bring to the reading act.

extradiegetic narrator: a narrator who does not take part in the events of the story.

focalization: the perceptual center from which the events in the story are presented; **external** focalization is restricted to what is visible to an outside observer, **internal** focalization presents the mental processes (thoughts, feelings, etc.) of characters; so-called **zero** (or **neutral**) focalization presents the narrative information from an indeterminate location, usually associated with an **omniscient** narrator.

free indirect discourse: the representation of a story character's speech or thought in such a way, that the utterance stays close to the character's oral syntax, but with adjustment to the past tense and without the tag clause ("said he," "she whispered," etc.). This type of discourse is strongly context-dependent, and therefore difficult to define in general; for a more thorough analysis of the concept, see Prince (1987: 34–35).

heterodiegetic narrator: a narrator who tells a story not about him-/herself.

homodiegetic narrator: a narrator who shares the spatiotemporal world of the characters.

implied reader: the reader presupposed by the text, as can be reconstructed from the implied author's norms and values.

implied author: the implicit author of a text, as can be reconstructed from the text, and to be distinguished from the real author, who can "pose" as a different implied author in several of his texts.

internal point of view: see **focalization.**

intradiegetic narrator: a character telling an embedded narrative in which s/he participates, while participating in a primary narrative, told by an extradiegetic narrator.

mood: according to Genette, the modalities of narrative information, such as "showing" versus "telling," internal versus external focalization.

narratee: a person who is narrated to (in the text).

narrative: see **text**; for a definition, see chapter 1.

omniscient narrator: a narrator who seems to know all about the characters' inner thoughts and feelings.

paralepsis: providing the reader more information that could be expected on the basis of the focalization; the term is Genette's (1980).

paralipsis: providing the reader less information that could be expected on the basis of the focalization; the term is Genette's (1980).

perspective: the location from which events in a story are presented to the reader. "Location" here can have both a literal and a figural meaning. Literally, "perspective" refers to the spatiotemporal coordinates of an agent or observer; figuratively, it signifies the norms, attitudes, and values held by such an agent or observer.

picaresque: fictional stories dealing with the adventures of rogues.

situation model: a mental representation of the situation described in a text; categories that populate such a situation are agents, actions, space, time, events, and causal relations.

story: the content of a narrative, the "what" of a story (in contrast to "discourse," the "how" of a narrative).

text: used here to refer to any symbolic representation of a narrative through a particular medium, whether that be oral or written language, gesture, film, television, or computer animation. The term *narrative* is equally employed here as medium-independent.

voice: according to Genette, what characterizes the narrator (who speaks, as opposed to who perceives).

Bibliography

Abelson, Robert P. & Carroll, J. D. 1965. "Computer simulation of individual belief systems," *American Behavior Scientist* 8, 24–30.

Adamson, S. M. 1994a. "Subjectivity in Narration: Empathy and Echo." In M. Yaguello (ed.), *Subjecthood and Subjectivity*. Paris, France: Ophrys, 183–98.

———. 1994b. "From empathetic deixis to empathetic narrative: Stylisation and (de)subjectivisation as processes of language-change." *Transactions of the Philological Society* 92, no. 1, 55–88. (Reprinted in S. M. Wright & D. Stein [eds.], *Subjectivity and Subjectivisation*. Cambridge, England: Cambridge University Press, 1995.)

———. 1995. "Empathetic Narrative: A Literary and Linguistic Problem." In W. Ayres-Bennett & P. O'Donovan (eds.), *Syntax and the Literary Text*. Cambridge, England: Cambridge French Colloquia.

Albrecht, J. E., O'Brien, E. J., Mason, R. A., & Myers, J. L. 1995. "The role of perspective in the accessibility of goals during reading." *Journal of Experimental Psychology: Language, Memory, and Cognition* 21, 364–72.

Allbritton, D. W. & Gerrig, R. J. 1991. "Participatory responses in prose understanding." *Journal of Memory and Language* 30, 603–26.

Allen, James F. & Perrault, J. D. 1980. "Analyzing intention in utterances." *Artifical Intelligence* 15, no. 3, 143–78.

Alvarado, Sergio Jose. 1990. *Understanding Editorial Text: A Computer Model of Argument Comprehension*. Boston: Kluwer Academic Publishers.

Anand, Mulk Raj. 1940. *Untouchable*. Harmondsworth, England: Penguin.

Anderson, David D. 1981. "Sherwood Anderson's Moments of Insight." In David D. Anderson (ed.), *Critical Essays on Sherwood Anderson*. Boston: Hall, 155–71.

Anderson, J. 1980. *Cognitive Psychology*. San Francisco: Freeman.

Anderson, Sherwood. 1978. "The Egg." In R. V. Cassill (ed.), *The Norton Anthology of Short Fiction, Shorter Edition*. New York: Norton, 1–9.

Andringa, Els. 1986. "Perspektivierung und Perspektivenübernahme." *SPIEL* 5, no. 1, 135–46.

———. 1996. "Effects of 'Narrative distance' on readers' emotional involvement and response." *Poetics* 23, 431–52.

Andringa, Els & Davis, S. 1994. "Literary Narrative and Mental Representation or How Readers Deal with 'A Role for Emily.'" In H. van Oostendorp & R. Zwaan (eds.), *Naturalistic Text Comprehension*. Norwood, NJ: Ablex, 247–68.

Appel, Alfred Jr. (ed.). 1970. *The Annotated Lolita* by Vladimir Nabokov. New York: McGraw-Hill (1955).

Armah, Ayi Kwei. 1973. *Two Thousand Seasons*. Nairobi: East African Publishing House.

Auerbach, E. 1953. *Mimesis: The Representation of Reality in Western Literature*, trans. W. R. Trask. Princeton: Princeton University Press. (Original edition 1946.)

Bakhtin, Mikhail M. 1981. *The Dialogic Imagination*, ed. Michael Holquist. Austin: University of Texas Press.

Bally, C. 1912. "Le style indirect libre en français moderne." *Germanisch-Romanische Monatsschrift* 4, 549–56, 597–606.

Bal, Mieke. 1977. *Narratologie*. Paris, France: Klincksieck.

———. 1985. *Narratology. Introduction to the Theory of Narrative*, trans. Christine van Boheemen. Toronto: University of Toronto Press.

Banfield, Ann. 1982. *Unspeakable Sentences: Narration and Representation in the Language of Fiction*. Boston and London: RKP.

———. 1987. "Describing the Unobserved: Events Grouped Around an Empty Centre." In Fabb et al. (1987: 265–85).

Baron, H. V. 1998. "'Disseminated consciousness' in Lawrence's *Sons and Lovers*." *Essays in Criticism* 48, 357–78.

Barth, John. 1982. *Sabbatical*. New York: Putnam.

Barthes, Roland. 1957. "Critique muette et aveugle." In *Mythologies*. Paris, France: Seuil, 36–37.

Bartlett, F. C. 1932. *Remembering*. Cambridge, England: Cambridge University Press.

Bate, W. J. 1945. "The sympathetic imagination in eighteenth-century English criticism." *English Literary History* 12, 144–64.

Bayen, Ute J., Murname, Kevin, & Erdfelder, Edgar. In press. "Source discrimination, item detection, and multinomial models of source monitoring." *Journal of Experimental Psychology: Learning, Memory, and Cognition.*

Bell, A. 1991. *The Language of News Media.* Oxford, England: Basil Blackwell.

Benveniste, Emile. 1966. *Problèmes de linguistique générale.* Paris, France: Gallimard.

Biber, Douglas. 1988. *Variation across Speech and Writing.* Cambridge, England: Cambridge University Press.

Birkerts, S. 1994. *The Gutenberg Elegies.* Boston: Faber and Faber.

Birnbaum, Laurence, Flowers, Margot, & McGuire, Rod. 1980. "Towards an AI Model of Argumentation." *Proceedings of the First National Conference on Artificial Intelligence.* Stanford, CA, 313–15.

Black, J. B., Turner, T. J., & Bower, G. H. 1979. "Point of view in narrative comprehension, memory, and production." *Journal of Verbal Learning and Verbal Behavior* 18, 187–98.

Bloch, Gilles & Farrel, Robert. 1998. "Promoting Creativity through Argumentation." *Proceedings of Intelligent Tutoring Systems.* Montreal, 243–49.

Böhm, C. 1990. "Die psychologische Realität der Tiefenstruktur filmischer Narrationen: Inferenzbildung und Protagonistenrepräsentation." In G. Schumm & H. J. Wulff (eds.), *Film und Psychologie.* Münster, Germany: Maks, 1, 143–78.

Booth, Wayne C. 1961a. *The Rhetoric of Fiction.* Chicago: University of Chicago Press.

———. 1961b. "Distance and point of view: An essay in classification." *Essays in Criticism,* 11, 60–79.

———. 1983. *The Rhetoric of Fiction* (2nd ed.). Chicago: University of Chicago Press.

Bordwell, David. 1985. *Narration in the Fiction Film.* London, England: Methuen.

Borges, Jorge Luis. 1970. *Labyrinths, Selected Stories, and Other Writings.* Donald A. Yates and James E. Irby (eds.). Harmondsworth: Penguin.

Bouvrie, Synnøve Des. 1990. *Women in Greek Tragedy: An Anthropological Approach.* Oslo: Norwegian University Press.

Boyle, T. C. 1993. *The Road to Wellville.* New York: Penguin Books.

Branigan, Edward. 1984. *Point of View in the Cinema*. New York and Berlin: Mouton.

———. 1992. *Narrative Comprehension and Film*. London and New York: Routledge.

Brau, Jean-Louis & Lavergne, Gérard, (eds.). 1992. *La focalisation. Actes du colloque international sur la focalisation narrative* (Nice 12–13–14 Juin 1991). Cahiers de narratologie, 3. Nice, France: Publications de la faculté des Lettres et sciences humaines de Nice.

Brechon, Arlette & Brechon, Robert. 1974. *Les noces d'or*. Paris: Albin Michel.

Bremond, Claude. 1966. "La logique des possibles narratifs." *Communications* 8, 60–76.

Brenner, Gerry. 1995. "More than a Reader's Response: A Letter to 'De Ole True Huck.'" In Graff and Phelan, 450–68.

Brewer, W. F. & Lichtenstein, E. H. 1982. "Stories are to entertain: A structural-affect theory of stories." *Journal of Pragmatics* 6, 473–86.

Brinton, L. 1980. "Represented perception: A study in narrative style." *Poetics* 9, 363–81.

Broek, P. van den. 1988. "The effects of causal relations and hierarchical position on the importance of story statements." *Journal of Memory and Language* 27, 1–22.

———. 1990. "Causal Inferences in the Comprehension of Narrative Texts." In A. C. Graesser & G. H. Bower (eds.), *Psychology of Learning and Motivation: Inferences and Text Comprehension*. San Diego, CA: Academic, 175–94.

Broek, P. van den, Rohleder, L., & Narvaez, D. 1994. "Cognitive Processes in the Comprehension of Literary Texts." In H. van Oostendorp & R. Zwaan (eds.), *Naturalistic Text Comprehension*. New Jersey: Ablex, 229–46.

Bronzwaer, W. J. M. 1970. *Tense in the Novel*. Groningen, Netherlands: Wolters-Noordhoff.

———. 1975. "A hypothesis concerning deictic time-adverbs in narrative structure." *Journal of Literary Semantics* 1, no. 4, 53–72

Brooks, Cleanth & Warren, Robert Penn. 1943. *Understanding Fiction*. New York: Crofts.

Brooks, D. H. M. 1981. "Joint Action." *Mind* 90, 113–19.

Brooks, P. 1984. *Reading for the Plot: Design and Intention in Narrative*. Cambridge, MA: Harvard University Press.

Bruner, Jerome S. 1986. *Actual Minds, Possible Worlds*. Cambridge, MA: Harvard University Press.

Bryant, D. J., Tversky, B., & Franklin, N. 1991. "Internal and external spatial frameworks for representing text." *Journal of Memory and Language* 31, 74–98.

Bühler, K. 1934. "The Deictic Field of Language and Deictic Words." In R. J. Jarvella & W. Klein (eds.), *Speech, Place, and Action*. New York: Wiley, 1982, 9–30.

Bunyan, John. 1966. *Grace Abounding to the Chief of Sinners*. R. Sharrocle (ed.). London: Oxford University Press.

Burch, Noël. 1973. *Theory of Film Practice*. New York: Praeger. (Original French edition 1969.)

Butler, Christopher (ed.). 1992. *Computers and Written Texts*. Oxford, England: Blackwell.

Callinicos, Alex. 1995. *Theories and Narratives. Reflections on the Philosophy of History*. Durham, NC: Duke University Press.

Canary, Robert H. & Kozicki, Henry Kozicki (eds.). 1978. *The Writing of History. Literary Form and Historical Understanding*. Madison: University of Wisconsin Press.

Carbonell, J. 1979. "Subjective Understanding: Computer Models of Belief Systems." Ph.D. diss., New Haven, CT: Yale University Computer Science Department, Technical Report 150.

Cassill, R. V. 1977. *The Norton Anthology of Short Fiction: Instructor's Handbook*. New York: Norton.

Chafe, Wallace. 1994. *Discourse, Consciousness, and Time*. Chicago and London: University of Chicago Press.

Chatman, Seymour B. 1978. *Story and Discourse: Narrative Structure in Fiction and Film*. Ithaca, NY: Cornell University Press.

———. 1986. "Characters and narrators: Filter, center, slant and interest-focus." *Poetics Today* 7, 189–204.

———. 1990. *Coming to Terms: The Rhetoric of Narrative in Fiction and Film*. Ithaca, NY: Cornell University Press.

———. 1995. "How loose can narrators get (and how vulnerable can narratees be)? *Narrative* 3, 303–6.

Ci, Jiwei. 1988. "An alternative to Genette's theory of order." *Style* 22, no. 1: 18–38.

Clark, Herbert H. & Gerrig, Richard J. 1991. "Quotations as demonstrations." *Language* 66, 764–805.

———. 1993. *Arenas of Language Use*. Chicago: University of Chicago Press.

Clark, H. H. & Schaefer, E. F. 1989. "Contributing to discourse." *Cognitive Science* 13, 259–94.

Cohn, Dorrit. 1966. "Narrated monologue: definition of a fictional style." *Comparative Literature* 18, 97–112.

———. 1978. *Transparent Minds: Narrative Modes for Presenting Consciousness in Fiction*. Princeton, NJ: Princeton University Press.

———. 1981. "The encirclement of narrative: On Franz Stanzel's Theorie des Erzählens." *Poetics Today* 2, no. 2, 157–82.

———. 1990. "Signposts of fictionality: A narratological perspective." *Poetics Today* 11, 775–804.

———. 1993. " 'I doze and I wake': The deviance of simultaneous narration." In Herbert Foltinek, Wolfgang Riehle, & Waldemar Zacharasiewicz (eds.): *Tales and their telling difference. Zur Theorie und Geschichte der Narrativik. Festschrift zum 70. Geburtstag von Franz K. Stanzel*. Heidelberg, Germany: Winter, 9–23.

Cohn, Dorrit & Gérard Genette. 1992. "A Narratological Exchange" [1985]. In Ann Fehn, Ingeborg Hoesterey, & Maria Tatar, (Eds.) *Neverending Stories. Toward a Critical Narratology*. Princeton, NJ: Princeton University Press, 258–66.

Coleridge, S. T. 1983. *Biographia Literaria*. J. Engell & W. J. Bate (eds.). Princeton, NJ: Princeton University Press. (Original 1817.)

Coles, C. 1994. "Critical periods for prenatal alcohol exposure." *Alcohol Health & Research World* 18, 22–29.

Comisky, P. & Bryant, J. 1982. "Factors involved in generating suspense." *Human Communication Research* 9, 49–58.

Conrad, Joseph. 1923. *The Secret Agent: A Drama in Three Acts*. London: Privately printed for subscribers only by T. Werner Laurie.

Cook, Guy. 1995. *Discourse and Literature: The Interplay of Form and Mind*. Oxford, England: Oxford University Press.

Coupland, Nikolas, Giles, Howard, & Wiemann, John M. 1991. *"Miscommunication" and Problematic Talk*. New York: Sage.

Culpeper, Jonathan. 1994. "Language and Characterization." Ph.D. diss., Lancaster University.

Cupchik, G. C. 1995. "Emotion in aesthetics: Reactive and reflective models." *Poetics* 23, 177–87.

———. 1996. "Suspense and Disorientation: Two Poles of Emotionally Charged Literary Uncertainty." In P. Vorderer, H. J. Wulff, &

M. Friedrichsen (eds.), *Suspense: Conceptualizations, Theoretical Analyses, and Empirical Explorations*. Hillsdale, NJ: Erlbaum, 189–97.

Cupchick, G. C. & Laszlo, J. 1994. "The landscape of time in literary reception: Character experience and narrative action." *Cognition and Emotion* 8, 297–312.

Cutting, D., Kupiec, J., Pedersen, J., & Sibun, P. 1992. "A Practical Part-of-Speech Tagger." *Proceedings of the Third Conference on Applied Natural Language Processing*. Trento, 133–40.

Davies, R. 1988. *The Lyre of Orpheus*. New York: Viking.

Davis, M. H., Hull, J. G., Young, R. D., & Warren, G. G. 1987. "Emotional reactions to dramatic film stimuli: The influence of cognitive and emotional empathy." *Journal of Personality and Social Psychology* 52, 126–33.

de Sousa, R. 1987. *The Rationality of Emotion*. Cambridge, MA: MIT Press.

Dickens, Charles. 1848. *Dombey and Son*. London, England: Chapman & Hall, 1907.

———. 1854. *Hard Times*, ed. David Craig. Harmondsworth, England: Penguin.

———. 1861. *Great Expectations*, ed. Angus Calder. Harmondsworth, England: Penguin.

Dihle, Albrecht. 1994. *Die Griechen und die Fremden*. München, Germany: C. H. Beck.

Dijk, T. A. van. 1988. *News as Discourse*. Hillsdale, NJ: Erlbaum.

———. 1995. "Cognitive Context Models and Discourse." In M. Stamenow (ed.), *Cognition and consciousness*.

Dijk, T. A. & Kintsch, W. 1983. *Strategies of Discourse Comprehension*. New York: Academic Press.

Dijkstra, K., Zwaan, R. A., Graesser, A. C., & Magliano, J. P. 1995. "Character and reader emotions in literary texts." *Poetics* 23, 139–57.

Dixon, Peter, Bortolussi, Marissa, Twilley, Leslie C., & Leung, Alice. 1993. "Literary processing and interpretation: Towards empirical foundations." *Poetics* 22: 5–33.

Dixon, P. & Bortolussi, M. 1996. "Literary communication: Effects of reader-narrator cooperation." *Poetics* 23, 405–30.

Doležel, Lubomír. 1973. *Narrative Modes in Czech Literature*. Toronto: University of Toronto Press.

Dray, William. 1985. *Narration and Knowledge*. New York: Columbia University Press.

———. 1993. *Philosophy of History*. Englewood Cliffs, NJ: Prentice-Hall.

Duchan, Judith F., Bruder, Gail A., & Hewitt, Lynne E. (eds.). 1995. *Deixis in Narrative: A Cognitive Science Perspective*. Hillsdale, NJ: Erlbaum.

Edmiston, William F. 1989. "Focalization and the first-person narrator: A revision of the theory." *Poetics Today* 10, 729–44.

Effe, B. 1975. "Entstehung und Funktion 'personaler' Erzählweisen in der Erzählliteratur der Antike." *Poetica* 7, 135–57.

Ehrlich, S. 1990. *Point of View*. London, England: Routledge.

Elias, Norbert & John L. Scotson. 1965. *The Established and the Outsiders: A Sociological Enquiry into Community Problems*. London, England: Cass.

Euripides. 1969. *Medea*, ed. Alan Elliott. New York: Oxford University Press.

Eysenck, M. W. & Keane, M. T. 1990. *Cognitive Psychology: A Student's Handbook*. Hillsdale, NJ: Erlbaum.

Fabb, N., Attridge, D., Durant, A., & MacCabe, C. (eds.). 1987. *The Linguistics of Writing: Arguments between Language and Literature*. New York: Methuen.

Faulkner, William. 1930. *A Rose for Emily*. New York: Jonathan Cape and Harrison Smith.

Fillmore, C. J. 1981. "Pragmatics and the Description of Discourse." In P. Cole (ed.), *Radical Pragmatics*. New York: Academic Press, 143–66.

Findahl, O. & Höijer, B. 1981. "Studies of News from the Perspective of Human Comprehension." In G. C. Wilhoit & H. de Bock (eds.), *Mass Communication Review Yearbook* 2. Beverly Hills, CA: Sage, 393–403.

Fleischman, S. 1990. *Tense and Narrativity*. London, England: Routledge.

Fletcher, C. R. & Chrysler, S. T. 1990. "Surface forms, textbases, and situation models: Recognition memory for three types of textual information." *Discourse Processes* 13, 175–90.

Fludernik, Monika. 1993a. *The Fictions of Language and the Languages of Fiction*. London, England: Routledge.

———. 1993b. "Second-person fiction: Narrative YOU as addressee and/or protagonist: Typological and functional notes on an increasingly popular genre." *Arbeiten aus Anglistik und Amerikanistik* 18, no. 2: 217–47.

———. 1994a. "Introduction: Second-person narrative and related issues." *Style* 28, no. 3: 281–311.

———, (ed.). 1994b. "Second-person narrative." Special issue. *Style* 28.3.

———. 1994c. "Second-person narrative as a test case for narratology: The limits of realism." *Style* 28, no. 3: 445–79.

———. 1994d. "Second-person narrative: A bibliography." *Style* 28, no. 3: 525–48.

———. 1995a. "Erzähltexte mit unüblichem Personalpronominagebrauch: Engl. one und it, frz. on, dt. man." In Dorothea Kullmann (ed.), *Erlebte Rede und impressionistischer Stil. europäische Erzählprosa im Vergleich mit ihren deutschen Übersetzungen*. Göttingen: Wallstein, 283–308.

———. 1995b. "Pronouns of Address and 'Odd' Third Person Forms: The Mechanics of Involvement in Narrative" In Keith Green (ed.), *New Essays on Deixis*. Amsterdam, Netherlands: Rodopi, 99–129.

———. 1996. *Towards a "Natural" Narratology*. London, England: Routledge.

Foerster, Heinz, von. 1984. "On Constructing a Reality." In Paul Watzlawick (ed.), *The Invented Reality: How do we know what we believe we know? Contributions to constructivism*. New York: Norton. 41–61.

Fowler, Alistair. 1982. *Kinds of Literature: An Introduction to the Theory of Genres and Modes*. Oxford, England: Clarendon Press.

Fowler, Roger. 1983. "Polyphony and Problematic in *Hard Times*." In Robert Giddings (ed.), *The Changing World of Charles Dickens*. London, England: Vision Press. 91–108.

———. 1986. *Linguistic Criticism*. Oxford, England: Oxford University Press.

Fowles, John. 1982. *Mantissa*. London, England: Jonathan Cape.

Franklin, N., Tversky, B., & Coon, V. 1992. "Switching points of view in spatial mental models." *Memory and Cognition* 20, 507–18.

Franklin, Stan. 1995. *Artificial Minds*. Cambridge, MA: MIT Press.

Frazier, L. & Rayner, K. 1982. "Making and correcting errors during sentence comprehension: Eye movements in the analysis of structurally ambiguous sentences." *Cognitive Psychology* 14, 178–210.

Friedman, Norman. 1967. "Point of View in Fiction." *PMLA* 70 (1955). (Reprinted in Philip Stevick [ed.], *The Theory of the Novel*. New York: Free Press, 108–37.)

Frijda, N. H. 1988. "The laws of emotion." *American Psychologist* 43, 349–58.

Gallie, W. B. 1964. *Philosophy and the Historical Understanding*. London, England: Chatto & Windus.

Gardner, J. 1984. *The Art of Fiction*. New York: Knopf.

Garrod, S. C. & Sanford, A. J. 1988. "Thematic subjecthood and cognitive constraints on discourse structure." *Journal of Pragmatics* 12, 519–34.

Geertz, Clifford. 1983. *Local Knowledge: Further Essays in Interpretive Anthropology*. New York: Basic Books.

Genette, Gérard. 1980. *Narrative Discourse: An Essay in Method*, trans. Jane E. Lewin. Ithaca, NY: Cornell University Press.

———. 1988. *Narrative Discourse Revisited*, trans. Jane E. Lewin. Ithaca, NY: Cornell University Press.

Gerrig, Richard. 1993. *Experiencing Narrative Worlds: On the Psychological Activities of Reading*. New Haven, CT: Yale University Press.

———. 1996. "Participatory Aspects of Narrative Understanding." In R. J. Kreuz & M. S. MacNealy (eds.), *Empirical Approaches to Literature and Aesthetics*. Norwood, NJ: Ablex, 127–42.

Gibbs, Raymond W. 1994. *The Poetics of Mind: Figurative Thought, Language, and Understanding*. Cambridge, England: Cambridge University Press.

Glasersfeld, Ernst, von. 1979. "Reflections on John Fowles's *The Magus* and the Construction of Reality." *The Georgia Review* 33, 444–48.

———. 1984. "An Introduction to Radical Constructivism." In Paul Watzlawick (ed.), *The Invented Reality: How Do We Know What We Believe We Know? Contributions to Constructivism*. New York: Norton, 17–40.

Glenberg, A., Meyer, M., & Lindem, K. 1987. "Mental models contribute to foregrounding during text comprehension." *Journal of Memory and Language* 26, 69–83.

Gold, J. 1973. "Hiketeia." *Journal of Hellenic Studies* 93, 74–103.

Goodwin, James. 1981. "Conrad and Hitchcock: Secret Sharers." In Michael Klein & Gillian Parker (eds.), *The English Novel and the Movies*. New York: Unger.

Graber, D. 1988. *Processing the News*. New York: Longman.

Graesser, Arthur C., Mio, Jeffery S., & Mills, Keith. 1989. "Metaphors in Persuasive Communication." In Dietrich Meutsch & Reinhold Viehoff (eds.), *Comprehension of Literary Discourse: Results and Problems of Interdisciplinary Approaches*. Berlin and New York: De Gruyter, 131–54.

Graesser, Arthur C., Singer, Murray, & Trabasso, Tom. 1994. "Constructing inferences during narrative text comprehension." *Psychological Review* 101, 371–95.

Graff, Gerald & Phelan, James (eds.). 1995. *Adventures of Huckleberry Finn: A Case Study in Critical Controversy*. Boston: Bedford.

Gray, Wilson, S., Rinck, M., McNamara, T., Bower, G., & Morrow, D. 1993. "Mental models and narrative comprehension: Some qualifications." *Journal of Memory and Language* 32, 141–54.

Greenspan, P. S. 1995. *Practical Guilt: Moral Dilemmas, Emotions, and Social Norms*. Oxford, England: Oxford University Press.

Grice, H. P. 1975. "Logic and Conversation." In P. Cole & J. L. Morgan (eds.), *Syntax and semantics,* Vol. 3. *Speech Acts*. New York: Seminar, 41–58.

Griffin, J. 1980. *Homer on Life and Death*. Oxford, England: Oxford University Press.

Guerard, Albert. 1958. *Conrad the Novelist.* Cambridge, MA: Harvard University Press.

Guillén, Claudio. 1971. "On the Concept and Metaphor of Perspective." In *Literature as System: Essays towards the Theory of Literary History*. Princeton: Princeton University Press, 283–371.

Gunter, B. 1987. *Poor Reception: Misunderstanding and Forgetting Broadcast News*. Hillsdale, NJ: Erlbaum.

Haller, W. 1938. *The Rise of Puritanism*. New York: Columbia University Press.

Hamburger, K. 1973. *The Logic of Literature*, trans. M. J. Rose, Bloomington, IN: Indiana University Press.

Hardin, J. (ed.). 1991. *Reflection and Action: Essays on the* Bildungsroman. Columbia, SC: University of South Carolina Press.

Hartman, Geoffrey. 1980. *Criticism in the Wilderness*. New Haven, CT: Yale University Press.

Haynes, Roslynn D. 1994. *From Faust to Strangelove: Representations of the Scientist in Western Literature*. Baltimore, MD: Johns Hopkins University Press.

Helprin, Mark. 1981. "North Light." In *Ellis Island and Other Stories*. New York: Delcorte Press/Seymour Lawrence, 63–67.

Hemingway, Ernest. 1986. "Hills Like White Elephants." In Charles H. Bohner (ed.), *Classic Short Fiction*. Englewood Cliffs, NJ: Prentice-Hall, 461–64.

Hempfer, Klaus W. 1973. *Gattungstheorie: Information und Synthese. (Theory of genre: Information and synthesis)*. München, Germany: Fink.

Herman, David. 1994. "Hypothetical focalization." *Narrative* 2, 230–53.

———. 1995. *Universal Grammar and Narrative Form*. Durham, NC: Duke University Press.

Herring, Henry D. 1985. “Constructivist interpretation: An alternative to deconstruction.” *Bucknell Review* 29, no. 2, 32–46.

Himmelfarb, Gertrude. 1995. *On Looking Into the Abyss: Untimely Thoughts on Culture and Society*. New York: Vintage Books.

Höijer, B. & Findahl, O. 1984. *Nyheter, Förståelse och Minne (News, comprehension and memory)*. Uppsala, Sweden: Uppsala University.

Horssen, Petra van & Jacobs, Astrid. 1995. *Beleving van Speelfilm: Verslag van een onderzoeksstage. (Experiencing Films: Report of an Investigation)*. Amsterdam, Netherlands: mimeo.

Hovy, Eduard H. 1988. *Generating Natural Language Under Pragmatic Constraints*. Hillsdale, NJ: Erlbaum.

Howe, Irving. 1968. *Sherwood Anderson*. Stanford, CA: Stanford University Press.

Hunter, R. L. 1993. *Jason and the Golden Fleece (The Argonautica)*. Oxford, England: Clarendon Press.

Hutchby, Ian. 1995. “Aspects of recipient design in expert advice-giving on call-in radio.” *Discourse Processes* 19, 219–38.

Ingoldby, Grace. 1994. “To Be a Pilgrim.” In Andrew Motion & Candice Rodd (eds.), *New Writing*. London, England: Minerva, 3: 450–56.

Isherwood, Christopher. 1964. *A Single Man*. London, England: Methuen.

Ishiguro, Kazuo. 1990. *The Remains of the Day*. London, England: Faber & Faber. (Original edition 1989.)

Jacobs, P. & Rau, L. 1993. “Innovations in text interpretation,” *Artificial Intelligence* 63, no. 1–2, 143–92.

Jacobson, J. L. & Jacobson, S. W. 1994. “Prenatal alcohol exposure and neurobehavioral development.” *Alcohol Health & Research World* 18, 30–36.

Jahn, Manfred. 1995. “Narratologie: Methoden und Modelle der Erzähltheorie.” In Ansgar Nünning (ed.), *Literaturwissenschaftliche Theorien, Modelle, Methoden: Eine Einführung*. Trier, Germany: Wissenschaftlicher Verlag Trier, 29–50.

———. 1996. “Windows of focalization: Deconstructing and reconstructing a narratological concept.” *Style* 30, 241–67.

Jahn, Manfred & Nünning, Ansgar. 1994. “A survey of narratological models.” *Literatur in Wissenschaft und Unterricht* 27, no. 4: 283–303.

Jahn, Manfred, Moliter, Inge, & Nünning, Ansgar. *Cognac. A Concise Glossary of Narratology from Cologne*. Cologne, Germany: mimeo.

Jakobson, Roman. 1973. *Questions de poétique*. Paris, France: Editions du Seuil.

Jakobson, Roman & Lévi-Strauss, Claude. 1962. "Les Chats de Baudelaire." *L'Homme* 2, 5–21.

James, Henry. 1979. "Daisy Miller." In Ronald Gottesman et al. (eds.), *The Norton Anthology of American Literature*. New York: Norton, 2: 338–88.

James, William. 1950. *The Principles of Psychology*. New York: Dover, vol. 1.

Jameson, Frederick. 1987. Foreword. In A. J. Greimas, *On Meaning: Selected Writings in Semiotic Theory*, trans. P. J. Perron & F. H. Collins. Minneapolis: University of Minnesota Press.

Jarvella, R. J. & W. Klein (eds.). 1982. *Speech, Place and Action: Studies in Deixis and Related Topics*. Chichester, England: Wiley.

Johnson, M. L. 1971. *The New Journalism*. Lawrence: University of Kansas Press.

Johnson, B. T. & Eagly, A. H. 1989. "Effects of involvement on persuasion: A meta-analysis." *Psychological Bulletin* 106, 290–314.

Johnson, H. M. & Seifert, C. M. 1993. "Correcting Causal Explanations in Memory." *Proceedings of the 15th Annual Conference of the Cognitive Science Society.* Boulder: University of Colorado, 581–86.

———. 1994. "Sources of the continued influence effect: When misinformation in memory affects later inferences." *Journal of Experimental Psychology: Learning, Memory and Cognition* 20, 1420–36.

Johnson, M. K., Hashtroudi, S., & Lindsay, D. S. 1993. "Source monitoring." *Psychological Bulletin* 114, 3–28.

Johnson-Laird, P. 1983. *Mental Models*. Cambridge, MA: Harvard University Press.

Jolles, André. 1930. *Einfache Formen* (Simple forms) (6th ed.). Tübingen, Germany: Max Niemeyer, 1982.

Jones, E. E. & Nisbett, R. E. 1972. "The Actor and the Observer: Divergent Perceptions of the Causes of Behavior." In E. E. Jones, D. E. Kanouse, H. H. Kelley, R. E. Nisbett, S. Valins, & B. Weiner (eds.), *Attribution: Perceiving the Causes of Behavior*. Morristown, NJ: General Learning Press, 79–94.

Jong, I. J. F. de. 1994. "Between Word and Deed: Hidden Thoughts in the *Odyssey*." In I. J. F. de Jong & J. P. Sullivan (eds.), *Modern Critical Theory and the Classics*. Leiden, Netherlands: Brill, 27–50.

———. 1985. "Eurykleia and Odysseus' scar: *Odyssey* 19.393–466," *Classical Quarterly* 35, 517–18.

———. 1987. *Narrators and Focalizers: The Presentation of the Story in the Iliad*. Amsterdam, Netherlands: John Benjamins (Grüner).

———. 1991. *Narrative in Drama: The Art of the Euripedean Messenger-Speech*. Leiden, Netherlands: Brill.

Josselson, Ruthellen & Lieblich, Amia. 1995. *Interpreting Existence: The Narrative Study of Lives*. London, England: Sage.

Joyce, James. 1916. *A Portrait of the Artist as a Young Man*. London, England: Penguin.

Just, M. A., Carpenter, P. A. 1992. "A capacity theory of comprehension: Individual differences in working memory." *Psychological Review* 99, 122–49.

Kawin, Bruce. 1978. *Mindscreen: Bergman, Godard, and First-Person Film*. Princeton, NJ: Princeton University Press.

Keysar, Boaz. 1994. "The illusory transparency of intention: Linguistic perspective taking in text." *Cognitive Psychology* 26, 165–208.

Kintsch, Walter. 1980. "Learning from text, levels of comprehension, or: Why anyone would read a story anyway." *Poetics* 9, 87–98.

———. 1988. "The role of knowledge in discourse comprehension: A construction-integration model." *Psychological Review* 95, 163–82.

Kintsch, Walter & Greene, E. 1978. "The role of culture-specific schemata in the comprehension and recall of stories." *Discourse Processes* 1, 1–13.

Kintsch, W., Welsch, D., Schmalhofer, F. & Zimny, S. 1990. "Sentence memory: A theoretical analysis." *Journal of Memory and Language* 29, 133–59.

Kittel, H. (ed.). 1992. *Geschichte, System, literarische Übersetzung*. Berlin, Germany: Erich Schmidt.

Kneepkens, E. W. E. M. & Zwaan, R. A. 1995. "Emotions and literary text comprehension." *Poetics* 23, 125–38.

Kovacs, David. 1986. "On Medea's Great Monologue Eur. *Medea* (1021–1080)." *Classical Quarterly* 36, 343–52.

———. 1994. *Cyclops, Alcestis, Medea*, ed. and trans. David Kovacs. Cambridge, MA: Harvard University Press-Loeb Classical Library 12.

Kozloff, Sarah. 1987. *Invisible Storytellers: Voice-Over Narration in American Fiction Film*. Berkeley, CA: University of California Press.

Kreuz, Roger J. & MacNealy, Mary Sue (eds.). 1995. *Empirical Approaches to Literature and Aesthetics*. Norwood, NJ: Ablex.

Lakoff, G. 1991. "Metaphor and war: The metaphor system used to justify the war in the gulf." *Journal of Urban and Cultural Studies* 2, no. 1, 59–72.

Lanser, Susan Sniader. 1981. *The Narrative Act: Point of View in Fiction*. Princeton, NJ: Princeton University Press.

Larsen, S. F. 1980. *Memory for Radio News: Discourse Structure and Knowledge Updating*. University of Aarhus, Institute of Psychology.

———. 1983. "Text processing and knowledge updating in memory for radio news." *Discourse Processes* 6, 21–38.

Latacz, J. 1984. "Das Menschenbild Homers." *Gymnasium* 91, 15–39.

Latour, Bruno. 1987. *Science in Action: How to Follow Scientists and Engineers through Society*. Cambridge, MA: Harvard University Press.

Lattimore, R. 1991. *The Odyssey of Homer*. New York: Harper Collins. (Original edition 1965.)

Lavie, Smadar. 1990. *The Poetics of Military Occupation*. Berkeley, CA: University of California Press.

Lazarus, R. S. & Alfert, E. 1964. "Short-circuiting of threat by experimentally altering cognitive appraisal." *Journal of Abnormal and Social Psychology* 69, 195–205.

Leavis, F. R. 1948. *The Great Tradition*. Harmondsworth, England: Penguin.

Lee-Sammons, W. H. & Whitney, P. 1991. "Reading perspectives and memory for text: An individual differences analysis." *Journal of Experimental Psychology: Learning, Memory, and Cognition* 17, 1074–81.

Leech, G. N. & Short, M. H. 1981. *Style in Fiction: Linguistic Introduction to English Fictional Prose*. London, England: Longman.

Lefkowitz, Mary R. & Fant, Maureen B. 1992. *Women's Life in Greece and Rome*. London, England: Duckworth. (Original edition 1982.)

Levinson, Stephen C. 1986. "Putting Linguistics on a Proper Footing: Explorations in Goffman's Concepts of Participation." In Paul Drew & Anthony Wootton (eds.), *Erving Goffman: Exploring the Interaction Order*. Cambridge, England: Polity Press, 161–227.

Liebow, Elliot. 1993. *Tell Them Who I Am: The Lives of Homeless Women*. New York: Free Press.

Lintvelt, Jaap. 1981. *Essai de typologie narrative: Le "point de vue."* Paris, France: Corti.

Lips, M. 1926. *Le style indirect libre*. Paris, France: Payot.

Lohmann, D. 1992. "Homer als Erzähler: Die Athla im 23. Buch der Ilias." *Gymnasium* 99, 289–319.

Long, T. 1987. *Repetition and Variation in the Short Stories of Herodotus*. Frankfurt am Main, Germany: Athenäum Verlag.

Lubbock, Percy. 1921. *The Craft of Fiction*. London, England: Cape.

Lyons, John. 1977. *Semantics*. Cambridge, England: Cambridge University Press.

———. 1982. "Deixis and subjectivity: *Loquor ergo sum*." In Jarvella, Robert & Wolfgang, Klein. Speech, Place and Action. Chichester: Wiley, 101–124.

Lyotard, Jean-François. 1984. *The Postmodern Condition*, trans. G. Bennington and B. Manumi. Minneapolis: University of Minnesota Press.

Mackie, J. L. 1976. "Causes and Conditions." In Myles Brand (ed.), *The Nature of Causation*. Urbana: University of Illinois Press, 307–44.

———. 1980. *The Cement of the Universe: A Study of Causation*. Oxford: Clarendon Press.

Mailer, Norman. 1968. *Armies of the Night*. London: Weidenfeld and Nicolson.

Mann, Thomas. 1930. *Mario und der Zauberer*. Berlin: Fischer.

———. 1982. Bei Lyons die Seiten-augabe aus dein Buch von Farvella/ Klein (o.s. 37n) noch hinzufügen.

Margolin, Uri. 1983. "Characterization in narrative: Some theoretical prolegomena." *Neophilologus* 67, 1–14.

———. 1987. "Introducing and sustaining characters in literary narrative: A set of conditions." *Style* 21, 107–24.

———. 1989. "Structuralist approaches to character in narrative: The state of the art." *Semiotica* 75, 1–24.

———. 1990a. "Narrative 'you' revisited." *Language and Style* 23, no. 4, 425–46.

———. 1990b. "The what, the when, and the how of being a character in literary narrative." *Style* 24, 453–68.

———. 1990c. "Individuals in narrative worlds: An ontological perspective." *Poetics Today* 11, 843–71.

Martin, W. 1986. *Recent Theories of Narrative*. Ithaca, NY: Cornell University Press.

McHale, Brian. 1978. "Free indirect discourse: A survey of recent accounts." *Poetics and Theory of Literature* 3, 249–87.

———. 1983. "Unspeakable sentences, unnatural acts: Linguistics and poetics revisited." *Poetics Today* 4, no. 1, 17–45.

McKoon, G., & Ratcliff, R. 1992. "Inference during reading." *Psychological Review* 99, 440–66.

Melville, H. 1981. *Moby-Dick*. New York: Bantam Books. (Original work published 1851.)

Meyer, E. Y. 1974. *In Trubschachen*. Roman. Frankfurt am Main, Germany: Suhrkamp. (Original edition 1973.)

Miall, D. S. 1989. "Beyond the schema given: Affective comprehension of literary narratives." *Cognition and Emotion* 3, 55–78.

Miall, D. S. & Kuiken, D. 1994a. "Foregrounding, Defamiliarization, and affect: Response to literary stories." *Poetics* 22, 389–407.

———, & Kuiken, D. 1994b. "Beyond text theory: Understanding literary response." *Discourse Processes* 17, 337–52.

———, & Kuiken, D. 1995. "Aspects of literary response: A new questionnaire." *Research in the Teaching of English* 29, 37–58.

Miller, Walter M. Jr. 1974. "I Made You." In Brian Aldiss (ed.), *The Penguin Science Fiction Omnibus*. London, England: Penguin, 485–96. (Original edition 1954.)

Miller, Seumas. 1992. "Joint action." *Philosophical Papers* 22, 275–97.

Miller, J. G. 1984. "Culture and the development of everyday social explanation." *Journal of Personality and Social Psychology* 46, 961–78.

Millis, Keith K. 1995. "Encoding discourse perspective during the reading of a literary text." *Poetics* 23, 235–53.

Minsky, Marvin. 1989. *Society of the Mind*. New York: Simon & Schuster.

Mitchell, W. J. T. 1981. *On Narrative*. Chicago: University of Chicago Press.

Montgomery, H. 1965. *Gedanke und Tat: Zur Erzählungstechnik bei Herodot, Thukydides, Xenophon und Arrian*. Stockholm, Sweden: P. A. Norstedt & Söner.

Moore, Lorrie. 1986. "How to Be an Other Woman." In *Self-Help: Stories by Lorrie Moore*. New York: Plume, 1–22. (Original edition 1985.)

Morrow, D. G. 1985a. "Prominent characters and events organize narrative understanding. *Journal of Memory & Language* 24, 304–19.

———. 1985b. "Prepositions and verb aspect in narrative comprehension." *Journal of Memory & Language* 24, 390–404.

———. 1986. "Grammatical morphemes and conceptual structure in discourse processing." *Cognitive Science*, 10, 423–455.

———. 1994. "Spatial Models Created from Text." In H. van Oostendorp & R. Zwaan (eds.), *Naturalistic Text Comprehension*. Norwood, NJ: Ablex, 57–78.

Morrow, D. G., Bower, G. H., & Greenspan, S. L. 1989. "Updating situation models during comprehension." *Journal of Memory and Language* 28, 292–312.

Morrow, D. G., Greenspan, S. L., & Bower, G. H. 1987. "Accessibility and situation models in narrative comprehension." *Journal of Memory and Language* 26, 165–87.

Morrow, D. G., Leirer, V., Altieri, P., & Fitzsimmons, C. 1994. "Age differences in updating situation models from narratives." *Language and Cognitive Processes* 9, 203–20.

Morrow D. G., Stine-Morrow, E. A. L., Leirer, V., Andrassy, J., & Kahn, J. 1997. "The role of reader age and focus of attention in creating situation models." *Journal of Gerontology: Psychological Sciences* 52B, 73–80.

MUC-3. 1991. *Proceedings of the Third Message Understanding Conference*, San Mateo, CA: Morgan Kaufmann Publishers.

Nelles, William. 1990. "Getting Focalization into Focus." *Poetics Today* 11, 365–82.

Nieragden, Gran. 1996. "Who Sees when 'I' Speak? Neuvorschläge zur Relation von homodiegetischer Erzählung und Fokalisierung." Manuscript.

Nünning, Ansgar. 1989a. *Grundzüge eines kommunikationstheoretischen Modells der erzählerischen Vermittlung: Die Funktionen der Erzählinstanz in den Romanen George Eliots. (Outline of a theoretical model of narratorial communication: The functions of the narratorial instance in the novels of George Eliot).* Trier, Germany: Wissenschaftlicher Verlag Trier.

———. 1989b. "Bausteine einer konstruktivistischen Erzähltheorie: Die erzählerische Umsetzung konstruktivistischer Konzepte in den Romanen von John Fowles." ("Steps toward a constructivist narratology: The narrative transformation of constructivist concepts in John Fowles's novels"). *DELFIN* 13, 3–17.

———. 1993. "Renaissance eines anthropomorphisierten Passepartouts oder Nachruf auf ein literaturkritisches Phantom? Überlegungen und Alternativen zum Konzept des *implied author*." ("Renaissance of an anthropomorphized passepartout, or: Obituary for a phantom of literary criticism? Reflections on, and alternatives to, the concept of the 'implied author' "). *Deutsche Vierteljahresschrift für Literaturwissenschaft und Geistesgeschichte* 67: 1–25.

———. 1994. " 'The Past Is the Fiction of the Present': Constructivist Reflections upon Susan Daitch's *L.C.* as a Novel about the Recording of History." In Bernd Engler & Kurt Müller (eds.), *Historiographical Metafiction in Modern American and Canadian Literature*. Paderborn, Germany: Schöningh. 279–98.

Nussbaum, Martha C. 1990. *Love's Knowledge: Essays on Philosophy and Literature*. New York: Oxford University Press.

———. 1995. *Poetic Justice. The Literary Imagination and Public Life.* Boston, MA: Beacon Press.

O'Brien, E. J. & Myers, J. L. 1987. "The role of causal connections in the retrieval of text." *Memory & Cognition* 15, 419–27.

O'Neill, Patrick. 1994. *Fictions of Discourse: Reading Narrative Theory*. Toronto: University of Toronto Press.

O'Reilly, Kate. 1994. "Mouth." *New Writing,* eds. Andrew Motion & Candice Rodd. London, England: Minerva, 3: 93–95.

Ohtsuka, Keisuke & Brewer, William F. 1992. "Discourse organization in the comprehension of temporal order in narrative texts." *Discourse Processes* 15, 317–36.

Oostdijk, Nelleke. 1990. 'The Language of Dialogue in Fiction.' *Literary and Linguistic Computing* 5, no. 3: 235–41.

Oostendorp, H. van. 1996. "Updating situation models derived from newspaper articles." *Medienpsychologie* 8, 21–33.

Oostendorp, H. van & Bonebakker, C. M. 1996. "Het vasthouden aan incorrecte informatie bij het verwerken van nieuwsberichten" ("Holding on to misinformation while processing news reports"). *Tijdschrift voor Communicatiewetenschap* 24, 57–75.

———, & Bonebakker, C. M. 1999. "Difficulties in Updating Mental Representations during Reading News Reports." In H. van Oostendorp & S. R. Goldman (eds.), *The Construction of Mental Representations during Reading*. Mahwah, NJ: Erlbaum.

Pascal, R. 1977. *The Dual Voice*. Manchester, England: Manchester University Press.

Patnoe, Elizabeth. 1995. "Lolita Misrepresented, Lolita Reclaimed: Disclosing the Doubles." *College Literature* 22, 81–104.

Paul, I. H. 1959. "Studies in remembering: The reproduction of connected and extended verbal material." *Psychological Issues* 1, no. 2, special issue.

Peer, Willie van. 1986. *Stylistics and Psychology: Investigations of Foregrounding*. London, England: Croom Helm.

———. 1992. "Literary Theory and Reader Response." In E. F. Nardocchio (ed.), *Reader Response to Literature. The Empirical Dimension*. Berlin and New York: De Gruyter, 137–52.

———. 1995. "Literature, Imagination, and Human Rights." *Philosophy and Literature* 19, no. 2, 276–91.

———. 1998. "Truth matters: A critical exercise in revisionism." *New Literary History* 29, no. 2, 329–46.

Peer, Willie van & Maat, Henk Pander. 1996. "Perspectivation and Sympathy: Effects of Narrative Point of View." In Roger J. Kreuz & Mary Sue MacNeally (eds.), *Empirical Approaches to the Arts and Literature*. New York: Ablex, 143–56.

———. In press. "Narrative perspective and the interpretation of characters' motives." *Language and Literature*.

Perfetti, C. 1985. *Reading Ability*. New York: Oxford University Press.

Petty, R. E. & Cacioppo, J. T. 1986. "The Elaboration Likelihood Model of Persuasion." In L. Berkowitz (ed.), *Advances in Experimental Social Psychology*. Orlando, FL: Academic Press, 19: 123–205.

Pfister, Manfred. 1974. *Studien zum Wandel der Perspektivenstruktur in elisabethanischen und jakobäischen Komödien*. München, Germany: Fink.

———. 1977. *Das Drama: Theorie und Analyse*. München, Germany: Fink.

———. 1988. *The Theory and Analysis of Drama*. Cambridge, England: Cambridge University Press.

Phelan, James. 1995. "On the Nature and Status of Covert Texts: A Reply to Gerry Brenner's 'Letter to De Ole True Huck.' " In Graff & Phelan (468–79).

Pier, John. 1995. Review of Fludernik (1993). *Style* 29, no. 2, 343–49.

Piercy, Marge. 1991. *He, She, and It*. New York: Knopf.

Pohler, Eva Mokry. 1996. "Floating in Space and Time: Where and When Is the Story?" *Narrative* 4, 278–86.

Popper, Karl R. 1994. "Reason or Revolution?" In *The Myth of the Framework: In Defence of Science and Rationality*. London, England: Routledge, 65–81.

Pouillon, Jean. 1946. *Temps et roman*. Paris, France: Gallimard.

Pratt, Mary Louise. 1977. *Toward a Speech Act Theory of Literature*. Bloomington, IN: Indiana University Press.

Prentice, D. A., Gerrig, R. J., & Bailis, D. S. 1997. *The Willing Construction of Disbelief in Fictional Information*. Manuscript.

———. 1977. "What readers bring to the processing of fictional texts." *Psychonomic Bulletin and Review* 4, 416–20.

Prince, Gerald. 1982. *Narratology: The Nature and Function of Narrative*. The Hague, Netherlands: Mouton.

———. 1987. *A Dictionary of Narratology*. Lincoln: University of Nebraska Press.

———. 1990. "On Narratology (Past, Present, Future)." In A. Maynor Hardee & Freeman G. Henry (eds.), *Narratology and Narrative*. Columbia: University of South Carolina Press, 1–14.

Propp, Vladimir. 1928. *Morphology of the Folk Tale*, trans. Laurence Scott. Austin: University of Texas Press, 1968.

Proust, Marcel. 1932. *Remembrance of Things Past*, trans. C. K. Scott Moncrieff. New York: Random House, vol. 2.

Rabinowitz, N. S. 1993. *Anxiety Veiled: Euripides and the Traffic in Women*. Ithaca, NY: Cornell University Press.

Reardon, B. P. 1989. *Collected Ancient Greek Novels*. Berkeley, CA: University of California Press.

Rehm, Rush. 1992. *Greek Tragic Theatre*. London and New York: Routledge.

Reifer, David M., Hu, Xiangen, & Batchelder, William H. 1994. "Response strategies in source monitoring." *Journal of Experimental Psychology: Learning, Memory, and Cognition* 20, 680–93.

Richards, I. A. 1929. *Practical Criticism*. London, England: Routledge and Kegan Paul.

Richardson, Brian. 1991. "The Poetics and Politics of Second Person Narrative." *Genre* 24, 309–30.

Ricoeur, Paul. 1984. *Time and Narrative*. Chicago, IL: University of Chicago Press.

Rimmon-Kenan, Shlomith. 1983. *Narrative Fiction: Contemporary Poetics*. London and New York: Methuen.

———. 1989. "How the model neglects the medium: Linguistics, language, and the crisis of narratology." *Journal of Narrative Technique* 19, 157–66.

Rinck, M. & Bower, G. H. 1995. "Anaphora resolution and the focus of attention in situation models." *Journal of Memory and Language* 34, 110–31.

Roche, Maurice. 1960. *Compact: Roman.* Paris, France: Seuil.

Roe, Emery. 1995. *Narrative Policy Analysis: Theory and Practice.* Durham, NC: Duke University Press.

Ronen, Ruth. 1994. *Possible Worlds in Literary Theory.* Cambridge, England: Cambridge University Press.

Ross, L. D. 1977. "The Intuitive Psychologist and His Shortcomings: Distortions in the Attribution Process." In L. Berkowitz (ed.), *Advances in Experimental Social Psychology.* New York: Academic Press, 10: 174–214.

Rossum-Guyon, Françoise van. 1970. "Point de vue ou perspective narrative." *Poétique* 4, 476–97.

Roth, Joseph. 1989. *Radetzkymarsch: Roman.* Cologne, Germany: Kiepenheuer & Witsch. (Original edition 1932.)

Rusch, Gebhard. 1987. *Erkenntnis, Wissenschaft, Geschichte: Von einem konstruktivistischen Standpunkt.* Frankfurt am Main, Germany: Suhrkamp.

Ryan, Marie-Laure. 1985. "The modal structure of narrative universes." *Poetics Today* 6, no. 4, 717–55.

———. 1986. "Embedded narratives and tellability." *Style* 20, no. 3, 319–40.

———. 1991. *Possible Worlds, Artificial Intelligence and Narrative Theory.* Bloomington, IN: Indiana University Press.

Sack, Warren. 1994a. "Indexing Multimedia by Ideology." Proceedings of the AAAI Workshop on Indexing and Reuse of Multimedia Systems, Seattle, WA, 73–81.

———. 1994b. *Actor-Role Analysis: Ideology, Point of View and the News* (Technical Report 94–005). Cambridge: MIT Media Laboratory, Learning and Common Sense Section.

Salthouse, T. A. 1991. *Theoretical Perspectives in Cognitive Aging.* Hillsdale, NJ: Erlbaum.

Sanders, J. & Redeker, G. 1996. "Perspective and the representation of speech and thought in narrative discourse." In G. Fauconnier, E. Sweetser, and E. S. Smith (eds.), *Spaces, Worlds, and Grammar (Cognitive Theory of Language).* Chicago, IL: University of Chicago Press.

Sanders, José. 1994. "Perspective in Narrative Discourse." Ph.D. diss. Catholic University of Brabant.

Schaeffer, J.-M. 1989. *Qu'est-ce qu'un genre littéraire? (What is a literary genre?)* Paris, France: Seuil.

Schmalhofer, F. & Glavanov, D. 1986. "Three components of understanding a programmer's manual: Verbatim, propositional, and situational representations." *Journal of Memory and Language* 25, 279–94.

Schmidt, Siegfried J. 1982. *Foundation for the Empirical Study of Literature: The Components of a Basic Theory*, authorized translation from the German and fully revised by Robert de Beaugrande. Hamburg, Germany: Buske.

———. 1984. "The fiction is that reality exists: A constructivist model of reality, fiction, and literature." *Poetics Today* 5, no. 2: 253–74.

——— (ed.). 1987. *Der Diskurs des Radikalen Konstruktivismus*. Frankfurt am Main, Germany: Suhrkamp.

——— (ed.). 1992. *Kognition und Gesellschaft: Der Diskurs des Radikalen Konstruktivismus*. Frankfurt am Main, Germany: Suhrkamp.

Schneider, C. 1974. *Information und Absicht bei Thukydides: Untersuchung zur Motivation des Handelns*. Göttingen, Germany: Vandenhoeck & Ruprecht.

Schober, Michael F. 1995. "Speakers, addressees, and frames of reference: Whose effort is minimized in conversations about locations?" *Discourse Processes* 20, 219–47.

Selden, Raman & Widdowson, Peter. 1993. *A Reader's Guide to Contemporary Literary Theory*. (3rd ed). New York: Harvester Wheatsheaf.

Sell, R. (Ed.). 1991. *Literary Pragmatics*. London, England: Routledge.

Semino, Elena. 1995. "Schema Theory and the Analysis of Text Worlds in Poetry." *Language and Literature* 4, no. 2: 79–108.

Semino, Elena, Short, Mick, & Culpeper, Jonathan. 1997. "Using a corpus to test a model of speech and thought presentation." *Poetics* 25, 17–43.

Semino, Elena, Short, Mick, & Wynne, Martin. 1999. "Hypothetical Words and Thoughts in Contemporary British Narrative." *Narrative* 7, 307–34.

Senesi, Mauro. 1963. "The Giraffe." In *Harper's Magazine*, 226, 80–82.

Shaw, Harry. 1995a. "Loose narrators: Display, engagement, and the search for a place in history." *Narrative* 3, 95–116.

———. 1995b. "Thin description: A reply to Seymour Chatman." *Narrative* 3, 307–14.

———. 1996. "Drawing the line: A response to Eva Mokry Pohler." *Narrative* 4, 287–91.

Short, M. H. 1986. "Speech Presentation, The Novel and the Press." In Willie van Peer (ed.), *The Taming of the Text*. London and New York: Routledge, 61–81.

———. 1996. *Exploring the Language of Poems, Plays and Prose*. London, England: Longman.

Short, Mick, Semino, Elena, & Culpeper, Jonathan. 1996. "Using a Corpus for Stylistics Research." In Jenny Thomas & Mick Short (eds.), *Using Corpora for Language Research*. London, England: Longman, 110–31.

Silvain, Pierre. 1971. *Les eoliennes*. Paris: Mercure de France.

Simonton, Dean K. 1988. "Aesthetic success in 36 Hungarian and American short stories." In Colin Martindale (ed.), *Psychological Approaches to the Study of Literary Narratives*. Hamburg, Germany: Buske, 66–73.

Sinclair, John McH. 1966. "Taking a Poem to Pieces." In Roger Fowler (ed.), *Essays on Style and Language*. London, England: Routledge and Kegan Paul, 68–81.

Smith, Barbara Herrnstein. 1981. "Narrative Versions, Narrative Theories." In W. J. T. Mitchell (ed.), *On Narrative*. Chicago: University of Chicago Press, 209–32.

Snell, B. 1953. *Discovery of the Mind: The Greek Origins of European Thought*. Trans. T. G. Rosenmeyer. Oxford, England: Oxford University Press. (Original edition 1946.)

Sommers, Christina Hoff. 1994. *Who Stole Feminism: How Women Have Betrayed Women*. New York: Simon & Schuster.

Sowell, Thomas. 1995. *The Vision of the Anointed: Self-Congratulation as a Basis for Social Policy*. New York: Basic Books.

Sperber, Dan & Wilson, Deirdre. 1986. *Relevance: Communication and Cognition*. Oxford, England: Blackwell.

Stam, Robert, Burgoyne, Robert, & Flitterman-Lewis, Sandy. 1992. *New Vocabularies in Film Semiotics. Structuralism, Post-Structuralism and Beyond*. London and New York: Routledge.

Stanzel, F. K. 1965. *Die typischen Erzählsituationen im Roman. Dargestellt an "Tom Jones," "Moby-Dick," "The Ambassadors," "Ulysses," u.a.*, Wien/Stuttgart. (Original edition 1955.)

———. 1966. *Typische Formen des Romans*. Göttingen, Germany: Vandenhoeck & Ruprecht.

———. 1984. *A Theory of Narrative*. Cambridge, England: Cambridge University Press. (Original edition 1979.)

Sternberg, Meir. 1991. "How Indirect Discourse Means: Syntax, Semantics, Poetics, Pragmatics." In Sell 1991, 52–93.

Stine, E. A. L. 1995. "Aging and the Distribution of Resources in Working Memory." In P. Allen & T. Bashore (eds.), *Age Differences in Word and Language Processing*. Amsterdam, Netherlands: North-Holland, 171–86.

Storms, M. D. 1973. "Videotape and the attribution process: Reversing actors' and observers' points of view." *Journal of Personality and Social Psychology* 27, 165–75.

Stotland, E., Mathews, K. E., Sherman, S. E., Hansson, O. R., & Richardson, B. Z. (eds.). 1978. *Empathy, Fantasy and Helping*. Beverly Hills, CA: Sage.

Suh, S. & Trabasso, T. 1993. "Inference during reading: Converging evidence from discourse analysis, talk-aloud protocols, and recognition priming." *Journal of Memory and Language* 32, 279–300.

Tan, E. 1994. "Story Processing as an Emotion Episode." In H. van Oostendorp & R. Zwaan (eds.), *Naturalistic Text Comprehension*. New Jersey: Ablex, 165–87.

———. 1996. *Emotion and the Structure of Narrative Film*. Mahwah, NJ: Erlbaum.

Tan, E., Eggermont, L., & Joosten, P. 1989. "On becoming a cinephile: A theoretical and empirical analysis." *Tijdschrift voor Theaterwetenschap* 7, nos. 27–28, 207–33.

Taplin, Oliver. 1978. *Greek Tragedy in Action*. London, England: Methuen.

Tellegen, A. 1982. "Brief manual for the multidimensional personality questionnaire." Manuscript. University of Minnesota, Department of Psychology, Minneapolis.

The Annual Register for 1967. I. Macadam (ed.). London: Longmas, 176.

Toolan, Michael. 1988. *Narrative: A Critical Linguistic Introduction*. London, England: Routledge.

Trabasso, T. & Sperry, L. 1985. "Causal relatedness and importance of story events." *Journal of Memory and Language* 24, 595–611.

Trabasso, T. & Suh, S. 1993. "Understanding text: Achieving explanatory coherence through on-line inferences and mental operations in working memory." *Discourse Processes* 16, 3–34.

Trabasso, T. & van den Broek, P. 1985. "Causal thinking and the representation of narrative events." *Journal of Memory and Language* 24, 612–30.

Trabasso, T., van den Broek, P., & Suh, S. Y. 1989. "Logical necessity and transitivity of causal relations in stories." *Discourse Processes* 12, 1–25.

Truffaut, François. 1967. *Hitchcock*. New York: Simon & Schuster.

Turner, Frederick. 1991. *Beauty: The Value of Values*. Charlottesville and London: University Press of Virginia.

Turner, Jane. 1653. *Choice Experiences*. London.

Uspensky, Boris. 1973. *A Poetics of Composition*. Berkeley: University of California Press.

Wade, Elizabeth & Clark, Herbert H. 1993. "Reproduction and demonstration in quotations." *Journal of Memory and Language* 32, 805–19.

Wakefield, D. 1966. "The personal voice and the impersonal eye." *The Atlantic Monthly*, June 1966, 86–90.

Walton, Kendall L. 1990. *Mimesis as Make-Believe: On the Foundations of the Representational Arts*. Cambridge, MA: Harvard University Press.

Watson, D. 1982. "The actor and the observer: How are their perceptions of causality different?" *Psychological Bulletin* 92, 682–700.

Watzlawick, Paul (ed.). 1984. *The Invented Reality: How Do We Know What We Believe We Know? Contributions to Constructivism*. New York: Norton.

Wellek, R. & Warren, A. 1977. *Theory of Literature*. New York-London: Harvest/Harcourt. (Original edition 1948.)

White, Edmund. 1978. *Nocturnes for the King of Naples*. New York: St. Martin's Press.

White, Hayden. 1973. *Metahistory: The Historical Imagination in Nineteenth-Century Europe*. Baltimore: Johns Hopkins.

White, Morton. 1965. *Foundations of Historical Knowledge*. New York: Harper.

Wiebe, J. 1994. "Tracking point of view in narrative," *Computational Linguistics* 20, no. 2, 233–88.

Wilkes, A. L. & Leatherbarrow, M. 1988. "Editing episodic memory following the identification of error." *Quarterly Journal of Experimental Psychology* 40A (2) 361–87.

Wittig, Monique. 1964. *L'Opoponax*. Paris, France: Minuit.

———. 1966. *The Opoponax*, trans. Helen Weaver. London, England: Peter Owen.

Wohmann, Gabriele. 1975. "Schilderung eines Aufenthaltes." In *Laendliches Fest*. Darmstadt/Neuwied, Germany: Sammlung Luchterhand, 76–77.

Wolfe, T. 1975. *The New Journalism*. London, England: Picador.

Zeldin, Theodore. 1994. *An Intimate History of Humanity*. New York: Harper Collins.

Zillmann, D. & Cantor, J. R. 1977. "Affective response to the emotions of a protagonist." *Journal of Experimental Social Psychology* 13, 155–65.

Zwaan, R. A. 1994. "Effect of genre expectation on text comprehension." *Journal of Experimental Psychology: Learning, Memory and Cognition* 20, 920–33.

Zwaan, Rolf, Magliano, Joseph P., & Graesser, Arthur C. 1995. "Dimensions of situation model construction in narrative comprehension." *Journal of Experimental Psychology: Learning, Memory, and Cognition* 21, 386–97.

Zwaan, Rolf A. 1993. *Aspects of Literary Comprehension*. Amsterdam and Philadelphia: Benjamins.

Contributors

Sylvia Adamson
School of English and Linguistics
University of Manchester

Els Andringa
Department of Literary Studies
Utrecht University

Ute J. Bayen
Department of Psychology
University of Memphis

Marisa Bortolussi
Department of Modern Languages and Comparative Studies
University of Alberta

Cheryl Bowers
Department of Psychology
University of Memphis

Noël Carroll
Department of Philosophy
University of Wisconsin-Madison

Seymour Chatman
Department of Rhetoric
University of California-Berkeley

Peter Dixon
Department of Psychology
University of Alberta

Monika Fludernik
English Department
University of Freiburg

Richard Gerrig
Department of Psychology
State University of New York-Stony Brook

Arthur C. Graesser
Department of Psychology
University of Memphis

Petra van Horssen
Theater and Film Studies
University of Amsterdam

Xiangen Hu
Department of Psychology
University of Memphis

Astrid Jacobs
Theater and Film Studies
University of Amsterdam

Irene de Jong
Department of Classics
University of Amsterdam

Don Kuiken
Department of Psychology
University of Alberta

Uri Margolin
Department of Comparative Literature and Film Studies
University of Alberta

David Miall
Department of English
University of Alberta

Dan Morrow
Department of Psychology
University of New Hampshire

Ansgar Nünning
Department of English
University of Giessen

James Phelan
Department of English
Ohio State University

Gerald Prince
School of Arts and Sciences
University of Pennsylvania

Warren Sack
Media Lab
Massachusetts Institute of Technology

Dan Shen
Department of English
Peking University

Mick Short
Department of Linguistics
Lancaster University

Ed Tan
Department of Art History
Free University of Amsterdam

Herre van Oostendorp
Department of Psychology
Utrecht University

Willie van Peer
Institute of German as a Foreign Language
University of Munich

Name Index

Subject Index